D1366474

GREAT AIRCRAFT

OF

WWII

GREAT AIRCRAFT
OF
WWII

ALFRED PRICE

MIKE SPICK

CHARTWELL
BOOKS, INC.

Published by
CHARTWELL BOOKS, INC.
A Division of **BOOK SALES, INC.**
114 Northfield Avenue
Edison, New Jersey 08837

Copyright © Bookmart Ltd. 1997

This edition printed 1997

All rights reserved.

This book is protected by copyright. No part of it may be reproduced, stored in a retrieval system, or transmitted in any form or by any means, without the prior permission in writing of the Publishers, nor be otherwise circulated in any form of binding or cover other than that in which it is published and without a similar condition including this condition being imposed on the subsequent publisher.

ISBN 0-7858-0669-5

This book created for Bookmart by Amazon Publishing Ltd
Design by wda
Editors Norman Franks, Tessa Rose, Diana Vowles
Reproduction by Optima Technologies Ltd
Printed in Spain

The Authors

Dr Alfred Price wrote the chapters on the Supermarine Spitfire and the Messerschmitt 109 and 262. Dr. Price served as an aircrew officer in the Royal Air Force and, during a flying career spanning 15 years, he logged some 4,000 flying hours. While in the RAF he specialised and instructed in electronic warfare and airfighting tactics. Now working full-time as an author, he has written more than forty books on aviation subjects including *Instruments of Darkness, Battle of Britain: The Hardest Day, Battle over the Reich, Blitz on Britain, Spitfire – A Complete Fighting History* and *The Spitfire Story*. He was often asked to compile questions on aviation matters for the popular BBC television programme *Mastermind*. Dr. Price holds a PhD in History and is a fellow of the Royal Historical Society.

Mike Spick wrote the chapters on the Avro Lancaster, the North American P-51 Mustang and the Boeing B-17 Flying Fortress. Mr. Spick has been a full-time writer and commentator in the aviation scene for the past 14 years. His specialities are fighter tactics and helicopter warfare, and he spent several years as a consultant to the Swiss-based Project Atlas. He has written over thirty books, including *The Ace Factor, Fighter Pilot Tactics, All-Weather Warriors, Designed for the Kill* and *Luftwaffe Fighter Aces*. An Associate of the Royal Aeronautical Society, he has advised on aviation matters for television, and has been a consultant to the magazine AirForces Monthly since its inception in 1988.

CONTENTS

INTRODUCTION

In writing this book we have aimed at producing a general interest account of the six truly outstanding combat aircraft of World War II. It has been no easy matter to decide which types to include, and which to omit. In the end, after much thought, we selected the Supermarine Spitfire, the Avro Lancaster, the Messerschmitt 109, the Messerschmitt 262, the North American P-51 Mustang and the Boeing B-17 Flying Fortress.

After describing their design and development, we devote much space to relating the combat career of each type. To present as vivid a picture as possible of how they performed their assigned combat tasks, we have included numerous first-person accounts from pilots who flew these planes in action.

When describing the German Messerschmitt 109 fighter, several published accounts have used the abbreviation Bf 109 for this aircraft. Bf stood for *Bayerische Flugzeugwerke*, Bavarian Aircraft Factory, and those intent on being pedantic insist on using this form. However, official Luftwaffe documents use both the 'Bf' and the 'Me' forms of abbreviation for this aircraft. So both are correct. In this account we have used the simpler and more direct form 'Me'.

Mike Spick
Alfred Price

THE SUPERMARINE SPITFIRE

PROLOGUE

Rheine, western Germany, 13.35 hours, 29 December 1944.

A dozen Spitfires of No. 411 (Canadian) Squadron, flying in three separate four-plane sections, traced lazy patterns in the sky high above the important Luftwaffe airfield. Leading Yellow Section was Flight Lieutenant Dick Audet, a 22-year old of French extraction flying his fifty-third operational sortie. During the previous months he had carried out numerous bombing and strafing attacks on ground targets, but he had yet to encounter enemy aircraft in the air.

The Spitfires' mission was to engage German aircraft taking off from the airfield or on the landing approach to it. Suddenly Audet caught sight of a dozen hostile fighters in loose formation far below. He gave a clipped radio call to inform his commander of the enemy presence and to say that he was about to engage. Then Audet led his Section into a steep diving turn, moving his force as rapidly as possible into a firing position behind the German planes. It was to be a classic fighter 'bounce', with no quarter asked or given. In his combat report Audet later wrote:

'The enemy were four Messerschmitt 109s and eight Focke Wulf 190s, flying line astern. I attacked an Me 109, the last aircraft in the formation. At 200 yards I opened fire and saw strikes all over the fuselage and wing roots. The 109 burst into flames and trailed black smoke.

'I now went around in a defensive circle until I spotted an FW 190. I attacked from 250 yards down to 100 yards and from 30 degrees from line astern. I

Below: Flight Lieutenant Dick Audet scored five victories during his first encounter with enemy aircraft, on 29 December 1944.
Right: Spitfire Mark IXs of Audet's unit, No. 411 Squadron, warming their engines at their base at Heesch in Holland, before a mission.

saw strikes all over the cockpit and to the rear of the fuselage. It burst into flames. I saw the pilot slumped in his cockpit.

'Ahead was a 109 going down in a slight dive. It pulled up sharply into a climb, and the cockpit canopy flew off. I gave a short burst at about 300 yards and the aircraft whipped down in a dive. The pilot attempted to bail out, but his chute ripped to shreds. I saw the 109 hit the ground and smash into flaming pieces.

'I next spotted an FW 190 being pursued by a Spitfire pursued in turn by an FW 190. I called this pilot – one of my Yellow Section – to break, and attacked the 109 from the rear. We went down in a steep dive. I opened fire at 250 yards and it burst into flames. I saw it go into the ground and burn.

'Several minutes later, while attempting to re-form my section, I spotted an FW 190 at about 2000 feet. I dived on him and he turned into me from the right. He then flipped around in a left-hand turn, and attempted a head on attack. I slowed down to wait for him to fly into range. At about 200 yards I gave a short burst. I could not see any strikes but he flicked violently and continued to do so until he crashed.'

Within 10 minutes Dick Audet had shot down five enemy aircraft, to gain for himself the coveted status of fighter ace. Other pilots in the squadron witnessed the feat and it would later be confirmed by analysis of his combat camera film. During the action other pilots in Audet's squadron destroyed three more enemy fighters.

Although the Spitfire had been in service for six years, the versions in service at the end of 1944 were still formidable fighting machines. Yet, paradoxically, the fighter was designed for a purpose quite different from that flown by Dick Audet on that December afternoon. The Spitfire was designed solely as an air defence interceptor, to engage and destroy enemy bombers attempting to attack targets in the British Isles. The Spitfire fulfilled that task brilliantly, and was equally effective in hunting down enemy fighters over their own territory. In those and a dozen other roles, the sleek-lined little fighter illustrated its versatility.

SUPERMARINE SPITFIRE VB

1 Aerial stub attachment
2 Rudder upper hinge
3 Fabric-covered rudder
4 Rudder tab
5 Sternpost
6 Rudder tab hinge
7 Rear navigation light
8 Starboard elevator tab
9 Starboard elevator structure
10 Elevator balance
11 Tailplane front spar
12 IFF aerial
13 Castoring non-retractable
   tailwheel
14 Tailwheel strut
15 Fuselage double frame
16 Elevator control lever
17 Tailplane spar/
   fuselage attachment
18 Fin rear spar
   (fuselage frame
   extension)
19 Fin front spar
   (fuselage frame
   extension)
20 Port elevator tab hinge
21 Port elevator
22 IFF aerial
23 Port tailplane
24 Rudder control lever
25 Cross shaft
26 Tailwheel oleo access place
27 Tailwheel oleo shock-absorber
28 Fuselage angled frame
29 Battery compartment
30 Lower longeron
31 Elevator control cables
32 Fuselage construction
33 Rudder control cables
34 Radio compartment
35 Radio support tray
36 Flare chute
37 Oxygen bottle
38 Auxiliary long-range fuel tank
   (29gal/132l)
39 Dorsal formation light
40 Aerial lead-in
41 HF aerial
42 Aerial mast
43 Cockpit aft glazing
44 Voltage regulator
45 Canopy track
46 Structural bulkhead
47 Headrest
48 Plexiglass canopy
49 Rear-view mirror
50 Entry flap (port)
51 Air bottles (alternative rear
   fuselage stowage)
52 Sutton harness
53 Pilot's seat (moulded Bakelite)
54 Datum longeron
55 Seat support frame
56 Wingroot fillet
57 Seat adjustment lever
58 Rudder pedal frame
59 Elevator control connecting tube
60 Control column spade grip
61 Trim wheel
62 Reflector gunsight
63 External windscreen armour
64 Instrument panel
65 Main fuselage fuel tank
   (48gal/218l)
66 Fuel tank/longeron
   attachment fittings

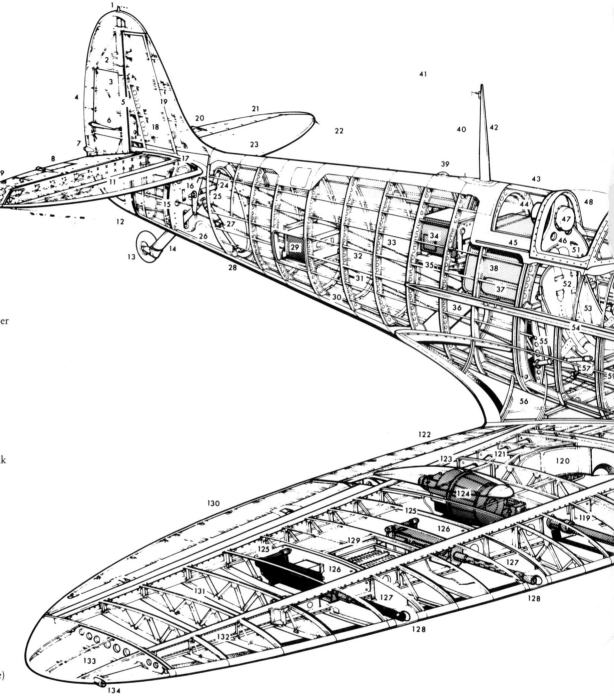

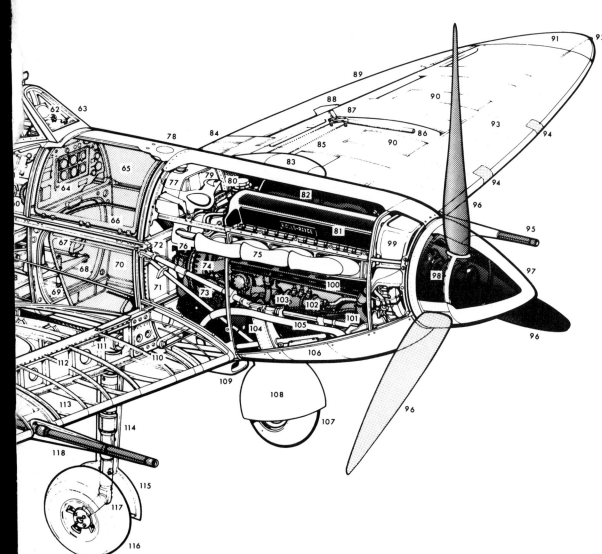

67 Rudder pedals
68 Rudder bar
69 King post
70 Fuselage lower fuel tank
    (37gal/168l)
71 Firewall/bulkhead
72 Engine bearer attachment
73 Steel tube bearers
74 Magneto
75 'Fishtail'/exhaust manifold
76 Gun heating 'intensifier'
77 Hydraulic tank
78 Fuel filler cap
79 Air compressor intake
80 Air compressor
81 Rolls-Royce Merlin 45 engine
82 Coolant piping
83 Port cannon wing fairing
84 Flaps
85 Aileron control cables
86 Aileron push tube
87 Bellcrank
88 Aileron hinge
89 Port aileron
90 Machine-gun access panels
91 Port wingtip
92 Port navigation light
93 Leading-edge skinning
94 Machine-gun ports (protected)
95 20mm cannon muzzle
96 Three-blade constant-speed
    propeller
97 Spinner
98 Propeller hub
99 Coolant tank
100 Cowling fastening
101 Engine anti-vibration
     mounting pad
102 Engine accessories
103 Engine bearers
104 Main engine support member
105 Coolant pipe
106 Exposed oil tank
107 Port mainwheel
108 Mainwheel fairing
109 Carburettor air intake
110 Stub/spar attachment
111 Mainwheel leg pivot point
112 Main spar
113 Leading-edge ribs (diagonals
     deleted for clarity)
114 Mainwheel leg shock-absorber
115 Mainwheel fairing
116 Starboard mainwheel
117 Angled axle
118 Cannon barrel support fairing
119 Spar cut-out
120 Mainwheel well
121 Gun heating pipe
122 Flap structure
123 Cannon wing fairing
124 Cannon magazine drum
     (120 rounds)
125 Machine-gun support brackets
126 Gun access panels
127 .303in machine-gun barrels
128 Machine-gun ports
129 Ammunition boxes (350rpg)
130 Starboard aileron construction
131 Wing ribs
132 Single-tube outer spar section
133 Wingtip structure
134 Starboard navigation light

A FIGHTER IS BORN

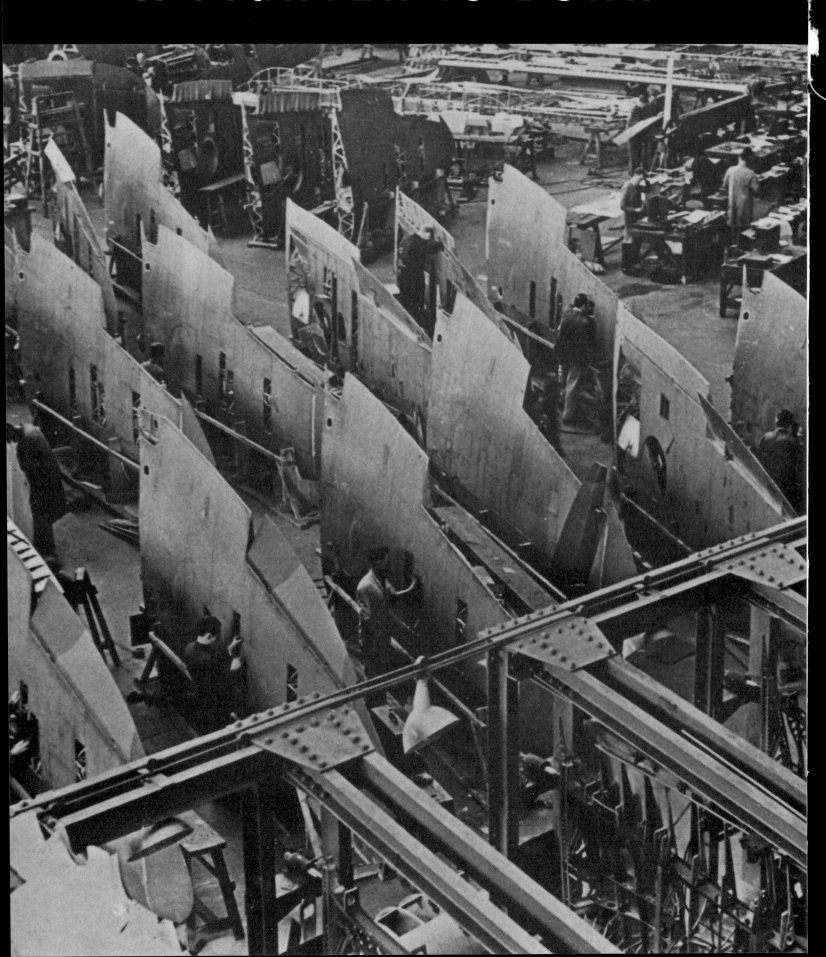

The story of the Spitfire began almost exactly ten years before Dick Audet's famous action, in December 1934. Then, at the Supermarine Aviation Company's works at Southampton, Reginald Mitchell and his team finalized the layout of their new high-speed fighter for the RAF.

Mitchell had already established his name as a highly successful designer of racing floatplanes for the Schneider Trophy competition. One of his designs – the Supermarine S.5 – had won that international contest in 1927. The S.6 won it two years later in 1929. After another two-year gap the Supermarine S.6B won the trophy outright for Britain in 1931 and later went on to raise the World Air Speed record to 407mph (655km/hr).

These had been magnificent achievements but, in the nature of things, the market for high-speed racing seaplanes was extremely limited. The Supermarine company's main 'bread and butter' products were its big Southampton and Scapa flying boats which now equipped seven RAF maritime patrol squadrons.

In 1934 the fastest fighter type in the Royal Air Force was the Hawker Fury, which had a maximum speed of 207mph at 14,000 feet (333km/hr at 4,270m). At that time Air Vice Marshal Hugh Dowding held the post of Air Member for Supply and Research, and was responsible for issuing to manufacturers the specifications for new aircraft required for the Royal Air Force. Dowding was an exceptionally farsighted innovator, what we would now call a 'technocrat'. He saw the vital need for a new fighter to bridge the huge gap in performance between the Schneider

Trophy racers and the biplanes that were then in service.

The early 1930s saw rapid advances in aviation technology. The Schneider Trophy racing seaplanes had demonstrated the performance advantages of using highly supercharged engines, streamlined all-metal airframes and the monoplane wing layout. These features were also being incorporated into the latest land planes, together with wing flaps to reduce the landing speeds, and retractable undercarriages.

■ MITCHELL'S FIRST FIGHTER ■

In February 1934 Reginald Mitchell's first fighter design appeared, the Supermarine Type 224. The aircraft took part in the competition to select a new fighter type for the Royal Air Force. Although it

Far left: **Production of wings at Woolston, early in 1939.**

THE SCHNEIDER TROPHY AND THE SPITFIRE

The Supermarine S.6B, Reginald Mitchell's final racing floatplane design, gained the Schneider Trophy outright for Great Britain in 1931. Later that year it raised the world absolute speed record to 407mph (655km/hr).

One frequently repeated myth about the Spitfire is that it was 'developed from' the Supermarine S.6B. This is simply not true. Certainly Mitchell learned a lot about high-speed flight from his work on the floatplanes, but that is quite different from saying that the Spitfire was 'developed from' them. In fact the two aircraft were quite different designs, intended for quite different roles. There was not a single component of any significance in the Spitfire that resembled its counterpart in the racing seaplane.

Type Single-seat racing floatplane.
Power Plant One Rolls-Royce 'R' engine developing 2,350hp.
Dimensions Span 30ft 0in (9.14m), length 28ft 10in (8.79m).
Weight Maximum loaded weight 6,086lb (2760kg).
Performance Maximum speed 407mph at 245 ft (655km/hr at 75m), a World record.

Right: **The Supermarine S.6B racing floatplane won the coveted Schneider Trophy outright for Great Britain in 1931. Later that year it captured the world absolute speed record at 40mph (655km/hr).**

SUPERMARINE TYPE 224

REGINALD MITCHELL'S FIRST FIGHTER DESIGN

This single-seat interceptor fighter used a novel type of evaporative cooling for the engine, employing a steam condenser built into the leading edge of each wing. The system gave continual trouble and would probably have precluded the fighter being ordered for the RAF even if its performance had been more impressive.

Type Single-seat interceptor fighter.
Armament Four Vickers .303in (7.7mm) machine guns synchronized to fire through the propeller arc.
Power Plant One Rolls-Royce Goshawk developing 680hp.
Dimensions Span 45ft 10in (13.97m) length 29ft 5¼in (8.97m).

Weight Maximum loaded weight 4,743lb (2,151kg).
Performance Maximum speed 228mph at 15,000ft (367km/hr at 4,575m); time to climb to 15,000ft, 9½ minutes.

Above: The Supermarine Type 224, Reginald Mitchell's unsuccessful first attempt at designing a fighter aircraft.

Right: The Hawker Fury, the fastest fighter type in the RAF in 1934, had a maximum speed of 207mph (333km/hr).

was a monoplane design of all-metal construction, the fighter had a fixed undercarriage and a rather clumsy appearance. The Type 224 proved a flop. Its maximum speed was only 228mph (367km/hr) and it took 9½ minutes to reach 15,000 feet (4,575m). The unusual system of evaporative cooling for the engine, using a steam condenser mounted along the leading edge of each wing, gave continual trouble. The winner of the competition, the Gloster entrant later named the Gladiator, had a maximum speed of 242mph (390km/hr) and it climbed to 15,000 feet in 6½ minutes. One thing was clear: a good biplane design would outperform an over-conservative monoplane design.

Having learned that painful lesson, Reginald Mitchell persuaded the company to allow him to design a smaller, lighter and more streamlined fighter. This time he would use the new 1,000 horse power V-12 engine, later

named the Merlin, then under test at the Rolls-Royce company in Derby. When Air Vice Marshal Dowding saw details of the proposed new fighter he gave it his full support, and issued an official Royal Air Force specification so that the government would meet most of the cost of building a prototype.

The new fighter made its maiden flight on 5 March 1936, with Chief Test Pilot

'Mutt' Summers at the controls. This was an altogether more effective machine than its predecessor and it aroused immediate interest. Not long afterwards the Air Ministry allocated a name to the new fighter – 'Spitfire'. Had the decision been left to its designer, the aircraft would certainly have been named differently. When Mitchell learned of the official choice of name, he was heard to

FASTEST FIGHTER

'It is claimed – and the claim seems indisputable – that the Spitfire is the fastest military aeroplane in the world. It is surprisingly small and light for a machine of its calibre (the structural weight is said to have been brought down to a level never before attained in the single-seat fighter class), and its speed and manoeuvrability are something to marvel at.

'Tight turns were made at high speed after dives, and the control at low speeds was amply demonstrated. The demonstration was cramped by low clouds, but after the main flying display the machine was taken up again and gave one of the smoothest displays of high-speed aerobatics ever seen in this country.'

FLIGHT MAGAZINE, 3 JULY 1936

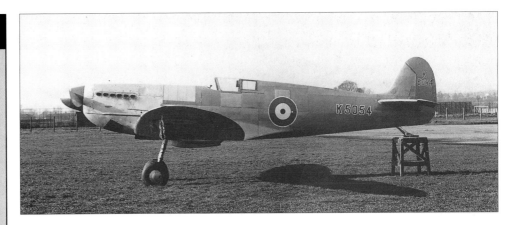

comment: 'It's the sort of bloody-silly name they would give it!'

During flight tests the new fighter attained a maximum speed of 349mph at 16,800 feet (562km/hr at 5,122m), and in the climb it reached 30,000 feet (9,145m) in 17 minutes. Not only was it the fastest fighter in existence but it was also one of the most heavily armed, for it was designed to carry eight Browning .303in (7.7mm) machine guns in the wings.

■ LARGE ORDER ■

The Spitfire became available at exactly the right time for the Royal Air Force. In Germany the recently re-formed Luftwaffe was building up its strength rapidly. Its new monoplane fighter type, the Messerschmitt 109, was on the point of entering large-scale production. To meet the mounting threat, in June 1936 the British Government signed a contract for 310 Spitfires.

The Spitfire made its first public appearance on 18 June 1936, during a press-day held at Eastleigh to show aircraft made by the Supermarine and Vickers companies. Other aircraft taking part included a Walrus amphibian (another of Mitchell's designs) and the prototype Wellington bomber. With press photographers eagerly snapping away, Jeffrey Quill started the Spitfire's engine and taxied to one end of

the grass runway. Then he pushed open the throttle to begin his take-off run and the lightly loaded aircraft rapidly gained speed. Before getting airborne the pilot made a brief scan of his instruments, and noticed the needle of the oil pressure gauge suddenly drop to zero. That left him in an unenviable position. He had no room to stop before reaching the airfield boundary, and on the other side of it lay the sprawling buildings of the Southern Railway Company's locomotive works. Fearing that the engine might seize up at any moment, the pilot eased the aircraft into the air and reduced power to the minimum necessary

Above: The prototype Supermarine F. 37/34, serial number K 5054, pictured at Eastleigh shortly before its maiden flight. The metal parts of the aircraft were unpainted, the aircraft carried no armament and the undercarriage was locked in the down position.

to hold it there. Then he took it round in a shallow turn, aiming to get it back to the airfield as soon as possible. The engine maintained its healthy roar, but as Quill lined up for the landing he saw he was a little too low. He eased open the throttle for one last burst of power, the engine responded and he made a safe landing.

PROTOTYPE SPITFIRE

Type Single-seat interceptor fighter.
Armament Eight 303in (7.7mm) Browning machine guns with 350 rounds per gun.
Power Plant One Rolls-Royce Merlin Type C liquid cooled V-12 engine with single-speed supercharger developing 990hp.
Dimensions Span 40ft (12.1m); length 29ft 11in (9.17m).
Weight Maximum loaded weight 5,395lb (2,446kg).
Performance Maximum speed 349 mph at 16,800 ft (562 km/hr at 5,122 m). Service ceiling 35,400ft (10,790m).

Below: The Supermarine works at Woolston on the outskirts of Southampton, close beside the River Itchen.
Above: Close to disaster! Jeffrey Quill taking off in the prototype Spitfire during the press day at Eastleigh on 18 June 1936.

A few seconds before this photograph was taken, when it was too late to abort the take off, an oil pipe had come adrift. In the background is the sprawling Southern Railway works over which the aircraft had to pass before it returned to the airfield. By

skilful flying Quill took the fighter in a wide circuit and landed before the engine seized. Had the prototype been lost that day, it is possible that the RAF might have cancelled its order in which case the Spitfire would not have gone into production.

Examination of the engine revealed that an oil pipe had come adrift, allowing the lubrication system to run dry. The engine was changed and sent to Rolls Royce for examination, but it had suffered remarkably little damage from this treatment.

Had the prototype been lost during its first air display, the consequences to the nation hardly bear thinking about. Only the one Spitfire existed and it had not completed its initial performance trials with the Royal Air Force. If it had crashed the Royal Air Force would probably have cancelled the contract and ordered other types of fighter instead. That would have had a disastrous effect on the capability of Fighter Command during the Battle of Britain, four years later.

Thanks to Jeffrey Quill's skilful flying, however, there had been no crash. Five days later the Spitfire resumed flying with a new engine. On 27 June Flight Lieutenant Hugh Edwardes-Jones demonstrated the aircraft before a large crowd at the Royal Air Force Pageant at Hendon. Two days later 'Mutt' Summers flew it at the Society of British Aircraft Constructors' air display at Hatfield. The demonstrations aroused enormous public interest in the fighter, and drew lyrical descriptions in the press.

■ ON DISPLAY ■

The prototype completed its initial service trials at Martlesham Heath in July 1936, and returned to Eastleigh for modification. The fighter received a newer version of the Merlin, giving slightly greater power, and eight machine guns were fitted in the wings.

Not all aspects of the Spitfire's flight trials went off smoothly. One of the most serious problems was that the fighter's guns did not work reliably at high altitude. During the initial firing trials in March 1937, all eight guns fired perfectly at 4,000 feet (1,220m). It was a different story a few days later, when an RAF pilot climbed the Spitfire to 32,000 feet (9,755m) over the North Sea for the first high-altitude firing. It nearly ended in tragedy. One gun fired 171 rounds before it failed, another fired 8 rounds, one fired 4 rounds and the remaining five guns failed to fire at all. That was bad enough, but when the Spitfire touched down at Martlesham Heath after the test the shock of the landing released the previously frozen-up breech blocks. Three of the weapons loosed off a round in the general direction of Felixstowe, fortunately without hitting anyone.

'...the Spitfires will be useless as fighting aircraft... '

During the next 18 months Supermarine engineers tried various schemes to solve the problem of gun freezing, using hot air ducted from the aircraft's glycol radiator. Yet the guns were still not functioning reliably in July 1938 when the first production Spitfires were delivered to the Royal Air Force. This led the Chief of the Air Staff, Marshal of the Royal Air Force Sir Cyril Newall, to comment during a secret meeting of the Air Council: 'If the guns will

"MY GOD, IT'S MADE OF TIN!"

Whenever the prototype Spitfire landed away from its base, it was the subject of great interest. At that time most airframes comprised a wood or light metal framework with a covering of linen fabric. The streamlined all-metal monoplane Spitfire with its enclosed cockpit and retractable undercarriage made every other aircraft in the Royal Air Force look positively prehistoric!

During a test flight in December 1936 Jeffrey Quill ran short of fuel, and he landed the Spitfire at the fighter airfield at Tangmere near Chichester. As he taxied in, a crowd of curious R.A.F. ground crewmen gathered to meet it. Then, Quill recalled:

'I taxied to a standstill and shut down, and could hear a tapping sound rather like raindrops hitting the aircraft. But it was a clear day. I checked I had shut everything down, but the tapping sound continued. Then as I climbed out I saw the reason. Several mechanics were standing around the rear fuselage, tapping it with their knuckles disbelievingly. "My God," one of them exclaimed, "It's made of tin!"'

not fire at heights at which the Spitfires are likely to encounter enemy bombers, the Spitfires will be useless as fighting aircraft . . .'

It took until October 1938 to resolve the problem. Then on the 14th, a service pilot took the prototype to high altitude and fired off the entire contents of the ammunition boxes without a single stoppage. The gun-heating modification was then incorporated in all Spitfires on the production line.

During the test programme the prototype Spitfire survived two serious accidents. During the first, in March 1937, it made an emergency wheels-up landing following an engine failure; and almost exactly a year later it suffered an undercarriage collapse on landing, following a fatigue fracture of one of the main wheel legs. On both occasions the aircraft resumed flying after repairs. By the end of 1938 production Spitfires

were emerging from the assembly hangar at Eastleigh at an encouraging rate, and the test programme of the prototype was complete. In those days there were no sentimental ideas about preserving historic aircraft, and the first Spitfire went to Farnborough for use as a 'hack' aircraft. On 4 September 1939, the day after Britain entered the Second World War, the aircraft suffered serious damage in a fatal landing accident. The venerable aircraft could have been repaired, but since there was no further use for it the machine was scrapped.

The prototype Spitfire had cost the public purse a mere £15,776. Rarely has the money of British taxpayers been better spent.

Below: The prototype Spitfire wearing drab military camouflage, in 1938. The muzzles of the two outer machine guns can be seen protruding from the wing.

SPITFIRE IN ACTION

Having gained the initial order for 310 Spitfires, the Supermarine Company found that fulfilling the contract was more difficult than expected. Previously the company had built small batches of flying boats for the Royal Air Force and its work force numbered only about 500. The new all-metal fighter required specialized manufacturing techniques, and at a time when the aircraft industry was expanding it was difficult to recruit workers with the necessary skills. As a result there were delays in getting the fighter into production.

In August 1938, twenty-nine months after the maiden flight of the prototype, No. 19 Squadron at Duxford received the first Spitfires. It took until December for the unit to get its full complement of aircraft, then other squadrons began to re-equip with the type. By this time Hugh Dowding had been promoted to Air Chief Marshal and held the post of Commander-in-Chief RAF Fighter Command. By a quirk of history, the man who had done so much to bring the Spitfire into being was now to direct these fighters into action.

When Great Britain declared war on Germany in September 1939, Royal Air Force Fighter Command possessed 187 Spitfires in front-line units. Nos 19, 41, 54, 65, 66, 72, 74, 602, 603 and 611 Squadrons were fully equipped with Spitfires and No. 609 Squadron was in the process of converting to the type.

Spitfires first saw action on 6 September 1939, during the so-called 'Battle of Barking Creek'. Because of a technical fault at the radar station at Canewdon in Essex, aircraft flying west of the station appeared on the screen as if their position was east of the radar (i.e., in the direction from which a German raiding force heading for London would make

Main left: **The cockpit of an early production Spitfire I.**
Inset: **Spitfires of No. 19 Squadron practise formation flying, early in 1939.**

SPITFIRE I

Type Single-seat interceptor fighter.
Armament: Eight Browning .303in (7.7mm) machine guns with 350 rounds per gun.
Power Plant One Rolls-Royce Merlin II liquid cooled V-12 engine with single-speed supercharger developing 1,030 horse power.
Dimensions Span 36ft 10in (10.98m); length 29ft 11in (9.11m).
Weight Maximum loaded weight 5,819lb (2,639kg).
Performance Maximum speed 362mph at 18,500ft (583km/hr at 5,640m). Service ceiling 31,900ft (9,725m).

Top: **Spitfires and Hurricanes from several squadrons lined up at Digby in Lincolnshire. The aircaft had assembled there prior to a massed flypast over cities in the Midlands, to mark Empire Air Day on 20 May 1939. (No. 72 Squadron Archive)**
Above and overleaf: **The 600th production Spitfire during its testing in April 1940. During the Battle of Britain this aircraft served with No. 64 Squadron.**

Spitfires first saw action on 6 September 1939, during the so-called 'Battle of Barking Creek'

its approach). The operators at Canewdon reported 20 unidentified aircraft heading towards London from the east, and to meet the threat several fighter squadrons were scrambled. Within

---

For the next hour chaos, utter and complete, reigned over the Thames estuary

---

minutes the 'incoming formations' being tracked on the radar, all of them now designated as 'hostile', increased to twelve. Despite the poor weather it looked as if the Luftwaffe was about to launch its expected onslaught on the capital. The defences came to full alert

A GERMAN PILOT'S OPINION OF THE SPITFIRE

Below: Spitfires in captivity: by the beginning of the Battle of Britain the Germans had captured four Spitfires in flying or repairable condition.
Bottom: A captured Spitfire painted in bogus British markings and used in propaganda photographs.

'I was able to fly a captured Spitfire at Jever. My first impression was that it had a beautiful engine. It purred. The engine of the Messerschmitt 109 was very loud. Also the Spitfire was easier to fly, and to land, than the Me 109. The 109 was unforgiving of any inattention. I felt familiar with the Spitfire from the very start. That was my first and lasting impression. But with my experience with the 109, I personally

would not have traded it for a Spitfire. I had the impression, though I did not fly the Spitfire long enough to prove it, that the 109 was the faster, especially in the dive. Also, I think the pilot's view was better from the 109. In the Spitfire one flew further back, a bit more over the wing.'

OBERLEUTNANT HANS SCHMOLLER-HALDY,
MESSERSCHMITT 109 PILOT, FIGHTER
GESCHWADER 54

and soon afterwards an anti-aircraft gun battery opened fire at 'twin-engined bombers' passing overhead. Shortly after that the leader of a Spitfire squadron broadcast a 'Tally Ho!' call, to indicate that he had enemy planes in sight and was about to engage. For the next hour chaos, utter and complete, reigned over the Thames Estuary. Squadrons of fighters cruised between the banks of cloud, seeking enemy planes but finding only friendly ones. There were several brief fire fights, each one broken off when it became evident that the 'opponents' were 'friendlies'. In the end shortage of

Right: Spitfires of No. 41 Squadron photographed during the Battle of Britain.

Above: Spitfires of Nos 222 and 603 Squadrons at Hornchurch at the time of the Battle of Britain. Note the steam roller in the background, to roll flat the filled-in bomb craters on the airfield.

Right: The Messerschmitt 109E was the most formidable opponent facing RAF Fighter Command during the Battle of Britain.

fuel forced the Spitfires and Hurricanes to return to their airfields, and then the situation resolved itself. In fact there had never been any German aircraft in the area. The fiasco cost the RAF three aircraft destroyed; two Hurricanes shot down by Spitfires of No. 74 Squadron and a Blenheim shot down by anti-aircraft fire. One RAF pilot was killed.

Following the action Fighter Command launched a thoroughgoing official inquiry to determine what had gone wrong and prevent a recurrence. One lesson, which has to be re-learned for each war, was the folly of opening

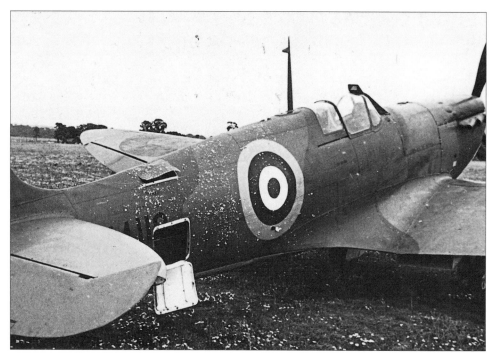

"YOU WON'T SURVIVE TEN MINUTES IN BATTLE"

'During the Battle of Britain one had to take every opportunity to train new pilots. Young pilots would arrive on the squadron with only six or seven hours' flying time on the Spitfire. One or two practice sorties could make all the difference to their ability to survive in combat. When we were at 30 minutes available, I might ring operations and ask permission to take one of the new pilots into the air for "follow my leader" practice. If one could take them up, one could point out their failings and tell them: "You won't survive ten minutes in battle if you fly like that!" The object was to tell them why and lead them round, not to frighten them.'

SQUADRON LEADER DONALD MACDONELL,
COMMANDER OF NO. 64 SQUADRON

Left: Spitfire X4110 had a service life of only 15 minutes! On the morning of 18 August 1940 this brand new aircraft arrived at No. 602 Squadron at Westhampnett as a replacement. Before there was time to paint on the squadron markings Flight Lieutenant Dunlop Urie took it into action and in an encounter with Me 109s the fighter suffered severe damage. Despite splinter wounds to both feet, Urie landed the machine at base. The Spitfire's back was broken and it never flew again.

Spitfires and Hurricanes flew large numbers of sorties to cover the evacuation of Dunkirk

fire on aircraft that had not been positively identified as 'hostile'. Another was the danger of looking at the reports from one radar in isolation (other stations along the coast had reported seeing no aircraft approaching from the east, but the absence of plots had been ignored). A further lesson was the need to fit IFF (identification friend or foe) radar equipment in all RAF fighters, and the programme to build and install this equipment received top priority.

Spitfires encountered genuinely hostile aircraft for the first time on 16 October 1939, when aircraft of Nos 602 and 603 Squadrons rose to intercept nine Junkers 88s running in to make a dive-bombing attack on Royal Navy warships in the Firth of Forth. Flight Lieutenant Pat Gifford of No. 603 Squadron shot down one of the bombers and Flight Lieutenants

Pinkerton and McKellar of No. 602 Squadron destroyed another. A third Ju 88 suffered damage.

The Spitfire first encountered German aircraft en masse on 21 May 1940, when the rapid advance of the German army into Belgium and France brought the war to within reach of Royal Air Force fighters operating from airfields in Kent. During the weeks that followed Spitfires and Hurricanes flew large numbers of sorties to cover the evacuation of Allied troops from Dunkirk.

■ BATTLE OF BRITAIN ■

At the beginning of July 1940 RAF Fighter Command possessed fifty squadrons of modern single-seat fighters, thirty-one with Hurricanes and nineteen with Spitfires. The Battle of Britain opened with Luftwaffe attacks on convoys of shipping passing through the

Above: **Pilot Officer Robert Doe of No. 234 Squadron was credited with eleven enemy aircraft destroyed and two shared destroyed. He then moved to a Hurricane squadron and shot down three more. Doe suffered serious injuries during a crash landing in January 1941, and these prevented him flying for several months.**
Above right: **Dunlop Urie, his feet bandaged, waiting to be taken to hospital.**
Right: **Squadron Leader Donald MacDonell commanded No. 64 Squadron during the Battle and was credited with nine enemy aircraft destroyed and one shared destroyed. He was shot down in March 1941 and spent the rest of the war in captivity.**

WAITING AT READINESS

During the Battle of Britain R.A.F. fighter squadrons waiting to go into action were held on the ground at what was known as Readiness 5 Minutes. The fighters sat in their earth-and-brick revetments around the perimeter of the airfield, and from time to time the ground crews would run the engines to warm the oil and ensure the planes could take off immediately. Squadron Leader Don MacDonell, commander of No. 64 Squadron during the Battle, explained what it was like having to wait on the ground until the next German attack was detected.

'When we were at Readiness the pilots would be relaxing at the dispersal area – reading, chatting, playing cards. Each Flight had a separate crew room, so no pilot was too far from his Spitfire. I would be out of my office, wearing flying kit and Mae West, with the Flight I was to lead on that day. Each pilot's parachute was laid out on the seat of his aircraft, with the straps laid over the armour plating at the back of the cockpit.

Every time the telephone rang there would be a ghastly silence. The orderly would answer it and often one would hear something like: "Yes, Sir ... yes, Sir ... Yes, Sir ... Sergeant Smith wanted on the phone." And everyone would breathe again.'

Above left: Flying Officer Leonard Haines of No. 19 Squadron was credited with eight enemy 'kills' and four shared destroyed. He died in a flying accident in April 1941.

Above right: Squadron Leader Derek Boitel-Gill commanding No. 152 Squadron was credited with eight aircraft destroyed. He died in a flying accident in September 1941.

English Channel. The purpose of the attacks was to disrupt the coastal traffic and also to force the Royal Air Force into action. As time passed the fighting over the Channel became progressively more ferocious, and the Luftwaffe began sending free hunting patrols over southern England.

These actions were but a prelude to the main campaign by the Luftwaffe, which began on 13 August, aimed at destroying Fighter Command as an effective force. That day German aircraft launched multi-pronged attacks on the Royal Navy bases at Portland and Southampton and on the airfields at Detling and Eastchurch.

There were repeated attacks on Fighter Command airfields in the south of England

During the next three and a half weeks there were repeated attacks on Fighter Command airfields in the south of England. The Luftwaffe failed in its aim of knocking out Fighter Command, however. Every major airfield in the No. 11 Group area took hard knocks.

'SCRAMBLE!'

In Fighter Command the code-word 'Scramble' meant 'get airborne as rapidly as possible'. When pilots received the order they ran as if their lives depended on it – because they did. Each 30-second delay in getting airborne meant 1,000 feet (305m) less altitude they had when they met the enemy. And everyone knew that a Spitfire caught in the climb was easy meat for a Messerschmitt attacking in a dive. Squadron Leader Donald MacDonell explained the procedure for getting airborne:

'The orderly answering the telephone would shout "SCRAMBLE!" at the top of his voice and each pilot would dash for his aircraft. By the time one got there a mechanic would already have started the engine; the other would be holding the parachute up and help me strap it on. Once that was done I would clamber into the cockpit. He would pass my seat straps over my shoulders and help me fasten them. When I gave the thumbs-up he would slam shut the side door and I would pull tight the various straps. Next I would pull on my helmet, plug in the R/T lead and check that the engine was running properly. If all was well I would wave to the groundcrew to pull away the chocks, open the throttle, and move forward out of my blast pen and across the grass to the take-off position. Once there I would line up, open the throttle wide open and begin my take-off run with the rest of my pilots following as fast as they could. The whole thing, from the scramble order to the last aircraft leaving the ground, took about a minute and a half.

'As soon as Spitfires were all off the ground and climbing, I would inform operations. The Sector Controller would come back and tell me where he wanted me to go and at what altitude. While the squadron was forming up I would climb in a wide spiral at low boost, until everyone was in place. Then I would open up to a high throttle setting to get to altitude as fast as possible.'

SPITFIRE FIGHTER DEPLOYMENT, SEPTEMBER 1940

Spitfire units on the afternoon of 14 September, before the decisive action of the Battle of Britain on the next day. First figure aircraft serviceable, in brackets aircraft unserviceable

NO. 10 GROUP, HQ BOX, WILTSHIRE
Middle Wallop Sector

No. 152 Squadron	17	(2)	Warmwell
No. 609 Squadron	15	(3)	Middle Wallop

St Eval Sector

No. 234 Squadron	16	(1)	St Eval
Group Total	48	(6)	

NO. 11 GROUP, HQ UXBRIDGE, MIDDLESEX
Biggin Hill Sector

No. 72 Squadron	10	(7)	Biggin Hill
No. 92 Squadron	16	(1)	Biggin Hill
No. 66 Squadron	14	(2)	Gravesend

Hornchurch Sector

No. 603 Squadron	14	(5)	Hornchurch
No. 41 Squadron	12	(6)	Rochford
No. 222 Squadron	11	(3)	Rochford

Tangmere Sector

No. 602 Squadron	15	(4)	Westhampnett
Group Total	**92**	**(28)**	

NO. 12 GROUP, HQ WATNALL, NOTTINGHAMSHIRE
Duxford Sector

No. 19 Squadron	14	(0)	Fowlmere

Coltishall Sector

No. 74 Squadron	14	(8)	Coltishall

Wittering Sector

No. 266 Squadron	14	(5)	Wittering

Digby Sector

No. 611 Squadron	17	(1)	Digby

Kirton-in-Lindsey Sector

No. 616 Squadron	14	(4)	Kirton-in-Lindsey
No. 64 Squadron	7	(3)	Leconfield
	6	(3)	Ringway
Group Total	**86**	**(24)**	

NO. 13 GROUP, HQ NEWCASTLE, NORTHUMBERLAND
Catterick Sector

No. 54 Squadron	15	(2)	Catterick

Usworth Sector

No. 610 Squadron	14	(5)	Acklington

Turnhouse Sector

No. 65 Squadron	15	(5)	Turnhouse
Group Total	**44**	**(12)**	

Spitfires at Operational Training Units

26	(24)

Spitfire Production During Week Prior to 14 September 38

Replacement Spitfires Held at Maintenance Units, 14 September 1940

Ready for immediate issue to units	47
Ready for issue within four days	10

Below left: Sergeant Basil Whall flew with No. 602 Squadron and was credited with seven enemy aircraft destroyed and two shared destroyed. In October 1940 he suffered fatal injuries when he tried to land his damaged aircraft after a combat sortie. *Below right:* Lieutenant Arthur 'Admiral' Blake, a Fleet Air Arm pilot loaned to RAF Fighter Command, flew with No. 19 Squadron. Credited with four enemy aircraft destroyed and one shared destroyed, he was shot down and killed in October 1940.

Above: **The wrecked shell of the Supermarine factory at Woolston, pictured after the devastating German air attack on 26 September 1940.**

However, there was an efficient damage-repair organization and in the event only one airfield, that at Manston in Kent, was put out of action for more than a few hours. Only in rare instances were the raiders able to catch RAF fighters on the ground. By the time the German bombers arrived to deliver their attack on an airfield, the Spitfires and Hurricanes based there were usually airborne and well clear. Fighters able to fly but not fight took off on 'survival scrambles'

with orders to keep clear of the area until the threat had passed. Aircraft unable to fly were wheeled into the protective revetments, or dispersed around the airfield where they were difficult to hit. As a result of these measures the front-line fighter units lost fewer than twenty fighters destroyed on the ground, despite the almost daily attacks on airfields throughout a 25-day period.

On 7 September the Luftwaffe shifted its attack to London, concentrating its main effort against the sprawling dock area to the east of the city. During the following week there were three further attacks on the capital. Then on 15 September, Battle of Britain Day, the Luftwaffe mounted two separate raids on London.

'IT DEMONSTRATED THE DETERMINATION AND BRAVERY WITH WHICH THE TOMMIES WERE FIGHTING OVER THEIR OWN COUNTRY'

Early on the afternoon of 15 September 1940, as the Heinkel 111s of Bomber Geschwader 26 were passing Maidstone on their way home, the formation suddenly came under attack from Spitfires. Leutnant Roderich Cescotti, one of the German pilots, recalled:

'A few Tommies succeeded in penetrating our fighter escort. I saw a Spitfire dive steeply through our escort, level out and close rapidly on our formation. It opened fire, from ahead and to the right, and its tracers streaked towards us. At that moment a Bf 109, which we had not seen before, appeared behind the Spitfire and we saw its rounds striking the Spitfire's tail. But the Tommy continued his attack, coming straight for us, and his rounds slashed into our aircraft. We could not return the fire for fear of hitting the Messerschmitt. I put my left arm across my face to protect it from the plexiglass splinters flying around the cockpit, holding the controls with my right hand. With only the thin plexiglass between us, we were eye-to-eye with the enemy's eight machine guns. At the last moment the Spitfire pulled up and passed very close over the top of us. Then it rolled on its back, as

though out of control, and went down steeply trailing black smoke. Waggling its wings, the Messerschmitt swept past us and curved in for another attack. The action lasted only a few seconds, but it demonstrated the determination and bravery with which the Tommies were fighting over their own country.'

Cescotti's Heinkel had taken several hits, but he was able to hold position in formation. He made a normal landing at his base at Wevelghem in Belgium.

Almost certainly the courageous Spitfire pilot was Flying Officer Peter Pease of No. 603 Squadron, who was shot down at the time, the place, and in the manner described by Cescotti. When the blazing fighter smashed into the ground a few miles south-east of Maidstone, Pease was still in the cockpit.

The son of Sir Richard Pease, Arthur Peter Pease studied at Eton and Cambridge University before joining the Royal Air Force at the beginning of the war. In July 1940 he was posted to No. 603 Squadron based at Dyce airfield near Aberdeen and later that month he shared in the destruction of a Heinkel 111. Early in August the Squadron moved to Hornchurch, north-east of London, to take part in the defence of southern

England. On 3 September Pease was credited with shooting down a Messerschmitt 109, and four days later his Spitfire suffered battle damage and he made a crash landing at Hornchurch. Just over a week later, on 15 September, Peter Pease died in action.

Above: **Flying Officer Peter Pease of No. 603 Squadron, whose courageous attack is described by Roderich Cescotti.**

'I FELT JOLLY GLAD TO BE DOWN ON THE GROUND WITHOUT HAVING CAUGHT FIRE'

'We were just going in to attack when somebody yelled "Messerschmitts" over the R.T. and the whole squadron split up. Actually it was a false alarm. Anyway, being on my own I debated what to do. The bombers were my object, so I snooped in under the 110s and attacked the bombers (about 40–50 Heinkel 111s) from the starboard beam.

'I got in a burst of about three seconds when – Crash! and the whole World seemed to be tumbling in on me. I pushed the stick forward hard, went into a vertical dive and held it until I was below cloud. I had a look round. The chief trouble was that petrol was gushing into the cockpit at the rate of gallons all over my feet, and there was a sort of lake of petrol in the bottom of the cockpit. My knee and leg were tingling all over as if I had pushed them into a bed of nettles. There was a bullet hole in my windscreen where a bullet had come in and entered the dashboard, knocking away the starter button. Another bullet, I think an explosive one, had knocked away one of my petrol taps in front of the joystick, spattering my leg with little splinters and sending a chunk of something through the backside of my petrol tank near the bottom. I had obviously run into some pretty good crossfire from the Heinkels. I made for home at top speed to get there before all my petrol ran out. I was about 15 miles from the aerodrome and it was a heart-rending business with all that petrol gushing over my legs and the constant danger of fire. About five miles from the 'drome smoke began to come from under my dashboard. I thought the whole thing might blow up at any minute, so I switched off my engine. The smoke stopped. I glided towards the 'drome and tried putting my wheels down. One came down and the other remained stuck up. I tried to get the one that was down up again. It was stuck down. There was nothing for it but to make a one-wheel landing. I switched on my engine again to make the aerodrome. It took me some way and then began to smoke again, so I hastily switched off. I was now near enough and made a normal approach and held off. I made a good landing, touching down lightly. The unsupported wing slowly began to drop. I was able to hold it up for some time and then down came the wing tip on the ground. I began to slew round and counteracted as much as possible with the brake on the wheel which was down. I ended up going sideways on one wheel, a tail wheel and a wing tip. Luckily, the good tyre held out and the only damage to the aeroplane, apart from that done by the bullets, was a wing tip that is easily replaceable.

'I hopped out and went off to the M.O. to get a lot of metal splinters picked out of my leg and wrist. I felt jolly glad to be down on the ground without having caught fire.'

PILOT OFFICER ERIC MARRS of No. 152 Squadron describing his action on 30 September 1940

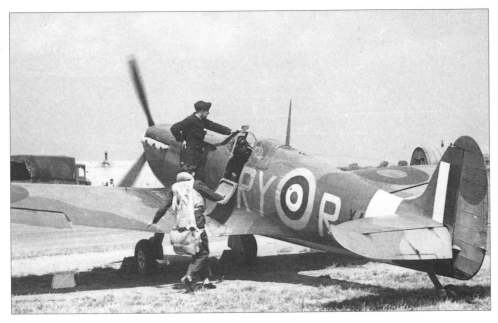

Left: **A pilot of No. 313 (Czech) Squadron running to his Spitfire during a scramble take off.**

No. 11 Group of Fighter Command, which bore the brunt of the defence of the capital, possessed 310 serviceable single-seat fighters. Of that total 218 were Hurricanes, and 92 were Spitfires. To meet the two attacks on London, the RAF fighter controllers used the same defensive tactics against each. About one-third of the available squadrons, Hurricanes and Spitfires, engaged the raiding forces as they made their way across Kent to the capital. The purpose of these attacks was twofold; first, to destroy as many German bombers as possible, and secondly to force the escorting Me 109s to fly at full throttle to ward off the British fighters and so deplete their limited supply of fuel. Meanwhile, the main body of defending fighters assembled over the east and south-east outskirts of London. It was there that the two great clashes occurred and most of the aircraft were shot down.

■ BATTLE OF BRITAIN DAY ■

The first attack took place shortly before noon. The raiding force comprised twenty-one Messerschmitt 109 fighter-bombers and twenty-seven Dornier 17 bombers, with an escort of about a hundred and eighty Me 109s. The fighter-bombers were to attack rail targets throughout the London area, while the Dorniers were to hit the concentration of rail lines and junctions at Battersea. Two hours later there was a much heavier attack on a series of targets in the London dock area, involving 114 Dornier 17s and Heinkel 111s escorted by some 450 Me 109s and a few Me 110s.

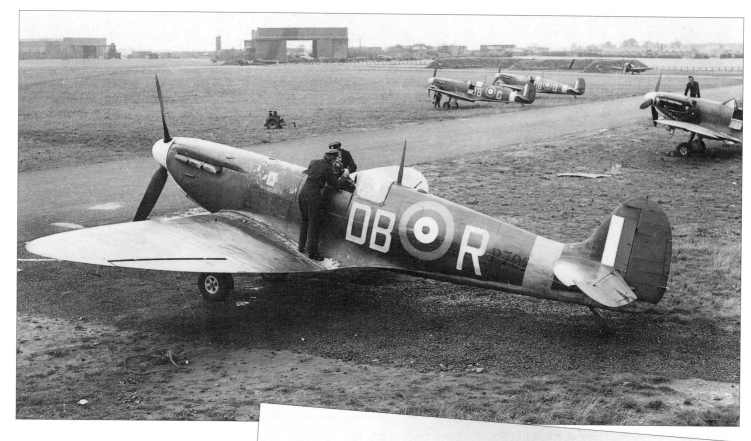

Above: WAAF mechanics helping the pilot strap into a Spitfire Mark II of No. 411 (Canadian) Squadron, at Digby in Lincolnshire in 1941.

Right: A few Mark II Spitfires were modified for the Air Sea Rescue role, and carried two cylindrical drums in parachutes in the rear fuselage containing an inflatable rubber dinghy and ration packs to drop to survivors.

During the late afternoon of the 15th the Luftwaffe also launched smaller attacks on targets on the south coast. Twenty-six Heinkels bombed the Royal Navy base at Portland, and a small force of Messerschmitt 109 and 110 fighter-bombers tried unsuccessfully to hit the Supermarine plant at Southampton.

That day fifty-five German aircraft were destroyed, most of them falling to fighter attack. The RAF lost eight Spitfires and twenty-one Hurricanes. The Spitfire force suffered a loss rate of 4.2 per hundred sorties, while the Hurricane force suffered a loss rate of 6.4 per hundred sorties. In action the Spitfire's superior performance meant it had a 50 per cent better chance of survival compared with the Hurricane.

The German losses on 15 September fell far short of the 185 aircraft the defenders claimed as destroyed. Yet the action is rightly deemed to mark the climax of the Battle. Two days later Adolf Hitler ordered an indefinite postponement of Operation Sealion, the planned invasion of Britain. The ships and barges concentrated at ports along the Channel coast returned to their normal tasks and it was clear that the threat of invasion had passed.

■ THE MARK II ■

Towards the end of the Battle of Britain the Spitfire Mark II entered service. Similar in most respects to the Mark I, the new variant was powered by the Merlin 12 engine giving an additional 110 horse power. With the installation of armour protection and additional items of equipment, however, the Mark II weighed 350lb (159kg) more than the early production Mark I. Because of this, the additional engine power merely restored the fighter's performance to its earlier level. The Spitfire emerged from the Battle of Britain with a proven record of success in the limited role of home-defence fighter. Yet this very success would inhibit its ability to achieve more in that role. Having suffered heavy losses during the Battle, the Luftwaffe gave up the idea of trying to mount large-scale daylight attacks on targets in Britain. If the Spitfire was to continue to play a major part in the war, it would have to do so in roles other than that of home-defence fighter. As we shall observe next, it had already started to do so.

MAINTAINING SPITFIRE PRODUCTION

On 26 September 1940 a raiding force of fifty-nine Heinkel 111s mounted a devastating attack on the two main Supermarine factories at Woolston and Itchen. The bombers wrecked most of the factory buildings at both sites, striking a body blow at Spitfire production.

On the day following the attack Lord Beaverbrook, Winston Churchill's tireless Minister of Aircraft Production, visited Southampton to inspect the damage. On his decision the two wrecked factories were abandoned. Production of Spitfires was to be dispersed into several smaller units in towns and cities. Fortuitously most of the machine tools and production jigs at Woolston and Itchen had survived the attack. Also, the final assembly hangers at Eastleigh airfield had not been touched. Supermarine executives toured Southampton, Winchester, Salisbury, Trowbridge, Reading and Newbury and the surrounding areas, looking at every large open building. Motor repair garages, laundries and bus stations were the obvious choices. Accompanying each Supermarine executive was a policeman who carried a letter of introduction from the Chief Constable of the area, requesting cooperation but giving no reason for the visit. Where a building was considered suitable for use in the dispersed production scheme, the not-always-delighted owner received official papers requisitioning the building. As each new site was acquired, the Spitfire production jigs and tools were brought in and set up.

By the end of October, thirty-five separate premises had been taken over for the programme and production had begun at sixteen of them. Also by this time, the large-scale production had started at the huge purpose-built Nuffield organization factory at Castle Bromwich near Birmingham.

Never again would Spitfire production be as vulnerable to air attack as it had been in September 1940.

Above right and below: **Following the attack on the Supermarine factories, Spitfire production was dispersed into several small units in the surrounding towns and cities. These photographs show Spitfire wing leading edges being manufactured at the requisitioned garage of Anna Valley Motors Ltd at Salisbury.**

Far right, below: **A remarkable photograph taken from a Messerschmitt 110 reconnaissance aircraft over Snodland, Kent, showing Spitfires of No. 64 Squadron climbing into position to intercept the aircraft. The Messerschmitt suffered severe damage in the ensuing engagement and the radio operator was killed.**

SPITFIRE SPYPLANES

In time of war it is difficult to exaggerate the importance of aerial reconnaissance. To plan effective air attacks, staff officers require the best possible information on each target. They need to know where bombs should be aimed to cause maximum damage. They also need to know the layout of the defences around each target, so they can route the bombers to avoid the worst of them. Without such information, attacking forces will inflict less damage, and suffer heavier losses, than would otherwise be the case. The best source of such information is aerial photography.

Today the idea of using an unarmed reconnaissance aircraft, to make a high speed dash through enemy territory to photograph targets, is well accepted. It was not always so. Before the Second World War most air forces employed modified bombers to fly long-range reconnaissance missions. Lacking the performance to avoid the defences, these machines had to carry guns and gunners to fight their way through to targets.

Shortly before the outbreak of war, Flying Officer Maurice 'Shorty' Longbottom, an enterprising young RAF officer, suggested a better means of securing reconnaissance photographs. In a memorandum he set down his views on the future of strategic aerial reconnaissance. Longbottom suggested that reconnaissance should be done 'in such a manner as to avoid the enemy fighters and AA defences as completely as possible'. The best way of doing that, he thought, was by 'the use of a single small machine, relying solely on its speed,

climb and ceiling to avoid detection . . .'. Longbottom believed the ideal aircraft would be a Spitfire with the guns, ammunition, radio and other unnecessary equipment removed. With additional fuel tanks and cameras installed in their place, he argued that such an aircraft would have the range to reach distant targets. It would, moreover, have the speed and altitude performance to penetrate the enemy defences at will.

The Air Ministry greeted Longbottom's memorandum with polite interest, but initially the paper was pigeon-holed. The RAF was desperately short of modern

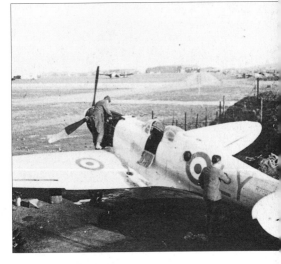

Main left: Compare the 1939 inset photograph with the main one, of Bullihgen, taken in April 1944 from a Spitfire at the same altitude, with a camera fitted with a 36in lens. Considerably more ground detail is visible. Comparison of these photos shows the great advances made in aerial cameras during the war years.

Top: Spitfire PR IC used for high-altitude photographic missions. This aircraft carried its vertically mounted cameras in a blister under the starboard wing, seen in the open position for the removal of the film magazines. **Middle:** Spitfire PR IF. This aircraft carried its vertically mounted cameras in the rear fuselage, and was fitted with blister fuel tanks

under the wings to give it increased range. **Above:** Spitfire PR IG used for low-altitude 'dicing' missions, to photograph targets beneath cloud. These aircraft wore a very pale shade of pink (the colour was the same as the bottom of cloud on overcast days). The window for the oblique camera is at the top left of the fuselage roundel.

RECONNAISSANCE VARIANTS

PR IA Original PR variant, one 5in (12.7cm) lens camera mounted in each wing. No additional fuel.

PR IB One 8in (20.3cm) lens camera in each wing. Additional fuel: 29-gallon (132l) tank in the rear fuselage.

PR IC As PR IB, but with the two 8in lens cameras mounted in tandem in a blister fairing under the starboard wing. Additional fuel: 29-gallon (132l) tank in the rear fuselage, 30-gallon (136.5l) blister tank under the port wing.

PR ID First major re-design of the Spitfire for the reconnaissance role. Carried two 8in or two 20in (50.8cm) lens cameras in the rear fuselage. Additional fuel: large fuel tank built integrally with the leading edge of the wing, capacity 114 gal (518l); 29-gallon tank in the rear fuselage. This variant replaced the Marks IA, IB, IC and IF in front-line service during 1941. When fitted with the Merlin 45 engine it became the PR 5D, then it was redesignated as the PR Mark 4.

PR IE Designed for the low-altitude reconnaissance role; only one example produced. Oblique camera under each wing, pointing at right angles to the line of flight. Additional fuel: 29-gallon (132l) tank in rear fuselage.

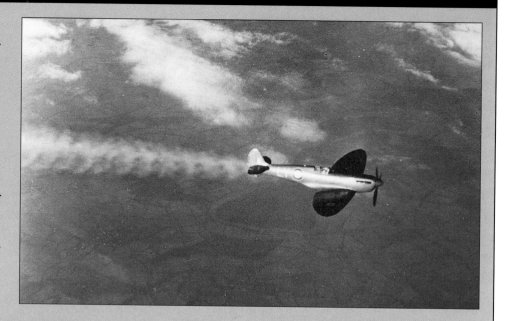

PR IF Carried two 8in or two 20in (50.8cm) lens cameras in the rear fuselage. Additional fuel: 30-gallon (136.5l) blister tank under each wing, 29-gallon (132l) tank in the rear fuselage.

PR IG Designed for low-altitude reconnaissance role. One oblique camera mounted in the rear fuselage, could point either to port or to starboard. In addition there was one 14in (35.6cm) and one 5in (12.7cm) mounted verti-

Above: A reconnaissance Spitfire at high altitude. When over enemy territory pilots went to great pains to avoid leaving condensation trails, since these betrayed their position and made them vulnerable to fighter interception.

cally in the rear fuselage. Additional fuel: 29-gallon (132l) tank in the rear fuselage.

Left and far right: Exterior and interior of the huge Spitfire production facility at Castle Bromwich, Birmingham. Morris Motors Ltd built the factory, under contract to the British Government. The plant produced some twelve thousand Spitfires, more than half of the total. At its peak it turned out 320 Spitfires per month.

Left: Dramatic low-altitude shot of the German cruiser *Hipper* in dry dock, at the heavily defended port of Brest.

fighters, and needed every available Spitfire for the defence of Great Britain. Air Chief Marshal Dowding was unwilling to release these precious aircraft for other roles, no matter how persuasive the arguments might appear.

It took only six weeks of war to change people's minds. The main RAF

SPYPLANE PILOT

'During the early [photographic reconnaissance] missions there was no such thing as cockpit heating in our Spitfires. For the high altitude missions we wore thick suits with electrical heating. Trussed up in our Mae West and parachute, one could scarcely move in the narrow cockpit of the Spitfire. When flying over enemy territory one had to be searching the sky the whole time for enemy fighters. On more than one occasion I started violent evasive action to shake off a suspected enemy fighter, only to discover that it was a small speck of dirt on the inside of my perspex canopy!

'A big worry over enemy territory was that one might start leaving a condensation trail without knowing it, thus pointing out one's position to the enemy. To avoid that we had small mirrors fitted in the blisters on each side of the canopy, so that one could see the trail as soon as it started to form. When that happened one could either climb or descend until the trail ceased. If possible, we liked to climb above the trail's layer because then fighters trying to intercept us had first to climb through the trail's layer themselves and could be seen in good time.'

PILOT OFFICER GORDON GREEN, SPITFIRE PILOT, PHOTOGRAPHIC RECONNAISSANCE UNIT

reconnaissance aircraft then in use, the low performance Blenheim, was quite inadequate for the task. Only rarely could they photograph targets any distance inside enemy territory, and they suffered heavy losses whenever they tried.

■ SECRET NEW UNIT ■

Following strong representations from the Air Ministry, Air Chief Marshal Dowding reluctantly agreed to release a couple of Spitfires for the reconnaissance role. The aircraft went to a highly secret new unit based at Heston north of London, headed by Wing Commander Sidney Cotton. Appropriately, one of the officers who helped him set up the unit was 'Shorty' Longbottom himself.

Cotton's first step was to modify the Spitfires for the new role and commence operations over enemy territory, to prove the validity of Longbottom's proposals. Each aircraft was fitted with a pair of cameras, mounted in each wing in the space previously occupied by the guns and ammunition boxes. Metal plates sealed off the empty gun ports, and groundcrewmen applied plaster of Paris to fill the joints in the skinning. Then each aircraft received a coat of polish to give it a smooth, high-gloss, finish. With these changes the maximum speed of the reconnaissance Spitfires was about 12mph (about 20km/hr) faster than the fighter version.

In November 1939 the Spitfire reconnaissance unit under the cover-designation 'No. 2 Camouflage Unit', moved to Seclin near Lille in France to begin operational trials. On the 18th Longbottom, now a Flight Lieutenant, took off to photograph the German city of Aachen and the nearby fortifications. Flying at 33,000 feet (10,000m), a very high altitude in those days, he found navigation more difficult than expected. When his films were developed, they showed a strip of Belgian territory to the south of Aachen. Longbottom learned the lesson well, and when he returned to the area four days later he made a successful photographic run over the German border defences.

During the weeks that followed the two Spitfires photographed several targets in western Germany, including the Ruhr industrial area. Significantly, and in distinct contrast to the Blenheims, the Spitfires flew their missions without loss or even serious interference from the German defences.

Photographs taken from 33,000 feet (10,000m) with 5in (12.7cm) focal-length cameras produced very small-scale pictures, however. The interpreters could pick out roads, railways, villages and major fortifications. But even with prints enlarged as much as the grain of the film allowed, it was not possible to see troop positions or individual vehicles. If the Spitfire's capabilities were to be fully exploited, longer lens cameras would be needed. Work began to develop these. Apart from that proviso, the flights proved the essential soundness of Longbottom's proposals. As a result Air Chief Marshal Dowding agreed to release a dozen more Spitfires for the reconnaissance role.

In January 1940 an improved photographic reconnaissance Spitfire was ready for operations, the PR IB (for details of this and other reconnaissance variants, see opposite; the earlier variant became known as the PR IA). In February

Left: Seamstresses applying the fabric covering to Spitfire rudders, in one of the component production halls at Castle Bromwich. The Spitfire's rudder weighed only 18lb (8kg), but was strong enough to withstand the side forces engendered when manoeuvring at high speed.

Longbottom demonstrated the usefulness of the PR IB's additional range capability when he photographed the important German naval bases at Wilhelmshaven and Emden.

Soon afterwards Cotton's unit was renamed the Photographic Development Unit, the new title revealing its true role for the first time. Early in 1940 the operations in France were reorganized and a further unit, No. 212 Squadron, formed at Seclin to conduct the Spitfire reconnaissance missions from there.

Below: A showpiece of the British aircraft industry, the Castle Bromwich plant had a constant stream of important visitors. Here Winston Churchill is seen chatting with Alex Henshaw, Chief Test Pilot at the factory. Between the summer of 1940 and 1946 Henshaw personally tested no fewer than 2,360 Spitfires, about one in ten of those built.

■ LONG-RANGE VISION ■

In March 1940 a so-called 'long range' reconnaissance version of the Spitfire appeared, the PR IC, with a further fuel tank to increase its reach. On 7 April Longbottom took this aircraft to Kiel, the first RAF aircraft to photograph the important naval base since the outbreak of war.

Little over a month later, on 10 May 1940, German forces launched their powerful Blitzkrieg attack on France, Holland and Belgium. During the hectic weeks that followed No. 212 Squadron photographed each stage of the relentless advance of the German Panzer columns. The squadron then withdrew to England, where its aircraft and personnel were incorporated in the PDU at Heston.

Thus far the reconnaissance Spitfires had flown their missions at medium or high altitude, and photographed their targets from directly above. Most of the RAF's aerial photography would continue to be done that way, but there was another technique that allowed close-up shots or photography of targets below cloud. A few Spitfires were fitted with the so-called oblique camera installation,

with a camera pointing at right angles to the line of flight and a few degrees below the horizontal. On 7 July 1940 Flying Officer Alistair Taylor proved the value of the new installation. Despite a 700-foot (213m) cloud base and heavy rain, which would have precluded vertical photography, he took good photographs of shipping inside Boulogne harbour as he flew past the outer mole. From then on low-altitude photography, nicknamed 'dicing' because of the risks involved, became an important additional role for the reconnaissance Spitfires.

Also in July 1940, the Photographic Development Unit underwent yet another name change. It became the Photographic Reconnaissance Unit (PRU) and at the same time Wing Commander Geoffrey Tuttle replaced Sidney Cotton as its commander. The changes of name and commander made no difference to the way the unit operated, however.

> *Longbottom took the PR IC to Kiel, the first RAF aircraft to photograph the important naval base*

At the end of July a further Spitfire reconnaissance variant appeared, the 'super-long-range' PR IF. This variant had a radius of action about 100 miles (160 km) greater than the Type IC. Operating from airfields in East Anglia, it could photograph targets as far afield as Berlin.

Throughout the summer of 1940, reconnaissance Spitfires kept a daily watch on the German preparations for the invasion of Britain. Each day they sallied forth to photograph each of the ports along the Channel coast, observing the growing assemblies of barges and shipping at each. Then on 20 September,

'IT WAS ALL RATHER LIKE A FOX HUNT . . . '

'During the early [photographic reconnaissance] missions to cover Brest [in 1941] we lost about five pilots fairly quickly. After the first couple had failed to return the Flight Commander, Flight Lieutenant Keith Arnold, asked Benson [the headquarters of the reconnaissance units] to send some reserve pilots. They duly arrived. Both took off for Brest that evening and neither came back. That was a very sobering incident.

'The important thing with any photographic mission was to take the photos if one could, and get them back to base. As the "boss" of PRU, Wing Commander Geoffrey Tuttle, often used to say, "I want you to get home safely not just because I like your faces, but because if you don't the whole sortie will be a waste of time!" So it was no use trying to play hide and seek with the Luftwaffe. If one had lost surprise during the approach to a heavily defended target, the best thing was to abandon the mission. One could go back another time when things might be better. Looking back at my time with the PRU, I get a lot of satisfaction from the knowledge that although I played my part in the war, I never had to fire a shot in anger. In one sense we in the reconnaissance business had things easy. All the time it was impressed on us: bring back the photographs or, if you can't, bring back the aeroplane. An infantryman taking part in the Battle of Alamein could not suddenly decide "This is ridiculous, I'm going home!" He just had to go on. But if we thought we had lost the element of surprise we were not only permitted to turn back, we were expected to do so. On the other hand there were times when I knew real fear. When one was 15 minutes out from Brest on a low altitude sortie, one's heart was beating away and as the target got nearer one's mouth got completely dry. Anyone who was not frightened at the thought of going in to photograph one of the most heavily defended targets in Europe, was not human.

'Whenever it was possible to photograph a target, flak could engage us: if we could see to photograph they could see to open up at us. But throughout my time as a reconnaissance pilot my luck held. I never once saw an enemy fighter, nor was my aircraft ever hit by flak. Indeed only once during the time we were flying those missions over Brest did one of our aircraft come back with any damage, and that was only minor. It was all rather like a fox hunt – either the fox got away unscathed or else it was caught and killed. There was rarely anything in between.'

PILOT OFFICER GORDON GREEN, SPITFIRE PILOT, PHOTOGRAPHIC RECONNAISSANCE UNIT

three days after Adolf Hitler's order to postpone the invasion, a reconnaissance Spitfire returned bearing the first hard evidence of the change in German plans. Its photographs of Cherbourg harbour showed that five destroyers and a torpedo boat had left the port since the previous reconnaissance. In the weeks that followed, almost every successive reconnaissance flight revealed fewer ships and barges in each port as the vessels resumed their normal tasks. The threat to Great Britain had passed.

■ TO STETTIN ■

The 'long range' and 'extra long range' versions of the Spitfire opened new vistas for photographic reconnaissance and the targets it could cover. Yet in terms of range, the modified fighter could do even better. Supermarine redesigned the wing to take a huge additional fuel tank that took up almost the entire leading edge back to the main spar. In October 1940 the first Spitfires modified in this way, the PR ID, became available for operations.

When carrying its full load of fuel the PR ID was difficult to handle, as Flight Lieutenant Neil Wheeler explained. 'You could not fly it straight and level for the

first half hour or hour after take off. Until you had emptied the rear tank, the aircraft hunted the whole time. The centre of gravity was so far back that you couldn't control it. It was the sort of thing that would never have got in during peacetime, but war is another matter.' Once part of the fuel load had been consumed, however, the Type D handled well and its extra range gave it a dramatic extension of reconnaissance cover. On 29 October 1940 one of these aircraft photographed the port of Stettin on the Baltic (now Sczecin in Poland) and returned after 5 hours and 20 minutes airborne. Other remarkable missions followed in rapid succession: to Marseilles and Toulon in the extreme south of France, and to Trondheim in Norway.

The final reconnaissance variant of the Spitfire I was the Type G, optimized for the low-altitude photographic role with an oblique camera mounted in the rear fuselage. This version retained the fighter's standard armament of eight .303in (7.7mm) machine guns to enable it to defend itself against enemy fighters.

By the beginning of 1941 the reconnaissance Spitfires possessed the range to photograph targets almost anywhere in

western Europe. At this point in the Spitfire story, however, this account must return to the new challenges facing the fighter version, because, following developments in the war situation in northern Europe and the Mediterranean theatre, the aircraft was about to face a further severe test.

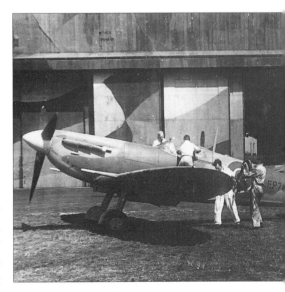

Above: **Test pilots striding out to fly brand new Spitfires off the production line at Castle Bromwich. Alex Henshaw is second from the right.**

THE SPITFIRE SPREADS ITS WINGS

In the spring of 1941 a new production version of the Spitfire appeared, the Mark V. This was fitted with the Merlin 45 engine which gave increases of, respectively, 440 and 330 horse power over the versions fitted to the Marks I and II. The main production version of the Spitfire V carried an armament of two 20mm cannon and four .303in (7.7mm) machine guns.

SPITFIRE V

Type Single-seat general purpose fighter.
Armament Four Hispano 20 mm cannon with 120 rounds per gun, or two Hispano 2 mm cannon with 120 rounds per gun and four Browning .303in (7.7mm) machine guns with 350 rounds per gun, or eight .303in (7.7mm) Browning machine guns with 350 rounds per gun. Maximum bomb load two 250lb (113kg) bombs.
Power Plant One Rolls-Royce Merlin 45 liquid cooled V-12 engine developing 1,470hp.
Dimensions Span 36ft 10in (10.98m), 32ft 6in (9.9m, clipped wings); length 29ft 11in (9.11m).
Weight Maximum loaded weight 6,070lb (2,752kg).
Performance Maximum speed 371mph at 20,000ft (597km/hr at 6,100m). Service ceiling 38,000ft (11,585m).

Left and inset: **Spitfire VC fitted with four 20mm cannon, being loaded on the aircraft carrier USS *Wasp* docked at Glasgow in April 1942. The wingtips had been removed and placed in the open cockpit, so that the aircraft could be brought by road from the nearby Abbotsinch airfield.**
Right, top: **A remarkable modification to a Spitfire carried out in Germany, when the Daimler-Benz company at Stuttgart fitted a DB 605 engine into a captured Mark V and carried out flight tests with the combination.**
Right, below: **Spitfire in trouble: a still from a combat film taken by the Luftwaffe fighter ace Major Gerhard Schoepfel of Fighter Geschwader 26, showing cannon shells bursting on the fuselage.**

Also during 1941 Fighter Command moved from the defensive to the offensive, mounting large-scale sweeps over occupied Europe. Simultaneously Spitfire production rose to a point where it exceeded losses, allowing an expansion in the number of units operating the fighter. During the Battle of Britain nineteen squadrons had operated Spitfires. By September 1941 there were twenty-seven. And by the end of 1941 Fighter Command had forty-six squadrons equipped with Spitfires.

The Mark V had a performance significantly better than the earlier variants of the Spitfire, yet it was not good enough. In the summer of 1941 the Luftwaffe introduced a new and even more effective fighter into service: the Focke Wulf 190.

When this new German fighter first appeared in action over northern France its performance came as a severe shock to

Fighter Command. The Focke Wulf was 25–30mph (40–48km/hr) faster than the Spitfire V at most altitudes and it could out-climb, out-dive and out-roll the British fighter. The Spitfire V's only advantage over its new opponent was that it could turn tighter.

Fortunately for the Royal Air Force, however, at this time the Luftwaffe was heavily committed to supporting the campaign in Russia. As a result the size of the fighter force retained in the west, and in particular that part of it operating FW 190s, would remain relatively small.

■ SPITFIRES TO MALTA ■

The next major challenge to face the Spitfire came early in 1942, and this time the venue was far to the south. Malta was the cornerstone of Britain's strategy in the central Mediterranean. Torpedo-bombers operating from the island took

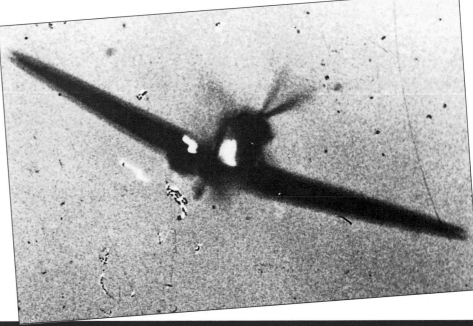

Left: In September 1942 the US manned 'Eagle' Squadrons of the RAF were officially transferred to the US Army Air Force with their aircraft. This aircraft went with No. 121 Squadron to become part of the 335th Fighter Squadron of the 4th Fighter Group.

a steady toll of ships carrying supplies and reinforcements to sustain the Axis ground forces in North Africa. Yet the beleaguered island lay within 100 miles (160km) of Axis airfields in Sicily and it suffered frequent and destructive air attacks. Malta's continued survival depended on the efficiency of her air defences, but the Hurricanes based on the island were outclassed by the Messerschmitt 109Fs opposing them.

Only the Spitfire V could engage the Me 109F on equal terms, but getting these aircraft to the island would be no easy task. The distance from Gibraltar to Malta was far beyond the Spitfire's

Right: US Army Air Force mechanics carry out an engine change on a Spitfire.
Below: Armourers of No. 72 Squadron cleaning the barrel and removing the ammunition drum from the Hispano 20mm cannon.

When the new German fighter first appeared, it came as a severe shock to Fighter Command

normal ferry range. Moreover, the strength of the Axis naval and air forces besieging the island precluded any large scale delivery of fighters by sea. The Hurricanes already on Malta had been transported half way by aircraft carrier, which launched them to fly the rest of the way to the island. The Spitfires would have to use the same method but even that would not be easy; from fly-off point to Malta was approximately 660 miles (1,062km).

To enable the Spitfire to reach Malta from a launch point, engineers at Supermarine designed a 90-gallon (409l) drop tank. The first delivery of Spitfires took place on 7 March 1942, when under

Operation Spotter fifteen of them took off from HMS *Eagle*. Before the end of the month the carrier made two further delivery runs, bringing to thirty-one the number of Spitfires flown to the island.

Above: The flight deck of *Wasp* pictured late on the afternoon of 19 April, as the carrier prepared to fly off her brood of Spitfires soon after first light the following morning. Ranged in front and to the left of them are the carrier's own Wildcat fighters, which would take off first to cover the operation.

Left: The Focke Wulf 190 fighter was a formidable opponent for the Spitfire Mark V.

SPITFIRE V VERSUS FOCKE WULF 190A

In July 1942 a Spitfire V was flown in a comparative trial against a captured Focke Wulf 190 fighter. During the past 10 months R.A.F. pilots had learned the hard way that they faced a formidable foe, but these trials revealed just how formidable that foe was. Excerpts from the official R.A.F. report on the trials are given below:

The FW 190 was compared with a Spitfire VB from an operational squadron for speed and all-round manoeuvrability at heights up to 25,000 (7,620m) feet. The FW 190 is superior in speed at all heights, and the approximate differences are as follows:

At 2,000ft (610m) the FW 190 is 25–30mph (40–48km/hr) faster than the Spitfire 5B

At 3,000ft (915m) the FW 190 is 30–35mph (48–56km/hr) faster than the Spitfire 5B

At 5,000ft (1,525m) the FW 190 is 25mph (40km/hr) faster than the Spitfire VB

At 9,000ft (2,744m) the FW 190 is 25–30 mph faster than the Spitfire 5B

At 15,000ft (4573m) the FW 190 is 20mph (32km/hr) faster than the Spitfire 5B

At 18,000ft (5,488m) the FW 190 is 20mph (32km/hr) faster than the Spitfire VB

At 21,000 (6,400m) the FW 190 is 20–25mph (32–40km/hr) faster than the Spitfire VB

Climb: The climb of the FW 190 is superior to that of the Spitfire VB at all heights. The best speeds for climbing are approximately the same, but the angle of the FW 190 is considerably steeper. Under maximum continuous climbing conditions the climb of the FW 190 is about 450ft/min (137m/min) better up to 25,000ft (7,620m).

Dive: Comparative dives between the two aircraft have shown that the FW 190 can leave the Spitfire with ease, particularly during the initial stages.

Manoeuvrability: The manoeuvrability of the FW 190 is better than that of the Spitfire VB except in turning circles, when the Spitfire can quite easily out-turn it. The FW 190 has better acceleration under all conditions of flight and this must obviously be most useful during combat.

When the FW 190 was in a turn and was attacked by the Spitfire, the superior rate of roll enabled it to flick into a diving turn in the opposition direction. The pilot of the Spitfire found great difficulty in following this manoeuvre and even when prepared for it, was seldom able to allow the correct deflection. A dive from this manoeuvre enabled the FW 190 to draw away from the Spitfire which was then forced to break off the attack.

The above trials have shown that the Spitfire VB must cruise at high speed when in an area where enemy fighters can be expected. It will then, in addition to lessening the chances of being successfully 'bounced', have a better chance of catching the FW 190, particularly if it has the advantage of surprise.

Left: Following the launch of the Spitfires on deck, those in the hangar were brought up by lift and followed them into the air. This required slick timing, as this photograph shows. A Spitfire is about to begin its take-off; the aircraft ahead of it can be seen climbing away, just above the starboard wing. Meanwhile, the lift is already on the way to the hangar to pick up the next aircraft.

■ AMERICAN HELP ■

The Spitfires arrived in the nick of time. The Luftwaffe had stepped up its onslaught on the island and the defending fighter units were heavily outnumbered. With the air situation over Malta deteriorating rapidly, on 1 April Winston Churchill sent a personal telegram to President Roosevelt asking for help:

'Air attack on Malta is very heavy. There are now in Sicily about 400 German and 200 Italian fighters. Malta can only now muster 20 to 30 serviceable fighters. We keep feeding Malta with Spitfires in packets of 16 loosed from EAGLE carrier from about 600 miles west of Malta.

'This has worked a good many times quite well but EAGLE is now laid up for a month by defects in her steering gear. . . Therefore there will be a whole month without any Spitfire reinforcements. Would you be willing to allow your carrier WASP to do one of these trips provided details are satisfactorily agreed between the Navy Staffs? With her broad lifts, capacity and length, we estimate that WASP could take 50 or more Spitfires . . .'

Within three days of receiving the telegram the US President agreed to the request. Six days after that *Wasp* docked at Port Glasgow to load 47 Spitfires for the island. The mission was code-named Operation Calendar.

On 13 April the American carrier set sail and five days later she and her escorts passed through the Strait of Gibraltar. At first light on the 20th, off the coast of Algeria, the carrier began launching the Spitfires. Forty-six of the 47 fighters that took off reached Malta safely. Such was the ferocity of the air fighting, however, during the next few days most of the precious Spitfires had been destroyed in the air or on the

Middle: Scene on the flight deck of USS *Wasp* on the morning of 9 May 1942, as the carrier prepares to launch her aircraft for the largest resupply of aircraft to Malta. In the background, preparing to launch her Spitfires also, is HMS *Eagle*.

Above: A soldier, a sailor and an airman carry out refuelling and rearming of a Spitfire of No. 603 Squadron at Takali, Malta, in the spring of 1942. The blast pen was constructed from empty petrol tins filled with sand.

Right and below: Spitfire Vs of No. 54 Squadron based at Darwin, Australia, early in 1943 providing air defence for the Northern Territory. (Australian War Memorial)

ground. Again Malta was in crisis, and again Mr Churchill asked the US President to help. And again the latter acceded. The next resupply operation was to be the largest of them all, Operation Bowery. The American carrier returned to Glasgow on 29 April and took on a further forty-seven Spitfires. By then HMS *Eagle* at Gibraltar had completed her repairs, and she took on a further seventeen fighters.

■ MALTA SAVED ■

As *Wasp* entered the Mediterranean a second time, *Eagle* set sail from Gibraltar to join her. The two carriers and their escorts headed east together and shortly after dawn on 9 May they launched their Spitfires. Sixty of the 64 fighters that set out reached Malta. It was sufficient to change the course of the battle. The island's air defences were now strong enough to resist Axis air attacks, and could be topped up with 'penny packets' of Spitfires delivered by the smaller Royal Navy carriers. Never again would the island be in such peril as it had been during the first week in May 1942.

By the autumn of 1942 the RAF possessed a more cost–effective method of delivering Spitfires from Malta from Gibraltar. Supermarine engineers had

modified the Mark V to fly the distance non-stop, by fitting a 170-gallon (772l) drop tank under the fuselage and a 29 gallon (132l) auxiliary tank in the rear fuselage. With a total fuel load of 284 gallons (1,290l) the modified Spitfire could fly the 1,100 mile (1,770km) distance in a single hop. That was as far as from London to St Petersburg in Russia, a remarkable feat for an aircraft designed originally as a short-range interceptor.

During October and November 1942 seventeen Spitfires took off from Gibraltar to fly to Malta. All except one of them made it.

Had more Spitfires been required they too would have flown to the island, but events in the North Africa theatre of operations had removed the need. The Allied victory at El Alamein, and the subsequent expulsion of Axis forces from Libya, lifted the siege of Malta.

Meanwhile, as we shall observe in the next chapter, engineers at Rolls Royce had solved Fighter Command's most pressing problem. With a new variant of the Merlin engine the Spitfire would be able to engage the much-feared Focke Wulf 190 on equal terms.

BY SPITFIRE TO MALTA

Pilot Officer Michael Le Bas of No. 601 Squadron described his take off in a Spitfire from the deck of USS *Wasp*. His heavily loaded aircraft carried a 90-gallon (409l) drop tank under the fuselage. Ahead lay a flight of 660 miles (1,062km), about as far as from London to Prague.

'The deck officer began rotating his checkered flag and I pushed forward the throttle to emergency override to get the last ounce of power out of my Merlin. The Spitfire picked up speed rapidly in its headlong charge down the deck, but not rapidly enough. The ship's bows got closer and closer and still I had insufficient airspeed and suddenly – I was off the end. With only 60 feet to play with before I hit the water, I retracted the undercarriage and eased forward on the stick to build up speed. Down and down went the Spitfire until, about fifteen feet above the waves, it reached flying speed and I was able to level out. After what seemed an age but was in fact only a few seconds, my speed built up and I was able to climb away. Nobody had told me about that at the briefing! It had been a hairy introduction to flying off an aircraft carrier. Things had happened so quickly that there was no time to think. Perhaps it was just as well.'

REGAINING CONTROL
OF THE SKIES

After the initial encounters with Focke Wulf 190s, Fighter Command made strong demands for an improved fighter with the performance to meet the new challenge. There could be no question of designing, building and bringing into service a completely new aircraft; on the most optimistic time scale that would have taken at least four years. Fighter Command could not wait that long.

In fact Rolls Royce already had the answer to the problem in a new version of the Merlin. Previous versions of the engine used a single-stage supercharger. The new engine employed a two-stage supercharger, in which the output from the first blower fed into the second to compress the charge of air further before it entered the carburettor. The two-stage supercharger gave a spectacular improvement in high-altitude performance. At 30,000 feet (9,145m) the Merlin 45 engine with a single-stage supercharger developed about 720 horse power. At the same altitude the same basic engine fitted with a two-stage supercharger developed about 1,020 horse power, an increase of more than 40 per cent. The extra plumbing added only about 200 pounds (90kg) to the weight of the engine and increased its length by 9 inches (23cm).

At the end of September 1941, three weeks after the debut of the Focke Wulf FW 190, an experimental Spitfire fitted with the Merlin incorporating the two-stage supercharger began flight testing.

There could be no question of designing, building and bringing into service a completely new aircraft

Far left: **A Spitfire VII, the high-altitude interceptor version of the famous fighter. Note the distinctive long-span wing with pointed tips, a recognition feature of this particular variant.**

SPITFIRE MARK IX

Type Single-seat general purpose fighter and fighter-bomber.
Armament Two Hispano 20 mm cannon with 120 rounds per gun, four Browning .303in (7.7mm) machine guns with 350 rounds per gun; or two Hispano 20mm cannon with 120 rounds per gun and two Browning .5in (12.7mm) machine guns with 250 rounds per gun. Maximum bomb load one 50-pound (226 kg) bomb and two 250 pounders (113kg).
Power Plant One Rolls-Royce Merlin 61, 63 or 70 liquid cooled V-12 engine with two-stage supercharger. Merlin 65 developed 1,565 hp.
Dimensions Span 40ft 2in (12.85, pointed wing tips), 36ft 10in (10.98m, normal wing tips) or 32ft 6in (9.9m, clipped wings); length 30ft 0in (9.14m).

Weight Maximum loaded weight 7,500lb (3,400kg).
Performance Maximum speed 40 mph at 25,000ft (657km/hr at 7,622m); service ceiling 43,000ft (13,110m).

Below: **Spitfire IX of No. 402 (Canadian) Squadron.**

TURNING POINT IN AN AIR WAR

On the afternoon of 30 July 1942 Flight Lieutenant Donald Kingaby of No. 64 Squadron scored his 16th aerial victory. Afterwards he reported:

'I sighted approximately 12 FW 190s 2,000 ft [610m] below us at 12,000ft [3,658m] just off Boulogne proceeding towards French coast. We dived down on them and I attacked a FW 190 from astern and below giving a very short burst, about half a second, from 300yd. I was forced to break away as I was crowded out by other Spits. I broke down and right and caught another FW as he commenced to dive away. At 14,000ft [4,268m] approx. I gave a burst of cannon and M/G, 400 yd range hitting E/A along fuselage. Pieces fell off and E/A continued in straight dive nearly vertical. I followed E/A down to 5,000ft [1,525m] over Boulogne and saw him hit the deck just outside the town of Boulogne and explode and burn up. Returned to base at 0ft.'

The combat report was little different from many others in the summer of 1942, yet this air combat marked a significant turning point in the air war over Europe. It was the first time the Spitfire Mark IX had encountered the Focke Wulf 190 in action. The latest variant of the British fighter showed that it could take on its once-feared opponent on equal terms. For the Luftwaffe, that action marked the beginning of the end of the easy going superiority its fighters had enjoyed for most of the previous year. It would never regain that position.

Initially there were difficulties in getting the supercharger to work properly, but by the end of the year these had been resolved. The Merlin 61 Spitfire showed itself to be considerably faster than any previous version, with a maximum speed of 414mph at 27,200 feet (667km/hr at 8,300m). Its rate of climb was also considerably better than that of the Spitfire V and its service ceiling was over 41,000 feet (12,500m).

■ THREE NEW VARIANTS ■

Fighter Command and Supermarine both knew a good thing when they saw it, and the new Merlin engine quickly spawned three more variants of the Spitfire. The Spitfire VII was a high-altitude interceptor version, with a pressurized cabin and a longer wingspan giving increased area. Its airframe was redesigned and strengthened to compensate for the increases in engine power and weight the fighter had incurred previously. The second of the new variants, the Spitfire VIII, was similar to the Mark VII but lacked the pressurized cabin of that type.

These two versions required a large amount of re-design, however, as well as retooling of the production lines. The changes would take time and neither version would be available in quantity until the spring of 1943.

In the meantime Fighter Command needed a fighter to counter the FW 190, and it needed it quickly. The solution arrived in the form of the Spitfire IX, which was essentially a Mark V with the minimum of modification necessary to take the Merlin 61 engine. Measured against peacetime stressing factors, the airframe of the Mark V was not really strong enough to accept the additional engine power and the increases in all-up weight. In wartime, however, the RAF was prepared to accept this deficiency in the name of operational expediency. No fighter pilot was going to reject the Spitfire IX in favour of the Mark V for that reason alone!

Left and above: A damaged aircraft repaired and returned to service was as valuable as a new aircraft built, and the R.A.F. salvage teams and repair organization played a valuable role. This Spitfire of No. 403 (Canadian) Squadron had crash-landed in a suspected minefield in Normandy. After a sweep of the area to ensure that it was safe to approach the aircraft, the fighter was dismantled and loaded on to a 'Queen Mary' transporter.

The first production Spitfire IXs arrived at No. 64 Squadron at Hornchurch during June 1942, and the unit resumed operations with the new variant at the end of July. The new Spitfire quickly demonstrated that it was the equal of the Focke Wulf 190 in combat. Proof of this came a few weeks later, when a German pilot inadvertently landed his FW 190 at Pembrey in South Wales. The RAF carried out detailed flight tests with the captured aircraft to determine its exact

SPITFIRE IX VERSUS FOCKE WULF 190A

In July 1942 a Spitfire IX was flown in a comparative trial against a captured Focke Wulf 190. Considering they were quite different aircraft, the similarities in performances were remarkable. Excerpts from the official trials report are given below:

Comparative Speeds: The FW 190 was compared with a fully operational Spitfire IX for speed and manoeuvrability at heights up to 25,000 feet (7,620m). The Spitfire IX at most heights is slightly superior in speed to the FW 190 and the approximate differences in speeds at various heights are as follows:

At 2,000ft (610m) the FW 190 is 7–8mph (11–13km/hr) faster than the Spitfire IX

At 5,000ft (1,524m) the FW 190 and the Spitfire IX are approximately the same

At 8,000ft (2,44 m) the Spitfire IX is 8mph (13km/hr) faster than the FW 190

At 15,000ft (4,573m) the Spitfire IX is 5mph (8 km/hr) faster than the FW 190

At 18,000 ft (5,488m) the FW 190 is 3mph (5km/hr) faster than the Spitfire IX

At 21,000 ft (6,400m) the FW 190 and the Spitfire IX are approximately the same

At 25,000 ft (7,622m) the Spitfire IX is 5–7mph 98–11km/hr) faster than the FW 190

Climb: During comparative climbs at various heights up to 23,000 feet (7,012 m), with both aircraft flying under maximum continuous climbing conditions, little difference was found between the two aircraft although on the whole the Spitfire IX was slightly better. Above 22,000 feet (6,707 m) the climb of the FW 190 is falling off rapidly, whereas the climb of the Spitfire IX is increasing. Dive: The FW 190 is faster than the Spitfire IX in a dive, particularly during the initial stage. This superiority is not as marked as with the Spitfire VB.

Manoeuvrability: The FW 190 is more manoeuvrable than the Spitfire IX except in turning circles, when it is out-turned without difficulty. The superior rate of roll of the FW 190 enabled it to avoid the Spitfire IX if attacked when in a turn, by flicking over into a diving turn in the opposition direction. As with the Spitfire VB, the Spitfire IX had great difficulty in following this manoeuvre.

The Spitfire IX's worst heights for fighting the FW 190 were between 18,000 and 22,000 feet (5,486m and 6,707m) and below 3,000ft (914m). At these heights the FW 190 is a little faster.

The initial acceleration of the FW 190 is better than the Spitfire IX under all conditions of flight, except in level flight at such altitudes where the Spitfire has a speed advantage. Then, provided the Spitfire is cruising at high speed, there is little to choose between the acceleration of the two aircraft.

The general impression gained by the pilots taking part in the trials is that the Spitfire IX compares favourably with the FW 190. Provided the Spitfire has the initiative, it undoubtedly has a good chance of shooting down the FW 190.

Left: The Spitfire VIII entered service some time after the Mark IX. This example belonged to No. 457 (Australian) Squadron and was one of the 410 purchased by that air force for operations in the South Pacific area.

MARK VII

Type Single-seat high-altitude interceptor fighter with pressurized cabin.
Armament Two Hispano 20 mm cannon with 120 rounds per gun, four Browning .303in (7.7mm) machine guns with 350 rounds per gun. Aircraft assigned to ultra high-altitude interception duties sometimes carried only the four .303in machine guns.
Power Plant One Rolls-Royce Merlin 61, 64 or 71 liquid cooled V-12 engine with two-stage supercharger. Merlin 61 developed 1,565hp.
Dimensions: Span 40ft 2in (12.85m, pointed wing tips) or 36ft 10in (10.98m normal wing tips); length 30ft 0in (9.15m).
Weight Maximum loaded weight 8,000lb (3,628kg).
Performance (Rolls-Royce Merlin 71 engine) maximum speed 424mph at 29,500ft (682km/hr at 8,994m); service ceiling 45,100ft (13,750m).

performance and then had it fly mock combats with each of the main Allied fighters. The comparison with the Spitfire IX (see preceding page) revealed that the two fighters were uncannily similar in performance.

■ MARK IX IN SERVICE ■

Initially the Mark IX units represented only a small proportion of the Spitfire force, but even so the new variant had an immediate impact on the air situation. In combat it was impossible to distinguish it from the Mark V, and FW 190 pilots could never be certain which Spitfire variant they faced. As a result the German fighters became markedly less aggressive and RAF fighter losses fell appreciably.

The first major action involving Spitfire IXs was on 19 August 1942, during the amphibious raid on Dieppe on the French coast. Four squadrons flew the new variant that day and in the course of intensive air operations they mounted 14 squadron-sized missions comprising about 150 sorties. These resulted in claims of six enemy aircraft destroyed and two probably destroyed, for the loss of seven fighters.

By the spring of 1943 the Spitfire IX equipped most of the RAF's single-seat fighter squadrons based in Great Britain. Perhaps surprisingly, the re-engineered variants of the Spitfire intended to replace the Mark IX saw rather less use. The feared high-altitude attacks on Great Britain failed to materialize, and the order for Mark VIIs was greatly reduced. Production ended early in 1944, after about 140 had been built.

By the time the Mark VIII

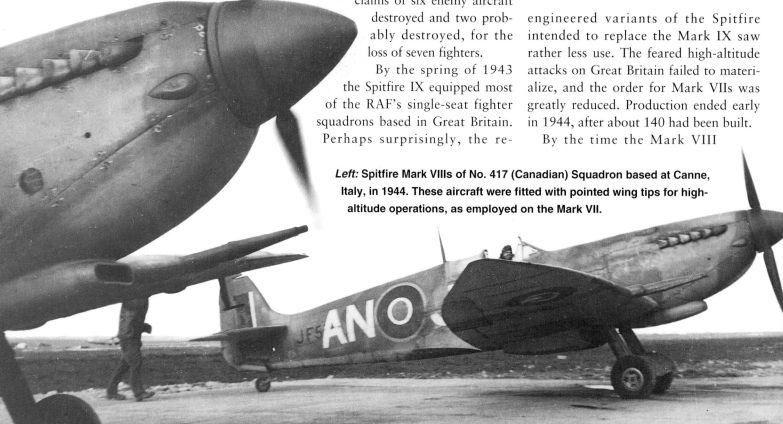

Left: Spitfire Mark VIIIs of No. 417 (Canadian) Squadron based at Canne, Italy, in 1944. These aircraft were fitted with pointed wing tips for high-altitude operations, as employed on the Mark VII.

Left: The Spitfire Mark XVI was similar to the Mark IX but was powered by the version of the Merlin engine built under licence by the American Packard Company. Late production Spitfire IXs and XVIs featured cut-down fuselages and bubble canopies, as seen on these Mark XVIs undergoing final assembly at Castle Bromwich in the spring of 1945.

Bottom left: Floatplane conversion of the Spitfire. A small number of aircraft were modified in this way but none saw action.

BUBBLE CANOPY

In most cases where Spitfires were shot down by enemy fighters, the victim never saw his assailant in time to take effective evasive action. Most such attacks were mounted from the fighter's blind zone, below and behind. Any modification that reduced the likelihood of a surprise attack would increase the fighter's chances of survival in combat.

The answer was to cutback the rear fuselage behind the cockpit, and fit the fighter with a bubble canopy. A Spitfire modified in this way flew for the first time in the summer of 1943. The manufacturer's trials showed the change brought no significant deterioration in the aircraft's handling characteristics. Experienced service pilots were hugely impressed with the improvement in view from the bubble canopy. Their report stated:

'This is an enormous improvement over the standard Spitfire rear view. The pilot can see quite easily round to his fin and past it, almost to the further edge of the tailplane, i.e. if he looks over his left shoulder he can practically see to the starboard tip of the tail. By banking the aircraft slightly during weaving action, the downward view to the rear is opened up well.'

Production Spitfire Mark IXs, XIVs and XVIs fitted with bubble canopies began reaching the operational squadrons early in 1945 and they immediately became popular with pilots.

became available in quantity, in the spring of 1943, the FW 190 menace over north west Europe had been contained. The entire 1,658-aircraft production run of this variant went overseas to units operating in the Middle East, the Far East and Australia.

The 'stop gap' version of the Merlin 61 Spitfire, the Mark IX, continued in production a lot longer than anyone had expected. Between them the Supermarine and Castle Bromwich plants turned out nearly six thousand of them.

The Spitfire XVI airframe was almost identical to that of the Mark IX, but it was powered by a version of the Merlin built by the American Packard Company. Late production Spitfire IXs and XVIs featured cut-down fuselages and bubble canopies, features which gave the pilot greatly improved vision behind and below the fighter.

The introduction of the Merlin 60 series improved the performance of the Spitfire to the point where it could fight the FW 190 on equal terms. Yet engineers at Rolls-Royce were not content to rest on their laurels. As we shall observe in the next chapter, they had something even better on offer.

ENTER THE GRIFFON

Mark XIV Spitfire of No. 402 (Canadian) Squadron. This version was the most effective variant to operate in the air superiority role during the Second World War.

In 1939 Rolls Royce had begun development of a larger engine than the Merlin, later named the Griffon. With a cubic capacity of 65 gallons (36.75l), the new engine was one-third larger than its predecessor. The initial production version, with a single-stage supercharger, developed 1,735 horse power. By clever positioning of components the designers kept the length of the Griffon to within 3 inches (7.5cm), and the weight to within 600 pounds (272kg), of the equivalent figures for the Merlin. Moreover, the new engine's frontal area was little greater than that of its predecessor.

The Spitfire was an obvious application for the new engine and in November 1941 an experimental Griffon prototype, the Mark IV, began flight testing. The aircraft had a maximum speed of 372mph at 5,700 feet (600km/hr at 1,740m) which increased to 397mph at 18,000 feet (640km/hr at 5,500m).

To counter the threat the RAF issued a requirement for a low-altitude interceptor

At about this time the Luftwaffe commenced tip-and-run attacks on towns on the south and east coasts of England. Small forces of fighter-bombers ran in at low altitude to avoid radar detection, giving the defenders little time to react. To counter the threat the RAF issued a requirement for a low-altitude interceptor. The Griffon Spitfire offered the best performance at low altitude, and this became the prototype for the Mark XII fighter. Supermarine received a production order to build one hundred examples.

Like the Mark IX, the early production Mark XIIs used Mark V airframes with the minimum of modification necessary to

SPITFIRE XII

Type Single-seat fighter optimized for operations at low and medium altitudes.
Armament Two Hispano 20mm cannon with 120 rounds per gun, four Browning .303in (7.7mm) machine guns with 350 rounds per gun.
Power Plant One Rolls-Royce Griffon 4 liquid cooled V-12 engine with single-stage supercharger developing 1,735 horse power.
Dimensions Span 32ft 7in (9.93m); length 30ft 9in (9.37m).

Weight Maximum loaded weight 7,400lb (3,356kg).
Performance Maximum speed 389mph at 12,500ft (626km/hr at 3,810m); service ceiling 37,350ft (11,387m).

Below: The first Griffon-powered Spitfire, pictured after the aircraft had been modified to become the prototype Mark XII low-altitude fighter.

SPITFIRE XIV

Type Single-seat fighter and fighter-reconnaissance aircraft.
Armament Two Hispano 20mm cannon with 120 rounds per gun, four Browning .303in (7.7mm) machine guns with 350 rounds per gun; or two Hispano 20mm cannon with 120 rounds per gun and two Browning .5in (12.7mm) machine guns with 250 rounds per gun. Fighter reconnaissance version carried an oblique-mounted camera in the rear fuselage.

Power Plant One Rolls-Royce Griffon 65 liquid cooled V-12 engine with two-stage supercharger developing 2,035hp.
Dimensions Span 36ft 1 in (10.98m normal wing tips) or 32ft 7in (9.93m, clipped wings); length 32ft 8in (9.96m).
Weight Maximum loaded weight 10,065 pounds (4,565kg).
Performance Maximum speed 439mph at 24,500ft (707km/hr); service ceiling 43,000ft (13,110m).

take the new engine. Production Mark XIIs all had clipped wings, to give greater speed at low altitude and greater rate of roll at all altitudes. Compared with the Mark IX, the Mark XII was 14mph (22km/hr) faster at sea level and 8mph faster at 10,000 feet (13km/hr at 3,050m). But above 20,000 feet (6,100m) performance fell away rapidly and the Mark XII became progressively slower than the Mark IX.

In the spring of 1943 Nos 41 and 91 Squadrons re-equipped with Mark XIIs and commenced operations from Hawkinge airfield near Folkestone. The units flew standing patrols against enemy fighter-bombers attacking coastal targets, and on 25 May No. 91 Squadron scrambled six fighters to engage FW 190 fighter-bombers attacking Folkestone. In the ensuing combat the Spitfires claimed the destruction of six raiders, without loss to themselves.

This action proved to be a rare success for the Mark XII, however. Although it was faster than the opposing fighter types at low and medium altitudes, this was of little value during offensive sweeps over France. German fighter pilots preferred to remain at altitude, coming down only to deliver high-speed diving attacks before making zoom climbs back to altitude. Rarely would they let themselves be drawn into turning fights with Spitfires below 20,000 feet.

An obvious next step for the Spitfire was to fit it with a Griffon with a two-stage supercharger. The new engine, the Griffon 65, appeared in the spring of 1943 and developed an impressive 1,540 horse power for takeoff and 2,035hp at 7,000 feet (2,134m). Six Spitfire VIIIs were modified to take the new engine and became prototypes for the Mark XIV.

Flight tests with pre-production Mark XIVs revealed it to be an extremely effective fighter, giving a huge improvement in performance over the Mark IX. During comparative trials against a captured FW 190 and a Messerschmitt 109G, the Spitfire XIV showed itself superior to the German fighters in almost every respect.

The new variant went into production in the autumn of 1943 and by the following spring Nos 91, 322 and 610 Squadrons had received Mark XIVs. All three units were fully operational in June when the V.1 flying bomb attacks on London commenced.

■ SPITFIRE v FLYING BOMB ■

Although the V.1s flew a straight and predictable path, usually they were not easy targets. The majority flew at speeds around 350mph (563km/hr), though the fastest reached 420mph (675km/hr) and the slowest came in at around 230mph (370km/hr). There were similar variations in altitude. Most flying bombs crossed the coast at between 3,000 and 4,000 feet (915 and 1,220m), but the highest came in at around 8,000 feet (2,440m) and the lowest flew at treetop height – which frequently led to their early demise!

Protecting the capital were four separate layers of defences. The first layer, extending from mid-Channel to about 10 miles (16km) short of the south coast, was the Outer Fighter Patrol Area where Spitfires and other fighters could engage the flying bombs. Next came the Gun Belt, with more than 2,500 AA guns of all calibres positioned along the strip of coast between Beachy Head and Dover; this was off-limits to fighters, allowing gunners freedom to shoot at anything that came within range. From 10 miles (16km) inland to 10 miles (16km) short of London was the Inner Fighter Patrol Area, where more fighters engaged the V.1s. The final layer, also off limits to fighters, was the barrage

> ## Although the V.1s flew a straight and predictable path, usually they were not easy targets

balloon zone. This began 10 miles short of the London built-up area and ended at its outskirts, and above it there hovered more than a thousand of the ungainly gasbags.

All available squadrons with Mark XIVs redeployed to airfields in Kent to defend the capital. Of the V.1s shot down by fighters, the great majority fell out of control and exploded on striking the ground. A few detonated in mid-air, but there was little risk of serious damage to the fighter unless it was within 150 yards (137m) of the explosion. Fighters often suffered minor damage, however, if they struck flying pieces from the missile or if they flew through the cloud of burning petrol from the fuel tank. Another method of bringing down a V.1 was to fly alongside it, place the fighter's wing under that of the flying bomb and then bank steeply to flip the missile out of control.

■ AIR SUPERIORITY FIGHTER ■

At the end of August 1944, Allied ground forces advancing along the north coast of

---

SPITFIRE XIV COMPARED WITH FOCKE WULF 190A

Early in 1944 the Air Fighting Development Unit at Duxford flew a Spitfire XIV in a comparative trial against a captured Focke Wulf 190A. Excerpts from the official trials report are given below:

Maximum Speeds: From 0–5,000ft (0–1,525m) and 15,000–0,000ft (4,573–6,100m) the Spitfire XIV is only 20mph (32km/hr) faster; at all other heights it is up to 60mph (97km/hr) faster.

Maximum Climb: The Spitfire XIV has a considerably greater rate of climb than the FW 190 A at all altitudes.

Dive: After the initial part of the dive, during which the FW 190 gains slightly, the Spitfire XIV has a slight advantage.

Turning Circle: The Spitfire XIV can easily turn inside the FW 190. Though in the case of a right-hand turn, this difference is not quite so pronounced.

Rate of Roll: The FW 190 is very much better.

Conclusions: In defence, the Spitfire XIV should use its remarkable maximum climb and turning circle against any enemy aircraft. In the attack it can afford to 'mix it' but should beware of the quick roll and dive. If this manoeuvre is used by an FW 190 and the Spitfire XIV follows, it will probably not be able to close the range until the FW 190 has pulled out of its dive

SPITFIRE XIV COMPARED WITH ME109G

Early in 1944 the Air Fighting Development Unit at Duxford flew a Spitfire XIV in a comparative trial against a captured Messerschmitt 109G, the latest sub-type of the famous German fighter. Excerpts from the official trials report are given below:

Maximum Speed: The Spitfire XIV is 40mph (64km/hr) faster at all heights except near 16,000ft (4,878m), where it is only 10mph (16km/hr) faster.

Maximum Climb: The same result: at 16,000ft (4,877m) the two aircraft are identical, otherwise the Spitfire XIV out-climbs the Me 109G. The zoom climb is practically identical when the climb is made without opening the throttle. Climbing at full throttle, the Spitfire XIV draws away from the Me 109G quite easily.

Dive: During the initial part of the dive, the Me 109G pulls away slightly, but when a speed of 380mph (611km/hr) is reached, the Spitfire XIV begins to gain on the Me 109G.

Turning Circle: The Spitfire XIV easily out-turns the Me 109G in either direction.

Rate of Roll: The Spitfire XIV rolls much more quickly.

Conclusion: The Spitfire XIV is superior to the Me 109G in every respect.

Below: During mock combats the Me 109G was no match for the Spitfire XIV.

France overran the last of the V.1 launching sites in the Pas de Calais. The 8,617th and last flying bomb launched from that area crossed the south coast of England on the morning of 1 September.

Following the capture of the V.1 sites, the Spitfire XIV squadrons redeployed to airfields in Belgium, to resume operations against conventional enemy aircraft. Four further squadrons joined them soon afterwards, Nos 41, 130, 350 and 403 Squadrons. For the remainder of the war the Mark XIV was the main air superiority fighter operated by the Royal Air Force in the skies over northern Europe.

The Mark XXI was intended as the 'definitive' fighter variant of the Spitfire, and had the war continued into 1946 it was set to become the RAF's main air superiority type. Powered by the Griffon 65 engine, it featured a completely redesigned wing with a much-strengthened internal structure. It carried the four 20mm cannon armament as standard. These changes added significant weight to aircraft, however, and early production machines had unpleasant handling characteristics. It took a few months to iron out these bugs and as a result the variant entered service only during the final few weeks of the war.

The delay in bringing the Mark XXI into action had no effect on the air war in Europe, for the Allied Air Forces defeated the Luftwaffe with the fighter types in service. Before we finish with the Second World War, however, it is necessary to review developments of the Spitfire for roles other than air combat. In the next chapter we shall observe the work done to improve the effectiveness of reconnaissance variants.

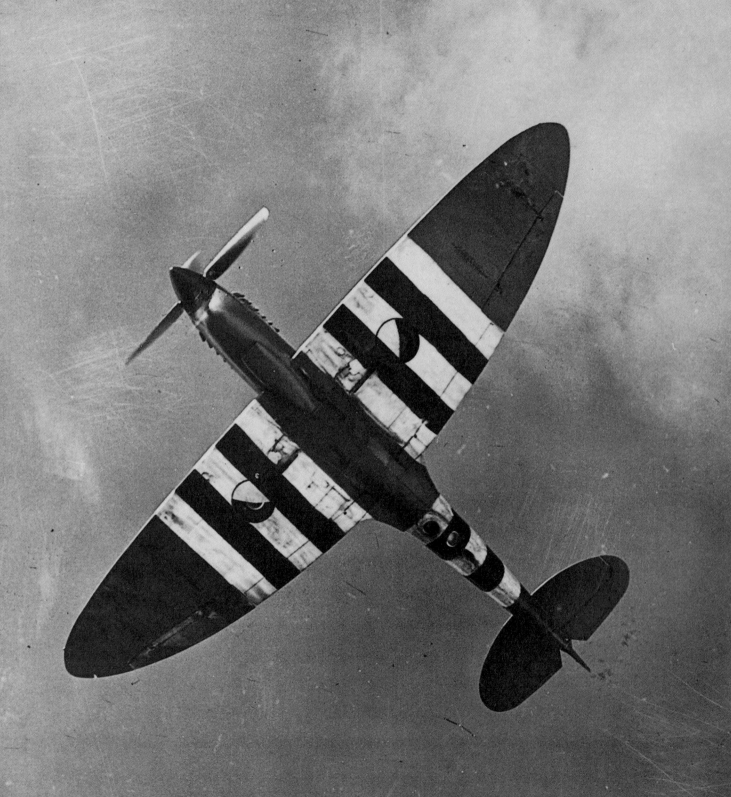

As the war progressed, the Royal Air Force faced increasing demands to provide reconnaissance photographs of targets deep inside occupied territory in Europe. Yet, by the summer of 1942, the improving German air defences inflicted mounting losses on the reconnaissance Spitfires. The obvious answer was to produce a higher-performance reconnaissance aircraft powered by the Merlin 61 engine. The new variant, the Spitfire PR XI, combined the strengthened airframe of the Mark VIII fighter with the integral wing fuel tank and rear fuselage camera installation of the PR Marks ID and VD.

Left: Spitfire PR XI in invasion markings. Note the ports in the rear fuselage for the two vertical cameras.

As an interim measure until the PR XI became available, fifteen Mark IX fighters underwent modification for the reconnaissance role. Designated PR IXs, these aircraft had the armament removed and a pair of vertical cameras installed in the rear fuselage. The version had no extra internal fuel tankage, and during operations it usually flew with a 90-gallon (409l) drop tank under the fuselage. No. 541 Squadron at Benson received the first PR Mark IXs in November 1942. Although the limited tankage confined the PR IX to operations over western Europe, it restored the ability to photograph defended targets without incurring serious losses.

In December 1942 the first Spitfire PR XIs began coming off the production line. The new variant could operate at altitudes above 42,000 feet (12,800m), some 10,000 feet (3,000m) higher than previous reconnaissance versions. The Mark XI replaced all other unarmed versions of the Spitfire in front-line reconnaissance units,

SPITFIRE MK XI

Type Single-seat long range reconnaissance aircraft.

War Load Two vertically mounted reconnaissance cameras, could also carry one oblique mounted camera. No armament.

Power Plant One Rolls-Royce Merlin 63 liquid cooled V-12 engine with two-stage supercharger developing 1,650 horse power.

Dimensions Span 36ft 10in (10.98m); length 31ft 1in (9.47m).

Weight Maximum loaded weight 8,519lb (3,863kg).

Performance Maximum speed 417mph at 24,000ft (671km/hr at 7317m); service ceiling 44,000ft (13,415m).

Below and overleaf: Spitfire XIs of the 10th Photo Group, US Army Air Force. The unit operated this variant on photographic reconnaissance missions over occupied Europe.

SPITFIRE XIX

Type Single-seat long-range reconnaissance aircraft.

War Load Two vertically mounted reconnaissance cameras, could also carry one oblique mounted camera. No armament.

Power Plant One Rolls-Royce Griffon 66 liquid cooled V-12 engine with two-stage supercharger developing 2,035hp.

Dimensions Span 36ft 10in (10.98m normal wing tips); length 32ft 8in (9.96m).

Weight Maximum loaded weight 10,450lb (4,739kg).

Performance Maximum speed 445mph at 26,000ft (716km/hr at 7,927m); operational ceiling in excess of 49,000ft (14,940m).

Top: PRXI of US 10th Photo Group.
Above: German pilots clamber over a captured PR XI, trying to learn its secrets.

and 471 examples were built. For more than a year after the variant entered service, it was almost immune to fighter interception while flying at high altitude. When aircraft were lost it was usually because they were forced to descend, due to technical failure or to go below cloud to take photographs.

During the autumn of 1943 the US

8th Air Force in Great Britain received a dozen Mark XIs. These formed the equipment of the 14th Photo Squadron, 10th Photographic Group, based at Mount Farm near Oxford. The unit's role was to take pre-strike and post-strike photographs of targets attacked by the US heavy bombers. Major Walt Weitner, commander of the 14th,

described his impressions of flying this version on operations:

'With all the extra clothing, the parachute, dinghy, life jacket and oxygen mask, the narrow cockpit of a Spitfire was no place for the claustrophobic! With a full load of fuel and that undercarriage, the Spit would "lean" disconcertingly during turns when one taxied. But once you were off the ground and got up a little speed she really perked up, she would leap away. Once the gear was up and you pulled up the nose, boy would she climb!'

During operational missions the Mark XI normally cruised at altitudes around 39,000, ascending above that altitude if enemy fighters attempted to intercept it. Weitner found the Spitfire easy to handle at very high altitude:

'For high altitude work the Spit was unequalled. One had always to have hold of the stick, but it needed hardly any pressure. In the reconnaissance business you did not fly straight and level for long. You were continually banking to search the sky all around for enemy fighters and to check the navigation.'

■ NEW VARIANTS ■

The system of allocating Spitfire numbers was anything but methodical, and the PR Mark X entered service more than a year later than the PR XI. The Mark X was similar to the Mark XI, but it was fitted with a pressurized cabin. Only sixteen examples were built, however, and the variant entered service with Nos 541 and 542 Squadrons in May 1944. The commander of the latter unit, Squadron Leader Alfred Ball, remembered the PR X without any great affection:

'I flew the PR X a few times on operations. They were not popular because of the poor visibility out of the very thick perspex canopy. Outside everything looked a slightly

discoloured yellow, the perspex was not as clear as on an ordinary Spitfire. Also, with the extra weight of the pressure cabin, the Mark X felt much heavier than the Mark XI. We preferred the unpressurized Mark XI to the Mark X.'

The Mark XI's near-immunity from fighter interception lasted until the spring of 1944. Then the Luftwaffe deployed its first jet fighter types, the rocket-propelled Messerschmitt 163 and the turbojet powered Me 262. High flying Allied reconnaissance aircraft, unarmed and alone, offered perfect targets on which the German jet pilots could make practice interceptions.

The period of immunity for the Mark Xs and XIs was drawing to a close, but the Spitfire was not finished yet. A fighter-reconnaissance version of the Spitfire XIV entered service in small numbers, fitted with an oblique camera in the rear fuselage. This variant retained the same armament as the fighter version, and made an excellent fighting scout.

■ THE MARK XIX ■

With the increasing threat of interception from German jet fighters, there was a requirement for a Griffon-powered long-range unarmed reconnaissance variant. This became the PR Mark XIX, with integral wing fuel tanks as fitted to the PR XI and its predecessors.

The new variant entered service in May 1944 and gave a huge advance in performance over the PR XI. Later production Mark XIXs had pressurized cabins, built to an improved design that eradicated the unpopular features of that fitted to the PR X. With the additional power from the Griffon engine, the Mark XIX could accept the extra weight of the pressurized cabin without any noticeable deterioration in performance. Comfortably ensconced in their pressurized

cabins, pilots often took this variant above 49,000 feet (above 15,000m).

When jet fighters tried to intercept Mark XIXs, the latter had little difficulty in outmanoeuvring them provided they were seen in good time. Squadron Leader Ball recalled:

> ## 'Once the gear was up and you pulled up the nose, boy would she climb!'

'I encountered Messerschmitt 262s on a couple of occasions. Unless your eyes were shut when they jumped you, you could usually get away from them. They had a long climb to reach us, and they could not stay with us for very long. I would wait until the 262 pilot was about to open fire, then pull into a tight turn. You had to judge the turn correctly – if you turned too soon it was not difficult for him to pull enough deflection and you were a sitting duck. Provided you handled your aircraft properly, it was very difficult for them to shoot you down.'

Altogether 225 examples of the PR XIX were built, before production of this version ended in the spring of 1946.

Photographic reconnaissance was one role that the Spitfire's designer had not envisaged. Another was that of fighter-bomber and, as we shall observe in the next chapter, this became an increasingly important aspect of Spitfire operations during the final phase of the war.

Below: **The Mark XIX was the final reconnaissance version of the Spitfire, and it remained in front-line service in this role until 1954. This example carries a 170-gallon (773l) ferry tank under the fuselage.**

SPITFIRE FIGHTER-BOMBER

Winston Churchill once commented that 'Air power is the most difficult of all forms of military force to measure, or even to express in precise terms.' One can apply those same words to air superiority. Certainly, once the enemy air force is driven from the skies, the side with air superiority possesses a great advantage. However, to exploit this advantage types of aircraft other than the pure fighter must be brought into play. Bombers, transports and reconnaissance aircraft can then capitalize on the situation and mount effective operations to support the land battle. To assist with this, part of the fighter force will relinquish air-to-air operations and join in the attack on ground targets.

By the time of the Normandy invasion, in June 1944, the Luftwaffe had been weakened to such a point that it was rarely able to operate over northern France. Having thus secured air superiority, many Spitfire units switched to the fighter-bomber role. These aircraft became the bane of the existence of German ground troops, as they bombed and strafed anything that moved in the rear areas. Such attacks made movement on the ground extremely hazardous during the daylight hours.

■ TARGET ROMMEL ■

An action by Spitfire fighter-bombers that had far-reaching consequences for the land battle occurred on 17 July 1944. That day Field Marshal Erwin Rommel, commander of German ground forces in Normandy, needed to travel urgently to a sector of the front where an Allied breakthrough seemed imminent. A flight of Mustangs on low-level reconnaissance observed the staff car speeding along a road near Lisieux, and reported their find. Spitfires of No. 602 Squadron, flying an armed reconnaissance over the area, were immediately ordered to investigate the sighting.

Squadron Leader Chris Le Roux, the formation leader, spotted the car and carried out a low altitude strafing attack with cannon and machine guns. He scored several hits and, its driver dead at the wheel, the car ran off the road and crashed into a tree. Rommel suffered a

Far left: **A pair of Spitfire IX fighter-bombers of No. 601 Squadron about to take off from Fano, Italy, to attack a target in enemy territory. The nearer aircraft carries a 500lb (226kg) bomb under the fuselage, the aircraft in the background carries one 250lb (113kg).** *Below and overleaf:* **Mark IXs fitted with two 250lb (113kg) bombs under the wings.**

' THE EFFECT OF AIR SUPERIORITY '

'... we always knew when we were flying over the front line either when starting out on a reconnaissance mission or when returning: the contrast was astonishing, for in German occupied territory not a thing moved; perhaps a solitary vehicle would be observed, but as soon as the driver or look-out saw an aeroplane the vehicle stopped. Over our own territory masses of tents and convoys were to be seen; and that was the effect that air superiority, or the complete lack of it, had on land forces and their everyday existence.'

GROUP CAPTAIN G. MILLINGTON, COMMAN-
DER NO. 285 (RECONNAISSANCE) WING IN
ITALY, 1944, IN HIS BOOK
THE UNSEEN EYE

fractured skull and severe concussion, and had to be replaced at a critical stage in the land battle.

■ BOMB LOADS CARRIED ■

The bomb loads carried by Spitfires flying ground attack missions depended on the nature of the target and its distance from base. The greater the distance the aircraft had to fly, the smaller the bomb load it could carry. Normally the Spitfires carried two 250 pound (113kg) bombs under the wings or a 500 pounder (226kg) under the fuselage. However, if the target was relatively close to base, the aircraft might carry the 500 pounder as well as two 250 pounders. Once the bombs had been dropped, the fighter could switch to the ground-attack role, its powerful armament making it an effective ground-strafing aircraft. When operating in the fighter-bomber role, Spitfires usually flew in sections of four or six, depending on the type of target and the weight of attack required.

Once the bombs had dropped, the fighter's powerful gun armament made it an effective ground-strafing aircraft

Flying Officer David Green flew Spitfires with No. 73 Squadron over Italy and Yugoslavia during the final months of the war. He describes the normal tactics for a dive-bombing attack in a Spitfire:

'Carrying two 250lb bombs, the Spitfire made a very fine dive bomber. It could attack accurately and didn't need a fighter escort because as soon as the bombs had been released it was a fighter. The briefing beforehand had to be good enough for us to be able to fly right up to the target even if we had never been there before, identify it and bomb it. Because

AIR SUPPORT FOR THE ARMY, MORNING OF 10 NOV 1944

SQUADRON	AIRCRAFT	TIME UP	REMARKS
No. 7 SAAF	6 Spitfire	0945	Bombed medium gun position.
No. 1 SAAF	6 Spitfire	1000	Bombed field guns near Forli.
No. 601	6 Spitfire	1015	Bombed field guns near Forli. Light AA fire. One aircraft failed to pull out of dive possibly due to flak hit, pilot killed.
No. 2 SAAF	6 Spitfire	1020	Two aircraft returned early. Rest bombed gun position and carried out strafing attacks. Heavy AA from target, no losses.
No. 92	6 Spitfire	1025	Bombed gun positions S. Faenza.
No. 92	6 Spitfire	1030	Bombed and strafed gun and mortar positions near Faenza.
No. 4 SAAF	6 Spitfire	1040	Dive-bombed gun positions.
No. 2 SAAF	6 Spitfire	1105	Bombed 3 gun positions, target well strafed. Light AA from target.
No. 4 SAAF	6 Spitfire	1135	Bombed gun positions.

the flak was often accurate we didn't want to spend time circling in the target area before we went down to attack. We normally operated in sections of four, and would fly to the target at 10,000 feet in finger-four battle formation.'

When the raiding force neared the target area the Spitfires closed up and moved into loose echelon formation to starboard of the leader. David Green continued:

'As the target came into view I would position it so that it appeared to be running down the line of my port cannon. As the target disappeared under the wing, I would hold my heading. When the target emerged from under the trailing edge I would pull the aircraft up to kill the forward speed, roll it over on its back and let the nose drop until the target was lined up in the gunsight graticule. That way, one got the Spitfire to go down in the correct angle of dive of 60 degrees. It was a pretty steep dive, it felt as if one was going down vertically. The other aircraft in the section, Nos 2, 3, and 4, would be following me down still in echelon.'

When the leader's dive took him to an altitude of 4,000 feet (1,219m) above the ground, he released his bombs.

'I would let go my bombs and call "Bombs gone!"; the other chaps in the section would then release theirs. If there had been little or no flak the desire to see the results of the bombing was usually so

> **'It was a pretty steep dive, it felt as if one was going down vertically.'**

great that I would pull hard on the stick to bring the aircraft out of the dive and into a slight climb, so that I could look over my shoulder to see where the bombs had gone. But if we were being fired at, we would use our high forward speed to get us down to ground level where there was cover.'

During the final months of the war almost every attack launched by the British army received strong fighter-bomber support. The example above shows the scale of air support for the British advance on the Montone River in Italy, on 10 November 1944. That morning, during a two-hour period, two RAF and four South African Air Force Spitfire squadrons flew 54 sorties to soften-up the German defences. Air operations continued in the same vein throughout the rest of the day.

■ VERSATILITY ■

Given the ability of the Spitfire in the fighter-bomber role, the reader should remember that attacks on ground targets were far from everyone's thoughts when the Spitfire was conceived. As so often with this aircraft, it was a case of the very good basic design proving very good at a wide range of different roles.

The Spitfire remained in front-line service in the RAF for nearly a decade after the end of the war. In the next chapter we shall observe the final stages of its lengthy career in that service and also in foreign air forces.

POST-WAR SPITFIRES

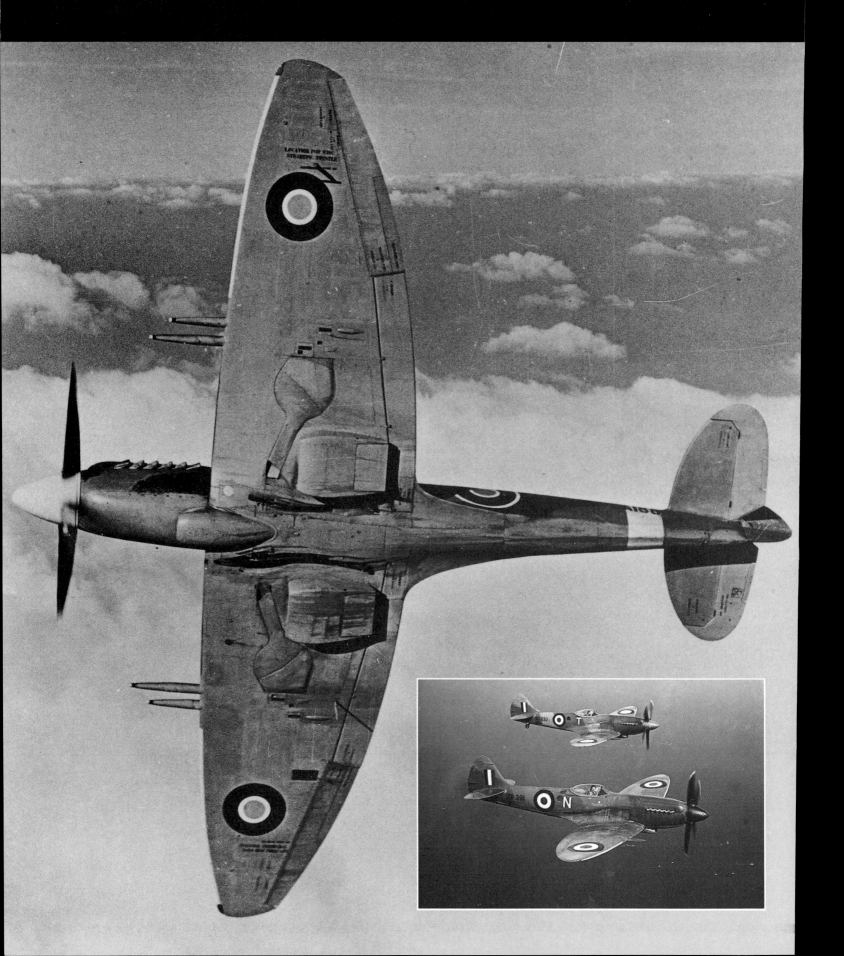

At the end of the war just over a thousand Spitfires were serving with RAF front-line units. About two-thirds of that total were Mark IXs (or the essentially similar Mark XVIs). For a 'stopgap' fighter put into production in a hurry, this had been a remarkably successful variant.

The Spitfire force was rapidly run down after the war as the RAF reduced its strength and many units converted to jet fighters. During the early post war period the Mark XVIII was the main fighter variant to equip fighter units in the Middle East and the Far East. Externally similar to the late production Mark XIV with bubble canopy and additional fuel tanks in the rear fuselage, this variant also featured a redesigned and strengthened wing. Production ran to some 300 aircraft and the variant equipped six front-line squadrons.

The Mark XVIII saw action with Nos 28 and 60 Squadrons in Malaya, engaging in bombing and strafing operations against Communist guerillas in that country. Serving in the Middle East with Nos 32 and 208 Squadrons, this variant became involved in clashes during the Arab-Jewish conflict leading up to the establishment of the state of Israel.

As mentioned earlier, the Mark XXI had been intended as the 'definitive' fighter variant of the Spitfire. At the peak more than 1,800 were on order, but with the end of the war most of these were cancelled. In the event production ended at 120 aircraft and this variant served with only four front-line squadrons.

Left: **A Spitfire XXI tips its wing to show the revised wing shape of this and later variants. Note also the fairing doors covering the main wheels and the armament of four 20mm cannon introduced as standard with this version.**
Above right: **After the war Spitfires served in several second-line units. This Mark XVI operated with the Central Gunnery School.**
Inset and right: **Spitfire XVIIIs of No. 208 Squadron based at Fayid in the Suez Canal Zone in 1947.**

THE SPITFIRE MARK XXII

Type Single-seat interceptor fighter.
Armament Four Hispano 20mm cannon with 150 rounds each for the inner weapons and 175 rounds each for the outer weapons.
Power Plant One Rolls-Royce Griffon 61 liquid cooled V-12 engine with two-stage supercharger developing 2,035hp.
Dimensions Span 36ft 1in (11.25m); length 32ft 11in (10.03m).
Weight Maximum loaded weight 10,086lb (4,574kg).
Performance Maximum speed 449mph at 25,000ft (723km/hr at 7,622m); service ceiling 45,500ft (13,872m).

Left: Mark XVIIIs of No. 28 Squadron pictured at Kai Tak, Hong Kong, late in 1950. The aircraft carries the black and white identification bands on the rear fuselage and above and below the wings, introduced soon after the start of the war in Korea.
Middle: Spitfire made for two. After the war small numbers of Spitfire XVIIIs and IXs were converted into two-seat trainers with dual controls. Trainer variants served with the Indian, the Dutch, the Egyptian and the Irish air forces, though the type was not adopted by the RAF.
Below left: Spitfire PP139 served as a development prototype for the Mark XXI, and incorporated several new features. The enlarged fin with the straight leading edge and the windscreen with revised contours were not incorporated into production aircraft.

During the post war period the Mark XVIII was the main fighter variant to equip fighter units in the Middle East and Far East

The next major production fighter variant, the Spitfire XXII, was essentially a Mark XXI with a bubble canopy and the new enlarged tail assembly. The majority of Mark XXIIs went to Royal Auxiliary Air Force squadrons, reserve units manned by the so-called 'weekend pilots'. During 1948 twelve of the twenty RAuxAF squadrons re-equipped with Spitfire XXIIs.

■ FINAL VARIANT ■

The final Spitfire variant, the Mark XXIV, looked little different from the Mark XXII. Its main points of difference were two additional fuel tanks fitted in the rear fuselage, and wing fittings to carry six 60lb (27kg) rockets. Supermarine built fifty-four Mark XXIVs and converted twenty-seven Mark XXIIs on the production line to this configuration. The final Mark XXIV, the last of more than twenty thousand Spitfires built, left the factory at South Marston near Swindon in February 1948.

Only one front-line unit received the

Right and below: Mark XXIs serving with No. 41 Squadron based at Luebeck in Germany shortly after the end of the war. (Adamson)

The majority of Mark XXIIs went to Royal Auxiliary Air Force squadrons

Spitfire XXIV, No. 80 Squadron based in Germany in January 1948. In July 1949, after the start of the Korean War, the unit moved to Hong Kong to provide air defence for the colony. The last RAF unit to operate Spitfires in the fighter role, it re-equipped with Hornets in January 1952. Photographic reconnaissance Mark XIXs continued in front-line service for a further two years, before this variant also ended its front-line career in the Far East. In April 1954, No. 81 Squadron in Malaya exchanged its trusty Spitfires for Meteors.

Although the Spitfire had passed out of front-line service, it would continue to perform second-line tasks in the RAF for three more years. The last full-time RAF unit to operate Spitfires was the civilian-manned Temperature and Humidity (THUM) Flight based at Woodvale in Lancashire. The unit's Mark XIXs, carry-ing meteorological measuring equipment, made daily flights to 30,000 feet (9,144m) to record the weather conditions in each altitude band. These flights continued until June 1957 when the unit disbanded. Even then the Spitfire's career in the RAF was not at an end. After the THUM Flight disbanded, one of its redundant Mark XIXs went to the Central Fighter Establishment at West Raynham to serve as a gate guardian. Service engineers lovingly maintained the aircraft in flying condition, however, and when the unit transferred to Binbrook the Spitfire went too.

During 1963 Indonesia launched its claim to parts of Malayan territory, and threatened to use force to secure it. To meet the threat the RAF sent reinforcements to the area, including detachments of Lightning fighters. The Indonesian Air Force operated Second World War Mustang fighters, and there was uncertainty on the best tactics for the Mach 2

Left and above: A few Spitfires were fitted with the contra-rotating propeller, comprising two three-bladed units rotating in opposite directions. Although this made the fighter easier to fly and a more steady gun platform, it came too late for general service use.
Below: The Mark XXII was similar to the Mark XXI, but featured a bubble canopy as well as a larger tailplane, fin and rudder.

Also during the years following the Second World War, several foreign air forces operated Spitfires. The largest such operator was the French Air Force, which took delivery of more than five hundred Mark Vs, VIIIs, IXs and XVIs. Some went to Vietnam and flew against Communist guerillas during the initial stages of the long conflict in that country.

■ SPITFIRES INTERNATIONAL ■

The Royal Dutch Air Force received seventy-six Mark IXs, some of which saw combat over what was then the Dutch East Indies. That conflict ran from 1947 to 1949, and ended with the foundation of the modern state of Indonesia.

Other major post-war Spitfire users were the Turkish Air Force, which received 273, the Royal Greek Air Force with 242 and the Royal Belgian Air Force with 203. The Indian Air Force received 159, the Italian Air Force 140 and the Czechoslovak Air Force 77.

Almost a century has elapsed since Orville Wright made the first manned flight in a heavier-than-air flying machine. In the turbulent history of military aviation, no aircraft has carved a deeper niche than Mitchell's little fighter – which somebody else chose to call 'Spitfire'.

fighters to engage these. To discover the answer, the CFE ran a combat trial using the Spitfire XIX as a stand-in for the Mustang. Mock combats between the two aircraft revealed that the older fighter stood little chance in a wartime encounter. The Lightning was almost invulnerable while it maintained high speed and did not enter a turning fight with the more nimble opponent. The best tactic for the Lightning was to position itself a few thousand feet below the piston-engined fighter, and make a steep climbing attack from there. This gave a good chance of getting into a missile-firing position on the Spitfire (or Mustang) without being seen. The trial at Binbrook took place twenty-seven years after the maiden flight of the Spitfire, and probably represented the final warlike act in the aircraft's long and distinguished career.

Above: Spitfire XXIIs formed the main equipment of the Royal Auxiliary Air Force units during the late 1940s. These aircraft belonged to No. 613 (City of Manchester) Squadron based at Ringwood, which converted to the variant in the summer of 1948.

Left: Spitfire XXII of No. 607 (County of Durham) Squadron. The '4' painted on the fin, fuselage and wing was the aircraft's racing number for the Cooper Trophy air race in 1948.

Above: Mark IX of the Royal Dutch Air Force, which received seventy-six examples of this variant.

Left: From its external appearance the final variant of the Spitfire, the Mark XXIV, was little different from the Mark XXII. The main changes were that it carried two additional fuel tanks in the rear fuselage, and wing fittings to carry six 60lb (27kg) rockets. Only No. 80 Squadron equipped with this variant and after a brief spell in Germany the unit took its Mark XXIVs to Hong Kong.

Above: One of seventy-seven examples of Mark IX passed to the Czechoslovak Air Force.

Left: The French Air Force was the largest foreign operator of Spitfires after the war, when that service took delivery of some 500 Mark Vs, VIIIs, IXs and XVIs.

Above: Three Spitfire PR Mark XIs of the Royal Norwegian Air Force, which also received seventy-one Mark IXs.

Left: The Italian Air Force received 140 Spitfire IXs after the war.

Right: Spitfire XIVs of the Royal Belgian Air Force which received 134 examples of this variant, in addition to sixty-nine Mark IXs and Mark XVIs.

Left: The Southern Rhodesian Air Force received twenty-two Spitfire XXIIs from surplus RAF stocks in 1951.

Above and below: Partners in war, and also in peace. A Hurricane pictured with a Spitfire XIX of the Royal Air Force Battle of Britain Memorial Flight. These aircraft are firm favourites at present-day airshows.

APPENDIX
THE SPITFIRE FAMILY

The main driving force for the development of the Spitfire came from the progressive increases in power from the Merlin, and later the Griffon, series of engines. In developing the extra power the engines guzzled fuel faster, requiring larger capacity (and therefore heavier) fuel tanks to restore the fighter's range. Also, the more powerful engines required propellers with more blades to convert that rotational power into thrust. During its life the Spitfire progressed from a two-bladed propeller to a three-blader, then to a four-blader and finally to a five-bladed propeller. The greater the number of propeller blades, the greater the weight and also the greater the twisting forces they exerted on the airframe when the engine ran at full power. At the end of the fighter's career it was necessary to fit an entirely new and larger tail assembly, to overcome these twisting forces.

Application of the hard-won lessons of air combat led other problems. The RAF demanded the installation of armour to protect the pilot and vulnerable parts of the aircraft's structure, as well as additional equipment and more powerful (and therefore heavier) weaponry.

THE PRICE OF SUCCESS

'I loved the Spitfire, in all of her many versions. But I have to admit that the later Marks, although they were faster than the earlier ones, were also much heavier and so did not handle so well. You did not have such positive control over them. One test of manoeuvrability was to throw the Spitfire into a flick roll and see how many times she rolled. With the Mark II or the Mark V one got two and a half flick rolls, but the Mark IX was heavier and you got only one and a half. With the later and still heavier versions one got even less.

'The essence of aircraft design is compromise, and an improvement at one end of the performance envelope is rarely achieved without a deterioration somewhere else.'

ALEX HENSHAW, CHIEF TEST PILOT AT THE CASTLE BROMWICH SPITFIRE FACTORY

When the fighter sat on the ground these increases in weight did not matter much, but in the stress of combat it was an entirely different matter. If the pilot pulled 6G in the turn, every part of the aircraft weighed six times as much. If the wings and the rest of the structure were not strong enough to withstand these increased forces, the airframe would be overstressed and weakened. In extreme cases the structure might collapse altogether. So, to cope with each major increase in the fighter's weight, the airframe was continually being redesigned to increase its strength and maintain a safe load factor. In addition, and inevitably, each such redesign brought with it a further increase in weight. Thus every improvement in performance, fire power, range or capability gave a further twist in the spiral of increased weight. And that in turn led to a further deterioration in the fighter's handling characteristics.

K 5054	Prototype Spitfire, first flew in March 1936. Only one aircraft built.
Mark I	Similar to the prototype but with some revisions to the structure, this was the first production fighter version. The Mark I made its maiden flight in May 1938 and entered service in the following September.
Mark I Recon Variants	Mark Is modified for the reconnaissance role, designated from IA to IG depending on the Reconnaissance configuration of the cameras and fuel tanks carried. First such aircraft entered service in November 1939.
Mark II	Fighter version similar to the Mark I, but fitted with the more powerful Merlin 12 engine. Entered service in September 1940.
Mark III	Fighter version similar to the Mark I but with a redesigned internal structure and fitted with a retractable tail wheel. This variant did not go into production. In September 1941 the prototype Mark III served as a test bed for the Merlin 61 engine with two-stage supercharger.
Mark IV	Designation initially applied to the prototype Griffon-engined Spitfire. In 1941 the designation system was revised and the Griffon aircraft became the Mark XX for a short time, before finally ending up as the Mark XII. The Mark IV designation was then re-allocated to reconnaissance versions.
Mark V	Fighter version similar to the Mark I, but fitted with the more powerful Merlin 45-series engine. The Mark V entered service in February 1941 and was built in very large numbers. It was the first variant to be fitted with bomb racks and operated in the fighter-bomber role.
Mark VI	High-altitude interceptor fighter, similar to the Mark V but fitted with a pressurized cabin and longer-span wing. The Mark VI was built in small numbers and entered service in April 1942.
Mark VII	High-altitude interceptor fighter, similar to the Mark VI but powered by the Merlin 61-series engine with two-stage supercharger. Built in moderate numbers, the first squadron equipped with this variant became operational in April 1943.
Mark VIII	General-purpose fighter similar to the Mark VII but without the pressurized cabin. Entered service in the summer of 1943. Built in large numbers, all Mark VIIIs went to units based outside the United Kingdom. This variant also operated in the fighter-bomber role.
Mark IX	General-purpose fighter version based on the Mark V, but fitted with the Merlin 61-series engine. Entered service in June 1942. This variant was intended as a stop gap, pending large scale production of the Mark VIII. In the event the Mark IX remained in production until the end of the war. With the externally similar Mark XVI, it was built in greater numbers than any other variant. Late production aircraft were fitted with bubble canopies. This variant also operated in the fighter-bomber and fighter-reconnaissance roles.
Mark X	Photographic reconnaissance variant generally similar to the PR ID, but fitted with the Merlin 61 series engine and a pressurized cabin. Entered service in May 1944, built in small numbers.
Mark XI	Photographic reconnaissance variant similar to the Mark X but without the pressurized cabin. Entered service in December 1942 and became the most-used photographic reconnaissance variant.
Mark XII	Fighter version based on the Mark V but fitted with the early Griffon 2 engine with a single-stage supercharger. Originally it was designated the Mark IV, then it was redesignated the Mark XX,

before finally receiving this designation. Built in moderate numbers as a low-altitude fighter, all production aircraft had clipped wings. Entered service in February 1943.

Mark XIII Low-altitude fighter-reconnaissance variant fitted with vertical and oblique cameras, armed with four .303in (7.7mm) machine guns. Only 26 examples produced, it entered service in the summer of 1943.

Mark XIV Fighter version similar to the Mark VIII but fitted with the Griffon 61-series engine with two-stage supercharger. It entered service in February 1944. A fighter-reconnaissance version of the Mark XIV also appeared. The variant was built in large numbers and the final production aircraft had bubble canopies.

Mark XV Designation not applied to the Spitfire.

Mark XVI Fighter version similar to the Mark IX but powered by the Merlin engine produced under licence by the American Packard Company. The two variants were produced side-by-side at the Castle Bromwich plant and their external appearance was almost identical. The Mark XVI entered service in September 1944 and late production aircraft were fitted with bubble canopies. This variant also operated in the fighter-bomber role.

Mark XVII Designation not applied to the Spitfire.

Mark XVIII Fighter-bomber version similar in external appearance to the late-model Mark XIV fitted with the bubble canopy, this variant featured a redesigned and strengthened wing and carried additional fuel tanks in the rear fuselage. A fighter-reconnaissance version of the Mark XVIII also appeared. Built in moderate numbers after the war, it entered service in January 1947. All Mark XVIIIs went to units based outside the United Kingdom.

Mark XIX Photographic reconnaissance variant which combined the Griffon 61 engine, the fuel tank layout of the Mark XI and a pressurized cabin that was a marked improvement over that fitted to the Mark X. It entered service in the summer of 1944 and became the most-used reconnaissance variant during the final year of the war. The Mark XIX remained in front-line service in the R.A.F. until 1954.

Mark XX Designation applied to the prototype Griffon-powered Spitfire, alias the Mark IV, following the re-allocation of Mark numbers. After a further re-allocation of Mark numbers this aircraft was re-designated as a Mark XII and the Mark XX designation fell vacant.

Mark XXI Fighter version with a redesigned and strengthened wing and fuselage, fitted with the Griffon 61-series engine. The Mark XXI entered service in April 1945 and saw some action before the war ended. Following the end of the conflict several large contracts for the Mark XXI were cancelled and the variant was built in only moderate numbers.

Mark XXII Fighter version similar to the Mark XXI, but with a bubble canopy. Production aircraft fitted with enlarged tailplane, fin and rudder. The Mark XXII entered service in November 1947 and became the main post-war production variant. It remained in service with Royal Auxiliary Air Force squadrons until March 1951.

Mark XXIII A projected fighter version that was to have been fitted with laminar-flow wing; not built.

Mark XXIV Fighter version based on the Mark XXII, but with two additional fuel tanks in the rear fuselage and wing fittings to carry six 60lb (27kg) rockets. Only one squadron operated this variant. The type remained in front-line service in the RAF until January 1952.

THE AVRO LANCASTER

Bielefeld, western Germany, 14 March 1945. The Lancaster B.1 (Special) heading towards its target had been unable to reach more than 14,000ft (4,250m). Beneath it bulked the outline of the largest and most destructive bomb ever used in war; the Grand Slam, weighing more than 22,000lb (10 tonnes). In the nose lay the bomb-aimer, holding the graticule of his sight on the target. The seconds ticked away interminably until at last the computer automatically released the huge bomb.

The pilot, Squadron Leader Calder, felt the bomber lift as the weight came off, and the wings, which previously had taken on a distinct upward curve, resumed their normal shape.

Lying prone in the nose, the bomb aimer watched as the huge weapon plunged downwards, dwindling in size as it did so, spinning as it went for greater accuracy. At first it appeared that it was going to fall short, but this was illusory. In the final seconds of its fall it seemed to sweep forward and hit about 90ft (30m) from the target.

■ TARGET COLLAPSED ■

The impact was not very spectacular; from that altitude there was just a tiny splash of mud as the Grand Slam, travelling faster than sound, penetrated something like 75ft (25m) into the earth. After an 11-second delay, however, a gigantic underground explosion erupted, flinging earth and mud some 500ft (150m) into the air, and forming an enormous cavity into which a large section of the target, a rail viaduct that was vital to German communications during the closing months of the war, collapsed.

The Lancaster had not been flying alone; that would have been far too risky, even at this late stage in the war. It was accompanied by 14 others,

Above: **The Bielefeld Rail Viaduct had survived previous raids, but succumbed to the first Grand Slam dropped.**

each armed with a Tallboy, a smaller (12,000lb/ 5.4 tonnes) version of the Grand Slam. Even as the huge bomb went off, Tallboys were falling around the viaduct, their combined effect destroying several more arches of the now sadly battered target, and ensuring that it would never again be used to carry German reinforcements to where they were most needed.

Above: Grand Slam, the largest bomb of all. Only 41 were dropped, all by Lancaster Specials of No. 617 Squadron.

The Lancaster had, in the space of three short years, become the backbone of RAF Bomber Command. A total of 7,366 were built, of which almost half were lost on operations. They carried out something like 156,000 operational sorties, an average of about 21 sorties each, which says much about the hazards they faced, and dropped more than 600,000 tons of bombs; an average of more than 81 tons each. They carried greater bomb loads farther than any other wartime bomber.

■ VERSATILITY ■

Lancasters formed the main equipment of the Pathfinder Force; they pioneered low-level marking and precision attacks, and, far more than any other heavy bomber type before or since, they proved amenable to modification to carry special weapons. With all this, the Lancaster retained its docile handling, even when badly damaged, which undoubtedly saved the lives of many crewmen. Long after the war, the Lancaster retains a mystique unequalled by any other bomber, and the affection of those that flew to war in it remains even now, over 50 years later.

Above: 1,000lb bombs in storage. Lancasters dropped no fewer than 217,640 of these between 1942 and 1945.

AVRO LANCASTER MK III

1 Two .303in (7.7mm)
   Browning machine guns
2 Frazer-Nash power-operated
   nose turret
3 Nose blister
4 Bomb-aimer's panel
   (optically flat)
5 Bomb-aimer's control panel
6 Side windows
7 External air temperature
   thermometer
8 Pitot head
9 Bomb-aimer's chest support
10 Fire extinguisher
11 Parachute emergency exit
12 F-24 camera
13 Glycol tank/step
14 Ventilator fairing
15 Bomb-bay doors forward
   actuating jacks
16 Bomb-bay doors forward
   actuating jacks
17 Control linkage
18 Rudder panels
19 Instrument panel
20 Windscreen sprays
21 Windscreen
22 Dimmer switches
23 Flight-engineer's folding seat
24 Flight-engineer's control panel
25 Pilot's seat
26 Flight-deck floor level
27 Elevator and rudder control rods
   (underfloor)
28 Trim tab control cables
29 Main floor/bomb-bay support
   longeron
30 Fire extinguisher
31 Wireless installation
32 Navigator's seat
33 Canopy rear/down-view blister
34 Pilot's head armour
35 Cockpit canopy emergency
   escape hatch
36 D/F loop
37 Aerial mast support
38 Electrical services panel
39 Navigator's compartment
   window
40 Navigator's desk
41 Aircraft and radio
   compass receiver
42 Wireless-operator's desk
43 Wireless-operator's seat
44 Wireless-operator's
   compartment window
45 Front spar carry-through/
   fuselage frame
46 Astrodome
47 Inboard section wing ribs
48 Spar join
49 Aerial mast
50 Starboard inboard engine nacelle
51 Spinner
52 Three-blade de Havilland
   constant-speed propellers
53 Oil cooler intake
54 Oil cooler radiator
55 Carburettor air intake
56 Radiator shutter
57 Engine bearer frame
58 Exhaust flame-damper shroud

59 Packard-built Rolls-Royce
   Merlin 28 liquid-cooled engine
60 Nacelle/wing fairing
61 Fuel tank bearer ribs
62 Intermediate ribs
63 Leading-edge structure
64 Wing stringers
65 Wingtip skinning
66 Starboard navigation light
67 Starboard formation light
68 Aileron hinge fairings
69 Wing rear spar
70 Starboard aileron
71 Aileron balance tab

72 Balance tab control rod
73 Aileron trim tab
74 HF aerial
75 Split trailing-edge flap
   (outboard section)
76 Emergency (ditching) exit
77 Crash axe stowage
78 Fire extinguisher
79 Hydraulic reservoir
80 Signal/flare pistol stowage
81 Parachute stowage box/spar step
82 Rear spar carry-through
83 Bunk backrest
84 Rear spar fuselage frame

85 Emergency packs
86 Roof light
87 Dinghy manual release cable
   (dinghy stowage in starboard
   wingroot)
88 Mid-gunner's parachute stowage
89 Tail turret ammunition box
90 Ammunition feed track
91 Emergency (ditching) exit
92 Flame floats stowage
93 Sea markers stowage
94 Roof light
95 Dorsal turret fairing
96 Frazer-Nash power-operated

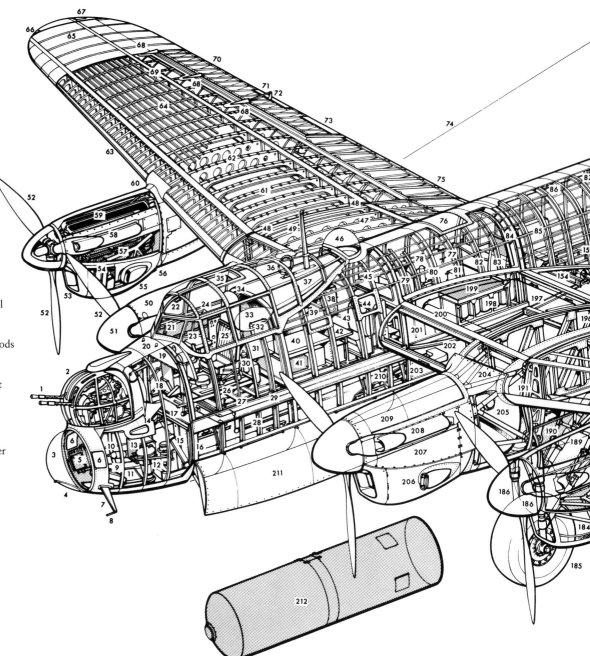

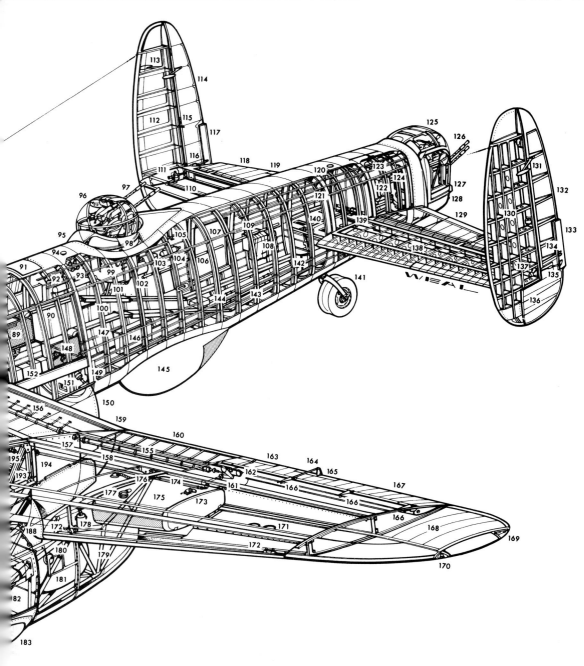

156 Flap toggle links
157 Flap tube connecting link
158 Rear spar
159 Split trailing-edge flap (inboard section)
160 Split trailing-edge flap (outboard section)
161 Aileron control lever
162 Aileron trim tab control cable linkage
163 Aileron trim tab
164 Aileron balance tab control rod
165 Aileron balance tab
166 Aileron hinge fairings
167 Port aileron
168 Port wingtip
169 Port formation light
170 Port navigation light
171 Retractable landing lights (port wing only)
172 Cable cutters
173 Fuel vent pipe
174 Aileron control rod
175 Port outer (No. 3) fuel tank (114 gal/518 litres)
176 Outboard engine support frame/rear spar pick-up
177 Fuel booster pump
178 Fire extinguisher
179 Engine sub-frame
180 Filler cap
181 Outboard engine oil tank
182 Firewall/bulkhead
183 Carburettor air intake
184 Outboard engine support frame
185 Port mainwheel
186 Undercarriage oleo struts
187 Flame-damper shroud
188 Outboard engine support frame/main spar pick-up
189 Undercarriage retraction jacks
190 Oleo strut attachment pin
191 Undercarriage support beam (light-alloy casting)
192 Centre-section outer rib/undercarriage support
193 Location of port intermediate (No. 2) fuel tank (383 gal/1741 litres)
194 Mainwheel well
195 Emergency retraction air valve
196 Retraction cylinder attachment
197 Port inner (No. 1) fuel tank (580 gal/2637 litres)
198 Oxygen bottle stowage
199 Rest bunk
200 Main spar
201 Hinged inboard leading-edge
202 Cabin heater installation
203 Air intake
204 Inboard engine support frame
205 Inboard engine oil tank
206 Carburettor intake anti-ice guard
207 Port inner nacelle
208 Flame-damper shroud
209 Detachable cowling panels
210 Bomb shackles
211 Bomb-bay doors (open)
212 8000lb (2532kg) bomb

dorsal turret
97 Two .303in (7.7mm) Browning machine guns
98 Turret mounting ring
99 Turret mechanism
100 Ammunition track cover plate
101 Turret step bracket
102 Header tank
103 Oxygen cylinder
104 Fire extinguisher
105 DR compass housing
106 Handrail
107 Crew entry door (starboard)
108 Parachute stowage
109 First-aid pack
110 Starboard tailplane
111 Rudder control lever
112 Starboard tailfin
113 Rudder balance weights
114 Starboard rudder
115 Rudder datum hinge
116 Rudder tab actuating rod

117 Rudder tab
118 Starboard elevator
119 Elevator balance tab
120 Roof light
121 Tail main frame
122 Parachute stowage
123 Fire extinguisher
124 Tail turret entry door
125 Frazer-Nash power-operated tail turret
126 Four .303in (7.7mm) Browning machine guns
127 Cartridge case ejection chutes
128 Rear navigation light
129 Elevator trim tab
130 Fin construction
131 Rudder balance weights
132 Port rudder frame
133 Rudder trim tab
134 Rudder tab balance weight
135 Rudder tab actuating rod
136 Rudder horn balance

137 Trim tab actuating jack
138 Tailplane construction
139 Elevator torque tube
140 Tailplane carry-through
141 Non-retractable tailwheel
142 Elsan closet
143 Ammunition track cover plate
144 Elevator and rudder control rods
145 H2S (radar-bombing) ventral antenna fairing
146 Dorsal turret step
147 Ammunition feed track
148 Tail turret ammunition box
149 Bomb-bay aft bulkhead
150 Bomb-bay doors
151 Bomb-bay doors aft actuating jacks
152 Reserve ammunition boxes
153 Main floor support structure
154 Flap operating hydraulic jack
155 Flap operating tube

THE MANCHESTER

The origins of the Lancaster lay in Air Ministry Specification P13/36, issued in September 1936, although a long and tortuous road had first to be followed before the definitive aircraft emerged. The requirements included a maximum bomb load of 8,000lb (3.63 tonnes), a six-man crew, which included a ventral gunner, and the ability to operate from existing 4,500ft (1,375m) long grass strips. Power was to be provided by two Rolls-Royce Vultures, a 24 cylinder liquid-cooled engine which was expected to develop about 2,000hp.

The Handley Page Company had early doubts about the Vulture, and switched to the proven Merlin, of which four were needed, for what was to become the Halifax. At A. V. Roe, chief designer Roy Chadwick persevered with the Vulture for the Type 679 bomber, with Napier's Sabre as a fall-back engine.

Two prototypes of the Avro Type 679,

Left: **The Lancaster Mk I, originally known as the Manchester III, was developed around the Manchester fuselage and wing centre section.**

AVRO 679

Dimensions
Wing span 80ft 2in (24.43m)
Tailplane span 22ft 0in (6.70m)
Length 70ft 0in (21.33m)
Height 19ft 6in (5.94m)

Weights
Maximum takeoff 45,000lb (20,400kg)
Maximum bomb load 10,000lb (4,500kg)

Power
Two Rolls-Royce 24 cylinder Vulture I liquid-cooled engines rated at 1,720hp each.

Performance
Maximum speed 256mph (412km/hr) at 12,500ft (3,800m)
Range with maximum bomb load c1,200 miles (1,930km)
Service ceiling c18,000ft (5,500m)

Armament
Two .303 Browning machine guns in each of three Nash and Thompson power-operated turrets, nose, tail, and a retractable ventral 'dustbin'. None fitted on first flight.

later to be named the Manchester, were ordered within a week of Specification P13/36 being issued, and the first flight took place at Ringway Airport on 25 July 1939. It was a large aircraft, with the wing in the mid position, and with twin fins and rudders. Handling

problems were immediately apparent; the controls were heavy, and lateral stability left much to be desired. Much more critical, however, was the fact that the take-off run was far longer than anticipated, even though the aircraft was being flown at a light all-up weight, with no bombload, with the gun turrets omitted and their positions faired over. Meanwhile the second prototype, already well advanced, was modified to try to cure these faults. The outer wing sections were redesigned, extending the span to 90ft 1in (27.46m); the control surfaces (ailerons and elevators) were improved, and larger fins and rudders fitted.

In the expectation that the faults of the first prototype would soon be overcome, contracts were placed for the production of 1,200 Manchesters. The first flight of the second prototype took place on 26 May 1940, and while the take-off run was appreciably shortened and handling considerably improved, directional stability, especially at low airspeeds, was still far from adequate. It was then decided to fit a central fin, which went some way towards improving matters.

Meanwhile, problems were being

Below: **The twin-engined Manchester was the forerunner of the Lancaster. This No. 61 Squadron aircraft failed to return from a raid on Hamburg in April 1942.**

1562
PHOTO "THE AEROPLANE"

Above: The Manchester IA dispensed with the central fin, but the span of the tailplane was greatly increased.

encountered with the Vulture. The design of this 24-cylinder monster had been started in 1935. In essence it consisted of two V-12 engines on a common crankcase, one upright, with the other inverted beneath it. With a capacity of 42.48 litres, it was expected to deliver over 2,000hp at 3,000rpm for take-off,

The Vulture was just that bit too clever for the time

and 1,710hp at an altitude of 15,000ft (4,570m); impressive figures for that era.

The truth was that it was just that bit too clever for the time. Lubrication, excessive wear, metal fatigue and over-heating all gave cause for concern. But with the build-up of RAF Bomber Command a matter of extreme urgency, it was decided to press on with the

Manchester, hoping that the problems would eventually be solved.

■ DEFENSIVE ■

The gun turrets were installed in the second prototype; two .303 Brownings in the nose, tail, and in a retractable ventral 'dustbin' arrangement. These also gave rise to handling problems. When rotated, they interfered with the slipstream. The nose turret caused the aircraft to yaw to one side, while the rear turret caused vibration in the elevators. Minor amendments reduced these effects to acceptable levels.

Meanwhile, actual battle experience in 1939 caused a rethinking of the defensive armament for bombers. The ventral turret was deleted and a twin-gun mid-upper turret installed. It was suggested that the armament of the tail turret was doubled to four machine guns, but various weight restrictions prevented this being put into practice for some considerable time.

Despite the problems encountered in the early flight test days, the Manchester had many good points. The layout of the spacious cabin was highly praised, while the capacious bomb bay could hold

either four 2,000 pounders (900kg) or four sea mines; or one of the new (not yet in service) 4,000lb (1,800kg) bombs together with six 1,000 pounders (450kg). The structure was sturdy, and various tweaks to the flight control system eventually resulted in an aircraft that in most respects was quite a pleasant one to fly.

The first production aircraft arrived at Boscombe Down for trials on 5 August 1940, but continuing problems with the Vulture engines limited it to 52,000lb (23.59 tonnes) rather than the 57,000lb (25.85 tonnes) for which it was stressed. The second production Manchester joined it in October and, carrying typical bomb loads, demonstrated that it could operate at altitudes of up to 13,500ft (4,100m) with no problems. But after one or two engine failures, the type was eventually operationally limited to 12,000ft (3,660m) with maximum bomb load and 50 per cent fuel.

■ STOP-GAP ■

Further testing revealed an average of only 76 flying hours between engine failures, and generally the Manchester was only able to maintain height on one engine at fairly light all-up weights. At some stage the decision seems to have been taken that the Manchester would be only an interim type with Bomber Command, but nevertheless it was still rushed into service.

The first operational Manchester squadron was No. 207, formed at Waddington late in 1940, even though further airframe modifications were needed. Composed mainly of experienced crews, conversion onto type proceeded despite bad weather, and the Manchester was released for short-range operations with a reduced bomb load.

The target was the German cruiser Admiral Hipper

The first operation was flown by six aircraft on the night of 24/25 February 1941. The target on that occasion was the German cruiser *Admiral Hipper*, which was in the French port of Brest at that time. None of these early aircraft were as yet fitted with the mid-upper gun turret, and the ventral dustbin remained unmanned for the raid. The bomb load consisted of twelve 500lb (225kg) semi-armour piercing bombs. Only moderate flak was encountered, and all aircraft returned safely, although

one crashed on landing. *Admiral Hipper* was not hit, which was only to be expected in those early days of the night-bombing war.

Several more raids followed, including some to targets in Germany. However, the first Manchester lost to enemy action came over England on 13 March, when a No. 207 Squadron aircraft was caught shortly after take-off by German intruder ace Hans Hahn. Only one crewman survived the crash, with its subsequent exploding bombload.

The unreliable Vultures claimed their first victim exactly a week later, when a Manchester crashed shortly after take-off following an engine fire. Then, on 13 April, all Manchesters were grounded for

engine changes. By this time, several aircraft entered service with the mid-upper turret, while the grounding period allowed others to have this fitted.

Despite the fitting of new engines, with their improved lubrication systems, the Manchester still continued to be plagued by engine problems. However, things were not all bad. During a raid on Berlin on 10/11 May, Squadron Leader Charles Kydd's Manchester was attacked by night fighters, which set one of the engines on fire. Successfully extinguishing the flames, Kydd jettisoned his bombs and managed to return safely to base on his one remaining operational engine.

The summer of 1941 saw the introduction of the Manchester 1A, which differed from the first model in having a tailplane of increased span, taller twin fins and rudders, and no central fin. This was done primarily to improve directional control in the event of a symmetric thrust caused by one engine failing. It was also to be powered by the improved Vulture V.

■ LANCASTERS ■

Meanwhile the Manchester was being overtaken by events. The first Lancasters reached the squadrons late in 1941, and with this, the fate of the twin-engined aircraft was sealed. It was finally withdrawn from Bomber Command operations after a raid on Bremen on 25/26 June 1942.

MANCHESTER SQUADRONS

Sqn No.	Bases	1st Operation	Last Operation
207	Waddington	24 Feb 1941	
	Bottesford		11/12 March 1942
97	Waddington	8/9 April 1941	
	Coningsby		9/10 Jan 1942
61	N. Luffenham	14/15 Aug 1941	
	Syerston		1/2 June 1942
83	Scampton	28 Jan 1942	1/2 June 1942
106	Coningsby	20 March 1942	25/26 June 1942
50	Skellingthorpe	8/9 April 1942	
	Swinderby		25/26 June 1942
49	Scampton	2/3 May 1942	25/26 June 1942

The operational careers of the last four squadrons listed were very short, but it should be considered that the similarities between the Manchester and the Lancaster which supplanted it were sufficient to ease the task of converting onto the latter type quite considerably.

MANCHESTER 1A

Dimensions
Wingspan 90ft 1in (27.46m); Tailplane span 33ft 0in (10.06m); Length 70ft 0in (21.33m); Height 19ft 6in (9.54m).

Weights
Maximum takeoff 56,000lb (25,400kg); Maximum bomb load 10,350lb (4,700kg).

Power
Two Rolls-Royce 24 cylinder Vulture II liquid-cooled engines rated at 1,845hp each.

Performance
Maximum speed 265mph (426km/hr) at 17,000ft (5,200 km/hr); Range with maximum bomb load 1,200 miles (1,930km); Service ceiling 19,200ft (5,850m).

Armament
Two Browning .303 machine guns in nose and dorsal turrets; four .303 Browning machine guns in tail turret.

It has often been said that the Lancaster arose from the failure of the Manchester. This is not entirely true; as early as the autumn of 1938, long before the first flight of the Manchester prototype, A.V. Roe's design office considered the possibility of a four-engined variant of the Type 679. But with other priorities in the design offices, only the most basic work was done at this stage on what was to become the Avro Type 683.

Early in the following year, a new specification was issued; B.1/39. Its ultimate purpose was to produce a heavy bomber which would start to replace the four-engined Stirlings and Halifaxes (neither of which had yet flown), and the Manchester itself in four to five years' time.

The requirements were stringent; a cruising speed of 280mph (450km/hr) at 15,000ft (4,570m) while carrying a bomb load of 9,000lb (4.08 tonnes); only slightly less than the maximum of 10,000lb (4.54 tonnes) specified. Range under these conditions was to be a

Left: **As a safeguard against a shortage of Merlins, the Mk II Lancaster was powered by Bristol Hercules radial engines. Only 300 were built.**

minimum of 2,500 miles (4,000km). This was pushing the state of the art very hard, and was not helped by the requirement for defensive armament, which was to consist of tail and ventral turrets each carrying four 20mm cannon. These turrets did not even exist at that time, and the complexity, weight and drag of such monsters eventually ensured that they never would. Prototype aircraft were ordered from both Handley Page and Bristol, but neither got past the mockup stage. The Air Ministry was however interested in A.V. Roe's proposal for a four-engined bomber developed from the Manchester, even though it would retain the same defensive armament as the latter. But with war looming, the twin-engined aircraft naturally had first priority, and initial

Above: **The first four-engined bomber to enter service with Bomber Command was the Short Stirling. It was inferior to the Lancaster in both performance and load-carrying.**

progress with the four-engined machine was slow. Not until the production Manchester was finalized could serious work start on its derivative.

With hindsight, the advantages of four-engined bombers seem glaringly obvious. Because they were bigger than their twin-engined counterparts, they could carry heavier loads of fuel and weaponry, which translated into larger bomb loads carried further. In 1939 this was less obvious, and in fact the twin-engined Manchester could carry a 40 per cent greater bombload than the

BRITISH BOMBER COMPARISONS 1941

A/C type	Cruise Speed at Altitude	Bomb Load for Max Radius	Radius with Max Bomb Load
Wellington	170mph (273km/hr) at 11,300ft (3,450m)	2,500lb (1,130kg) for 1,100 miles (1,770km)	560 miles (900km) with 4,500lb (2,040kg)
Stirling	208mph (335km/hr) at 13,800ft (4,200m)	3,500lb (1,590kg) for 855 miles (1,375km)	285 miles (460km) with 14,000lb (6,350kg)
Halifax	203mph (327km/hr) at 15,100ft (4,600m)	5,800lb (2,630kg) for 910 miles (1,465km)	580 miles (930km) with 8,000lb (3,630kg)
Manchester	205mph (330km/hr) at 13,650ft (4,160m)	8,100lb (3,675kg) for 885 miles (1,425km).	500 miles (805km) with 10,350lb (4,700kg)

From the above table it can be seen that the payload/range of the twin-engined Manchester was significantly better than either of its four-engined contemporaries whether judged by maximum radius or maximum bombload. It totally outclassed the earlier twin-engined Wellington in both departments.

Above: The Rolls-Royce Merlin XX engine installation package for the Beaufighter IIF was adapted for the Lancaster.

four-engined Halifax over a comparable distance, although, it must of course be said, this was provided that its Vultures kept running. There were other factors, although these were often rather problematical. Two engines required fewer systems, less installation weight, less maintenance, and lower costs for spares and replacements than four engines. Aerodynamically, with only two engines instead of four, there was the further advantage of having less drag to overcome in flight. The difficult bit was producing an engine that gave sufficient power to do the job, without it becoming too complex to be reliable. Rolls-Royce

was far from the only company to have problems with over-complex engines at this time. The Napier Sabre was scheduled to power the Manchester II, but delays in development ensured this aircraft variant was never built.

The overall wingspan was increased to accommodate engines

The Merlin was the obvious choice for the Type 683, but demand for this engine for Spitfires and Hurricanes, to say nothing of the Whitley and Halifax bombers, was high. As a backup, the

more powerful but heavier and draggier Bristol Hercules radial was selected. Ironically, increased demand for the Hercules caused by Stirling production eventually led to the Beaufighter, originally powered by the Bristol engine, being fitted with Merlin XXs, in its Mk IIF variant. For this, Rolls-Royce had developed an engine installation package, or power egg, which, with minor changes, proved eminently suitable for the new bomber.

Type 683, known in the design office as the Lancaster from a very early stage, was developed around the Manchester fuselage and wing centre section. The crew cabin had been highly praised, while the cavernous bomb bay met all current and not a few future requirements. The overall wingspan was substantially increased to accommodate the outboard engines, which also had the effect of improving take-off performance, while various other detail modifications were made.

■ FOUR ENGINES ■

A turning point came at the end of August 1940, when the decision was taken that Bomber Command's strategic force would be entirely equipped as soon

Left: The Avro Type 683 prototype was initially known as the Manchester III, and only later renamed the Lancaster I.

Above: The second Lancaster prototype introduced a ventral turret that was fitted to early production aircraft.

as possible with four-engined bombers. In retrospect this decision seems extraordinary, if only because the Stirling had barely started reaching its first squadron, while the service entry of the Halifax was still three months in the future, as was that of the Manchester. The four-engined heavy bomber had yet to prove itself, but there remained one sound operational reason for the decision. Even reliable engines failed occasionally, and all were vulnerable to flak and fighters. The failure of one engine in a four-engined type was much less serious than the same case in a twin, in which a full 50 per cent of the available power was lost, and asymmetric handling problems, with all the remaining power on one side, were far more extreme.

Trials at Boscombe Down showed good handling qualities but directional stability was lacking

The decision to proceed with the four-engined Avro bomber was taken, although as a security measure the name Lancaster was dropped and the Type 683 became known as the Manchester Mark III, the Mark II designation having been reserved for the Napier Sabre-powered

aircraft, which in fact was never built. The prototype used a Manchester I airframe powered by Merlin Xs, and retained the short-span tailplane and triple fin layout of that aircraft. The first flight took place on 9 January 1941.

Trials at Boscombe Down showed

good handling qualities although, as was only to be expected, directional stability was lacking. This was cured by a new tailplane of almost double the span of the original, and very much larger twin fins and rudders, with the central fin removed. With the new Merlin XXs fitted, the prototype reached a maximum speed of 310mph (500km/hr) at 21,000ft (6,400m) – an outstanding performance for a heavy bomber of that era. A new production contract was issued, limiting the output of Manchesters to 200 before switching to the Lancaster, as it had inevitably become known. The use of Manchester sub-assemblies speeded up this process.

■ SECOND PROTOTYPE ■

The second Lancaster prototype, which made its maiden flight on 13 May 1941, was rather nearer to the production machine standard, stressed for an all-up weight of 60,000lb (27.22 tonnes), and

LANCASTER

Dimensions
Wingspan 102ft 0in (31.09m); Length (tail up) 69ft 6in (21.18m); Height (tail up) 20ft 6in (6.25m); Wing area 1,297 sq. ft (120.45m²).

Weights
Empty 36,900lb (16,740kg); Normal loaded 53,000lb (24,040kg); Maximum overload 65,000lb (29,480kg) (B.I Special with 22,000lb (9,980kg) Grand Slam 70,000lb (31,750kg); Maximum internal bomb load 14,000lb (6,350kg).

Power
Four Rolls-Royce Merlin 12 cylinder liquid-cooled engines each rated at 1,460hp (variable depending on type) driving a three-bladed variable-pitch, constant-speed propeller. Lancaster B.III powered by four Bristol Hercules 14 cylinder air-cooled radial engines each rated at 1,650hp.

Fuel and Oil
Total fuel 2,154gal (9,790 litres) in six wing tanks. 580gal (2,637 litres) in each inboard wing tank; 383gal (740 litres) in each intermediate wing tank, and 114gal (518 litres) in each outboard wing tank. One or two overload 400 gal (1,818 litre) tanks could be mounted in the bomb bay. Oil tank capacity 150gal (682 litres) carried in four wing tanks.

Performance
Maximum speed 270mph (434km/hr) at 19,000ft (5,800m); Cruise speed 210mph (338km/hr); 19.3 min to 11,000ft (3,350m); 43.5min to 20,000ft (6,100m); Service ceiling 21,500ft (6,550m); Range with 14,000lb (6,350kg) bomb load 1,160 miles (1,870km); with 7,000lb (1,795kg) bomb load and one overload fuel tank 2,230 miles (3,590km).

Armament
Two .303 Browning machine guns with 1,000rpg in a Frazer-Nash power-operated turret in the nose; ditto in the mid-upper position, and four Browning machine guns with 2,500 rpg in a Frazer-Nash power-operated turret in the tail. A few aircraft retained the ventral gun position, while many others had the mid-upper turret removed. Others were fitted with a Rose-Rice tail turret with two .50 Browning heavy machine guns.

with a dorsal gun turret fitted. It retained the ventral turret for the time being. This was followed into the air by the third prototype on 26 November of that year, which was powered by Hercules VI radials, and as such became the prototype Lancaster Mark II. But long before the radial-engined machine took to the air, production Mark Is were rolling off the lines.

The production aircraft still showed their Manchester origins, but had been refined in many ways. All-up weight had been increased to 65,000lb (29.48 tonnes) maximum, although this could be exceeded in an emergency; maximum bomb load had been increased to 14,000lb (6.35 tonnes); two extra fuel tanks had been fitted in the wings, and the ventral turret had been deleted as being of no earthly use at night. A collar fairing had been added around the mid-upper turret to prevent the guns being depressed enough to damage the aircraft, and a four-gun turret was standard in the tail position. The crew consisted of seven men; the pilot, who was also the aircraft captain, regardless of rank; a second pilot, who was quickly replaced by the new category of flight engineer; a bomb-aimer, who also manned the front turret; a navigator, a wireless operator, and mid-upper and tail gunners.

■ THE LANCASTER ■ CLOSE UP

The Lancaster is a lady, and for that reason is never described as 'it', but always as 'she'. No empty-headed glamour queen this, frivolous and shallow, but very much the

Above: **The standard camouflage scheme was dark green and dark earth disruptive pattern above and matt black below.**

grand dame, the indomitable dowager, yet with a twinkle in her eye to hint at a racy past in her younger days. Her attire is sombre, a staid dull black on undersides of wings and tail and fuselage sides complemented by a tasteful camouflage scheme on top. Guns protrude from turrets in her nose and tail and mid-way down her upper fuselage, saying, as they said to many a German night fighter during the war 'Do not trifle with me, young man!' There she sits on the ground, nose high, seemingly sniffing at the sky, eager to take once more to the element for which she was designed.

As we walk towards

her, the first impression is that she is big. Her huge main wheels, suspended on sturdy legs beneath the inboard engine nacelles, are almost shoulder-height, while the front fuselage towers high above us. Her mid-mounted wings spread 50ft (15m) to either side, carrying the four sleek cowlings which house the Rolls-Royce Merlin engines with their shrouded exhausts, fronted by large three-bladed propellors.

We draw nearer. Right in the front of her nose is a hemispherical transparent dome, with a round optically flat panel looking downwards. This is where the real business is done; through this the bombs are aimed. Above is a turret from

Below: **Figures on the ground give scale to the first production Lancaster, seen prior to delivery to Boscombe Down for type testing.**

LANCASTER GUN TURRET

Type	FN 5	FN 50	FN 20	FN 64
Position	Nose	Mid-upper	Tail	Ventral*
Guns	2 x .303 Browning Mk II	2 x .303 Browning Mk II	4 x .303 Browning Mk II	2 x .303 Browning Mk II
Rounds per gun	1,000	1,000	2,500	500
Gunsight	Mk III Reflector	Mk IIIA Reflector	Mk III Reflector or Gyro Mk IIc	Periscopic
Traverse	+/-95°	360°	+/-94°	+/-90°
Elevation	60°	20°	60°	0°
Depression	45°	2°	45°	60°

Rarely used, mainly on early aircraft.

which project the muzzles of two .303 Browning machine guns. Immediately behind the turret is a glazed cabin for the pilot and his flight engineer, but we see little of this as we walk beneath the giant bird.

What we do see is the huge bomb bay, which starts almost immediately beneath the front of the cabin and reaches back beyond the wing trailing edge to a point almost level with the dorsal turret. As is usual before engine start-up, the bomb bay doors are open, revealing the sinister outlines of the contents. In the centre is a large, dark green cylinder, a 4,000lb (1,800kg) high explosive 'cookie'. It is surrounded by twelve SBCs (Small Bomb Containers) filled with incendiaries. This is the most usual Lancaster bomb load.

onto the sill, and we climb up and in, onto an inner step, then it's down onto the central catwalk.

■ REAR GUNNER ■

Once inside, it is difficult to see much until our eyes accustom themselves to the gloom. Not that there is a lot to see; to one accustomed to travel in modern airliners, the interior of a Lancaster is bleak indeed. The structure, fuselage formers and longerons are bare, showing the metal skin. Running the length of the fuselage walls are pipes, rods, all manner of plumbing and wiring. These are for carrying hydraulic fluid and power to where it is needed.

At this point, the first member of the

crew leaves us. He turns left and vanishes. He passes the primitive Elsan toilet to his right, scrambles over the tailplane spar structure, pauses for a moment to stow his parachute, then squeezes into his cold and cramped position, shutting the armoured doors behind him. He is the rear gunner, and his job is arguably the most dangerous, and certainly the coldest, the most lonely and isolated, of any Lancaster crewman.

From now until the end of the mission, his only human contact will be the disembodied voices of other crew members over the intercom. His brief is unceasing vigilance for however many hours the mission takes. The German night fighters almost always attack from astern. Yet his task is thankless; if he is lucky enough to survive a complete tour of operations, he may well do so without once so much as seeing a night fighter, but knowing that the one he doesn't see may well kill him and his crew. He is proud of his skills; his party piece is probably putting a pencil in the barrel of one of his guns, then using his power controls to sign his name on a piece of card held up by an obliging ground crewman. But the chances are that he will never get the opportunity to use these skills. Even if he does, his four rifle-calibre machine guns are far outranged by the cannon of the German night fighters which, if visibility is good enough,

Below: The open doors give some idea of the vast size of the bomb bay. The bombs were released in a preset sequence.

We climb up and in, then it's down onto the central catwalk

Astern of the bomb bay is a teardrop-shaped fairing. This houses the scanner for H2S, the latest radar bombing and navigational aid. We enter the Lancaster through a small hatch in the starboard side, just ahead of the leading edge of the tailplane. A short metal ladder hooks

Above: **Up the ladder and in. A crew from No. 9 Squadron board their Lancaster ready for a mission.**

about in flight. Next to reach his station is the mid-upper gunner. After stowing his parachute in its place high on the right, he climbs into his turret via a step on the left of the fuselage. Access is not easy however, due to the seat design which forces him to squeeze past it before he can enter.

The mid-upper gunner has only two machine guns, although his turret can be traversed through 360 degrees, giving him a grandstand view all round. His field of fire is obstructed, however, to the rear by the tailplane and fins, on each side by the wings, engines and propellors, and straight ahead by the navigator's astrodome. The turret is surrounded by a fairing which contains a cam track. By restricting the movement of the guns, this ensures that he cannot damage his own aircraft when firing. When the guns are elevated at 20 degrees or more, turret traverse is fast and smooth, but below this it is much slower. This is to avoid damage to the turret fairing at full

can stand off and shoot at him. Otherwise they can slip in below where, against the dark backdrop of the ground, they are difficult to see, and pull underneath the bomber where his guns cannot reach and pick it off with their upward-firing guns.

Even in defeat, with his aircraft going down in flames or out of control, the rear gunner's fate is a lonely one. The call to bale out is 'Abracadabra Jump, Jump! Abracadabra Jump, Jump!'. It sounds silly, but it has one advantage. It cannot possibly be misunderstood. Nevertheless, it was often not used, and the order given in plain language. On hearing the command to bale out, the rear gunner opens his armoured doors at the rear of his turret, reaches back for his parachute and clips it onto his chest harness. He swivels his turret right round until the open doors are facing outwards, then does a backward roll out into the night sky above a hostile country. This is of course presupposing that his parachute has not been burnt or shot to pieces, that he is still able to turn his turret to the escape position, and that the centrifugal forces exerted by his out-of-control bomber will allow him to make these necessary moves.

The rest of the crew turn to the right along the catwalk. On the far wall is a handrail, very necessary for moving

LANCASTER BOMB LOADS

Bombing, and especially night bombing, was a very imprecise art in the Second World War. Even finding the target was difficult enough; hitting it often seemed next to impossible. The solution adopted was to saturate the target area with bombs; high explosive to demolish buildings and incendiaries to set the ruins on fire. It was crude, but it was the only practicable means available to Bomber Command. There were of course specialized weapons which called for greater accuracy, but these were less common.

AREA BOMBING LOADS

Blast and demolition
1) 1 x 8,000lb (3,630kg) HE plus 6 (max) 500lb (225kg) HE.
2) 14 x 1,000lb (450kg) HE.

Blast, demolition and fire
3) 1 x 4,000lb (1,800kg) HE plus 3 x 1,000lb HE plus up to 6 SBCs (Small Bomb Containers) each holding either 236 4lb (2kg) or 24 x 30lb (14kg) incendiaries.
4) 1 x 4,000lb (1,800kg) HE plus up to 12 SBCs. The most common Lancaster load.

Maximum incendiary
5) 14 SBCs.

Deployed tactical targets
6) 1 x 4,000lb (1,800kg) HE plus up to 18,500lb (225kg) HE, some with delayed action fuses.

Low-level attacks
7) 6 x 1,000lb (450kg) HE with delayed action fuses.

Hardened targets, naval installations, ships etc.
8) 6 x 2,000lb (900kg) armour piercing with very short delay fuses.

Minelaying
9) Up to six 1,500lb (680kg) or 1,850lb (840kg) mines.

and his pencils and pads. He has a small window which is level with the leading edge of the wing, but at night keeps a curtain drawn across it. This is mainly because he needs artificial light by which to work, and this must not be allowed to betray the presence of the bomber to any roving fighters which might be in the area. In any case, over blacked-out enemy territory there is little to see, while above a heavily defended area the view can sometimes be a little too exciting for someone who has no immediate task to occupy him. The wireless operator has the warmest place in the aircraft; often he is overheated while other crew members are freezing.

H2S, a blind bombing aid which shows a radar picture of the ground

Above: Emergency escape from the rear turret was made by turning it sideways as seen here, then rolling out backwards.
Left: The mid-upper turret, showing the fairing which prevented the gunner from damaging his own aircraft.
Below: H2S position in the Lancaster. Top left is the curtain which shuts out light; to the right is the flight engineer's position, with his seat folded. (Alfred Price)

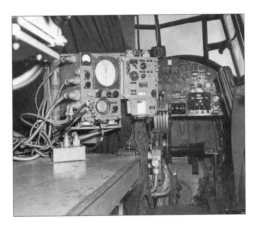

depression, but in action, it is a serious disadvantage as it makes tracking a fast-moving enemy fighter very difficult.

In an emergency the mid-upper gunner must squirm out of the turret, retrieve his parachute from stowage, and depart through the door by which he entered. Just ahead of the mid-upper turret is an escape hatch in the fuselage roof, which is used in the event of a crash landing or a ditching at sea. In the latter event, a dinghy is housed in the upper surface of the starboard wingroot, which hopefully can be released manually from inside the aircraft, and which should then inflate automatically if the Lancaster comes down in the 'drink', as it is generally known. The walls in this area of the fuselage are cluttered with fire extinguishers and flame float and sea marker canisters.

Further up the fuselage is an obstacle, the rear wing spar carry-through, with a step on the far side which contains more

parachute stowage. To the left of this is the rest bunk, which is normally used only for casualties.

A few feet along is yet another obstacle, the main wing spar carry-through. Larger than the rear spar, it has probably been the cause of more bad language by Lancaster crewmen than any other feature of this remarkable aircraft, being of a height to make their eyes sparkle. But once this has been negotiated, we arrive at the main crew positions via a 7mm-thick armoured door. Situated on the left is the wireless operator's post. He sits at a small table with his radio

In front of the wireless operator sits the navigator, sideways on. He also has a table, but larger than that of the wireless operator, on which he spreads out charts, pencils, protractors, computer (not quite like our modern variety), and all the other paraphernalia needed to find a specific location in a blacked-out and hostile Europe. Almost overhead is an astrodome, through which the navigator can 'shoot' the stars to arrive at a very approximate position, but in this machine he has something better and very different.

This is H2S, a blind bombing aid which shows a radar picture of the ground below on a television-type screen. It needs a fair bit of interpretation to get good results, and like all electronic aids of this era, it can be temperamental. But it helps. Like the wireless operator, the navigator has a window, out of which he rarely looks, and he is partitioned off from the pilot by another curtain which keeps light out of the main cabin.

■ THE PILOT ■

Up front, his seat on a raised floor section to the left of the main cabin, is the pilot, who is also the aircraft captain.

Above left: The H₂S scanner housing supplanted the ventral turret position on many aircraft. This is a late war model.
Above right: Lancaster pilot's position, showing the sliding hatch through which escape was barely possible. However, the extensively glazed cabin gave a good all-round view.

He has a good all-round view through the framed canopy, albeit slightly restricted to the rear and to starboard. There is a direct-vision panel on either side of the windshield, and in the canopy roof is an escape hatch, for use in a crash-landing or ditching. Behind him is a 4mm-thick sheet of armour, the top part of which can be folded down.

Straight in front of the pilot is the control column, topped with a wheel-type yoke. The column moves backwards and forwards to control the elevators in the tail, causing the aircraft to climb or dive, while the yoke moves like a car steering wheel, controlling the ailerons in the wings to make the aircraft bank to left or right. At his feet are the rudder pedals, which are used for flat turns to either side.

Low to the pilot's left is the compass, but to allow him to steer without constantly having to glance inside the cockpit, a compass repeater is mounted on the centre strut of the divided windshield. On the dash in front of him are many dials and switches, which include the essential flying instruments; air speed indicator, artificial horizon, turn and bank indicator and rate of climb/descent indicator among them, while the throttle levers and propellor speed controls are mounted on a central console where they can be reached by both the pilot and the flight engineer.

The flight engineer sits to the right of the pilot. He has a folding seat, which is necessary to allow access to the bomb aimer's and front gunner's positions, and a tubular footrest which pulls out from under the raised floor section beneath the pilot's position. His task is to look after the engines, throttle settings and propellor pitch settings, fuel flow, and generally act as the pilot's assistant.

He has two panels to monitor. The first is on the starboard side, and this contains oil and fuel gauges, booster pump switches, fuel pressure warning lights, fuel tank selector cocks, and many other things. The second is part of the main dash, which can also be seen by the pilot. This contains revolution counters, boost gauges, ignition switches, engine fire extinguisher buttons and propellor feathering buttons, plus much else. All in all, the flight engineer is a pretty busy man.

■ BOMB AIMER ■

Squeezing past the flight engineer's station, we clamber down into the nose. Down, because this is the first time that we have been ahead of the bomb bay, and the amount we clamber down gives us some idea of its depth. This is the territory of the bomb aimer, who usually mans the nose turret when not actually on the bombing run, although he can also be called upon to assist the navigator by map-reading, always assuming that the ground is in sight.

The bomb aimer lies prone, his chest propped on an adjustable support. Beneath him is the forward escape hatch, which may also be used by the flight engineer and the pilot, in the latter case if he can reach it in time before the aircraft goes completely out of control.

To the right of the bomb aimer is the bomb fusing and selection panel. It is essential that the bombs are released in a predetermined order from the long bay if unwanted changes of trim are to be avoided. For this, a selector box is used. The bombs themselves are released by a hand-held 'tit', which has a small guard above the button to prevent accidents. Also featured are camera controls and photo-flares which enable a picture to be taken of the aim point.

■ BOMBS GONE ■

The bomb sight itself is of the vector type, into which the aircraft speed and altitude are set, together with the ballistic data for the type of bombs carried, and the estimated wind speed and direction. The sight is gyro-stabilized, which allows banked turns to be made during the run-up to the target. Two lines of light on a reflecting screen form a cross which indicates where the bomb will drop at any given moment. Over the intercom, the bomb aimer guides the pilot to a

Left: Bomb release switch in hand, the bomb aimer lies prone facing his Mk XIV vector sight.

Below left: All late-production Lancasters, regardless of mark, were fitted with an enlarged nose transparency.

position where the extension of the vertical line passes through the aim point. When the bomber is lined up correctly, the aim point appears to slide gradually down the vertical line. Then when the cross touches the target, the bomb aimer presses the button and down go the bombs, bringing destruction to the target below. When not engaged in dropping the bombs, the bomb aimer occupies the nose turret, with its two machine guns. At night he will probably have little to do; rarely is visibility clear enough to allow the night fighters to attack from head-on. In daylight or at low level the situation may well be different, and it may even be that the turret must be occupied even on the bombing run. This gives rise to a problem; the gunner has no footrest, and in moments of excitement may well tread on the bomb aimer's head, to say nothing of showering him with hot 'empties' when he fires.

This then is the Lancaster, a bomber in which many thousands of men went to war, and for which many thousands of crewmen had affection, and faith that she was the best.

Below: When not actually on the bombing run, the bomb aimer normally manned the front gun turret. This Lancaster was visiting the USA on a goodwill mission in 1942.

The first unit to receive the Lancaster was No. 44 (Rhodesia) Squadron at Waddington. To provide initial experience, the first Lancaster prototype arrived in mid-September 1941, while several Manchester pilots were transferred to the squadron to ease the task of conversion. Not until Christmas Eve did the first three operational aircraft arrive, followed by four more on 28 December.

Above: This former No. 44 Squadron aircraft flew the Atlantic to Canada to serve as a pattern aircraft for Lancaster production there.

Far left: Fitters swarm all over the port inner engine of this Lancaster Mk II of No. 408 'Goose' Squadron, RCAF.

No. 44 Squadron had previously flown Hampdens, but from January 1942, seven Manchester squadrons were progressively re-equipped with the Lancaster. Unusually, three of the seven had not even started to receive the Manchester at this time, but this decision was not as strange as it seems. Brand-new Manchesters, with their excellent payload/range capability, were still coming off the production lines, and Lancaster production was not yet in full swing. Also, the similarities of the two aircraft made it relatively easy to convert Manchester crews to the Lancaster; the latter could therefore be introduced into service faster by bringing more Manchesters on stream. The first Lancasters reached No. 97 Squadron in January, and No. 207 Squadron in March 1942.

The first Lancaster operation took place on the night of 3/4 March 1942. Four Lancasters of No. 44 Squadron, led by Squadron Leader John Nettleton, laid mines (an operation codenamed 'Gardening') off the German coast. All returned safely. The first excursion over Germany was made a week later, two aircraft of the same squadron joining a raid on Essen, again without loss. This run of good fortune was not to last; the first Lancaster to be lost in action failed to return from another Gardening sortie on 24/25 March.

■ THE AUGSBURG RAID ■

In the Spring of 1942 U-boat production facilities became priority targets, and one of the most important was the MAN works at Augsburg, where their diesel engines were made. Augsburg was not far from Munich, a round trip of some 1,250 miles (2,000km), mostly over enemy territory. The works was little bigger than the average football pitch, which ruled out a night attack. The attack would have to be in daylight.

On the afternoon of 17 April, 12 Lancasters took off for Augsburg. The first wave of six, flying in two Vics of three, was from No. 44 Squadron, led by John Nettleton. Two miles (3km) astern and about 3 miles (5km) to starboard was the second wave, six Lancasters from No. 97 Squadron led by Squadron Leader John Sherwood. Each aircraft carried four 1,000lb (450kg) bombs with 11-second delayed action fuses.

Leaving the English coast near Selsey Bill, they flew low over the Channel to cross the French coast near Trouville, and continued hugging the ground southwards for about 100 miles (160km) before turning east.

Diversionary attacks were planned to keep German fighters occupied, but

AUGSBURG RAID REPORT, EXTRACT

Aircraft Attacking	Bombs Dropped	Release Height	Time at Target	Results Observed
8	14.3 tons	50/400ft	1955/2015	Huge red flames seen. One a/c claimed hits on main building, two others claim bombs in target area.

Owing to poor light and low altitude, photographs lacked all essential detail. No bomb bursts are shown, but a large fire is seen probably in the city of Augsburg, and it is clear that at least one and probably all the aircraft passed directly over the target. A PR photograph taken on 25/4 reveals severe damage chiefly to the S end of the works. The main Diesel Assembly Shop has suffered heavy damage.

Above: Squadron Leader John Nettleton led the daring daylight raid on the U-boat engine factory at Augsburg, for which he was awarded the Victoria Cross.

LANCASTER SQUADRONS, OPERATION MILLENNIUM

Sqn No	Base	Date of 1st Op
l44	Waddington	3 March 1942
97	Woodhall Spa	20/21 March 1942
207	Bottesford	24/25 April 1942
83	Coningsby	29/30 April 1942
61	Syerston	5/6 May 1942
106	Coningsby	30/31 May 1942
50	Skellingthorpe	30/31 May 1942
		(one a/c only)

these miscarried. Between 20 and 30 Messerschmitt 109s of JG.2 returning to base encountered the rear Vic of Nettleton's wave. Attacking, they quickly shot down all three before turning their attention to the leading trio. One more Lancaster went down and the others were damaged before the Germans, by now low on fuel and ammunition, broke off the running battle. The second wave, although only a few miles away, was not spotted.

At this point Garwell's aircraft was hit by flak

Nettleton and Flying Officer J. Garwell, the other survivor of the first wave, bored eastwards on track for Munich until over the Ammer lake they swung north towards Augsburg, followed at a distance of about 10 miles (16km) by the No. 97 Squadron formation.

Augsburg finally hove into sight, and the two remaining Lancasters of No. 44 Squadron detoured around some tall factory chimneys and commenced their bombing run. At this point Garwell's aircraft was hit by flak and, shortly after releasing his bombs, he had to slide the burning Lancaster onto the ground. Four of the seven crewmen aboard survived, to be taken prisoner. Nettleton's Lancaster alone escaped into the gathering gloom.

Minutes later, the first Vic of the second wave from 97 Squadron arrived to find a thoroughly alerted defence. Unlike Nettleton, Sherwood did not attempt to dodge around the factory chimneys, but climbed above them, his two wingmen pulling into line astern behind him. All three aircraft bombed accurately, but Sherwood's Lancaster was mortally hit by ground fire, and crashed in flames shortly after. By some miracle, Sherwood himself survived with only minor injuries.

Meanwhile the final Vic, which had dropped back still further, now came racing in from the south. They were met by a storm of anti-aircraft fire, and all three were badly damaged. One blew up just as its bombs fell clear, but the other two got through. Wearily the survivors

Below: Wellingtons were the most numerous bombers participating in Operation Millennium. However, they were soon to be phased out in favour of the Avro Lancaster. (via Flypast)

Above: No. 83 Squadron Lancasters took part in the 1,000 bomber raid on Cologne. This unit was also the first Lancaster Pathfinder squadron.

Right: Cologne at the end of the war, showing the devastation around the cathedral. Wrecked bridges block the Rhine.

climbed into the darkening sky, one with only three engines operative, and straggled back to base, where one of the surviving 97 Squadron aircraft was struck off charge.

Seventeen bombs hit the factory buildings, inflicting extensive damage on them. Nettleton was awarded the Victoria Cross for his exploit, and many other survivors were decorated for this, the first Lancaster raid to be made public. But with a loss rate exceeding 50 per cent it was not, by the very nature of things, repeatable, even though the interception by German fighters which had caused such havoc to the first wave had largely been a matter of ill fortune.

■ OPERATION ■ MILLENNIUM

By the end of May 1942, seven squadrons had Lancasters on strength. This was just in time for them to take part in a raid which for Bomber Command was a turning point in the night air offensive.

The strategic bombing of the Third Reich was, in its early days, an extremely haphazard affair, with individual crews plotting their own courses and timings. Navigation was inexact, and only one crew in three managed to place their bombs within 5 miles (8km) of the target. Any damage caused was a mere pinprick. To make matters worse, the German night fighter defences had taken the measure of this form of attack, and losses were steadily rising. Bomber Command's future looked increasingly uncertain. This was the situation when Air Marshal Arthur Harris assumed command in February 1942.

Harris realized that only a spectacular success could save his command from being broken up. Previous raids had neglected the cardinal principle of concentration of force. This had to be corrected. An unprecedentedly heavy raid on a single target was needed, concentrated in time and space. A raid by 1,000 bombers would be the biggest raid ever; the magic number of 1,000 would attract interest and demonstrate that RAF Bomber Command was truly a force to be reckoned with.

The target chosen was Cologne. The city was within range of a new radio navigational device called Gee, and on a moonlit night the serpentine coils of the Rhine made it easily identifiable from

All aircraft would follow the same route from a merge point off the coast

the air. To achieve concentration of force, all aircraft would follow the same route from a merge point off the coast (the first use of the bomber 'stream'), and the entire attack was to last just 90 minutes, an average of more than 11 aircraft bombing every minute! The German defences would be saturated by

Above: Mk I R5609 flew with No. 97
Squadron on the Cologne and Essen
thousand-bomber raids. Later it took part in
the Battles of the Ruhr, Berlin, Hamburg
and Peenemunde. It survived the war.
(Alfred Price)

weight of numbers, minimizing losses.

The Cologne raid took place on the night of 30/31 May, 1942. The attack was in three waves, the first consisting of Gee-equipped Wellingtons and Stirlings with selected crews; their task was to locate the target and start fires to guide the main force in. The second wave consisted of the remaining Stirlings and Wellingtons, and the other twin-engined types; Hampdens, Whitleys and Manchesters. The third and most concentrated wave consisted of the new heavy bombers; more than 125 Halifaxes and about 75 Lancasters were scheduled to be over the target during the final 15 minutes of the attack. It has been suggested that this was to maximize the devastation in an already hard-hit city, but the fact is that operationally it was the best place for them. As the fastest and most heavily armed aircraft in the force, they were the least vulnerable to German night fighters, and equally were least likely to straggle on the homeward leg. This was borne out by events; losses to the third wave amounted to a mere 1.9 per cent, compared with 4.8 per cent to the first wave and 4.1 per cent to the second.

Post-war analysis by German generals described the Cologne raid as 'alarmingly effective'. For Bomber Command, it opened a new era in strategic bombing, with marked targets and highly concentrated attacks. Within three years, Lancasters would make up virtually the whole of the raiding force, and the damage they wrought upon German industry and communications was incalculable. From the Cologne raid onward, the history of the Lancaster was inextricably bound up with the development of Bomber Command's strategy and tactics.

The secret of success for Operation Millennium had been the ability to find the target and mark it for the following crews. While Gee was a useful navigation aid, it not only lacked the accuracy needed for blind bombing, but was too short-ranged to cover many important targets. The idea was mooted of a special target-finding force, and this was eventually formed in July 1942.

■ THE PATHFINDERS ■

Competition promotes increased efficiency, and Bomber Command introduced this in the form of a photographic ladder. It became standard procedure for each bomber to photograph its aim point, and each squadron's position on the ladder was determined by the accuracy of these. The ladder indicated which squadrons (and also which crews) were consistently finding their targets.

The first proposal was to form one or more elite units with selected crews. For various reasons this was abandoned, and Path Finder Force (PFF) was formed, commanded by Group Captain Don Bennett, an Australian navigation expert and prewar trail-blazer.

Bomber Command was divided into operational areas called Groups. The squadron heading the photographic ladder in each of the four Bomber Groups was transferred to the newly formed No. 8 Pathfinder Group, based on Huntingdon. Inevitably one Lancaster squadron was among them, No. 83. The others flew aircraft representative of the Groups in which they normally operated, but this was not to last. No. 156 Squadron traded its Wellingtons for Lancasters in January 1943; No. 7 Squadron its Stirlings in July of the same year, and finally No. 35 Squadron its Halifaxes in April 1944. By the end of the war, there were 14 Lancaster-equipped PFF Squadrons. But this was still three years in the future.

The first loads to go down contained a high proportion of incendiaries

Regrettably PFF did not manage to bring about an instant improvement in bombing effectiveness. This had to wait for new navigational devices, for special pyrotechnic markers, and the development of methods which made the best use of them.

The former duly arrived in the shape of Oboe, an accurate but range-limited radio bombing device carried by Mosquitos. Dependent on signals from ground transmitters in England, it took in the highly industrialized Ruhr area but not much else.

The heavy bombers were fitted with H2S, a radar navigation and blind bombing aid, although initially only a few aircraft carried it. It was much less accurate than Oboe, but as it was not dependent on external aids it was not range-restricted.

Parachute flares had long been used as an aid to target finding. They had however two drawbacks. Unless visibility was

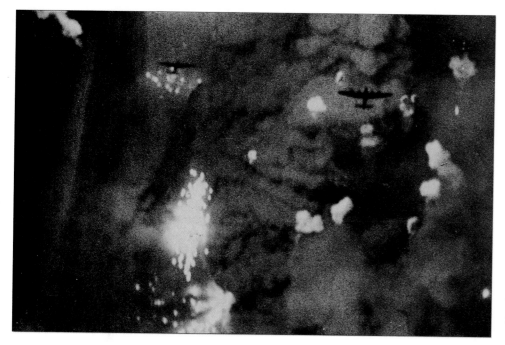

Above: Flak bursts punctuate the night sky over Germany as Pathfinder markers go down on a target in Germany. Two other bombers are just visible.

good, they would not light up the ground sufficiently well for crews to visually identify a target, or even pinpoint their own location. Then, of course, unless the flares were released in the right area, they simply illuminated a strange and often unrecognizable area of Germany, which was not a lot of help. Used in conjunction with Oboe or H2S, flares became far more effective.

In Operation Millennium, the first loads to go down contained a high proportion of incendiaries, to start fires which would lead the following bombers to the target area. Something more accurate was needed, and this duly arrived in the form of markers, known as Target Indicators, or TIs.

Each TI contained 60 pyrotechnic candles. A barometric fuse preset to operate at low altitude blew the TI open, cascading the candles onto the ground, igniting as they went. Seen from above, the contents of each TI would appear as an intense pool of light, about 900ft (275m) in diameter. Burning time was about three minutes, so they needed to be replenished at frequent intervals.

By now the Germans had started to produce dummy targets to mislead the bombers. Their obvious reaction to TIs

was to copy them and, when a raid was imminent, set them off on a dummy target. To circumvent this, TIs were produced in a combination of colours; red, yellow, green, etc., and used in a predetermined order which varied from raid to raid.

When cloud covered the target, sky markers were used. These were parachute flares in a variety of colours, and sometimes throwing off coloured stars. Dropped by Oboe or H2S aircraft, they demanded a rather complicated offset bombing technique. While skymarking was nowhere near as accurate as ground marking, it gave accuracy far superior to the early years of the

war, when 'agricultural bombing' – the accidental bombing of fields – was a common occurrence.

With the new equipment available, all that remained was to find the best methods of employing it. Oboe Mosquitos were used for the initial marking of all targets within its range. Outside Oboe reach, H2S was used. Tactics were roughly as follows. The first aircraft to arrive, typically five minutes before the main attack was scheduled to start, were the Finders, backed by a few Supporters. The Finders dropped flares where they thought that the aiming points were likely to be. Having visually identified the aim point, they would drop further flares directly above it.

The Finders would be followed by the Illuminators, who would drop sticks of flares directly across the aim point. Then would come the Primary Markers, to put TIs on the aim point itself. Backers-Up would continue to drop TIs at intervals, to give the Main Force an aiming point throughout the attack.

This form of visual marking was code-named Newhaven. When, due to poor visibility or broken cloud, the marking was carried out using H2S, it became Parramatta, while skymarking was dubbed Wanganui.

As with all new methods, teething

Below: Flak damage sustained by a Lancaster of No. 50 Squadron over Leipzig. Miraculously nothing vital was hit.

troubles occurred, mainly due to the precise timing required. The first real success achieved by PFF came during the Barmen-Wuppertal raid on 29/30 May 1943. The target was accurately marked, and the subsequent bombing highly concentrated. How was this done?

■ BARMEN/WUPPERTAL ■

A total of 719 aircraft were despatched. Of these, 272 were Lancasters (the force had been building up rapidly, and a further 12 squadrons now operated the type). Of these, 20 aircraft were Lancaster Is and IIIs of PFF, and the attack was spearheaded by 11 Mosquito IVs fitted with Oboe.

Main Force, following on behind, included 31 Lancaster Is and IIIs of No. 8 Pathfinder Group; 76 Lancaster Is and IIIs of No. 1 Group; 16 Hercules-engined Lancaster IIs of No. 3 Group; and 129 Lancaster Is and IIIs of No. 5 Group. Loads consisted of a mixture of high explosives; 4,000lb (1,800kg) cookies in the case of the Lancasters, and incendiaries.

Above: **Incendiary bomb containers are loaded. Fires on the ground drew other bombers like moths to a candle.**

The bombing was heavy and concentrated

Visibility in the target area was poor, due to industrial haze and smoke, but the first Mosquitoes marked accurately at 00.47 hours, with red target indicators. They were followed by PFF backers-up with green TIs, and PFF 'fire-raisers' with incendiaries. Four of these, equipped with H2S, also marked with yellow TIs.

Main Force aircraft were instructed to aim at the reds if visible; otherwise at the centre of the greens.

The bombing was heavy and concentrated; 611 aircraft claimed to have bombed the primary target. A total of 33 aircraft were lost on this raid, about 4.6 per cent. Lancaster losses amounted to seven, or about 2.6 per cent of those despatched; barely half the average losses for the raid.

A factor common to all forms of warfare is confusion, and the Pathfinder-led attacks on Germany were no exception. If a Pathfinder put down his TIs in the wrong place, for whatever reason, inevitably a proportion of Main Force would use them as an aim point. In addition, the Germans, by dint of much practice, grew adept at decoys. A third factor was creep-back; the tendency of crews over a heavily defended target to release their bombs at the earliest possible moment, with the result that the Main Force bomb pattern would extend further and further back from the original aim point until in extreme cases it

ended in open countryside. What was needed was a raid controller to direct the marking, giving a continuous running commentary on which TIs were to be used for aiming and which should be ignored; which was the real target and which a decoy; and generally keeping the bombing pattern tidy.

A possible solution appeared to be that pioneered by Wing Commander Guy Gibson for Operation Chastise, the destruction of the Mohne and Eder dams in the Ruhr. He controlled his force, albeit a small one, very effectively using VHF voice radio to communicate. Possibly a Master Bomber could control an orthodox raid in the same way. There was only one way to find out; lay on a small-scale experiment.

■ OPERATION ■ BELLICOSE

An easy target would have proved little; in the event the one chosen called for a high degree of precision. Friedrichshafen lies on the north shore of the Bodensee (Lake Constance), the south shore of which is in Switzerland. In the 1914–18 war it had been notorious as the home of the Zeppelin factory, a building complex about 1,500ft (460m) long by 1,050ft (320m) wide. In 1943, it was the largest production centre for radar parts in the whole of the Third Reich, and its destruction would be a severe blow to

---

EXTRACT FROM BOMBER COMMAND NIGHT RAID REPORT NO. 340

611 aircraft, out of a force of 719, attacked the Barmen district of Wuppertal with very great success. The fire-raising technique was effectively employed, as a complement to ground marking, resulting in the best concentration yet achieved by the Pathfinder Force. Immense damage was caused in the town, covering over 1,000 acres and affecting 113 industrial concerns, as well as totally disrupting the transport system and public utilities.

Left: Laden with equipment, a crew strolls out to its No. 61 Squadron Lancaster. Normally transport would be laid on.

the German air defences and much else.

Continuous marking of such a small target was next to impossible. Special tactics were needed. Main Force crews were to orbit the target at between 4 and 6 miles (6–10km), with no more than two aircraft at the same altitude. The instant a TI landed on the target, the Master Bomber would issue a special signal, and as many aircraft as possible would attack immediately. It was of course possible that the target could quickly become obscured by smoke; in this case the crews were to make their attack run from a certain point, sighting on a second point, but delaying bomb release long enough for the aircraft to cover 6,000ft (1,800m) to the actual target.

This raid was sufficiently different for special training and picked crews to be needed. No. 5 Group supplied 56 Lancaster IIIs with experienced crews drawn from 12 squadrons. No. 8 Group provided four hand-picked Pathfinder crews from 97 Squadron, based at Bourn, also with Lancaster IIIs. Piloted by Flight

Below: **Prototype Lancaster Mk III. Externally indistinguishable from the Mk I, the main difference was American-built Packard Merlins with Hamilton propellers.**

Lieutenants Rodley, a survivor of the Augsburg raid, and John Sauvage, and Pilot Officers D.I. Jones and Jimmy Munro, the latter a Canadian, they were flown north to Scampton for two days' intensive training.

It was perhaps significant that for this trial mission the Master Bomber was not a Pathfinder, but the very experienced Group Captain Leonard Slee. His deputy was the Australian squadron commander, Wing Commander G.L. Gomm. In addition there were two controllers, either of whom could take charge in the event of an emergency. The force took off late in the evening of 20 June 1943 and headed south, crossing the Channel at maximum altitude. Once over France they progressively lost height down to 10,000ft (3,050m) as they passed Orléans, then lower still to between 2,500 and 3,000ft (750–900m). After crossing the Rhine they began to climb to attack altitude, which was 5,000ft (1,500m) for the Pathfinders and 10,000ft (3,050m) for the Main Force. At about this time, Group Captain Slee's Lancaster lost an engine and was unable

to keep its place at the head of the stream. Wing Commander Gomm, of No. 467 (Australian) Squadron, took over as Master Bomber.

Exactly on time, Munro and Jones released a string of flares parallel to, and on either side of, the target. The gun defences opened up at once, more strongly than expected, and Gomm ordered all aircraft to gain another 5,000ft (1,500m). Realizing that this would make visual identification very difficult, the four Pathfinders stayed at their original altitude.

The Master Bomber ordered all aircraft to attack at once

Sauvage put down a green TI just north of the Zeppelin sheds. He was followed by Rodley, who dropped a green TI accurately. On seeing this, the Master Bomber ordered all aircraft fitted with the Mk XIV bombsight to attack at once. An attempt to renew this marker failed. Jones later commented that he had to abandon one run because it was impossible to hold his aircraft steady in the concussions from the bombs. More flares were dropped along the shoreline

Above: Aircraft of No. 50 Squadron at Swinderby. The nearest was struck off charge when it crashed at Thurlby, Lincs, on 19 September 1942.

around the two predesignated points in order to enable the remainder of Main Force to bomb indirectly.

After the attack, all 59 Lancasters (one had been driven off track by thunderstorms) orbited the target to form up before heading for Maison Blanche and Blida airfields in Algeria, where they arrived safely.

For 'Rod' Rodley, however, it was an eventful trip. Unknown to him, a TI had hung up. When, far out over the Mediterranean he lost height, the barometric fuse operated and the candles ignited. The first intimation that all was not well came when an evil red glow suddenly appeared beneath his Lancaster. Thinking he was under attack from a night fighter, Rodley took evasive action, while Sergeant Duffy, his flight engineer, checked for damage. The bomb bay was a mass of flames, but the cause was obvious. A quick pull on the jettison toggle and the blazing remnants of the TI fell clear, leaving the Lancaster damaged but flyable.

Considerable destruction was caused to the target, and the Master Bomber concept was rated a success. Six of the Lancasters were damaged by anti-aircraft fire, one beyond repair. The

'shuttle' concept of flying on to North Africa was also rated a success, and was later used by both Bomber Command and the USAAF. As a footnote, intercepts of German night fighter radio traffic revealed that patrols were flown in the Florennes/Juvincourt area, presumably waiting for the bombers to return. They did of course, several nights later, bombing La Spezia on the way for good measure.

As the strategic bombing of the Third Reich continued, PFF methods became ever more sophisticated, with contingency plans for almost every eventuality. At the same time, the proportion of Lancasters to other heavy bomber types grew ever greater. Moving forward in time to just over a year later, on 23/24 July 1944, a force of 619 heavy bombers was sent against the German naval base at Kiel. Of these, no fewer than 84 per cent were Lancasters.

■ PATHFINDER ■ PROGRESS

By this time the concept of the Master Bomber was tried and proven. His function was to check on the accuracy of the marking, call by radio for adjustments or back-up where necessary, and, while loitering in the area until the bombing was completed, do everything possible to ensure that the munitions went down exactly where they were intended to go.

Whereas in the Friedrichshafen raid the Master Bomber had flown a Lancaster, loitering over heavily defended targets for extended periods in a four-engined bomber could not be considered a good insurance risk. It was not long before the standard aircraft for this purpose became the fast and agile twin-engined Mosquito. This was the case

BOMBER COMMAND AIRCRAFT IN RAID ON KIEL, 23/24 JULY 1944

Group	Type	No	Missing
8	Mosquito IX	1	-
	Mosquito XVI	6	-
	Mosquito XX	3	-
	Lancaster III	89	1
1	Lancaster I	85	1
	Lancaster III	104	1
6	Lancaster II	14	-
	Lancaster X	28	-
5	Lancaster I	46	1
	Lancaster III	53	-
3	Lancaster I	59	-
	Lancaster II	14	-
	Lancaster III	27	-
4	Halifax III	100	-

TOTAL
10 Mosquitos, 519 Lancasters, 100 Halifaxes

Top: **To assist target identification, detailed models were made by the Central Intelligence Unit. Seen here is Kiel harbour.** *Above:* **Lancaster Mk I of No. 83 Squadron. After a distinguished career with PFF, this aircraft came down in Holland after raiding Essen on 3/4 April 1943.**

for the Kiel raid, in which the Master Bomber and his deputy flew two of the 10 Mosquitos allocated for primary marking. Some idea of PFF progress can be given by quoting the Plan of Attack in full.

'The method employed for the raid on Kiel was controlled Newhaven marking. Blind Illuminators, 21 Lancasters, were to drop red TIs at H-6 (six minutes before zero hour), and white flares if the weather was suitable. If there was more than 6/10ths cloud, they were to retain their white flares, and drop green flares with red stars instead. If their H2S

should prove unserviceable, they were to retain their markers and act as Main Force. These were to be followed by the Primary Visual markers, 6 Lancasters, at H-4, who were to drop red and green TIs using the red TIs dropped by the Illuminators as a guide, but only after definite visual identification. If they could not identify the target visually they were to retain their markers and act as Main Force. Visual Centerers, 16 Lancasters, distributed throughout the attack, were to aim green TIs with one second overshoot at: 1) the centre of mixed red and green TIs; 2) the centre of red TIs; 3) the centre of green TIs; in that order of priority. If no TIs were visible, they were to act as Main Force. The marking was to be kept up during the attack by the Secondary Blind Markers, 7 Lancasters at H+10 and 4 at H+11. They were to drop red TIs by H2S. If there was more than 6/10ths

cloud they were to release skymarking flares green with red stars. If their H2S was unserviceable they also were to act as Main Force. 28 Lancasters of 8 Group were to act as supporters, bombing at H-6 on H2S, or if that was unserviceable, visually or on a good dead reckoning.'

■ KIEL ■

The Main Force was scheduled to attack in four very concentrated waves, putting 516 heavy bombers over the target in the space of just 15 minutes. Scattered among them would be 15 ABC (Airborne Cigar) Lancasters of No. 101 Squadron, each carrying an extra crewman whose function was to jam the German night fighter radio frequencies. Bombing instructions were, in order of priority: 1) centre of mixed red and green TIs or red TIs; 2) centre of green TIs; 3) centre of skymarking flares.

Rarely does anything go precisely according to plan, and the raid on Kiel was no exception. The target was covered with 10/10ths cloud. No contact could be made with the Master Bomber, and his deputy assumed control of proceedings. Marking was checked by H2S and considered accurate, although rather scattered in the early stages. Main Force bombed on the glow of TIs as seen through the cloud, but both marking and bombing appeared to become more concentrated towards the end of the attack, and many explosions and fires were reported.

Severe damage was caused to the north-east portion of the Deutsche Werke shipyards, and hangars at the Holtenau airfield were partially destroyed. A considerable amount of damage was done to the facilities and barrack area near the Torpedo Boat Harbour, and moderate damage to a torpedo components and electrical signalling works. Sixteen medium-sized buildings in the Marine Artillery Depot were partially destroyed. Only four Lancasters were lost on this mission; a mere 0.7 per cent of the total.

PFF led the way to the targets, but Main Force, huge and largely anonymous, was the mighty sledgehammer that came crashing down on them.

For all practical purposes Main Force was Bomber Command. Main Force delivered the greatest weight of bombs against the war machine that was the Third Reich, and Main Force took the greatest number of casualties. Nor should it be forgotten that Main Force was the training ground for those who became Pathfinders or who smashed the Ruhr Dams and sank the *Tirpitz*. Although it was occasionally diverted to tactical aims, by far the greatest effort was strategic.

As the war continued, the Lancaster progressively became the backbone of Main Force. In numbers of sorties flown and tonnages of bombs delivered, it outstripped all other bombers in service by a considerable margin.

The strategic bombing of Germany, and to a lesser extent its Axis partner Italy, consisted of a number of what amounted to protracted set-piece battles, interspersed with many highly individual actions. The thousand-bomber raids of May and June 1942 had only been achieved by milking training units of aircraft and crews, and pressing every possible reserve machine into service. This tremendous effort could not, by the very nature of things, be sustained. During the months following June 1942, Bomber Command restricted itself to raids of up to 300 aircraft against single targets roughly twice a week, weather permitting.

The number of Lancaster squadrons steadily grew. Prior to October 1942, conversion onto the new type was carried out by a specially formed third flight within each squadron. This allowed squadrons to operate old and new types side by side until conversion was complete, with them thus remaining fully operational. After this conversion flights were centralized and merged into Heavy Conversion Units.

Top: Squadron crew returns from a raid. Two are Canadians and one a New Zealander, reflecting an ever-increasing influx from the Dominions.
Above: Wing Commander Guy Gibson (right) led No. 106 Squadron to Gdynia, dropped the first 8,000 pounder, and took part in Operation Robinson before forming the Dam Busters.
Far Left: The devastated oil refinery at Harburg, just to the south of Hamburg.

Special weapons feature often in the Lancaster story. One of these was the huge Capital Ship Bomb, which featured a shaped charge designed to cut through armour. This monstrosity was turnip-shaped, and possessed appalling ballistic qualities for a role where accuracy was essential.

FRIEDRICHSHAFEN, BOMB LOADS

Leader and Deputy Leader	2 x Lancaster III	1 x 4,000lb (1,800kg) 7 x 500lb (227kg)
97 Sqn PFF	2 x Lancaster III	3 x red TI; 3 x green TI 16 x white flares 2 x 500lb (227kg) 2 x red TI, 2 x green TI 32 x white flares 2 x 500lb (227kg)
9, 49, 50, 57, 61, 106 Sqns, No. 5 Grp	32 x Lancaster III	1 x 4,000lb (1,800kg) 7 x 500lb (227kg)
44, 207, 467, 619 Sqns, No. 5 Grp	Lancaster III fitted with Mk XIV bombsight	14 x 500lb (227kg)
44, 207 Sqns, No. 5 Grp	Lancaster III not fitted with Mk XIV bombsight	Full incendiary load

SEARCHLIGHTS

'One of my most anxious moments of the whole raid was when, during one of my five successful runs over the target, T-Tommy was caught in a cone of searchlights. I fought desperately to lose those probing beams of light which had caught my aircraft in their web. Shrapnel rattled along the fuselage like hailstones until, by diving at near maximum speed, I escaped into the friendly darkness. Poor Jack Hannah, my wireless operator, stationed at the astrodome on the lookout for enemy fighters, protested in vigorous terms as he was tossed about like a pea in a pod.'

PILOT OFFICER D.I. JONES, No. 97 SQUADRON.

Targets for the Capital Ship Bomb were soon found. In August 1942, the German's only aircraft carrier *Graf Zeppelin* and the battle cruiser *Gneisenau* were reported at Gdynia in Poland. A raid was mounted on 27 August by Lancasters of No. 106 Squadron adapted to carry the special bomb. It was led by Wing Commander Guy Gibson, already possessed of a formidable reputation, with a specialist bomb aimer, Squadron Leader Arthur Richardson, for this mission only.

■ ANTICLIMAX ■

The result was, perhaps inevitably, an anticlimax. Visibility was poor, and the defences stronger than expected. Arriving over Gdynia, 106 Squadron was unable to locate *Graf Zeppelin*, but managed to find what was believed to be *Gneisenau*.

Top: To carry bombs of 8,000lb (3,600kg) or more, Lancaster bomb bay doors were bulged, as seen on this Mk II.

Above: A gaggle of Lancasters at low level. Not the Le Creusot raid, but these in Far Eastern finish show up much better.

PARTICIPANTS IN OPERATION ROBINSON

Squadron	No. of A/C	Base
N.o 9	10*	Waddington
No. 44	9	Waddington
No. 49	10	Scampton
No. 50	12	Skellingthorpe
No. 57	10	Scampton
No. 61	7*	Syerston
No. 97	9	Woodhall Spa
No. 106	12*	Syerston
No. 207	15	Langar

NB. * denotes two aircraft to Montchanin.

Gibson made numerous runs over the harbour, and despite Richardson's best efforts, the bomb missed the battle cruiser by about 1,200ft (360m). The rest of the squadron fared no better. In the event, the German aircraft carrier never entered service.

Early in September, 8,000lb (3,600kg) bombs started to arrive on the squadrons. These needed bulged doors and other modifications to the bomb bay, and Gibson's squadron, its aircraft already adapted for the Capital Ship Bomb, pioneered their use. The following month saw another Bomber Command set-piece attack.

Left: **Close examination reveals ice cream cornets among the bombs denoting raids on** *Dante's Daughter* **of No. 103 Squadron. These symbolized Italian targets.**
Below: **Greetings from Canada! A tastefully decorated 8,000lb (3,600kg) bomb on its loading trolley in front of a Mk II of No. 426 Squadron RCAF.**
Bottom: **Lancaster Mk II of No. 426 Thunderbirds Squadron RCAF, one of the many Canadian Lancaster units. It was lost over Stuttgart on 7/8 October 1943.**

After take-off, on 17 October, some 96 Lancasters from 5 Group assembled in a loose gaggle over Upper Heyford in Oxfordshire, and from there proceeded to Land's End. Descending to 1,000ft (300m) over the sea to avoid radar detection, they gave Ushant a wide berth before turning south-easterly over the Bay of Biscay. When about 60 miles (95km) from the French coast, they dropped down to 300ft (90m) and turned almost due east.

Crossing the coast near the Isle d'Yeu, they swept over the sparsely populated Vendée, passed a few miles south of Tours, and picked up the River Cher at Montrichard. German fighters were absent, and unhindered by the defences, the low-level armada thundered on. The sole incident occurred as a Lancaster of No. 57 Squadron took a partridge through the windscreen, injuring the flight engineer.

4,000ft, the minimum release height for the 4,000lb cookies

■ OPERATION ■ ROBINSON

Vital targets were not always in Germany. One such was the Schneider armaments factory at Le Creusot in south-eastern France, roughly halfway between Dijon and Lyon. Although it covered nearly 300 acres, the need to avoid civil casualties demanded a standard of accuracy that could only be attained in daylight. The nine Lancaster squadrons operational in No. 5 Group began to practise low-level flying early in October.

The lessons of the Augsburg raid had been well learnt. As in that ill-fated attack, the bombers were scheduled to reach the target just before dusk, making their escape into the darkening sky. This time, however, the inbound route of the raiding force was carefully planned to minimize the possibility of fighter interception.

Reaching the Loire near Nevers, the formation climbed to its briefed attack altitude of 4,000ft (1,200m), the minimum release height for the 4,000lb (1,800kg) cookies that were carried by 15 aircraft. As they climbed, they edged a few degrees southwards in the direction of Le Creusot and took up their attack formation.

Navigation and timing were spot on, and surprise

OVERSEAS LANCASTER SQUADRONS

Sqn No	Nationality	First Op	Base
460	Australian	22/23 Nov 42 Stuttgart	Breighton
467	Australian	2/3 Jan 43 Gardening	Bottesford
426	Canadian	17/18 Aug 43 Peenemunde	Linton-on-Ouse
405	Canadian	17/18 Aug 43 Peenemunde	Gransden Lodge
408	Canadian	7/8 Oct 43 Stuttgart	Linton-on-Ouse
432	Canadian	18/19 Nov 43 Sea Search	East Moor
463	Australian	26/27 Nov 43 Berlin	Waddington
75	New Zealand	9/10 April 44 Villeneuve St George	Mepal
300	Polish	18/19 April 44 Rouen	Faldingworth
419	Canadian	27/28 April 44 Friedrichshafen	Middleton St George
428	Canadian	July 44	Middleton St George
431	Canadian	December 44	Croft
434	Canadian	2/3 Jan 45 Nuremburg	Croft
424	Canadian	February 44	Skipton-on-Swale
433	Canadian	1/2 Feb 45 Ludwigshaven	Skipton-on-Swale
427	Canadian	11 March 45 Essen	Leeming
429	Canadian	April 45	Leeming

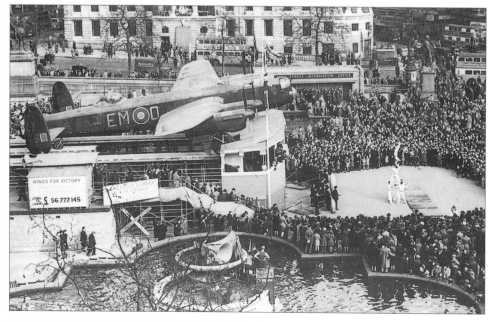

was virtually complete. The raiders arrived shortly after sunset, but the target was clearly visible despite the gathering dusk. In an attack lasting just nine minutes, over 200 tonnes of high explosive and incendiaries rained down.

At the same time, six Lancasters led by Guy Gibson broke away from the main force and attacked a transformer station at Montchanin, a few miles to the southeast. They carried ten 500lb (225kg) bombs each, and were briefed to attack from 500ft (150m). The transformer station was wrecked, but two of the pilots were over-enthusiastic and attacked from well below the minimum safe height. One aircraft was damaged and the other crashed, both victims of their own bomb explosions.

These were the only losses of the day, although one Lancaster forced to turn back with engine failure was intercepted by three Arado Ar 196 floatplanes of the Kriegsmarine. The flight engineer was killed in the attack, but the Lancaster gunners drove off the Germans, claiming two shot down.

In all, damage to the Lancasters was remarkably light, with just a few holes in some aircraft. Although limited production was resumed at Le Creusot after a period of about three weeks, major repair work was still in progress eight months later. Given the minimal casualties that were sustained, Operation Robinson must be reckoned an outstanding success.

The battle of El Alamein commenced just five days after the raid on Le Creusot, while Operation Torch, the Allied landings in north-west Africa, were scheduled for 11 November. Lancaster squadrons played an indirect part in these operations by bombarding targets in northern Italy, keeping the Italian Navy in port, and other reinforcements at home. Between 22/23 October and 11/12 December, 936 sorties were

Above left: The projection at the bottom of the turret is the Monica aerial; the damage was caused by flak.
Left: Star of Wings for Victory Week in Trafalgar Square, this No. 207 Squadron Lancaster was one of the first production aircraft. It survived the war.

flown. Genoa was raided five times, Turin seven times, and Milan once, this last in daylight. Italian air defences were ineffective and losses were light, even though France was often crossed in daylight on the outbound leg. But the long distances involved, plus a double crossing of the Alps, all carried out in late autumn weather frequently with icing conditions, made raiding Italy a tremendous test of endurance for the Lancaster crews.

If the weather was too bad for the Alpine crossing to be attempted, German targets were substituted instead at the last moment, causing, as Guy Gibson recorded, 'Last minute flaps, a new briefing, new maps, and bad tempers all round.' Hamburg, Duisburg, Stuttgart and Mannheim were among the German targets attacked during this period.

Lancaster output soon reached the stage where squadrons from No. 1 Group, based in North Lincolnshire and South Yorkshire, could start equipping with the type. The first three to do so were No. 460 (Australian) Squadron at Breighton; No. 101 Squadron at Holme-on-Spalding Moor, the first operation of which was the long haul to Turin on 20/21 November; and No. 103 Squadron at Elsham Wolds.

The conversion of the Australian squadron onto the Lancaster highlighted a trend. Although No. 44 Squadron had been dubbed 'Rhodesia', there were not enough Rhodesians to man it fully. Of the 48 aircrew on the Augsburg raid, only eight were Rhodesians. Two, including Nettleton himself, were South Africans. Two Canadians, two New Zealanders, and a single Australian completed the overseas contingent. The remaining 33 were British.

From the outbreak of war, volunteers from the British Empire, or Commonwealth, as it is now called, had hastened to the aid of the mother country. Their governments followed suit, and from quite an early stage, squadrons with national affiliations were formed. It is doubtful whether the personnel of these units was ever drawn entirely from just one country, but a high proportion of Australians, Canadians or New Zealanders in one squadron gave it a uniquely national flavour. No. 460 was the first of many such Lancaster squadrons, but numerically the Canadians took pride of place; No. 6 Group was for all practical purposes an all-Canadian Bomber Group.

■ ELECTRONIC ■ WARFARE

The year of 1943 commenced with raids on Berlin, with the Pathfinders honing their marking techniques on the city. Electronic warfare took on greater significance with the introduction of new jamming and threat detection systems. Of these, Tinsel could be tuned to transmit engine noise on the German fighter control frequencies; Monica was a tail warning radar; while Boozer could detect German radar emissions. Many other systems followed in the years to come.

Tinsel was initially successful, though the Germans gradually introduced measures to limit its effectiveness. Monica, in contrast, was a minor disaster from the outset. Quite unable to discriminate between friend and foe, it constantly gave false alarms as friendly aircraft in the bomber stream blundered into and out of its search area. Worse still, the Germans developed a detector codenamed Flensburg which could home on Monica's emissions from very long ranges. Naxos-Z was another German detector, designed to home on H_2S. The latter would have been no great problem had H_2S been used intermittently for navigation, and for blind bombing in the target area, but many crews kept it switched on throughout the sortie,

Above right: Lancaster Mk 1 of No. 106 Squadron damaged by a night fighter during the Battle of the Ruhr in April 1943.
Right: Danger came not only from the air. This Lancaster collided on the ground with an American B-17 Fortress.

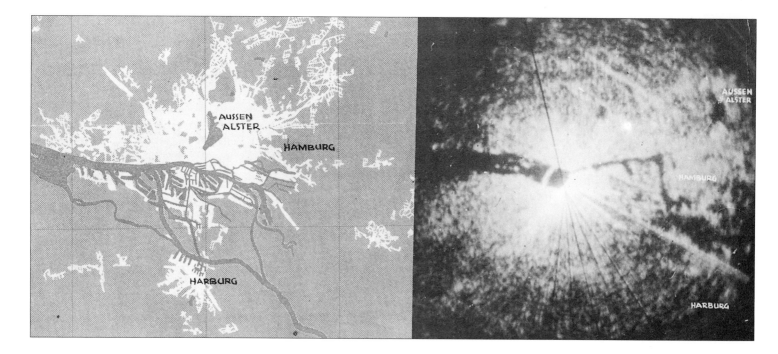

Above: Hamburg, with the distinctive River Elbe running through it, showed up well on the H₂S screen, as can be seen by comparing it with the map at left. (Alfred Price)

making the task of the night fighters much easier.

Boozer, however, was rather better; if the bomber was illuminated by ground radar, a red warning light came on in the cockpit. If fighter radar emissions were detected, an orange light glowed. There were two snags. Illumination by ground radar was too frequent for the warning to be of much value, while once a night fighter gained visual contact its radar was often switched to standby, upon which the warning light went out precisely at the moment of greatest danger.

WINDOW OVER HAMBURG

Many references to the difficulties caused by Window to the ground and fighter defences were overheard in intercepted wireless traffic. Some enemy aircraft reported interference. One very interesting remark was "it is impossible, too many hostiles". This indicates that the Window echoes, besides producing general interference of the (German) display tube, were also confused with true aircraft echoes.

115 sorties by night fighters were overheard, 33 of which mentioned British aircraft. Our crews reported 49 interceptions, but only seven of these developed into attacks. Enemy aircraft frequently seemed unaware of the presence of bombers in their vicinity. Only two instances of fighter damage were reported, and all of the five bombers seen to be shot down in combat were at least 20 miles (32km) away from Hamburg.

BOMBER COMMAND NIGHT RAID REPORT No. 383.

Below: Centurion! This 550 Squadron Lancaster survived the war with a tally of over 100 sorties against targets which included the Ruhr and Berlin.

■ THE BATTLE ■ OF THE RUHR

The Ruhr was the industrial heart of Germany, invariably heavily cloaked by industrial haze, making targets notoriously difficult to locate. However, with the introduction of Oboe it could be attacked accurately for the first time.

The Battle of the Ruhr opened on 5/6 March with a heavy raid on Essen, the home of the Krupps steelworks, one of the most important targets in Germany. It was marked by PFF, then bombed by Main Force in three waves. The final wave consisted of 145 Lancasters from 14 squadrons, about half the Main Force total. One-third of the Krupps works was heavily damaged, more than all previous raids on this target combined had achieved.

Raids on Munich, Nuremberg and Stuttgart followed, to avoid setting a pattern which would allow the defences to concentrate, then, just over a week later, Bomber Command returned to Essen. A third raid on Essen took place on 3/4 April, and a fourth on 30 April/1 May. Barmen/Wuppertal, described in the preceding chapter, also fell into this period. Another Ruhr target, Duisburg, had been raided twice. Dortmund and Dusseldorf were hit during May with over 300 Lancasters on each raid, the first time this figure had been exceeded. Raids on targets in the Ruhr continued until 14/15 June, culminating in a heavy attack on the steel and coal centre of Oberhausen.

The Battle of the Ruhr conclusively demonstrated Bomber Command's ability to hit targets in this area even in poor visibility, while taking only moderate casualties. But the Ruhr was within range of Oboe. The pressing need was to carry the battle deeper into Germany with similar results.

■ OPERATION ■ GOMORRAH

Hamburg was the second largest city in Germany, and the largest port in Europe. Its strategic importance lay in its ship-building activities, most notably the manufacturing of U-boats. Situated close to the coast, and with a large and very easily recognizable river running through it, Hamburg was suitable for locating by H2S.

In addition, a new counter-measure codenamed Window was made available for the first time. It consisted of bundles of aluminium foil strips, which would each give the appearance of a heavy bomber on German radars, making tracking impossible.

On the night of 24/25 July 1943, 791 bombers set course for Hamburg. Of these, 347, or slightly less than half, were Lancasters, but they carried nearly three-quarters of the total tonnage of bombs. As they approached they were monitored by German ground radar until the bomb aimers started to drop bundles of Window down their flare chutes at one-minute intervals.

The result was complete chaos for the

Above: Time exposure of German flak over a defended area. This is what the Lancaster crews faced nightly.
Right: Flight Lieutenant William Reid VC of No. 61 Squadron. Twice wounded, his aircraft badly damaged and two crewmen dead, he continued the mission and bombed the target.

defenders. One minute they could see many contacts, indicating a heavy raid was underway. The next the radar screens filled up, giving the appearance of a raid by 11,000 bombers! All semblance of control was lost, and fighters already airborne were ordered to the vicinity to hunt independently. They spent most of their time fruitlessly chasing clouds of Window, while the flak was reduced to firing at random, in the hope of scoring a lucky hit.

PFF marked accurately with Newhaven, and Main Force, now virtually unhampered by the defences, sent their bombs whistling down. Bombing accuracy was marred only by an element of 'creepback' in the later stages, caused by over-eager crews releasing their bombs a fraction too early on the attack run. Cumulatively, this extended for 7 miles (11km).

The loss rate for Hamburg had previously been around 6 per cent, but on this night only 12 aircraft were missing, a rate of 1.5 per cent. Only four Lancasters failed to return, but three of these were from the high-flying No. 103 Squadron, which had gained least protection of all—from Window.

■ FOLLOW-UPS ■

Hamburg's ordeal was far from over. Daylight raids by the USAAF 8th Air Force were made on 25 and 26 July, while on the night of 27/28, Bomber Command returned in force with 787 aircraft, 353 of them Lancasters. The same tactics were used, and losses were still very light at 2.2 per cent. A third raid followed on 29/30 July, and the fourth and final one on 2/3 August. The damage assessment report stated: 'The city of Hamburg is now in ruins. The general destruction is on a scale never before seen in a town or city of this size.'

The next event of note was a heavy raid upon the weapons research centre at Peenemunde. This was a high-risk mission; Peenemunde was a small target on the Baltic coast, and good visibility was needed for bombing accuracy, so much so that a full-moon night was chosen, 17/18 August. Deep penetrations were seldom made at this time of year, as the northern sky was never completely dark. Conditions were therefore ideal for the night fighters.

The force despatched consisted of 324 Lancasters, 219 Halifaxes and 54 Stirlings, with Group Captain John Searby of No. 83 Squadron as Master Bomber. The course to the target was planned to make it look as if the bombers were heading for Berlin. This impression was reinforced by eight PFF Mosquitos, which carried out a diversionary attack. It worked, and over 200 German fighters converged on the capital. But once bombs started going down on Peenemunde there was no disguising the real

Top: Most Lancasters died in flames, as did this Heavy Conversion Unit aircraft following a training accident.
Left: Lancaster Mk I ME703 of No. 576 Squadron survived the holocaust of the Nuremburg raid in March 1944, only to receive a direct flak hit five weeks later.
Below: Chaos in the Juvissy marshalling yards after a raid by 200 Lancasters on 18/19 April 1944.

In what amounted to a short campaign, some 3,095 sorties were flown, 1,373 of them by Lancasters. In total, more than 8,600 tons of bombs fell on Hamburg, of which Lancasters alone contributed over 6,000 tons. Losses were 86 bombers, 39 of them Lancasters. Apart from the damage inflicted on the target, the German defence system, fire and rescue services had been left in complete disarray.

The defenders proved more resilient than expected. Measures taken included a looser form of fighter control, new airborne radar of a different wavelength, emission detectors as described earlier, and saturating the target area with 'cat's-eye' single seaters. Before long, bomber losses started to rise again.

Top: **This Canadian Lancaster visited Berlin on at least seven occasions, flying with three different squadrons; Nos 432, 426 and 408.**
Above: **Casualty! Shot down over Berlin, a Lancaster broke up in mid-air and its tail landed in a garden. (Alfred Price)**

target, and those fighters with sufficient fuel stormed north to intercept, arriving in time to encounter the final two waves.

Peenemunde was heavily damaged, but the price paid for the raid upon it was high. Losses amounted to 40 aircraft, of which 24 were Lancasters. It is

believed that the majority fell to fighters, but how much worse this could have been had the fighters not been lured elsewhere first. Diversions and feints became a standard tactic in Bomber Command's armoury, followed later as strength increased by simultaneous attacks on multiple targets.

■ THE BATTLE ■ OF BERLIN

The operations so far described were successful, but Bomber Command also had setbacks. The Battle of Berlin was one such. It commenced on 18/19 November

1943 with an attack by an all-Lancaster force, but on this occasion PFF marking was not up to scratch, and the bombing was scattered. The absence of a Master Bomber did not help matters. Four days later they tried again, this time with better results.

A further 11 heavy raids on the German capital were carried out by the middle of February, interspersed with other targets. Results were indeterminate; while at first losses were light, they gradually increased. In all, 6,209 Lancaster sorties were flown in this period, losing 321 aircraft in action. This represented an unsustainable loss rate of 5.2 per cent, which rose to 8 per cent for a final raid in March.

Peenemunde was heavily damaged, but the price was high

These figures do not include operational attrition. Fog and low cloud over England in the small hours of 17 December caused the loss of 28 Lancasters, in addition to 25 missing, while two more had collided after takeoff. The loss rate for this one mission was an appalling 11.4 per cent.

The success of Hamburg could not be repeated. Berlin was too large an area, too heavily defended, too far inland, and much harder to identify with any precision. And by this time, the advantages of Window were much less as the German defences adapted themselves to it. While extensive damage was caused, the concentrated destruction of Hamburg was not repeated.

■ NUREMBERG ■

If the Battle of Berlin was a defeat for Bomber Command, the raid on Nuremberg on 30/31 March 1944 was a disaster. For Bomber Command, the Nuremberg raid was the night when it all went wrong.

Deception attacks on Kassel and Cologne were recognized early, which enabled the defences to concentrate on

of the bombers was visible from miles away, and the fighters needed no further invitation.

94 bombers failed to return that night, while 13 crashed on their return

An incredible total of 94 bombers failed to make the return journey from Germany that night, while 13 crashed on their arrival at base. Yet another was written off with battle damage, for an attrition percentage of 13.83. Seventy more aircraft returned with varying degrees of damage.

Most of the losses occurred on the outward leg. Night fighters accounted for 78 aircraft, including 55 Lancasters; flak claimed 11 (five of them Lancasters); two bombers collided and another one was lost to an unknown cause. Of the 440 Lancaster crewmen who failed to return home, only 107 survived. Worst of all was that the raid was an almost complete failure.

Top: The remains of the V-weapons site at Wizernes after a raid by Lancasters of No. 5 Group, 20 July 1944.
Left: Repair was a vital part of aircraft replacement. The nearest fuselage section belonged to an aircraft badly damaged by a night fighter in June 1944.
Below left and right: Before and after. A raid on the oil storage depot at Bec d'Ambes on 4 August 1944.

the main raid of 781 heavy bombers, of which 569 were Lancasters from 34 different squadrons. The twin-engined night fighters were scrambled, and ordered to assemble over a certain radio beacon. Unfortunately the course of the bombers took them towards this beacon, running them straight into the trap. Forecast winds were incorrect, and the bomber stream became spread out. Then, by mischance, atmospheric conditions were such that long condensation trails formed behind the bombers, shining white in the clear air under a half moon. The track

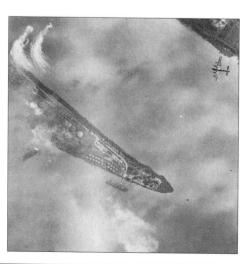

■ RETURN TO EUROPE ■

The outcome of the entire war in Europe hinged on the successful invasion of Normandy. From April 1944 the majority of Lancaster sorties were against targets in France and Belgium, mainly railway centres and airfields, radar stations and coastal gun batteries.

The weeks following D-Day saw Main Force heavily engaged in France and the Low Countries. Road and rail communications, enemy troop concentrations and fuel depots were all accorded priority, but meanwhile the V-1 and V-2 assault on London had begun, and a great deal of effort was diverted to their launching sites. Nor were targets in the Third Reich neglected; the Germans could be given no opportunity to move their home defence fighters forward.

This period saw a large-scale return to daylight operations for Bomber Command, made possible by Allied air superiority in the area, although the need to keep up the pressure around the clock made great demands on the bomber crews. Then, as the Allied armies pushed further inland, heavy attacks were made on German-held airfields in Holland. As the German defences were ground down, losses became progressively lighter; barely one percent for December 1944.

During the concluding six months of the war, the Lancaster force grew to an

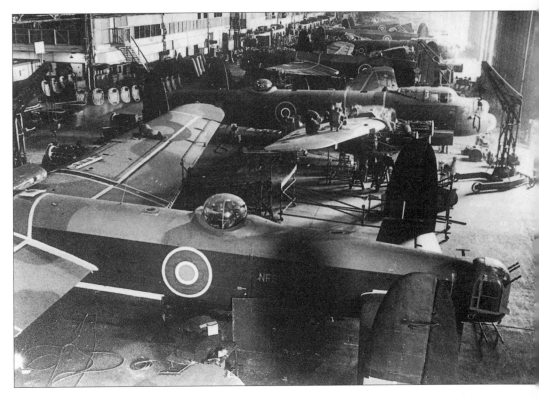

Above: Lancaster assembly line at Baginton. The wartime censor has rather clumsily airbrushed out the aircraft number.

enormous 57 squadrons; over 1,200 aircraft in all. As the area of occupied Europe shrank, so targets in Germany featured more and more. Concentrated attacks on synthetic oil plants were made during the winter of 1944/45, vastly reducing supplies. Dresden, at that time a

key road and rail target, was attacked in strength on 13/14 February 1945; Essen by more than 1,000 bombers in daylight on 11 March, and Kiel on 9/10 April. Berlin, once the most heavily defended area in Germany, was raided five nights later by more than 500 Lancasters, of which only two (0.4 per cent) failed to return. But by this time major targets were in short supply and the majority of raids were on a comparatively small scale, and as the Allied armies pushed into Germany the strategic bombing war gradually drew to a close.

■ FINAL OPERATIONS ■

The Lancaster ended the war on more peaceful tasks. Operation Manna saw 17 Lancaster squadrons dropping containers of food to the population of Holland; Operation Exodus involved the repatriation of released British prisoners of war, with basic accommodation for 24 passengers in each aircraft. This was followed by Operation Dodge, the return of 8th Army veterans from the Mediterranean area. It was an honourable finish to a hard-fought campaign.

Left: Edith, veteran of 84 sorties during which she destroyed a German fighter, completed a further 14 trips dropping food and repatriating prisoners of war.

A heavily defended target could put up a storm of light flak, but most bombing was carried out at altitudes beyond its reach. Heavy flak could not be avoided by high flying, but it had a far slower rate of fire than the light automatic guns. Not only were far fewer shells coming up at any one time, but they took between 20 and 30 seconds to arrive at typical operational altitudes. Radar-predicted heavy flak was pretty accurate, but one method of avoiding it was to change course and altitude at frequent intervals. Hopefully the shells would then burst in the spot where the bomber would have been had it not evaded.

This improved the odds a bit, but if shells came up in the wrong place or burst at the wrong height, Lady Luck became the sole arbiter. Many pilots felt that the best course was to take no evasive action at all, but to drop the nose and accelerate out of the flak zone as fast as possible. It was also undesirable to make radical changes of course and altitude while on the attack run, if bombing accuracy was to be maintained. But having said that, the Lancaster's deadliest enemy was the fighter, whether met by day or by night. As the vast majority of Lancaster

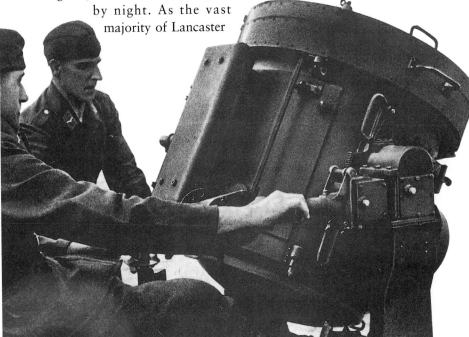

sorties were made under cover of darkness, we will concentrate on the night fighter threat.

As we saw in the preceding chapter, countermeasures were widely used to hinder the defenders. While these were often very effective, what they could not do was prevent a fighter from searching visually. If a night fighter succeeded in working its way into the bomber stream, it was in a target-rich environment. Even with its radar and radio communications jammed solid, it was often possible for the fighter to make a visual

Above: Radar-predicted heavy flak guns were mainly deployed along the coast or around cities.
Below left: Searchlights illuminated the bomber for flak or fighters; they could also dazzle the pilot and disorient him.
Opposite: Two .50 calibre machine guns in the tail gave a mightier punch than the usual four .303 Brownings.

sighting without these aids. And once the fighter was in visual contact, an attack usually followed.

Normal Lancaster defensive armament consisted of two machine guns in each of nose and dorsal positions, and four more in the tail, all in power-operated turrets. The guns were Browning .303 calibre, with a high cyclic rate of fire. They could pour out a lot of rounds, but the bullets themselves were small and lacked hitting power. Four types of ammunition were in general use; ball, tracer, armour-piercing and incendiary.

The four guns in the rear turret were usually harmonized on a point at 750ft (225m) for night missions, and on a 7ft 6in (2.29m) square pattern at 1,200ft (365m) by day. The nose and mid-upper turrets were normally harmonized 5ft (1.52m) apart at 1,200ft (365m), although it was generally accepted that the maximum effective range of the .303 Browning was 900ft (275m). The main defence at night was the tail and

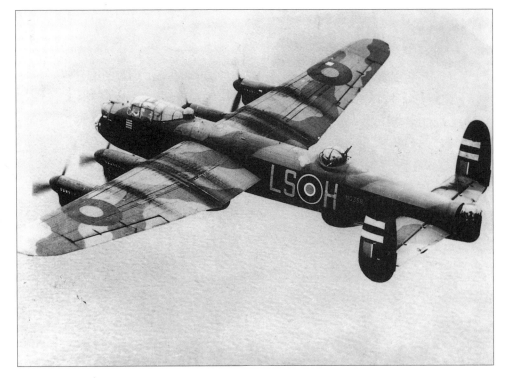

Left: The tail and mid-upper turrets were the Lancaster's main defensive armament. This example, from No. 15 Squadron, also carries G-H radar bombing equipment.
Below: Mk I Lancaster used for trials of a periscopically sighted ventral turret in 1942. It was not a success.

was such that the German fighters often had to get very close before they could see the bomber clearly enough to identify it and take aim. This brought them well into the effective range of the British machine guns, which could to a degree compensate for their small projectiles by their high rate of fire.

From June 1944, a number of Lancasters were fitted with the Rose Rice tail turret, which mounted two .50 calibre Brownings. While the combination of a much heavier projectile and a slightly higher muzzle velocity gave a rather better effective range, the cyclic rate of fire of this weapon was at most 850 rounds per minute. The standard four-gun Lancaster turret could spew out no less than 306 bullets in a four second burst, compared with just 113 for the Rose Rice turret. It must however be admitted that the weight of fire of the latter was about 50per cent heavier provided that all bullets struck home, but the former was more likely to score multiple hits.

The primary task of the Lancaster was to deliver bombs and return safely

Operationally, what were the implications? The primary task of the Lancaster was to deliver bombs on target and return safely. Given this, it was sufficient to foil the fighter's attack. Shooting it down was the cherry on the cake. On dark nights, when the fighters were forced to get in close, sometimes to less than 200ft (60m), the four-gun turret, with nearly triple the rate of fire of the Rose Rice, had much to commend it. Few German night fighter pilots would press home an attack while they were taking hits themselves. The final advantage of

mid-upper turret, in that order. Rarely were the nights clear enough to allow fighters to make frontal attacks, and it was unlikely that a Lancaster would overhaul a fighter from astern, so the nose turret was of most use in discouraging the ground defences during low-level missions.

Wartime British bomber armament has often been criticized as inadequate, because it was both out-ranged and out-gunned by the German fighter weapons. There are however two factors to consider: British bombers were far more heavily defended than those of any other nation except the Americans, and that included their German counterparts. For example, the Heinkel He 111 typically carried a single rifle-calibre machine gun in each of just five positions, with limited fields of fire and no power-operated turrets. Then at night, visibility

LANCASTER, DEFENSIVE GUNS

		.50 calibre
Browning MG	.303 calibre	.50 calibre
Cyclic rate of fire	1,150rpm	750/850rpm
Weight	22lb (10kg)	64lb (29kg)
Muzzle Velocity	2,660ft/sec (811m/sec)	2,750ft/sec (838m/sec)
Projectile Weight	174 grains	710 grains

Above: The nose turret was rarely of use at night, but daylight raids became more frequent. No. 100 Squadron – 128 ops.

the standard four-gun turret was that it had no less than 130 seconds' firing time, compared with a mere 24 seconds for the Rose Rice. However, unless shooting up ground targets was on the agenda, this was rarely called for; against enemy fighters 24 seconds' firing time was usually adequate.

If however the object of the exercise was to shoot down German fighters, then the heavier gun was preferable. This was also the case on clear nights with good visibility, when the German fighters could stand off at long range and shoot. In daylight – and from late 1944 Lancasters carried out a surprising number of daylight operations – it was no contest; the heavier gun with its longer range was by far the most preferable. Among the squadrons equipped with the Rose Rice rear turret were Nos 83, 101, 153 and 170.

The other major variation in Lancaster defensive armament was the Glenn Martin 250 mid-upper turret, which also

mounted two .50 calibre Brownings. This was carried by the Lancaster B.VII, of which a total of 150 were built. But as deliveries of this model did not commence until April 1945, it was just too late to see action.

■ GUNSIGHTS ■

Guns are not a lot of use unless they can be accurately aimed. The main gunsight used in Lancaster turrets was the Barr & Stroud G Mk III reflector sight. In use, this showed an illuminated orange circle with a central dot, both focused at infinity. A brightness control adjusted it according to conditions; bright in sunlight, dim at night. The radius of the circle was approximately equal to the wingspan of a single-engined fighter at a range of 1,200ft (365m), while the radius of the circle gave the deflection (the amount of aiming ahead) needed to hit a target with a relative crossing speed of 50mph (80km/hr).

In 1944, the Mk IIc gyroscopic sight entered service as a turret sight. This could actually predict the point of aim, although only if the approaching fighter could be tracked for a short while, and

its wingspan set on a dial. For this reason, it was very much a daylight sight, as it was rare for a gunner to have time to do such things at night. Finally, a gun-laying radar code-named Village Inn was introduced in the final months of the war, which allowed opponents to be engaged from beyond visual range. While potentially devastating, the problem was obtaining positive identification of the radar contact as hostile. The means were to hand, but the war ended before unrestricted blind firing could be permitted as a general rule.

The essence of effective defence against fighters was always to see them first. At night this was far from easy. As

ROSE RICE TURRET

2 x .50 Browning MGs
335 rounds per gun
Mk IIIA reflector sight
Traverse +/-94°
Elevation 49°
Depression 59°

Above: **Mk I fitted with an experimental arrangement of remote barbettes with the sighting position in the tail.**

a general rule, they came from below, where they were masked by the dark ground and most difficult to see. By contrast the bomber would be limned against the sky, which is always a fraction lighter, even on a starless night. Attacks generally came from astern, with the fighter swimming up from the depths and attacking in a slight climb with its fixed frontal armament. Its target was rarely the fuselage, as if the bombs detonated the resulting explosion could quite

easily destroy the night fighter too. Normally the wings, with the vulnerable engines and fuel tanks, were selected as the aiming point, although many a time silencing the rear gunner was a priority.

Later in the war, the German night fighters used Schrage Musik, cannon pointing upwards at an angle of about 60 degrees, aimed by a reflector sight mounted in the cabin roof. This allowed them to attack from almost directly underneath, out of the arcs of fire of all except those few Lancasters which had retained ventral turrets, and generally out of sight of the gunners also. All the fighter had to do was to formate beneath

the bomber and take careful aim at the fuel tanks between the engines. A short burst of fire was then usually sufficient.

■ SCHRAGE MUSIK ■

Because the German fighters did not use tracer in a Schrage Musik attack, Bomber Command was rather slow in identifying it. If a bomber set out then failed to return there was no one to tell the tale. Only those few aircraft that survived such attacks limped back bearing the tell-tale scars, and gradually the tactic became known.

Methods of dealing with night fighters varied. Often, if one was sighted that was not making any overtly aggressive moves, the policy was to leave it well alone, hoping that the bomber had not been seen. Other crews maintained that an aggressive attitude was best, opening fire even at long range in order to show the fighter the kind of welcome it could expect if it made an attacking move. Sometimes these ploys worked; at other times they didn't.

Flight Lieutenant Tony Weber's Pathfinder crew developed their own unique brand of defence against attack from below. The Lancasters of No. 405 Squadron had had their dorsal turrets removed to improve performance, which left the mid-upper gunner as a spare bod. A small viewing hole was cut in the fuselage floor aft of the bomb bay, fitted with safety straps, oxygen connection and power for a heated flying

Below: **Canadian-built Mk X, fitted with the small and neat Glenn Martin mid-upper turret.**

Above: 'Village Inn' gunlaying radar was fitted to a few tail turrets towards the end of the war.

Left: The most widely used German night fighter was the radar-equipped Messerschmitt Me 110G.

The result was a steep descent right on top of the offending fighter, accompanied by the fervent hope that the German pilot's reflexes were fast enough for him to get out of the way in time. Negative 'g' made the Merlins cut through fuel starvation, temporarily extinguishing the exhaust flames and probably adding to the German pilot's visual problems. One dose of this nerve-racking treatment usually convinced him to go look for someone who didn't play so rough. No. 405 Squadron later adopted the ventral viewing hole on all its aircraft.

The other, official counter to fighter attack was the corkscrew. Few people (and fighter pilots are no exception) are

suit. This position was then manned by the erstwhile mid-upper gunner. When a fighter was spotted coming in below, the pilot was warned. He immediately throttled back and lowered 10 degrees of flap, which killed a lot of speed and gave the aircraft greater manoeuvrability. As the Lancaster slowed, the fighter started to overshoot beneath it. Then, at the critical moment, Weber shoved the yoke fully forward, putting his huge bomber into a dive.

Above: The upward slanting cannon installation known as Schrage Musik allowed the night fighters to attack from the blind spot below the Lancaster. (Alfred Price)

any good at deflection shooting, and the object of the corkscrew was to give the fighter a difficult target rather than a sitting duck.

It consisted of a steep turn of about 30 degrees combined with a dive of about 500ft (150m), followed immediately by a steep turn of about 30 degrees in the opposite direction combined with a climb of about 500ft (150m). These manoeuvres would be repeated as long as the fighter was in an attacking position. In this way, course and altitude could both be maintained, at the expense of speed over the ground, while few German fighter pilots were good enough to follow

a corkscrewing Lancaster and still get into a good firing position.

Instructions for the corkscrew were given by the man best placed to see what was happening; usually the rear gunner, although the mid-upper gunner or the bomb aimer, from a position in the astrodome, could also act as controller for the engagement. On spotting a fighter moving into position, the man making the sighting would call over the intercom, 'Prepare to corkscrew left [or right]', the rule being to break into the direction of the attack where possible. Then as the fighter moved into firing range, the executive order of 'Go' would be given, launching the bomber into a series of wild gyrations. The controls had to be handled roughly, making the corkscrew violent, if it was to be really effective. The Lancaster could corkscrew very well

even with a 12,000lb (5,400kg) bomb on board, while unladen it was extremely manoeuvrable for such a large machine.

McLean was credited with five German fighters shot down plus one probable

Survival depended on teamwork; total co-operation and trust between pilot and gunners. A classic engagement occurred on 15/16 March 1944, following an abortive raid on an aero engine factory at Metz, near the Franco-German border.

The Lancaster was from No. 617 Squadron, the Dam Busters, and had a mainly Canadian crew. The rear gunner

THE CORKSCREW MANOEUVRE

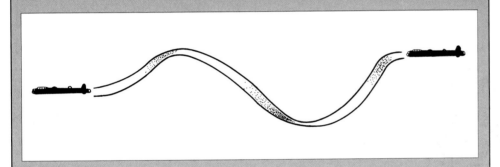

The corkscrew was a manoeuvre designed to make it very difficult for an enemy fighter to gain a firing position.

Above: Some Lancaster squadrons removed their dorsal turrets to improve performance.

up a contact to port at a range of about 3,600ft (1,100m). McLean strained his eyes, finally making out a dark shape which appeared to be four-engined. At first it was assumed to be another returning bomber. Gradually the shape closed, which was unusual, and when it was about 2,700ft (820m) away, McLean realized that it was actually two night fighters in close proximity to one another. Following standard procedure, he told his pilot: 'Prepare to corkscrew port!'

■ THREE FIGHTERS ■

The next shock came quickly; a Messerschmitt 109 single-seater fighter was sighted, flying abreast of the Lancaster about 1,500ft (450m) distant with navigation lights burning! The only explanation for this behaviour seemed to be that it was trying to distract the gunners from the fighters astern. At this moment, one of the two broke towards the Lancaster with obviously aggressive intentions.

As it closed, McLean gave the order 'Go!' and Duffy commenced a violent corkscrew just as the fighter opened fire at extreme range. The Lancaster was hit, but not seriously, and the German pilot broke away before lining up for another firing pass.

was a Scot with original ideas about defensive tactics and only that morning the crew had been on a fighter affiliation exercise to try them out.

Men are born with differing abilities. Some have a natural flair for ball games; others play the piano outstandingly well. Flight Sergeant T. J. McLean's individual talent, and indeed his whole instincts, were for air-to-air gunnery. Credited with five German fighters shot down plus a probable on a previous tour of operations, he had volunteered to join No. 617 Squadron, widely regarded at that time as a suicide outfit, and had been assigned to Flying Officer Bill Duffy's crew as the tail gunner.

Past experience had convinced Tom McLean that the most effective loading

for his guns was 45 per cent tracer and 55 per cent armour piercing, rather than the ball, tracer, incendiary and armour-piercing mix laid down in regulations. On this trip he had unofficially arranged for his preferred mix to be loaded for the first time, to his rear turret only. Not even the crew knew about this; the nose turret and the mid-upper, which was manned by Canadian Red Evans, both had standard loadings.

All aircraft were recalled without bombing when it was found that the target was under heavy cloud, but on the return trip across France the sky was cloudless, the stars shone brightly, and visibility was exceptionally good.

The first warning came from Monica, the tail warning radar, which picked

Above: German night fighters were largely dependent on ground control to position them in the bomber stream.

Having drawn no return fire from the bomber, the Me 110 was more venturesome on its second attack, closing right in. Once again the big bomber corkscrewed, spoiling its aim, while McLean poured an angry burst of fire at it, hitting its port engine, then called 'Drop' over the intercom. Immediately, the flight engineer throttled back all four engines and the Lancaster rapidly lost speed, reducing the range faster than the German pilot had expected, or was prepared for. McLean drew a bead on the cockpit and once more let fly. On hearing his guns, the flight engineer once more opened the throttles in what was a very well-rehearsed manoeuvre.

The second fighter plunged earthwards, trailing a comet-like fiery tail

On fire, the first Me 110 fell away into the void, and after making sure that the second fighter still remained in its original position, the rear gunner passed the word 'Easy' over the intercom. Upon hearing this, Bill Duffy relaxed the corkscrew manoeuvre.

They were not left in peace for long. The second night fighter, made cautious by seeing the fate of its partner, moved out to a position almost abeam of the Lancaster before commencing a curving attack from slightly below it. Again a violent evasive corkscrew, again a torrent of fire from both rear and mid-upper turrets, and the second fighter plunged earthwards, trailing a comet-like fiery tail.

Still the Me 109 shadowed them, just out of range. A renewed visual search (Monica had been switched off) showed yet another Me 110 coming up behind, moving from port to starboard, then finally to almost dead astern.

At this point Duffy spotted some cloud ahead and below, and pushed over into a shallow dive towards it. As he did so, the 110 came in, and once more the Lancaster went into a hard corkscrew, this time to starboard. Almost immediately McLean called: 'Drop!' The combination of corkscrew and speed loss spoiled the German pilot's aim completely, and he came hurtling in, to be met by a barrage of tracer and armour-piercing bullets at close range. With pieces flying off, his aircraft nosed up with flames bursting from its port wing and starboard engine, before entering a jerky flat spin down into the abyss. A red glow lit the cloud layer below.

At this, the Me 109 switched off its lights and turned in for an attack from abeam of the Lancaster. The tail turret could not be brought to bear, but Red Evans in the mid-upper position returned fire, then, as the Me 109 passed beneath

Below: In March 1944, a Lancaster of No. 617 Squadron accounted for three Me 110 night fighters like these in a single action. (Alfred Price)

the bomber, quickly traversed his turret to speed it on its way on the far side. It never returned.

At this stage of the war, night fighters were encountered quite frequently. Sometimes, by dint of hard manoeuvring or escaping into cloud, the bomber managed to shake them off. At other times, the air gunners managed to beat off the attack, while just occasionally they shot one down. In the general scheme of things, four against one was impossible odds; to survive such an encounter, let alone shoot down three fighters and beat off a fourth, bordered on the miraculous.

There are several footnotes to this outstanding action. As noted in the preceding chapter, Monica could be homed on from very long ranges. It was almost certainly this which drew as many as four fighters to a single Lancaster.

The corkscrew saved the lives of hundreds of bomber crewmen

The role of the Me 109 was more mysterious. Was it a deliberate decoy, or had it left its lights on accidentally? It seems hardly likely that it was acting as a controller, and it is extremely doubtful that it was acting as a station-keeping aid for the twin-engined fighters; they had their radars, which they were using, and presumably Flensburg as well. The most probable explanation is that it was a day fighter on a night cross-country that had forgotten to switch off its navigation lights, that just happened to be in the right place at the right time.

Flight Sergeant McLean's ammunition mix had much to commend it, inasmuch as the 'fright factor' of so much tracer, combined with the penetrative power of armour-piercing bullets, was potentially very effective. But not all bomber crews thought this way; some preferred to fire no tracer at all on the grounds that this merely demonstrated the inadequate range of the .303 Brownings, thereby encouraging the night fighters to stand off and shoot back. In fact, McLean's

idea would only be effective if the fighter could be lured in close, which of course was done.

There can be no doubt that the corkscrew saved the lives of hundreds of bomber crewmen. However, to be really effective it had to be violent, as if it was too gently executed, an experienced fighter pilot could simply follow the bomber through the manoeuvre. Properly carried out, it made the bomber a very difficult target, even by day.

In the closing months of the war, Lancasters carried out many daylight raids over Germany. Whereas American heavy bombers flew in tightly packed formations to take advantage of the massed firepower of their heavy machine guns, the reach of the Lancaster guns was less. The latter therefore flew in loose gaggles rather than tight formation, and corkscrewed when attacked by fighters. The combination of fire and movement generally proved an effective defence.

RAF LANCASTER SQUADRONS FORMED NOV 42–DEC 45

Sqn	First Op	Base Formed
101	20/21 Nov 42 Turin	Holme-on-Spalding Moor
103	21/22 Nov 42 Gardening	Elsham Wolds
12	3/4 Jan 43 Gardening	Wickenby
156	26/27 Jan 43 Lorient	Warboys
100	4/5 March 43 Gardening	Grimsby
115	20/21 March 43 Gardening	East Wretham
617	16/17 May 43 Dams Raid	Scampton
619	11/12 June 43 Dusseldorf	Woodhall Spa
7	8/9 July 43 Cologne	Oakington
514	3/4 Sept 43 Dusseldorf	Foulsham
166	22/23 Sept 43 Hanover	Kirmington
625	18/19 Oct 43 Hanover	Kelstern
626	10/11 Nov 43 Modane	Wickenby
550	26/27 Nov 43 Berlin	Grimsby
576	2/3 Dec 43 Berlin	Elsham Wolds
630	18/19 Dec 43 Berlin	East Kirkby

RAF LANCASTER SQUADRONS FORMED JAN 44–MAY 45

Sqn	First Op	Base
622	14/15 Jan 44 Brunswick	Mildenhall
15	January 44 not known	Mildenhall
635	22/23 March 44 Frankfurt	Downham Market
35	April 44 not known	Graveley
582	9/10 April 44 Lille	Little Staughton
90	June 44 not known	Tuddenham
149	17 Sept 44 Boulogne	Methwold
218	Sept 44 not known	Methwold
153	7 Oct 44 Emmerich	Kirmington
227	11 Oct 44 Walcheren	Bardney
186	18 Oct 44 Bonn	Tuddenham
170	19/20 Oct 44 Stuttgart	Kelstern
195	26 Oct 44 Leverkusen	Witchford
189	1 Nov 44 Homburg	Bardney
150	2 Nov 44 not known	Fiskerton
138	29 March 45 Hallendorf	Tuddenham

SPECIAL SQUADRONS

s a weapon of war the Lancaster was a bludgeon rather than a rapier. But circumstances alter cases, and when precision weapons were devised for special targets, the Lancaster became a scalpel.

Ruhr industry was dependent on hydro-electric power and water, supplied by several huge dams. The destruction of the largest of these would have a devastating effect on German armaments output. But no ordinary bomb was capable of smashing these concrete monsters. In the Weybridge offices of Vickers, a quiet genius called Barnes Wallis applied himself to the problem.

The solution he came up with was a large mine, which had to be placed with absolute precision against the inner face of the dams by flying at exactly 220mph (354km/hr) and 60ft (18m), releasing the weapon to an accuracy of less than one-fifth of a second. This called for a special

Right: Provisioning Lancaster, with modified bomb bay for Upkeep, and dorsal turret removed.
Below: An inert Upkeep falls clear of the dropping aircraft during trials at Reculver.
Left: To mark the 34th anniversary of the raid on the dams, a Lancaster reflew the mission in 1977.

squadron, trained specifically for the task. To lead it, the very experienced and dynamic Wing Commander Guy Gibson was chosen, and his aircrews were hand-picked from the best that Bomber Command could offer. They were a mixed bag; predominantly British, but including 26 Canadians, 12 Australians, two New Zealanders and a single American. It is less widely known that the ground crews and support tradesmen were also hand-picked, which made for an exceptionally efficient unit. Thus was the birth of No. 617 Squadron at Scampton in March 1943.

The mine, codenamed Upkeep, was a large cylindrical weapon weighing 9,250lb (4,200kg), over two-thirds of which was high explosive. Aircraft were taken from squadrons in No. 5 Group, as it had been found that 'low mileage, one careful owner' machines had better serviceability rates than those fresh from the factory, and modified. The bomb bay doors were removed and special brackets fitted, together with an electric motor to get Upkeep rotating at 500 revolutions per minute before release. The bomb bay was faired to front and rear of the mine in order to reduce drag and the mid-upper turret was removed. Transformed in this manner, Mk Is

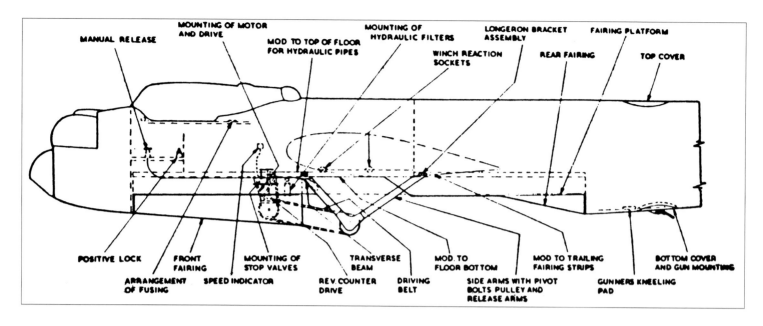

became Type 464 Provisioning Lancasters.

Other changes were made as they were found necessary. The entire raid was to be flown at low level, so bomb aimers assisted navigation using a specially prepared roller map. The nose turret had to be manned continually, which gave a role to the otherwise redundant mid-upper gunner, and stirrups were fitted to prevent him treading on the bomb-aimer's head in moments of excitement.

Achieving the exact height over water at night proved difficult, but was overcome by fitting Aldis lamps in the nose camera port and behind the bomb bay, angled so that the two spots of light touched at exactly 60ft (18m) and offset to starboard where they were easily seen by the navigator, who monitored height on the attack run.

This was the first use of the 'Master Bomber' technique, later to become standard

Standard bombsights could not be used, but the Dann sight, rigged up from a plywood triangle, an eyepiece and a couple of nails, worked well in practice, while pilots had marks on the windshield

Above: Diagram of the modifications required to carry Upkeep. Surviving aircraft were converted back to original standard.

to aid them in lining up on a target.

Close control of the operation was vital, and for this Gibson had all Lancasters fitted with fighter-type VHF radios. This was the first use of the 'Master Bomber' technique, later to become standard throughout Bomber Command.

At low level, the Lancasters might have to fight their way into and out of the target area, while the Mohne Dam at least was known to be defended. Three thousand rounds per gun was carried, giving 157 seconds of firing time. All of it was tracer, to keep the heads of the German gunners down.

■ OPERATION ■ CHASTISE

The attack on the dams was set for 16/17 May, when good weather was forecast, the moon was full, and the water level behind the dams was at its highest. Nineteen Lancasters took off in three waves. The first wave consisted of nine aircraft in three Vics of three, led by

Left: **Dr Barnes Wallis, creator of Upkeep, Tallboy and Grand Slam, pictured with the standard of No. 617 Squadron.**
Below: **Provisioning Lancaster at dispersal, showing the drive belt that rotated Upkeep at 500rpm before release.**

Above: **Gibson leads his crew aboard Lancaster ED932, AJ-G, prior to taking off on the Dams Raid. His aircraft survived the war, only to be scrapped.**
Left: **ED825, AJ-T, was the reserve aircraft for the Dams Raid, and was flown by Flight Lieutenant McCarthy when his own machine went unserviceable.**

Gibson. Its primary targets were the Mohne and Eder Dams. The second wave, of five Lancasters flying individually, took a more northerly route. Their target was the Sorpe Dam, of different construction to the first two and needing a different mode of attack, albeit with the same weapon. The third and final wave of five aircraft also flew individually. Taking off two hours after the others, it was a reserve to be used against the main targets if needed, otherwise to attack secondary dams in the area.

Opposition to the passage of the first wave was moderate, but Bill Astell's Lancaster fell to light flak. The remainder arrived over the Mohne Dam on time. Gibson later wrote, 'In that light it looked squat and heavy and unconquerable; it looked grey and solid in the moonlight, as though it were part of the countryside itself and just as immovable. A structure like a battleship was showering out flak all along its length.'

After circling to make an assessment of the situation, Gibson began his attack run, curving in down-moon, past the hills and low over the water. He had his spotlights on for height and the light flak saw him coming and opened up with everything they had, answered by Deering in the front turret. Bomb Aimer Spam Spafford released the mine and they swept low over the dam. From the air it looked like a perfect drop, but in fact the mine had fallen short. The dam remained standing.

Next came Hopgood. He was not so lucky. Hit by flak, his aircraft was set on fire and crashed, while his mine bounced

Above: **Dams Raid debrief. Standing L to R; Air Chief Marshal Arthur Harris, Air Marshal Cochrane. Seated; intelligence officer, Spafford and Taerum of Gibson's crew.**

clear over the dam. Gibson then made a critical move. Ordering Australian Mick Martin to attack, he flew slightly ahead of him and to one side to draw the enemy fire, and to add his own guns to Martin's in suppressing the defences. Even so, Martin's Lancaster was hit, and its mine was released off course to detonate harmlessly.

Fourth to attack was Dinghy Young, and with both Gibson and Martin distracting the defenders, he made a perfect run unscathed and deposited his Upkeep right against the dam wall. Still the dam stood, but even as Maltby made his run, the parapet crumbled and the dam burst. His mine added to the breach made by Young.

■ ON TO THE EDER ■

Martin and Maltby now set course for home, while Gibson and Young, the latter acting as deputy leader, led the three remaining armed Lancasters to the Eder Dam.

This was undefended, for the Eder was surrounded by steep hills, making an attack very hazardous. Australian David Shannon made three attempts at it without being able to line up correctly. Henry Maudslay then tried twice, with no better luck. Shannon's fourth attempt run was accurate; his mine exploded against the dam, causing a small breach.

Maudslay tried once more, but his mine hit the parapet with him just above it. For years it was assumed that he and his crew died in the explosion, but it appears that, badly damaged, he limped some 130 miles (210km) towards home before falling to flak.

Only one armed Lancaster remained, and on the second attempt its Australian pilot, Les Knight, made a perfect run. His mine punched a hole clean through the giant dam wall, and under the enormous pressure of water, the breach gradually widened.

The second wave of Lancasters had been less fortunate. The first aircraft to be lost during Operation Chastise was that of Byers, a Canadian, which was shot down by flak as it crossed the coast. In almost the same place, New Zealander Les Munro's Lancaster was damaged by flak and forced to abandon the mission, while Geoff Rice, flying as low as possible, hit the sea and lost his mine. Recovering by a hair's breadth, he also was forced to return. Barlow, an

OPERATION CHASTISE, PARTICIPANTS

PILOT	LETTERS	A/C No.
First Wave		
Wg Cdr G.P. Gibson	AJ-G	ED 932/G
Flt Lt J.V. Hopgood	AJ-M	ED 925/G
Flt Lt H.B. Martin	AJ-P	ED 909/G
Sqn Ldr H.M. Young	AJ-A	ED 887/G
Flt Lt D.J.H. Maltby	AJ-J	ED 906/G
Flt Lt D.J. Shannon	AJ-L	ED 929/G
Sqn Ldr H.M. Maudslay	AJ-Z	ED 937/G
Flt Lt W. Astell	AJ-B	ED 864/G
Plt Off L.G. Knight	AJ-N	ED 912/G
Second Wave		
Flt Lt J.C. McCarthy	AJ-T	ED 825/G
Flt Lt R.N.G. Barlow	AJ-E	ED 927/G
Flt Lt J.L. Munro	AJ-W	ED 921/G
Plt Off V.W. Byers	AJ-K	ED 934/G
Plt Off G. Rice	AJ-H	ED 936/G
Third and Reserve Wave		
Plt Off W.H.T. Ottley	AJ-C	ED 910/G
Plt Off L.J. Burpee	AJ-S	ED 865/G
Flt Sgt K.S. Brown	AJ-F	ED 918/G
Flt Sgt W.C. Townsend	AJ-O	ED 886/G
Flt Sgt C.T. Anderson	AJ-Y	ED 914/G

NB: McCarthy was originally scheduled to fly ED 923/G, but this aircraft developed a hydraulic leak.

Australian, was claimed by flak just inside the German border, and of the ill-fated second wave, only the American, Joe McCarthy, survived. After making nine runs against the Sorpe he dropped his mine on the tenth, but without any visible results.

The final wave fared only slightly better. Burpee, a young Canadian from Gibson's previous squadron, went down over Holland, while Ottley lasted only a little longer. Both fell to light flak. Of the other three, all Flight Sergeants, Anderson was the least lucky. Last off, the fates conspired to force him to abandon the mission without attacking.

One Victoria Cross and no fewer than 33 other awards were made

Brown attacked the Sorpe after several attempts, like McCarthy with no visible result, while Townsend, on course for the Mohne Dam, was diverted to the Ennerpe Dam instead. After several brushes with flak, he emerged into an area made unrecognizable by floods from the already breached Mohne and Eder. Finally Townsend arrived at what appeared to be the Ennerpe and dropped his mine, but post-war evidence seems to indicate that he attacked the Bever Dam 5 miles (8km) away.

Although the entire German air defence system was by now alert to the events, losses were lighter on the run home. Apart from Maudslay, the only other loss was Dinghy Young. Hit by flak as he recrossed the coast, he went down into the sea. Others, including McCarthy, Brown and Townsend, had eventful return flights, but recovered safely to Scampton.

Success had been dearly bought. Eight Lancasters failed to return home; of the 56 men on board them, only three survived. Gibson was awarded the Victoria Cross, Britain's highest decoration, and no fewer than 33 other awards were made to participants in the raid.

The Dams Raid has long passed into

Above: The Dortmund-Ems Canal, scene of the Dam Busters' worst disaster, was finally breached in 1944. (Alfred Price)
Below: Under the leadership of Group Captain Leonard Cheshire VC, No. 617 Squadron became the most accurate heavy bomber squadron of the war.

legend. No. 617 Squadron had established itself as an elite unit; truly a special squadron. Over the next two years, it would fully maintain this reputation.

The dams raid over, a new role was sought for No. 617 Squadron. The modified Lancasters were replaced by standard Mk IIIs, and the crews started intensive high- and low-level training. Wing Commander Guy Gibson was replaced by Squadron Leader George Holden. A few unexciting trips to Italy followed; then, on 30 August 1943, the squadron was ordered to Coningsby to concentrate on low-level attacks.

■ DORTMUND-EMS ■

The next target was the heavily defended Dortmund-Ems canal, a strategic artery in the German transport system. Bomber Command had often attempted to breach its banks, but without success. Now 617 was to try, using the new 12,000lb (5,440kg) high-capacity bomb.

Low cloud in the target area caused the first attempt to be recalled, minus Maltby, who went into the sea after hitting someone's slipstream at low level. On the following night they tried again. It was a disaster. Heavy mist in the target area foiled all attempts to bomb accurately, while the defences claimed five

Above: No. 9 Squadron, pictured here with its famous W4964 *Johnny Walker*, was something of an elite outfit. Its total of 106 operations took in the Ruhr, Hamburg, Berlin and Peenemunde and *Tirpitz*.

Lancasters, among them those of Holden and Les Knight. The squadron rapidly gained the reputation of being a suicide outfit. This notwithstanding, six aircraft, in company with six more from No. 619 Squadron, went out again the following night to attack the Antheor Viaduct in southern France at low level. This was another failure and the squadron was withdrawn from operations while changes took place.

One was the introduction of the extremely accurate Stabilizing Automatic Bomb Sight, or SABS, introduced by Arthur 'Talking Bomb' Richardson, whom we last saw over Gdynia with Guy Gibson. No. 617 was now to become a medium- and high-level 'sniper' squadron. The other was the arrival of Wing Commander Leonard Cheshire to command on 11 November.

A more exacting test came on the night of 8/9 February

Cheshire was an enigma. Introspective and unconventional, he was arguably the most inspirational bomber leader of the war. Always leading from the front, he has been described by David Shannon as a pied piper; people followed him gladly. He now set out to make the squadron live, breathe and eat bombing accuracy.

Several missions followed against pinpoint targets, but they were not a great success. Oboe marking was too inaccurate against small targets. Cheshire and Martin worked out between them that only low-level marking in a dive would be good enough, and on 3/4 January 1944, they tried it against a flying bomb site at Freval. By the illumination of flares, they marked from 400ft (120m), and 12,000lb (5,440kg) bombs from the remainder of the formation obliterated the target.

A more exacting test came on 8/9 February, by which time No. 617 had moved to Woodhall Spa. The aero engine works at Limoges were almost totally destroyed after being marked at low level, while damage to French houses close by was minimal. Other raids followed with equal success, the only failure during this time being another attempt against the Antheor Viaduct.

To mark heavily defended targets, a smaller and faster aircraft was needed. The obvious choice was a Mosquito, which Cheshire duly acquired, bringing the low-level marking career of the Lancaster to an end. At the same time, 617 became pathfinders and Main Force leaders to No. 5 Group. But other plans for them were afoot.

■ D-DAY DECEPTION ■

The first of these was Operation Taxable, a deception ploy that was designed to make the Germans think that a vast invasion fleet was moving towards Cap d'Antifer, some 20 miles (30km) north of Le Havre. This was done by 16 Lancasters, flying precise speeds and courses, dropping Window at five-second intervals. Packed to the gills with Window bundles, they maintained the deception for some eight hours until dawn broke to reveal only an empty sea to the expectant Germans.

The second was the introduction of the Tallboy, a new 12,000lb (5,440kg) bomb with exceptionally good ballistic qualities and penetrative power. Like Upkeep, Tallboy was the brainchild of Dr Barnes Wallis, and only the SABS-equipped Dam Busters could bomb accurately enough to make the best use of this new and devastating weapon.

Above: Lurking in the Norwegian fjords, the German battleship *Tirpitz* kept strong British naval forces tied down.

MOHNE DAM

'The gunners had seen us coming. They could see us coming with our spotlights on for over two miles away. Now they opened up and tracers began swirling towards us; some were even bouncing on the smooth surface of the lake. This was a horrible moment: we were being dragged along at four miles a minute, almost against our will, towards the things we were going to destroy. I think at that moment the boys did not want to go. I know I did not want to go.'

WING COMMANDER G. PENROSE GIBSON
VC, DSO, DFC.

One of the few south-to-north rail routes still open in France at this time passed through a tunnel near Saumur, on the Loire. Shortly after midnight on 8/9 June the squadron arrived overhead, and Cheshire placed two red spot fires in the mouth of the tunnel. Nineteen Tallboy-armed Lancasters moved in, plus another six with more conventional loads. The result was a series of enormous craters that tore the line to pieces. One Tallboy, however, had impacted the hillside and bored its way down to explode actually inside the tunnel almost 60ft (18m) below, completely blocking it.

Other precision raids followed; concrete E-boat pens at Le Havre, and V-Weapon sites scattered around the Pas-de-Calais and elsewhere. Then, in July, command of the squadron passed from Cheshire to Wing Commander Willie Tait DSO DFC.

■ 617 VERSUS *TIRPITZ* ■

The German battleship *Tirpitz* had long been a thorn in the side of the Royal Navy. Lying in Alten Fjord in northern Norway, by its very existence it tied down British naval units which would have been better employed elsewhere.

Even from the most northerly of British airfields Alten Fjord was outside Lancaster range. A deal was struck with the Russians, who made Yagodnik, near

EVADING RADAR

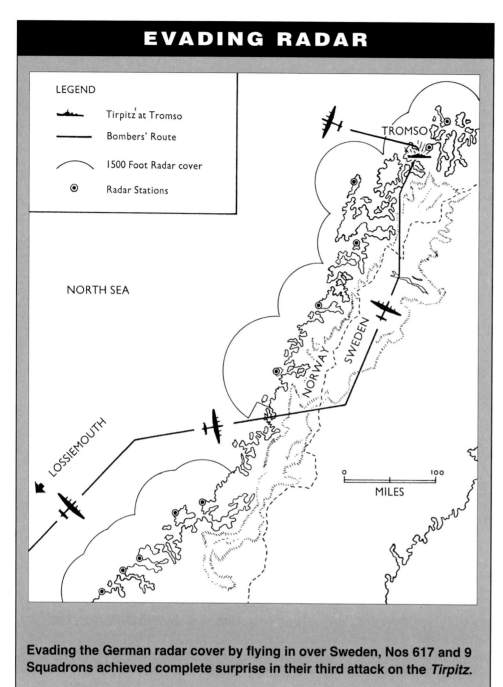

LEGEND

⬛ Tirpitz' at Tromso

─── Bombers' Route

⌒ 1500 Foot Radar cover

◉ Radar Stations

TROMSO

NORTH SEA

NORWAY

SWEDEN

LOSSIEMOUTH

0   100
|————————|
MILES

Evading the German radar cover by flying in over Sweden, Nos 617 and 9 Squadrons achieved complete surprise in their third attack on the *Tirpitz*.

system proved equal to the task, and a smokescreen quickly obscured the battleship. This notwithstanding, a single Tallboy hit was scored, but *Tirpitz* was still afloat. The Kriegsmarine moved her south to Tromsø for use as a floating gun battery; she would never sail again, but this was not known either.

Calculations showed that fitting internal fuel tanks in the fuselage of the Lancasters would just allow the monster to be attacked from Lossiemouth. On 20 October, 40 aircraft of 617 and 9 Squadrons set out on the long haul to Tromsø. A combination of poor weather and enemy fighters made this attack a failure, and few crews even so much as saw the battleship.

They achieved complete surprise and scored multiple hits

The final attack on *Tirpitz* was mounted on 12 November, with 31 Lancasters from both squadrons. Approaching from the neutral (Swedish) side, they achieved complete surprise and scored multiple hits. The *Tirpitz* slowly turned turtle, but the water was too shallow for her to sink completely.

*Below: "Twas a famous victory!" **Tirpitz** lies belly up in Tromsø Fjord, having capsized after multiple bomb hits.*

Arkhangelsk, available as a refuelling stop. For this and subsequent anti-*Tirpitz* operations, No. 617 was joined by No. 9 Squadron, which, although fitted with the Mk XIV vector bombsight, was also something of an elite outfit. Of the 36 Lancasters detailed, 24 carried Tallboys; the others were loaded with 12 Johnny Walker Diving Mines each, an original but ineffective weapon.

The raid nearly ended in disaster as bad weather over Russia forced many Lancasters to land where they could. Six were abandoned in the marshes. When on 15 September the attack was finally mounted, the German early warning

Above: **Lancasters of No. 101 Squadron were identifiable by their Air-borne Cigar masts. This one is unloading incendiaries.**

Tait was now replaced by 617's final wartime commander, Group Captain John Fauquier, a Canadian. Tallboys now rained down on the U-boat pens at Bergen, and the Bielefeld Viaduct. In common with most bridges, the latter proved singularly hard to hit and 54 Tallboys were aimed at it during February 1945 without result. But now Barnes Wallis' 22,000lb (10 tonne) Grand Slam was ready for use.

Only the Lancaster B.I Special could carry Grand Slam. This aircraft had strengthened main gear, nose and dorsal turrets deleted, and the bomb doors removed, plus other minor modifications. The crew was reduced to four.

The first Grand Slam raid took place on 14 March 1945, as related earlier. Five days later, six Grand Slams and 13 Tallboys were hauled to the rail viaduct at Arnsberg, where, incredibly, every bomb fell within a 600ft (180m) radius. To underline the astounding level of bombing accuracy, when the bridge at Nienberg was attacked on 22 March the first four aircraft sent in to bomb scored direct hits from a Grand Slam at one end and a Tallboy at the other and lifted the entire centre span into the air, where it was hit straight in the middle by another Tallboy!

The final mission was against Berchtesgaden, Hitler's redoubt

One more bridge was smashed, then the U-boat pens at Farge were attacked. Two Grand Slams went clean through the 23ft (7m) thick reinforced concrete roof and exploded inside, while shock waves from 10 near misses shattered the foundations. 617 Squadron's final mission was against Berchtesgaden, Hitler's southern redoubt, in the final days of the war.

There was one other special Lancaster squadron, No. 101, whose aircraft, distinguished externally by three large aerials, carried the top secret ABC (Air-borne Cigar) from October 1943. ABC was a jammer working on the German night fighter frequency, and required an additional member of crew to operate it. Lancasters of No. 101 Squadron carried a full load of bombs and, scattered throughout the bomber stream, accompanied Main Force on nearly every raid. In the later stages of the war, with multi-pronged raids the norm, 101 became the biggest Lancaster squadron of all, with a final complement of 42 aircraft.

APPENDIX
THE LANCASTER FAMILY

Although built in large numbers and with many variants, the Lancaster's external appearance changed little during its production, and its overall dimensions not at all.

LANCASTER MK I

Basic data for the Lancaster given in tabular form in Chapter 2 applies to the Mk I Merlin XX or XXII engines. Production continued past the end of the war, and the final Lancaster ever built was a Mk I. Many were later fitted with H2S, others had bulged bomb bay doors to allow them to carry 8,000 and 12,000 lb (3,600 and 5,440kg) HC bombs.

Lancaster Mk I raided Nuremberg and Dresden while with No. 170 Squadron. It is seen here post-war, testing tyres for Dunlop.

LANCASTER MK I VARIANTS

Provisioning Lancasters used on the Dams Raid were converted Mk Is. Mk I Special was designed to carry 22,000lb (10 tonne) Grand Slam with a maximum overload weight of 70,000lb (31,750kg). No nose or mid-upper turret. Only 32 built. Mk I (FE) intended for the Far East against Japan, but the war ended before they could arrive. Internal fuel capacity was increased to 2,554gal (11,600 litres); range with 7,000lb (3,175kg) bombload 3,180 miles (5,100km); FN 82 rear turrets were standard.

A saddle tank was designed to increase fuel capacity for Far East operations, but in high temperatures, take-off became marginal. (Alfred Price)

LANCASTER MK II

Powered by four Bristol Hercules VI or XVI 14 cylinder radial engines each rated at 1,735hp. Rate of climb was about five per cent less than that of the Mks I and III; service ceiling was lower at 22,000ft (6,700m); maximum and cruising speeds were rather lower, mainly due to the extra drag of the radial engines. Range with 12,000lb (5,440kg) was 1,000 miles (1,600km). Maximum overload weight was 63,000lb (28,600kg). A few Mk IIs were fitted with a single .50 calibre machine gun in the ventral position.

LANCASTER MK III

Virtually identical to the Mk I, the main difference being Packard-built Rolls-Royce Merlin 28s or 38s. These were popular with the engine fitters because of the lavish tool kits provided by the Americans. As with the Mk I, bulged bomb bay doors and H2S were often fitted. Many late-build aircraft carried the Rose-Rice tail turret.

The Lancaster Mk III was virtually identical to the Mk I.

Lancaster IIs of No. 408 'Goose' Squadron RCAF based at Linton-on-Ouse in October 1943.

The Lancaster Mk IV and V were so different from the original that they were renamed Lincoln B.1 and B.2.

LANCASTER MK IV AND V

Essentially a stretched Lancaster, longer, with greater wingspan, and better performance, the Mks IV and V differed so much that they were renamed Lincoln I and II.

The engine cowlings to the Merlin 85/87s on the Mk VI differed appreciably from those of earlier models.

LANCASTER MK VI

Nine aircraft only, converted from Mk Is and IIIs, used in the Pathfinder and ECM roles by No. 635 Squadron. Powered by Merlin 85s or 87s rated at 1,635hp enclosed in redesigned cowlings, driving four-bladed propellers. Performance was significantly better than that of the Mk III. No production undertaken.

LANCASTER MK VII

Final production variant. Martin mid-upper and Rose-Rice tail turrets. Entered service April 1945. A few Mk VII (FE)s were built.

The final production variant was the Mk VII, with .50in guns in mid-upper and tail turrets. This is a Mk VII (FE) intended for Tiger Force.

LANCASTER MK X

Canadian-built Mk III.

The Mk X was a Canadian-built Mk III. This machine, seen at the Malton works still minus its mid-upper turret, served with No. 428 'Ghost' Squadron RCAF.

POSTWAR LANCASTER CONVERSIONS

ASR III, Mk III converted for air-sea rescue with an airborne lifeboat fitted to the bomb bay, and ASV radar. Dorsal turret was removed, and guns removed from rear turret. Small windows to both sides of rear fuselage. Re-engined with Merlin 224s.

Conversion to ASR III standard, with paradroppable airborne lifeboat. Most later converted to MR/GR III.

GR III/MR III, Mk III converted for general reconnaissance or maritime reconnaissance similar to ASR III, but no lifeboat.

Experimental ASV radar aerial mounting, intended for use in the anti-shipping role. (Alfred Price)

PR I, Mk I converted for photo reconnaissance/survey work. All gun turrets were removed and faired over.

Into the jet age. This Mk II spent its life at the RAE Farnborough as a test bed for early jet engines.

many of her Lancasters home, while the French Aeronavale acquired a considerable number for maritime reconnaissance and search and rescue, a few of which remained in service up until the early Sixties. Other users were Argentina and Egypt.

In Britain the writing was on the wall. The Lincoln largely replaced the Lancaster in the few remaining front line bomber squadrons, and the last RAF Lancaster, an MR III, was retired in February 1954.

The end of the war saw dozens of Bomber Command Lancaster squadrons disbanded and hundreds of aircraft scrapped, but this did not prevent another 21 squadrons from other RAF commands operating the type. Other countries used them too; Canada took

Jet Age II; a Canadian Mk X-DC drone carrier, with Ryan Firebees beneath the wingtips.

This propeller from a shot-down Lancaster of No. 12 Squadron makes a fitting memorial at Dronten in Holland.

BIBLIOGRAPHY

AVRO LANCASTER
Francis K. Mason, Aston Publications, 1989.

BATTLE OVER THE REICH
Alfred Price, Ian Allan, 1973.

BRITISH AIRCRAFT ARMAMENT, Vols 1 and 2
R.Wallace Clarke, Patrick Stephens Ltd, 1993/94.

DAM BUSTERS
Paul Brickhill, Pan, 1954.

ENEMY COAST AHEAD
Guy Gibson VC, Pan, 1955.

FAMOUS BOMBERS OF THE SECOND WORLD WAR
William Green, MacDonald & Janes, 1975.

INSTRUMENTS OF DARKNESS
Alfred Price, MacDonald & Janes, 1977.

NUREMBERG RAID
Martin Middlebrook, Fontana, 1975.

PATHFINDER
D.C.T. Bennett, Frederick Muller, 1958.

617 SQUADRON, THE DAM BUSTERS AT WAR
Tom Bennett, Patrick Stephens Ltd, 1985.

Magazines.
Various issues of *Air International, Flypast* and *RAF Flying Review*.

THE MESSERSCHMITT
109 AND 262

PROLOGUE

Canterbury, Kent, 13.05 hours, 18 August 1940

Oberleutnant Gerhard Schoepfel was flying his favourite type of mission. He had eight aerial victories to his credit already, and was leading a free hunting patrol 4 miles (6.5km) high over southern England. It was the sort of mission that did not come his way often enough. With some 25 Me 109Es of IIIrd Gruppe of Fighter Geschwader 26 arrayed in battle formation behind and above him, he felt invincible. His task was to clear a path in front of raiding formations making for the important Fighter Command airfields at Kenley and Biggin Hill. The nearest bombers were some 20 miles (32km) behind him and they were not his concern. Today others had the frustrating task of flying close escort for the slow-flying Dorniers and Heinkels to ward off attacks by the Spitfires and

Above: Me 109Es of Gerhard Schoepfel's unit, IIIrd Gruppe of Fighter Geschwader 26, pictured in their camouflaged dispersal points at Caffiers near Calais during the Battle of Britain.

Hurricanes. Schoepfel's role was that of a hunter, pure and simple. His orders were to engage and destroy any British fighters he found, and he had complete tactical freedom to do so in any way he chose. Over enemy territory the German pilot's practised eyes quartered the sky continually and systematically, seeking out his quarry.

■ COVER THE LEADER ■

'Suddenly I noticed a Staffel of Hurricanes underneath me. They were using the English tactics of the period, flying in close formation of threes, climbing in a wide

Above: Oberleutnant Gerhard Schoepfel. At the end of the war he was credited with forty aerial victories. (Schoepfel)

spiral. About 1,000 m above them I turned with them and managed to get behind the two covering Hurricanes, which were weaving continually.'

In deciding his tactics, Schoepfel knew it was important to retain the element of surprise for as long as possible. Several aircraft diving to attack would almost certainly be spotted. But a single aircraft might sneak unobserved into a firing position behind the enemy fighters. The German ace ordered his pilots to remain at high altitude and cover him, while he delivered a lone attack on the formation from out of the sun. The Hurricanes, belonging to No. 501 Squadron, were climbing into position to engage the bomber formations nearing the coast. Picking up speed rapidly in the dive, Schoepfel remained unseen as he swung behind one of the two 'weaver' Hurricanes covering the rear of the formation. He placed his sighting graticule over the fighter, loosed off an accurate burst and saw it go down in flames. Then he pulled to one side and repeated the process with

Right: The tail of Gerhard Schoepfel's aircraft photographed on the afternoon of 18 August 1940, including the victory bars for the four Hurricanes of No. 501 Squadron

the second 'weaver'. Still the formation continued on its ponderous way. The German pilot moved in behind the main formation, fired again and a third Hurricane fell out of the sky.

'The Englishmen continued on their way having noticed nothing. So I pulled behind a fourth machine and took care of him also. But this time I went in too close. When I pressed the firing button, the Englishman was such a short distance in front of my nose that pieces of wreckage struck my propeller. Oil streaming back from the fourth plane spattered over my windscreen and the right side of the cabin, so that I could see nothing. I had to break off the action.'

Finally aware of their peril, the surviving Hurricanes broke formation and turned to engage the Messerschmitts diving to support their leader. There followed an inconclusive dogfight without loss to either side. Within a space of four minutes Gerhard Schoepfel, single handed, had destroyed a third of a squadron of Hurricanes. One pilot was killed, the other three jumped from their stricken aircraft and landed safely by parachute. In the summer of 1940 both the Luftwaffe and the Me 109 were at the peak of their effectiveness relative to the air forces and fighter types opposing them. Only the Spitfire was as fast as the German fighter, while all the other fighters it encountered in action were a good deal slower. It was a clear indication of Schoepfel's unbounded confidence in his aircraft and his ability that, alone and without hesitation, he took on an entire enemy squadron and emerged victorious from the encounter. Small wonder the very name of Messerschmitt was one that struck fear in Germany's enemies throughout the whole of the Second World War.

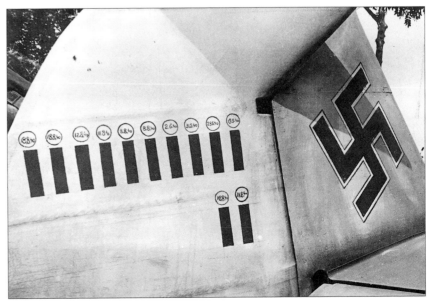

MESSERSCHMITT ME 109G-14

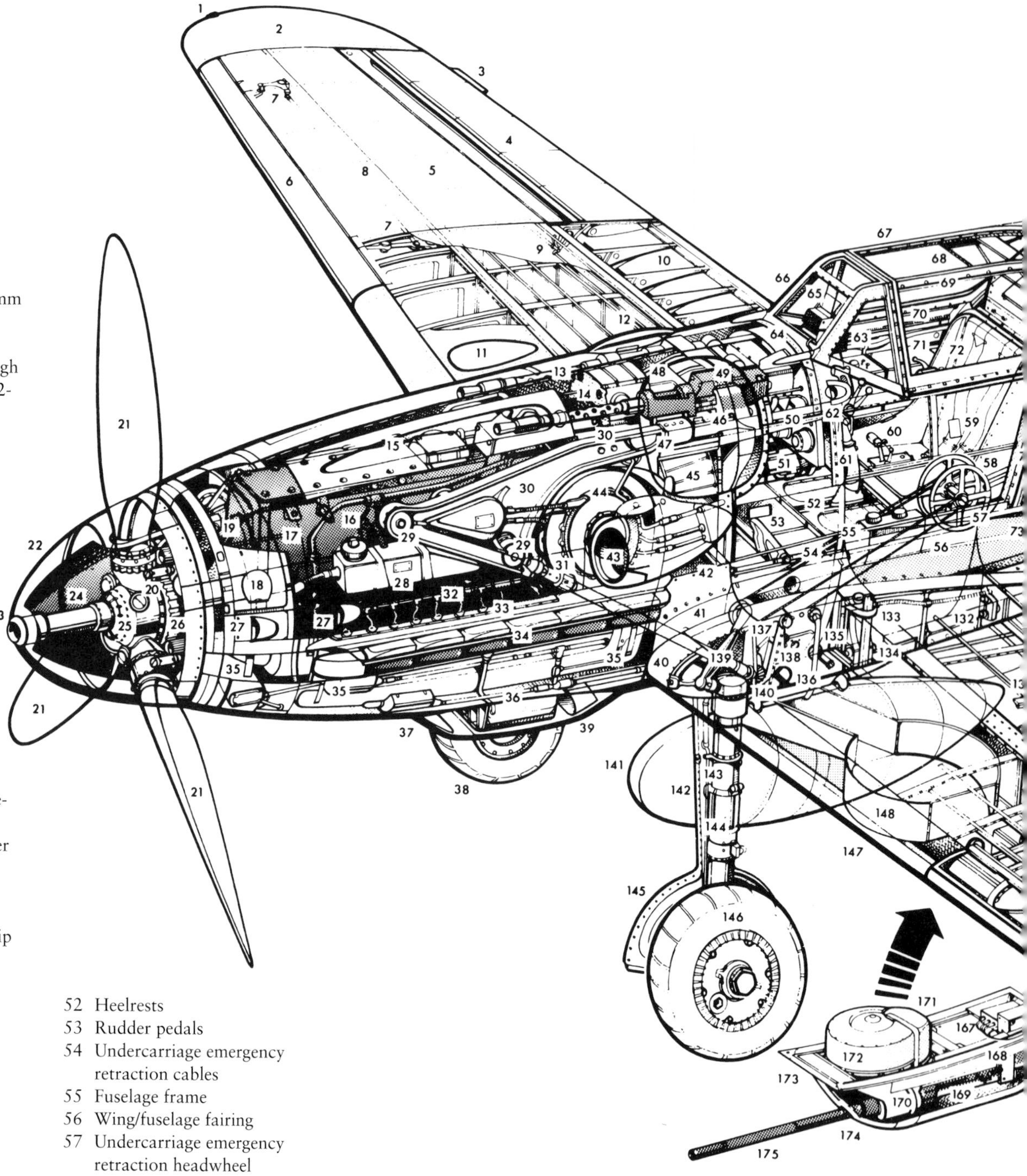

1 Starboard navigation light
2 Starboard wingtip
3 Fixed trim tab
4 Starboard Frise-type aileron
5 Flush-riveted stressed wing-skinning
6 Handley Page leading-edge automatic slot
7 Slot control linkage
8 Slot equalizer rod
9 Aileron control linkage
10 Fabric-covered flap section
11 Wheel fairing
12 Port fuselage machine-gun ammunition-feed fairing
13 Port Rheinmetall-Borsig 13mm MG 131 machine-gun
14 Engine accessories
15 Starboard machine-gun trough
16 Daimler Benz DB 605AM 12-cylinder inverted-vee liquid-cooled engine
17 Detachable cowling panel
18 Oil filter access
19 Oil tank
20 Propeller pitch-change mechanism
21 VDM electrically-operated constant-speed propeller
22 Spinner
23 Engine-mounted cannon muzzle
24 Blast tube
25 Propeller hub
26 Spinner back plate
27 Auxiliary cooling intakes
28 Cooling header tank
29 Anti-vibration rubber engine-mounting pads
30 Elektron forged engine bearer
31 Engine bearer support strut attachment
32 Plug leads
33 Exhaust manifold fairing strip
34 Ejector exhausts
35 Cowling fasteners
36 Oil cooler
37 Oil cooler intake
38 Starboard mainwheel
39 Oil cooler outlet flap
40 Wing root fillet
41 Wing/fuselage fairing
42 Firewall/bulkhead
43 Supercharger air intake
44 Supercharger assembly
45 20mm cannon magazine drum
46 13mm machine-gun ammunition feed
47 Engine bearer upper attachment
48 Ammunition feed fairing
49 13mm Rheinmetall-Borsig MG 131 machine-gun breeches
50 Instrument panel
51 20mm Mauser MG 151/20 cannon breech

52 Heelrests
53 Rudder pedals
54 Undercarriage emergency retraction cables
55 Fuselage frame
56 Wing/fuselage fairing
57 Undercarriage emergency retraction headwheel (outboard)
58 Tail trim handwheel (inboard)
59 Seat harness
60 Throttle lever
61 Control column
62 Cockpit ventilation inlet
63 Revi 16B reflector gunsight (folding)
64 Armoured windshield frame
65 Anti-glare gunsight screen
66 90 mm armourglass windscreen

67 Galland-type clear-vision hinged canopy
68 Framed armourglass head/back panel
69 Canopy contoured frame
70 Canopy hinges (starboard)
71 Canopy release catch
72 Pilot's bucket-type seat (8 mm back armour)

73 Underfloor contoured fuel tank (88 Imp gal/400 litres of 87 octane B4)
74 Fuselage frame
75 Circular access panel
76 Tail trimming cable conduit
77 Wireless leads
78 MW50 (methanel/water) tank (25 Imp gal/114 litres

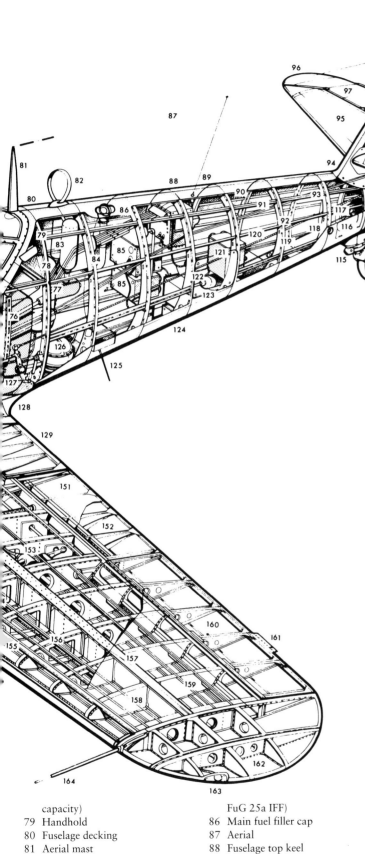

125 Ventral IFF aerial
126 Master compass
127 Elevator control linkage
128 Wing root fillet
129 Camber-changing flap
130 Ducted coolant radiator
131 Wing stringers
132 Wing rear pick-up point
133 Spar/fuselage upper pin joint (horizontal)
134 Spar/fuselage lower pin joint (vertical)
135 Flaps equalizer rod
136 Rüstsatz R3 auxiliary fuel tank ventral rack
137 Undercarriage electrical interlock
138 Wing horizontal pin forward pick-up
139 Undercarriage retraction jack mechanism
140 Undercarriage pivot-bevel
141 Auxiliary fuel tank (Rüstsatz R3) of 66 Imp gal (3000 litre) capacity
142 Mainwheel leg fairing
143 Mainwheel oleo leg
144 Brake lines
145 Mainwheel fairing
146 Port mainwheel
147 Leading-edge skin
148 Port mainwheel well
149 Wing spar
150 Flap actuating linkage
151 Fabric-covered control surfaces
152 Slotted flap structure
153 Leading-edge slot actuating mechanism
154 Slot equalizer rod
155 Handley Page automatic leading-edge slot
156 Wing stringers
157 Spar flange decrease
158 Wing ribs
159 Flush-riveted stressed wing-skinning
160 Metal-framed Frise-type aileron
161 Fixed trim tab
162 Wingtip construction
163 Port navigation light
164 Angled pitot head
165 Rüstsatz R6 optional underwing cannon gondola
166 14-point plug connection
167 Electrical junction box
168 Cannon rear mounting bracket
169 20mm Mauser MG 151 20mm cannon
170 Cannon front mounting bracket
171 Ammunition feed chute
172 Ammunition magazine drum
173 Underwing panel
174 Gondola fairing
175 Cannon barrel

construction)
93 Tail trimming cables
94 Tailfin root fairing
95 Starboard fixed tailplane
96 Elevator balance
97 Starboard elevator
98 Geared elevator tab
99 All-wooden tailfin construction
100 Aerial attachment
101 Rudder upper hinge bracket
102 Rudder post
103 Fabric-covered wooden rudder structure
104 Geared rudder tab
105 Rear navigation light
106 Port elevator
107 Geared elevator tab
108 Tailplane structure
109 Rudder actuating linkage
110 Elevator control horn
111 Elevator connecting rod
112 Elevator control quadrant
113 Tailwheel leg cuff
114 Castoring non-retractable tailwheel
115 Lengthened tailwheel/leg
116 Access panel
117 Tailwheel shock-strut
118 Lifting point
119 Rudder cable
120 Elevator cables
121 First-aid pack
122 Air bottles
123 Fuselage access panel
124 Bottom keel (connector stringer)

capacity)
79 Handhold
80 Fuselage decking
81 Aerial mast
82 D/F loop
83 Oxygen cylinders (three)
84 Filler pipe
85 Wireless equipment packs (FuG 16ZY communications and

FuG 25a IFF)
86 Main fuel filler cap
87 Aerial
88 Fuselage top keel (connector stringer)
89 Aerial lead-in
90 Fuselage skin plating sections
91 U-stringers
92 Fuselage frames (monocoque

MESSERSCHMITT Me 262A-1A

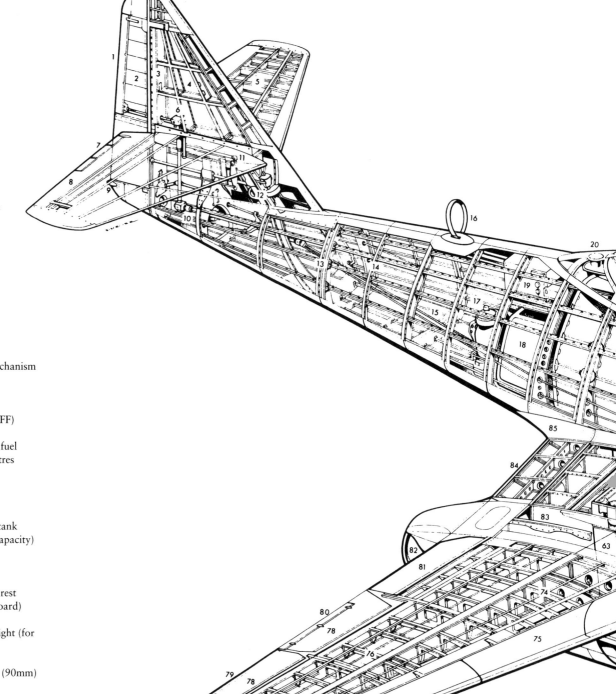

1 Flettner-type geared trim tab
2 Mass-balanced rudder
3 Rudder post
4 Tail fin structure
5 Tailplane structure
6 Rudder tab mechanism
7 Flettner-type servo tab
8 Starboard elevator
9 Rear navigation light
10 Rudder linkage
11 Elevator linkage
12 Tailplane adjustment mechanism
13 Fuselage break point
14 Fuselage construction
15 Control runs
16 FuG 25a loop antenna (IFF)
17 Automatic compass
18 Aft auxiliary self-sealing fuel tank (132 Imp gal/600 litres capacity)
19 FuG 16zy R/T
20 Fuel filler cap
21 Aft cockpit glazing
22 Armoured aft main fuel tank (198 Imp gal/900 litres capacity)
23 Inner cockpit shell
24 Pilot's seat
25 Canopy jettison lever
26 Armoured (15mm) head rest
27 Canopy (hinged to starboard)
28 Canopy lock
29 Bar-mounted Revi 16B sight (for both cannon and R4M missiles)
30 Armourglass windscreen (90mm)
31 Instrument panel
32 Rudder pedal
33 Armoured forward main fuel tank (198 Imp gal/900 litres capacity)
34 Fuel filler cap
35 Underwing wooden rack for 12 R4M 55mm rockets
36 Port outer flap section
37 Frise-type aileron
38 Aileron control linkage
39 Port navigation light
40 Pitot head
41 Automatic leading-edge slats

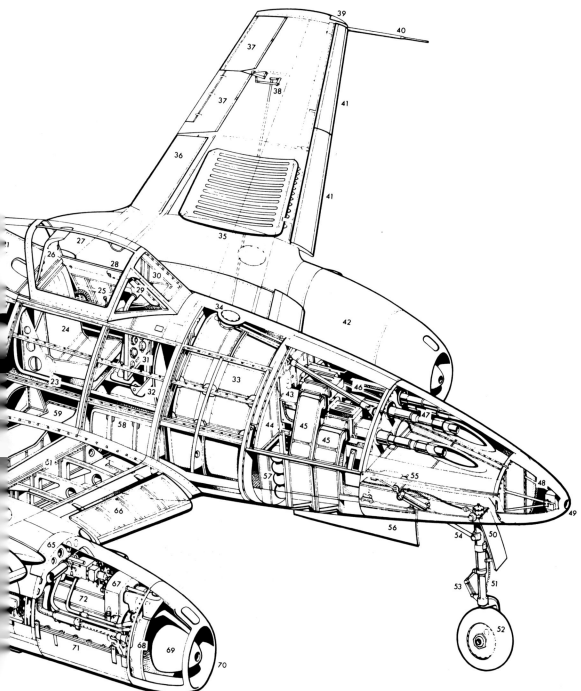

42 Port engine cowling
43 Electrical firing mechanism
44 Firewall
45 Spent cartridge ejector chutes
46 Four 30mm Rheinmetall-Borsig
   Mk 108 cannon (100rpg belt-fed
   ammunition for upper pair and
   80rpg for lower pair)
47 Cannon muzzles
48 Combat camera
49 Camera aperture
50 Nosewheel fairing
51 Nosewheel leg
52 Nosewheel
53 Torque scissors
54 Retraction jack
55 Hydraulic lines
56 Main nosewheel door (starboard)
57 Compressed air bottles
58 Forward auxiliary fuel tank
   (37 Imp gal/170 litres capacity)
59 Mainwheel well
60 Torque box
61 Main spar
62 Mainwheel leg pivot point
63 Mainwheel door
64 Mainwheel retraction rod
65 Engine support arch
66 Leading-edge slat structure
67 Auxiliaries gearbox
68 Annular oil tank
69 Riedel starter motor housing
70 Engine air intake
71 Hinged cowling section
72 Junkers Jumo 004B-2
   axial-flow turbojet
73 Starboard mainwheel
74 Wing structure
75 Automatic leading-edge slats
76 Mainspar
77 Starboard navigation light
78 Frise-type ailerons
79 Trim tab
80 Flettner-type geared tab
81 Starboard outer flap section
82 Engine exhaust orifice
83 Engine support bearer
84 Starboard inner flap structure
85 Faired wing root

The story of the Messerschmitt 109 began in 1934, more than a year before the German government revealed the existence of the clandestine air force that it had built up. Early that year the Air Ministry issued a requirement for an advanced monoplane fighter to replace the Heinkel 51 and Arado 68 biplanes then about to enter service, and invited aircraft companies to submit designs.

The early 1930s saw rapid advances in aviation technology, which revealed themselves most clearly in the design of fighter planes. The new generation of fighters was quite different in shape and in performance from those that had gone before. Out went the fabric-covered strut-braced biplane with its open cockpit and fixed undercarriage. In its place came the sleek low-wing monoplane with an all-metal structure, enclosed cockpit and a retractable undercarriage. These new fighters were much faster than their predecessors in the climb, in the dive and in level flight. Also, in their developed versions, they were more heavily armed.

Chief designer Willi Messerschmitt had no previous experience of designing fighter aircraft

At that time the Bavarian Aircraft Company (Bayerische Flugzeugwerke) at Augsburg was a little-known aircraft firm with about five hundred employees. It had never built a military aircraft of its own design, though it was turning out small batches of planes built under licence for the Luftwaffe. Willi Messerschmitt, the company's brilliant young chief designer, had no previous experience of designing a fighter. He did have great flair and originality, however, and he was very ambitious. When he saw the Luftwaffe requirement he jumped at the chance to turn his hand to a state-of-the-art fighter plane.

Messerschmitt's new fighter employed almost every innovation of the period. It was a clean-lined all-metal low-wing monoplane with a retractable undercarriage and an enclosed cockpit. To keep the landing speed to reasonable limits, the small wing was fitted with retractable flaps and leading-edge slots. Messerschmitt designed the fighter around the new 610hp Junkers Jumo 210 engine. Work on the airframe advanced more rapidly than that on the power plant, however, and it was clear that the latter would not be ready in time. Messerschmitt had to look elsewhere for an engine to get his prototype into the air. Ironically, in view of later events, his choice of engine was a 695hp Rolls Royce Kestrel imported from Great Britain.

Opposite: **Ground crewmen pictured reloading the wing and engine-mounted 7.9 mm machine guns of a 'Caesar' of IIIrd Gruppe of Fighter Geschwader 51. Scrupulous cleanliness was necessary for this operation, since any grit or dirt on the rounds was liable to cause a stoppage during firing.** *Below:* **The first prototype Me 109 ground-running its Rolls Royce Kestrel engine, at about the time of its maiden flight in September 1935. (via Ethell)**

MESSERSCHMITT 109 B-1

Type Single-seat interceptor fighter.
Armament Two Rheinmetall-Borsig 7.9mm machine guns mounted on top of the engine and synchronized to fire through the airscrew (500 rounds per gun).
Power Plant One Junkers Jumo 210 Da inverted V-12 liquid cooled engine developing 635 horse power for take off.
Dimensions Span 32ft 41/2 in (9.87m); length 28ft (8.55m).
Weight Normal operational take off, 4,741lb (2150kg).
Performance Maximum speed 289mph at 13,100ft (465km/hr at 4,000m). Service ceiling 26,900ft (8,200m).

MESSERSCHMITT 109 C-1

Type Single-seat interceptor fighter.
Armament Four Rheinmetall-Borsig MG 17 7.9 mm machine guns. Two synchronized to fire through the airscrew (500 rounds per gun), two mounted in wings (420rpg).
Power Plant Junkers Jumo 210 Ga inverted V-12 liquid cooled engine developing 700 hp for take off. This and subsequent versions were fitted with direct fuel injection engines.
Dimensions Span 32ft 4in (9.87m); length 28ft (8.55m)
Weight Normal operational take off 5060lb (2,29kg).
Performance Maximum speed 292mph (470km/hr) at 14,770ft (4,500m). Service ceiling 27,570ft (8,400m).

Initially called the Bayerische Flugzeugwerke (Bf) 109, the new fighter made its maiden flight in September 1935. That was one month before the prototype Hurricane and six months before the prototype Spitfire, its two main rivals during the early part of the forthcoming conflict.

The Arado, Heinkel and Focke Wulf companies also built prototypes of monoplane fighters for the Luftwaffe design competition. Messerschmitt's more-ambitious design quickly demonstrated that it had a clear edge over the other three, however. Its maximum speed of 290mph (467km/hr) was 17mph (27km/hr) faster than that of its nearest rival and its handling characteristics were also superior.

Below: **Line up of early production Me 109 'Bertas', awaiting delivery at the Bayerische Flugzeugwerke factory at Augsburg early in 1937. At this time the aircraft was the most potent fighter in service anywhere in the world. (via Schliephake)**

Above: **An Me 109 'Caesar' of Fighter Gruppe 152.**

■ INTO PRODUCTION ■

Following the service trials, the Luftwaffe placed an order for ten more Me 109 prototypes. A second prototype, powered by the Jumo 210A engine, joined the test programme in January 1936. In the autumn of 1936 the Luftwaffe announced that the Me 109 was to be its standard single-engined fighter type. The Me 109B, the 'Berta', was the initial production variant. It was powered by the Jumo 210 engine and carried an armament of three (later four) 7.9 mm machine guns.

In February 1937 production Me 109Bs began emerging from the Augsburg factory. The first Luftwaffe unit to receive the new fighter was IInd

Gruppe of Fighter Geschwader 132 based at Jueterbog near Berlin.

Early in 1938 the next major version of the Me 109 appeared, the Me 109C 'Caesar'. This featured several detailed improvements and its Jumo 210 engine was fitted with fuel injection. The initial version carried four machine guns, two on top of the engine and one in each wing close to the root. The 'Caesar' was built in moderately large numbers and the variant equipped several fighter units.

MESSERSCHMITT 109 D-1

Type Single-seat interceptor fighter.
Armament Two Rheinmetall-Borsig MG 17 7.9 mm machine guns mounted on top of the engine synchronized to fire through the airscrew (500 rounds per gun). One Oerlikon MG FF 20mm cannon mounted under the engine and firing through the spinner (60 rounds).
Power Plant One Daimler Benz DB 600Aa inverted V-12 liquid cooled engine developing 986hp for take off.
Dimensions Span 32ft 4in (9.87m); length 28ft 2in (8.60m).
Weight Normal operational take off, 5,336lb (2,420kg).
Performance Maximum speed 356mph (574km/hr) at 11,490ft (3,500m). Service ceiling 32,800ft (10,000m).

Left: Scramble take off by Me 109Cs of Fighter Geschwader 51.
Below: Testing the guns of an Me 109 at the firing butts.

Following hard on the heels of the 'Caesar' came the Me 109D 'Dora'. This was fitted with the new Daimler Benz 600 engine which developed 960 horse power. The more powerful engine gave

The fine performance of the 'Dora' was undermined by difficulties with the DB 600 engine

greatly enhanced performance and the 'Dora' could achieve a maximum speed of 356mph at 11,400feet (574km/hr at 3,500m). This variant also had greater fire power than its predecessors, with a 20 mm cannon firing through the propeller spinner and two machine guns mounted on top of the engine cowling. The DB 600 engine suffered serious teething troubles, however, and despite its fine performance the 'Dora' was not

MESSERSCHMITT 109 E-1

Type Single-seat general purpose fighter.

Armament Four Rheinmetall-Borsig MG 17 7.9mm machine guns in fuselage and wings. Or two MG17 machine guns and two MG FF cannon. Some aircraft were modified to carry a rack for single 110lb (45kg) bomb.

Power Plant One Daimler Benz DB 601A inverted V-12 liquid cooled engine developing 1,175hp for take off.

Dimensions Span 32ft 4in (9.87m); length 28ft 4in (8.64m).

Weight Normal operational take off, 5,535lb (2,510kg).

Performance Maximum speed 356mph at 13,130ft (573km/hr at 4,000m). Service ceiling 34,450ft (10,500m).

Above: The Heinkel 51 biplane was the main fighter type serving with the Condor Legion during the early stages of the Civil War in Spain. It was outclassed by the Soviet-built fighter types that it came up against.

popular with pilots. Fewer than two hundred were built before this variant passed out of production.

In September 1938 the so-called Munich Crisis broke, as a result of Adolf Hitler's claim that the Sudetenland area of Czechoslovakia should be incorporated into Germany. For a time it seemed that Great Britain might go to war to help the Czechs retain this territory, but in the end the British prime minister, Neville Chamberlain, acceded to Hitler's demand. Several commentators have said that the move was necessary to allow Britain time to re-arm. They neglect the fact that the Luftwaffe, too, was in no state to engage in a major conflict. Its fighter force possessed 583 Me 109s of all versions, of which 510 were serviceable. Most of these aircraft were the 'Bertas', with smaller numbers of the

later 'Caesar' and 'Dora' variants. Eight fighter Gruppen had equipped, or were in the process of re-equipping, with the Me 109. The rest operated outdated biplane fighter types. The Luftwaffe bomber force was no better placed to fight a major war. At the time many people were frightened by the barrage of misleading German propaganda regarding the size and invincibility of the Luftwaffe. Even now, more than half a century later, these canards are still repeated.

The next version of the Me 109, the first built in really large numbers, was the 'Emil' powered by the new Daimler Benz 601 engine. Based on the DB 600 engine that powered the 'Dora', the new engine was fitted with fuel injection and a more effective supercharger. And, most important of all, it was far more reliable than the earlier engine. The initial batches of Me 109Es reached the Luftwaffe early in 1939. The main production version was armed with two 7.9 mm machine guns in the fuselage and two 20 mm cannon in the wings.

■ MESSERSCHMITT AG ■

With the success of the new fighter assured, the management of the Bayerische Flugzeugwerke decided to capitalize on the international reputation won by its now-famous chief designer, and so they appointed Willi Messerschmitt to the posts of Chairman and Managing Director, and changed the company's name to Messerschmitt AG. The firm's two factories were turning out the fighter in large numbers, yet there were insufficient to meet the needs of the expanding Luftwaffe. Four other aircraft companies, Arado, Erla, Fieseler and Focke Wulf, were producing the Me 109E under licence. Production of the fighter reached 130 per month and it quickly replaced most of the earlier versions in front line units.

■ IN ACTION IN SPAIN ■

In the summer of 1936 civil war broke out in Spain. General Franco, the Nationalist leader, appealed to Adolf Hitler for help in his revolt against the left-wing government. This was soon forthcoming and the Luftwaffe dispatched a force, the Condor Legion, to fight alongside the Nationalists. Meanwhile the Soviet Union had been supplying aircraft to Spain's Republican government. When the Luftwaffe began operations over Spain, its pilots found that the Soviet-built Polikarpov I-16 monoplane had a clear edge in performance over their Heinkel 51 biplanes.

The new 109s of the Condor Legion were operated from a primitive airfield near Seville

Generalmajor Hugo Sperrle, the commander of the Condor Legion, impressed on his superiors the need to get Me 109s into the theatre as rapidly as possible. To test the new fighter under combat conditions, late in 1936 the Luftwaffe shipped three Me 109 prototypes to Spain. These operated from a primitive airfield near Seville and there were severe problems. Each of the handmade prototypes had components unique to itself, which made it difficult to keep

Below: **The Soviet Polikarpov I-16 was the best fighter operated by the Nationalist Air Force in Spain. It was clearly superior to the He 51, and came as a shock to the German pilots when they first met it over Spain.**

them serviceable. After a few weeks, and without seeing action, the fighters returned to Germany.

■ THE 109 TRIUMPHS ■

The trial highlighted the need for better ground support for the Me 109, if it was to perform effectively in action. Several Luftwaffe pilots flew the prototypes in Spain, and they had no doubt that the Me 109 was superior to any of the Soviet-built fighters opposing them.

As noted in the previous chapter, production Me 109 'Bertas' began to emerge from the Augsburg factory in February 1937. Sixteen of these machines were loaded, in crates, on a freighter which delivered them to the Condor Legion.

The first unit in Spain to re-equip with the Me 109B was the 2nd Staffel of Fighter Gruppe 88. When it became operational in April 1937 there was a lull in the ground fighting and initially the new fighter saw little action. Then, in July, the Republican forces launched a powerful offensive near Madrid. The Me 109 Staffel joined the battle, escorting Junkers 52 bombers delivering attacks on Republican troop positions.

As predicted, the Me 109 proved greatly superior to the Soviet-built I-16. It was faster in level flight, had a higher operational ceiling and was much faster in the dive. For its part the I-16 was more manoeuvrable, especially at altitudes below 10,000 feet (3,048m). Republican fighter pilots tried to lure

the Messerschmitts into turning fights below 10,000 feet, but with little success. German fighter pilots soon learned that their machine's better performance at altitude gave them the advantage of being able to accept or refuse combat, as they chose.

The new German fighter carried radios which might have been very useful during air-to-air actions. The sets gave such poor reception, however, that many pilots flew with them turned off.

The Me 109s would deliver a series of high-speed diving attacks to break up the enemy

Normally the Me 109s would patrol at altitudes between 16,000 feet (4,877m) and 20,000 feet (6,096m), which gave them a substantial height advantage over their opponents. On sighting enemy aircraft, the German formation leader would usually move his force into an attacking position above the prey. The Messerschmitts then delivered a series of high-speed diving attacks, pulling up and zooming back to altitude after each. They repeated the process until the enemy formation broke up, or

Above: **The arrival of the Me 109B in Spain in the spring of 1937 gave German pilots a machine in which they could engage the I-16 with confidence. This example belonged to 2nd Staffel of Fighter Gruppe 88 and wears the markings carried by aircraft of the Condor Legion.**

the German fighters ran low on fuel or ammunition. Provided the Me 109s maintained their high speed and did not get drawn into turning fights, they were almost unbeatable.

Some of the fiercest aerial fighting over Spain took place early in 1938, during the Republican offensive near Teruél. By then both Staffeln of Fighter Gruppe 88 had re-equipped with the Me 109. On 7 February Hauptmann Gotthardt Handrick, the Gruppe commander, was leading his unit during a bomber escort mission. Over the battle area he sighted a formation of twenty-two Soviet-built Tupolev SB-2 bombers moving in to attack a Nationalist troop position. Seeing no Republican fighters in the area, he led a concerted attack on the

enemy bombers. Several of the latter were shot down, and when I-16s finally arrived on the scene they too suffered losses. The Me 109s destroyed ten enemy bombers and two fighters, without loss to themselves.

Elsewhere that day another Me 109 pilot fought a noteworthy action.

Leutnant Wilhelm Balthasar shot down three bombers and a fighter within six minutes

---

Leutnant Wilhelm Balthasar delivered a succession of diving attacks on an escorted bomber formation and shot down three bombers and a fighter, all within a space of six minutes.

The Me 109 achieved striking success over Spain, although the number of these fighters sent to fight in the conflict was never large. Up to December 1938 only fifty-five 'Bertas', 'Caesars' and 'Doras'

had reached Spain and only thirty-seven were currently on the strength of Fighter Gruppe 88. However, such was the 109's superiority that these few aircraft had been sufficient to establish air supremacy over the entire country.

In March 1939, after suffering a succession of major reverses, the Republicans were forced to surrender. Following the cessation of hostilities the Condor Legion returned home to Germany, leaving behind some fifty Me 109s for incorporation in General Franco's Air Force.

■ POISED FOR POLAND ■

By the summer of 1939 Adolf Hitler judged that he had gained as much as he could in Europe by bluff alone. To advance his aims further, he would have to demonstrate Germany's military might and commit its armed forces. Now his forces were poised to launch an all-out onslaught against Poland. In the next chapter we shall observe how the Me 109 units fared during the early months of the Second World War.

On 1 September 1939 German ground forces invaded Poland, with powerful support from the Luftwaffe. At that time the Me 109 force comprised twenty-four Gruppen and five independent Staffeln, with a total of nearly 1,100 fighters. More than two-thirds of the units flew the 'Emil', the rest operated the older 'Berta', 'Caesar' and 'Dora' versions.

Only about one-fifth of the Me 109 force, five of the twenty-four Gruppen operating the type, was earmarked to take part in the campaign in Poland. The other units remained at their airfields in western Germany, ready to meet a possible onslaught from the Royal Air Force and the French Air Force. There was no large-scale Allied reaction, however, and the German fighters saw little action. The relatively small proportion of Me 109s assigned to support the attack on Poland proved quite sufficient to counter the meagre forces at the disposal of the Polish Air Force. The latter possessed only about three hundred combat planes, almost all of them outdated types. The PZL 11, the most modern Polish fighter type then in service, had a maximum speed of only 242 mph (389 km/hr). It was no match even for the early versions of the Me 109. After a few days the Polish Air Force was out of the fight and unable to give any assistance to its hard-pressed army. Two weeks into the campaign the Luftwaffe felt sufficiently confident to move two Me 109 Gruppen from Poland to bolster the air defences in the west. On 28 September the Polish forces laid down their arms and the campaign came to an end.

In the west the aerial activity was on a small scale, as each side probed the other's strengths and weaknesses. On 30 September the Royal Air Force learned a

Left: **Instrument panel of an Me 109 'Emil'. Although the cockpit was cramped and the view of the outside restricted, pilots came to love the machine as a highly capable air superiority fighter.**

Me 109 FRONT-LINE UNITS

2 SEPTEMBER 1939 – Units marked with asterisk took part in the campaign in Poland.

Unit	Total aircraft	Aircraft serviceable
Tactical Development Division		
Tactical Development (Lehr) Geschwader 2		
Staff Flight	3	3 Me 109E*
I.Gruppe	36	34 Me 109E*
10.Staffel	12	9 Me 109E
Air Fleet 1 (NE Germany)		
Fighter Geschwader 1		
I. Gruppe	54	54 Me 109E*
Fighter Geschwader 2		
II. Gruppe	42	39 Me 109E
10 Staffel	9	9 Me 109C, night-fighting unit
Fighter Geschwader 3		
Staff Flight	3	3 Me 109E
I. Gruppe	48	42 Me 109E
Fighter Geschwader 20		
I. Gruppe	21	20 Me 109E
Fighter Geschwader 21		
I. Gruppe	29	28 Me 109C and E*
Destroyer Geschwader 1		
II. Gruppe	36	36 Me 109B* (a)
Destroyer Geschwader 2		
I. Gruppe	44	40 Me 109D* (a)
Air Fleet 2 (NW Germany)		
Fighter Geschwader 26		
I. Gruppe	48	48 Me 109E
II. Gruppe	48	44 Me 109E
10. Staffel	10	8 Me 109C, night-fighting unit
Destroyer Geschwader 26		
I. Gruppe	52	46 Me 109B and D (a)
II. Gruppe	48	47 Me 109B and D (a)
III. Gruppe	48	44 Me 109B and C (a)
Air Fleet 3 (SW Germany)		
Fighter Geschwader 51		
I. Gruppe	47	39 Me 109E
Fighter Geschwader 52		
I. Gruppe	39	34 Me 109E
Fighter Geschwader 53		
I. Gruppe	51	39 Me 109E
II. Gruppe	43	41 Me 109E
Fighter Geschwader 70		
I. Gruppe	24	24 Me 109E
Fighter Geschwader 71		
I. Gruppe	39	18 Me 109C and E
Destroyer Geschwader 52		
I. Gruppe	44	43 Me 109B (a)
Air Fleet 4 (SE Germany)		
Fighter Geschwader 76		
I. Gruppe	49	45 Me 109E
Fighter Geschwader 77		
I. Gruppe	50	43 Me 109E
II. Gruppe	50	36 Me 109E
Destroyer Geschwader 76		
II. Gruppe	40	39 Me 109B and C
Assigned to German Navy		
Traegergruppe 186		
5., 6. Staffeln	24	24 Me 109C (b)

(a) These units had been formed to operate the Me 110 twin-engined fighter, but until these became available they operated Me 109s.
(b) Unit operating standard Me 109Cs, formed to train pilots earmarked to operate the Me 109T from the aircraft carrier *Graf Zeppelin* when she was completed.

IN ACTION OVER FRANCE

'Relatively few Me 109s were lost in combat and only at the end of the campaign, during the Dunkirk evacuation, was there much in the way of fighter-versus-fighter combat. During the campaign in France it was difficult to compare our [Me] 109 with the French Morane or Curtiss fighters, because I never had a dogfight with either of them. I saw only one Morane during the entire campaign and it was disappearing in the distance. Our Geschwader had very little dogfighting experience until the Dunkirk action, where we met the Royal Air Force for the first time in numbers. Our pilots came back with the highest respect for the [new] enemy.'

OBERLEUTNANT JULIUS NEUMANN, ME 109 PILOT, FIGHTER GESCHWADER 27

Above: **Me 109 'Emil' of Fighter Geschwader 27 pictured early in the war. The oversized markings on the wings were to assist recognition, following a series of incidents when aircraft had been engaged in error by 'friendly' forces.**

hard lesson when five Fairey Battle light bombers flew a daylight armed reconnaissance mission over the Saarbrucken area. Me 109s of Fighter Geschwader 53 intercepted the force and shot down four bombers without loss to themselves. Towards the end of the year the Me 109 again showed its effectiveness as a bomber-destroyer. On 18 December 1939 a force of Vickers Wellingtons flew an armed reconnaissance mission off the coast near Wilhelmshaven, intending to attack any German warships located at sea. The twenty-four bombers flew in close formation and depended on their

Right: **A pilot boards his Me 109 'Emil' for a scramble take off. The aircraft, which bears the 'Scalded Cat' insignia of Fighter Geschwader 20, was pictured during the summer of 1939.**

combined crossfire to deter fighter attacks. Thirty-four Me 109s, drawn from Fighter Geschwader 26 and 77 and Destroyer Geschwader 1, engaged the bombers, together with sixteen Me 110s. The German fighters pressed home their attacks despite heavy return fire, and shot down twelve of the Wellingtons. Two more bombers suffered such severe damage that they crashed on landing. For their part, the Wellingtons' gunners shot down only two Me 109s. After this

action the RAF made the policy decision that in future its attacks on targets in Germany would take place almost exclusively at night.

On 10 May 1940 German forces launched their long-prepared offensive in the west. By that time there were 1,346 Me 109s serving with the front line units, of which just over a thousand were serviceable. Three-quarters of these

Everywhere the Me109 reigned supreme, with no effective opposition

aircraft were assigned to support the offensive, while the rest remained in position to defend targets in Germany. The Luftwaffe quickly established air superiority over the Dutch, Belgian and French Air Forces, and over the Royal Air Force units based in France. Everywhere the Me 109 reigned supreme, with no effective fighter opposition. Without hindrance from the air or the ground, Luftwaffe bombers and dive-bombers carried out destructive attacks on airfields and other targets ahead of the fast-moving Panzer thrusts.

At the end of May the German advances pushed the battle front to within range of RAF fighter units flying from bases in southern England. Only during the Dunkirk evacuation was there any serious fighter-versus-fighter combat.

In the course of the evacuation the Luftwaffe learned the

THE FIRST PHASE OF THE BATTLE OF BRITAIN

Typical of the scrappy actions of the period was that on 13 July, when a convoy of freighters passed through the Strait of Dover. Half a dozen Junkers 87 'Stuka' dive bombers were attacking the ships when they were engaged by eleven Hurricanes of No. 56 Squadron.

'Unfortunately for them [the Hurricanes], they slid into position directly between the Stukas and our close-escort Messerschmitts. We opened fire, and at once three Hurricanes separated from the formation, two dropping and one gliding down to the water smoking heavily. At that instant I saw a Stuka diving in an attempt to reach the French coast. It was chased by a single Hurricane. Behind the Hurricane was a 109, and behind that, a second Hurricane, all of the fighters firing at the aircraft in front. I saw the deadly dangerous situation and rushed down. There were five aircraft diving in a line towards the water. The Stuka was badly hit and both crewmen wounded, it crashed on the beach near Wissant. The leading Messerschmitt, flown by Feldwebel John, shot down the first Hurricane into the water, its right wing appearing above the waves like the dorsal fin of a shark before it sank. My Hurricane dropped like a stone close to the one that John had shot down.'

MAJOR JOSEF FOEZOE, LEADING ME 109S OF FIGHTER GESCHWADER 51 ESCORTING THE STUKAS

[No. 56 Squadron lost two Hurricanes destroyed and two damaged. On the German side two Ju 87s were seriously damaged but Fighter Geschwader 51 suffered no losses.]

same hard lesson as that impressed on the RAF earlier: bombers operating by day without fighter escort could expect heavy losses if they came under attack from well-handled enemy fighters. From then on the Me 109 force would fly an increasingly large proportion of its missions in the fighter escort role.

■ BATTLE OF BRITAIN ■

The Battle of Britain was the first major action in which Me 109s confronted similar numbers of enemy fighters of comparable performance and flown by pilots with equal determination and skill.

During the Battle of Britain Me 109 fighter units flew three types of operation in support of German bombers. First, and most popular with the German pilots, was the free hunting sweep across enemy territory. Its purpose was to break up the defending fighter formations and chase them out of the area, to clear the sky for a bomber formation coming behind. German pilots assigned to this mission had full tactical freedom to engage and pursue RAF fighters as they wished. Second, and slightly less popular, were the 'intermediate escort' operations. In this case the fighters stayed with their assigned bomber formation until enemy fighters approached their charges, and only then were they free to break away and go into action. Third, and least popular of all, were the close escort operations which occupied the greater part of the fighter force during any large-scale attack. German fighter units assigned to this role had to remain with their allotted bomber formation at all times. Frequently the Me 109s would drive the Spitfires or Hurricanes away from the bombers, but had then to break off the pursuit and return to positions close to their allocated bomber unit. The British fighters would then return to the

Below: **A pair of 'Emils' in factory markings, probably photographed during a delivery flight to a Luftwaffe aircraft park.**

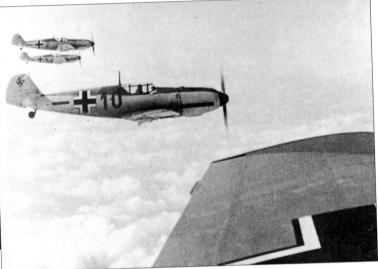

Me109 VERSUS SPITFIRE AND HURRICANE

'I cannot compare the Me 109 with the Spitfire or the Hurricane – I never flew either of those. We were told that there was no better fighter in the world than the 109 and we believed it. Why shouldn't we – it was certainly a very effective fighter. We knew that the Spitfire and the Hurricane were good fighters too and thought they might be closely comparable with our aircraft. So everything depended on the tactics used and how experienced and aggressive the pilots were. Of course, the RAF had some young and inexperienced pilots. But we had the feeling that there was a strong backbone of very well-trained and experienced pilots. The longer-serving RAF pilots had considerable flying experience. We in the Luftwaffe did not have this advantage. Very few of those who fought on our side in the Battle of Britain had more than four years' flying experience. Overall, we felt that we were dealing with an aircraft-pilot combination as good as our own.'

OBERLEUTNANT JULIUS NEUMANN, ME 109 PILOT,
FIGHTER GESCHWADER 27

Left: Julius Neumann pictured in the cockpit of the Me 109 at the R.A.F. Museum at Hendon in 1979. He recalled 'Immediately I sat in the cockpit I felt at home. Everything came easily to hand. Had the tank been full and there been enough room in front of me, I should have loved to have been allowed to take it up.'

Opposite (top left): 'Emils' of Fighter Geschwader 27 at their airfield at Boenning-hard near Wesel, shortly before the campaign in the west in May 1940. (Neumann)

(top right): Me 109s of Fighter Geschwader 27 at St Trond in Belgium, during the campaign in the west.

(bottom left): Me 109 'Emils' of IInd Gruppe of Fighter Geschwader 53 preparing to take off from Dinan in western France during the Battle of Britain.

(bottom right): Battle formation of Me 109Es of IInd Gruppe of Fighter Geschwader 27, photographed early in the Battle of Britain when the unit was based at Crepon in western France as part of Air Fleet 3. (Neumann)

fray and the frustrating process had to be repeated. From these duels between the two air forces the strengths and weaknesses of the 'Emil', compared with the Mark I versions of the Spitfire and the Hurricane, quickly became evident.

At altitudes above 20,000 feet (6,000m) the 'Emil' was slightly faster in level flight and in the climb than the Spitfire. At all altitudes the German fighter was much faster than the Hurricane. Below 15,000 feet (4,600m) the

---

Both the British Spitfire and the Hurricane could out-turn the Messerschmitt 109

Spitfire was the faster in level flight. Both British fighter types could out-turn the Me 109 at any altitude. Me 109 pilots found the fuel injection system fitted to the Daimler Benz 601 gave a useful advantage when they had a Spitfire or a Hurricane on their tail. The Messerschmitt pilot would push down the nose of his fighter and 'bunt' away from his pursuer. If an RAF fighter attempted to follow this manoeuvre, the negative 'G' shut off the fuel supply from the float carburetter fitted to the Merlin engine. There would be an ominous warning

---

Me 109 FRONT-LINE UNITS

7 SEPTEMBER 1940

Unit	Aircraft total	Serviceable	
Air Fleet 2 (Holland, Belgium, NE France)			
Fighter Geschwader 1			
Staff Flight	4	3	Pas de Calais area
Fighter Geschwader 3			
Staff Flight	3	3	Samer
I. Gruppe	23	14	Samer
II. Gruppe	24	21	Samer
III. Gruppe	25	23	Desvres Fighter
Geschwader 26			
Staff Flight	4	3	Audembert
I. Gruppe	27	20	Audembert
II. Gruppe	32	28	Marquise
III. Gruppe	29	26	Caffiers
Fighter Geschwader 27			
Staff Flight	5	4	Etaples
I. Gruppe	33	27	Etaples
II. Gruppe	37	33	Montreuil
III. Gruppe	31	27	Sempy
Fighter Geschwader 51			
Staff Flight	5	4	Saint Omer
I. Gruppe	36	33	Saint Omer, Saint Inglevert
II. Gruppe	22	13	Saint Omer, Saint Inglevert
III. Gruppe	44	31	Saint Omer
Fighter Geschwader 52			
Staff Flight	2	1	Laon/Couvron
I. Gruppe	21	7	Laon/Couvron
II. Gruppe	28	23	Pas de Calais area
III. Gruppe	31	16	Pas de Calais area
Fighter Geschwader 53			
Staff Flight	2	2	Pas de Calais area
II. Gruppe	33	24	Wissant
III. Gruppe	30	22	Pas de Calais area
Fighter Geschwader 54			
Staff Flight	4	2	Holland
I. Gruppe	28	23	Holland
II. Gruppe	35	27	Holland
III. Gruppe	28	23	Holland
Fighter Geschwader 77			
I. Gruppe	42	40	Pas de Calais area
Trials Gruppe 210	26	17	Denain (fighter-bombers unit, also flew Me 110s)
Air Fleet 3 (NW France)			
Fighter Geschwader 2			
Staff Flight	5	2	Beaumont-le-Roger
I. Gruppe	29	24	Beaumont-le-Roger
II. Gruppe	22	18	Beaumont-le-Roger
III. Gruppe	30	19	Le Havre Fighter
Geschwader 53			
I. Gruppe	34	27	Brittany area Tactical
Development (Lehr) Geschwader 2			
II. Gruppe	32	27	Saint Omer (fighter-bomber unit)
Air Fleet 5 (Norway)			
Fighter Geschwader 77			
II. Gruppe	44	35	Southern Norway

WAR DIARY OF 1ST GRUPPE OF FIGHTER GESCHWADER 3

The entry for 15 September 1940, now commemorated as Battle of Britain Day. At the time this unit was part of Air Fleet 2, based at Samer near Boulogne under the command of Hauptmann Hans von Hahn.

On 7 September the unit reported a strength of twenty-three Messerschmitt 109Es of which 14 were serviceable after four weeks of heavy fighting.
1200 [hours, take-off time] Escort (by 12 aircraft) of Do 17s against London. Oblt Keller shot down a Spitfire, Leutnant Rohwer a Hurricane. Fw Wollmer dived into the Channel, the impact was seen by Lt Springer. This crash appears not to have been caused by enemy action. After a long dive Vollmer's machine rolled a quarter turn into a vertical dive and he did not succeed in bailing out. A motor boat detached from a German convoy near Cap Gris Nez and went to the scene of the crash. 1510 [hours] Operation by 9 aircraft to escort He 111s against

London. At 1500 m there was almost total cloud cover. Over the Thames estuary and to the north of London there were gaps in the cloud. During the flight in there was contact with Spitfires. The bombers flew in loose formation to the north of London. Strong and accurate Flak. The Spitfires came from above, fired, and dived away. Hauptmann von Hahn shot down a Spitfire, Lt Rohwer probably destroyed a Hurricane. During an attack by Spitfires Oberleutnant Reumschuessel became separated from his wing man, Obfw Olejnik, and has not returned [this aircraft crashed near Charing, Kent; the pilot bailed out and was taken prisoner]. After he was separated from the formation Obfw Hessel was heard on the radio, but he failed to return [this aircraft crashed near Tenterden; the pilot bailed out and was taken prisoner]. Obfw Buchholz's aircraft was hit in the cooling system and forced down in the Channel. Oblt Keller made contact with a rescue aircraft nearby, which picked up Buchholz. He had [minor] injuries and was taken to the military hospital at Boulogne. The body of Lt Kloiber has been washed ashore near St Cecile, and buried. Lt Meckel and 2 feldwebels attended the funeral. During the last few days news has been received from the Red Cross in Geneva that Oblt Tiedmann, Oblt Rau, Oblt Loidolt, Lt Landry (these last two wounded) and Obfe Lamskemper have been captured by the British.

Scenes at the airfield at Caffiers near Calais, home of the Me 109 'Emils' of IIIrd Gruppe of Fighter Geschwader 26 during the Battle of Britain. The photos come from the personal album of Gerhard Schoepfel. *Top left:* **Ground crewmen constructing a sandbag blast pen to protect a fighter on the ground.** *Above left and middle right:* **Aircraft in their camouflaged blast pens.** *Top right:* **Engine change of a fighter in the open.** *Bottom right:* **Officers of IIIrd Gruppe of Fighter Geschwader 26 discussing the next mission. Seated second from left is the unit commander, Major Adolf Galland. To his immediate left is Gerhard Schoepfel.**

Above and right: '*Emils*' loaded with 550-pound bombs during attacks on England in the closing stages of the Battle of Britain.

splutter, and unless the RAF pilot restored positive 'G' immediately his engine would stop dead. Several German pilots owed their survival to the Me 109's ability to bunt away from a pursuer.

■ RADIUS OF ACTION ■

While such marginal differences in performance and capability decided some actions during this critical period, it is important to view them in the overall context. Throughout the Battle of Britain, and particularly during its final phases when the capital was the target, the Me 109's limited radius of action was of crucial importance. During that contest the Me 109, the Spitfire and the Hurricane each had an effective radius of action of about 100 miles (160km). For RAF fighters engaged in home defence operations, fighting over airfields where they could land to refuel, that distance was adequate. However, for Me 109s

flying in the bomber escort or support roles deep into enemy territory, it was inadequate. The German fighter pilots could not afford to spend long engaged in combat, their engines running at full throttle and guzzling fuel. If they were close to the limit of their radius of action the Messerschmitts had to break off the action, often prematurely, and head for home. This factor greatly reduced the effectiveness of the German single-engined fighter force.

There is another point to consider. The cliché image of the Battle of Britain is that of a sky full of Me 109s, Spitfires and Hurricanes engaged in one-to-one turning fights with Me 109s. That might make for a spectacular painting or film shot, but it was far from the reality of air combat. Any pilot who fastened his attention too long on one enemy fighter ran the serious risk of setting himself up for a surprise attack by another.

PROVIDING CLOSE ESCORT FOR THE BOMBERS

'Sometimes we were ordered to provide close escort for a bomber formation, which I loathed. It gave the bomber crews the feeling they were being protected, and it might have deterred some of the enemy pilots. But for us fighter pilots it was very bad. We needed the advantages of altitude and speed so we could engage the enemy on favourable terms. As it was, the British fighters had the initiative of when and how to attack. The Heinkels cruised at about 4,000 metres [13,000 feet] at about 300km/hr [190mph]. On close escort we flew at about 370km/hr [230mph], weaving from side to side to keep station on them. We needed to maintain speed, otherwise the Me 109s would have taken too long to accelerate to fighting speed if we were bounced by Spitfires. I hated having to fly direct escort. We had to stay with the bombers until our formation came under attack. When we saw the British fighters approaching we would want to accelerate to engage them. But our commander would call "Everybody stay with the bombers." We handed to the enemy the initiative of when and how they would attack us. Until they did we had to stay close to the bombers, otherwise their people would complain and there would be recriminations when we got back.'

OBERLEUTNANT HANS SCHMOLLER-HALDY, ME 109 PILOT, FIGHTER GESCHWADER 54

Above: **At the end of the Battle of Britain the top-scoring pilot in the Luftwaffe was Major Werner Moelders, the commander of Fighter Geschwader 51. On 22 October 1940 he scored his fiftieth aerial victory.**

On both sides, the really successful fighter pilots stalked their prey like hunters. They used the sun and cloud to remain unseen for as long as possible, as they edged into a favourable position before launching an attack. They then dived on their often unsuspecting prey, announcing their presence with a sudden and accurate burst of fire. There was no thought of chivalry. Usually the first thing the victim knew of the danger was when his aircraft shuddered under the impact of hits. A textbook example of this type of action appears in the Prologue to this book.

From the start of the Battle of Britain one Gruppe operated the Me 109 in the fighter-bomber role, attacking targets in southern England. The fighter carried a bomb load of up to 550 pounds (249kg). In the final part of the Battle, from the end of September, several Me 109 units flew aircraft modified for the fighter-bomber role. The defending fighters found the fast, high-flying German fighter-bombers difficult targets to engage. As a result the latter suffered minimal losses. On the other hand the Me 109 carried only a small weight of bombs, and their scattered bombing meant that the attacks had only nuisance value.

■ REPUTATION INTACT ■

The Me 109 force emerged from the Battle of Britain with its reputation still intact. True, it had suffered losses at the hands of the RAF pilots. But during these hard-fought engagements the Me 109 force had usually dealt out blows at least as hard as those it took.

Alongside the Spitfire Mark I, the 'Emil' was still a contender for the title of most effective fighter plane in the world. The new variant of the German fighter about to enter service, the Me 109 'Friedrich', would be even better.

Left: **Hauptmann Horst Tietzen, the commander of 5th Staffel of Fighter Geschwader 51, with his personal 'Emil' with eighteen victory bars on the tail. On the afternoon of 18 August 1940, when his victory score stood at twenty, he was shot down and killed during an action with Hurricanes of No. 501 Squadron.**

THE MOST SERIOUS AND UNPARDONABLE ERROR

'On 23 September our mission was a free hunting sweep in the triangle Ramsgate – Canterbury – Folkestone, where British fighter activity had been reported. With three of my pilots I took off at 10.27 and headed towards Ramsgate in a slow climb to 4,500 metres [about 15,000 feet]. The weather was strange, with layers of cloud in which aircraft could easily hide. There were several flights of aircraft about which we saw for a moment before they disappeared, we never knew if they were British or German. It was uncanny. We flew in wide curves, always changing altitude, never flying straight for long. We had been flying for 60 minutes, I thought that was enough and we were turning for home when I suddenly observed Hurricane squadron between Ramsgate and Dover, twelve aircraft in four "pulks" flying one behind the other. They were about 1,000 metres (2,873ft) below us and climbing in wide curves, like a creeping worm. My impression was that it was a Hurricane squadron on a training mission. The Hurricane pilots had no idea that four 109s were above them following each of their movements, like an eagle looking down on its prey. The spectacle was so fascinating that we completely forgot what was going on around us. That is the most serious and unpardonable error a fighter pilot can commit, and catastrophe immediately followed. Four Spitfires, of which we had been unaware due to our carelessness, attacked us from out of the sun. They fired at us from behind, roared close over our heads at high speed and disappeared back into the sky. As we broke formation fearing another attack from the Spitfires, I saw a 109 going down in flames on my right. It was Oberfeldwebel Knipscher, we never heard what happened to him.'

OBERLEUTNANT HANS SCHMOLLER-HALDY, ME 109 PILOT, FIGHTER GESCHWADER 54

Top: An 'Emil' crash-landed on a French beach. During the Battle of Britain this fighter was not fitted with drop tanks and lacked the range to penetrate far into southern England. Several were lost when they ran out of fuel on their way home following air combats or after encountering strong headwinds.
Above: Me 109E-7s of Fighter Geschwader 1, a unit that spent most of the war operating in the defence of the German homeland. (via Obert)
Right: Major Adolf Galland climbing out of the cockpit of his 'Emil' after a sortie over England during the Battle of Britain.

During 1940 the Messerschmitt company initiated a programme to clean up the airframe of the Me 109 and improve its fighting capability. The new variant became the Me 109 'Friedrich'. Compared with the 'Emil', the more obvious external changes were the more rounded spinner and nose contours, the rounded wing tips and the partially retractable tail wheel. The main production version was fitted with the new Mauser 15mm cannon, one of which fired through the propeller hub. This weapon had nearly twice the firing rate of the older 20mm Oerlikon cannon, and its far higher muzzle velocity made it a much more effective weapon than its predecessor.

Luftwaffe pilots who flew the 'Friedrich' remembered this variant with affection. It was faster than the 'Emil' and it handled rather better in the air. It was, in the truest sense of the expression, a 'fighter pilot's fighter'. The 'Friedrich' entered service in the spring of 1941 and by the middle of the year two-thirds of the Luftwaffe fighter force flew this type. Also at this time the Royal Air Force introduced the Mark V Spitfire into its home defence squadrons, a move that restored the balance between the fighter forces of the two sides.

■ NORTH AFRICA ■

That balanced existed only over north-west Europe, however. Until the spring

MESSERSCHMITT 109 F-2

Type Single-seat general purpose fighter.
Armament One Mauser 15mm cannon firing through the propeller spinner (200 rounds). Two Rheinmetall-Borsig 7.9mm MGs synchronized to fire through airscrew (500 rounds per gun).
Power Plant One Daimler Benz DB 601N inverted V-12 liquid cooled engine developing 1,200hp for take off.
Dimensions Span 32ft 6in (9.92m); length 29ft 4in (8.94m).
Weight Normal operational take off, 6,174lb (2,800kg).
Performance Max. speed 373mph at 19,700ft (600km/hr at 6,000m). Service ceiling 36,100ft (11,000m).

Top: A brand new Me 109 'Friedrich' in factory markings shows off its distinctive rounded wing form above the Alps.
Above: A 'Friedrich' of Fighter Geschwader 26 returning to its base at Liegescourt in northern France in the summer of 1941. (Schoepfel)
Opposite: Two 'Emils' of Fighter Geschwader 27 on patrol over the North African desert.

Top: 'Friedrich' wearing the personal markings of the commander of IIIrd Gruppe of Fighter Geschwader 2 based in northern France, photographed in 1941.
Above: An Me 109F of Fighter Geschwader 26 outside its camouflaged dispersal hangar in northern France.

of 1942 the Spitfire fighter units operated only from bases in Great Britain. Meanwhile, units equipped with the 'Friedrich' were heavily involved in the campaigns in North Africa and the Soviet Union where the new fighter easily outflew the less modern types opposing it. For the German fighter pilots this was a 'happy time' when many of them amassed large victory scores.

The foremost successful 'Friedrich' fighter pilot was Leutnant Hans-Joachim Marseille. He gained seven victories during the Battle of Britain while flying the 'Emil' before moving to the North African theatre to join Fighter Geschwader 27. From the beginning of

THE ATTACK ON RUSSIA

During the weeks following the invasion of Russia packs of German fighters ranged far and wide over enemy territory. Close to the ground the Polikarpov I-16, the main Soviet fighter type, was almost as fast as the Me 109F that equipped the majority of Luftwaffe fighter units. But the Type 24's radial engine was optimized for low-altitude operations and as height increased its performance fell away steadily; at 20,000 feet (6,096m) the I-16 was about 100mph (160km/hr) slower than the German fighter. Although the Soviet fighters were more manoeuvrable than their adversaries, in a fighter-versus-fighter combat that advantage did no more than allow a pilot to avoid being shot down, provided he saw his attacker in good time. For the most part, the Soviet fighter pilots had to dance to their enemies' tune. Typical of the scrappy actions taking place that morning was one near Brest-Litovsk, described by Unteroffizier Reibel of Ist Gruppe of Fighter Geschwader 53: 'I was flying as wing man to Lt Zellot. We flew in the direction of Brest from Labinka. As my leader ordered a turn about, I saw two biplanes in front of us. I immediately reported them and we brought them under attack. When we were about 200m [61ft] from them they both pulled into a tight turn to the right. We pulled up high and then began a new attack, but though we both opened fire it was without success. Soon there were about ten other [enemy] machines in the area. My leader ran in to attack one of the planes while I remained high in order to cover him. Then an I-15 became separated from the others. I immediately prepared to attack it, but I had to break away when another enemy machine, which I had not seen, suddenly appeared 50 metres [15ft] in front of me. I opened fire with machine guns and the cannon and it burst into flames and spun out of control. Apparently the pilot had baled out. Then I had to turn away, as I had two [enemy] machines behind me.' Using their superior speed, the German fighters easily pulled away.

Me 109 'Emils' of Fighter Geschwader 52 pictured at Kabaracie, Rumania, in the spring of 1941 shortly before the attack on the Soviet Union. The 'snake' marking on the rear fuselage indicated that these aircraft belonged to the IIIrd Gruppe.

Top left: Me 109 'Emil' fighter-bomber of Fighter Geschwader 54 operating over the Eastern Front in 1942.
Middle: Me 109 'Friedrich' of Fighter Geschwader 54 pictured beside a captured Soviet I-16 fighter. The more powerful and cleaner-lined German fighter had a considerable speed advantage over its enemy counterpart, especially at high altitude.
Bottom: Me 109 'Friedrich' of Fighter Geschwader 53, with the unit's 'Ace of Spades' insignia on the cowling, at a forward airfield in the Leningrad sector on the Eastern Front during the winter of 1941–2.

1942 his victory total rose rapidly. With no Spitfires yet operating in that area, the 'Friedrich' was superior to the Hurricane and Tomahawk fighters flown by the RAF and its allies. During a remarkable action on 3 June 1942, Marseille shot down six Tomahawks in rapid succession. The action is well documented and the combat is confirmed in the records of the victim unit, No. 5 Squadron South African Air Force. By the time of his death in September 1942, Marseille's tally of 'kills' stood at 158.

Early on the 15mm cannon fitted to the 'Friedrich' was replaced with a fast-firing 20mm Mauser cannon. With the two machine guns mounted above the engine cowling, the closely grouped weapons gave a

Me 109S IN NORTH AFRICA

Opposite page:

1. Hauptmann Karl-Wolfgang Redlich of Ist Gruppe Fighter Geschwader 27 (left, holding papers), briefing pilots before taking off from Catania in Sicily to fly to North Africa. The 'Emil' in the background is fitted with a dust filter over the engine air intake. (Schroer)

2. Ground running an 'Emil' at Catania, to warm the engine before setting out for North Africa. (Schroer)

3. Me 109 'Emils' of Fighter Geschwader 27 dispersed around the forward landing ground at Gambut in Libya. The photograph gives a good impression of the primitive conditions under which the unit had to operate. (Schroer)

4. Ground crewmen turning the handle for the inertia starter of the Daimler Benz 601 engine. The handle rotated a heavy flywheel which, when it was turning fast enough, was clutched to the engine to turn it over and start it.

5. 'Emils' of Fighter Geschwader 27 on patrol over the desert.

6. Me 109F of Fighter Geschwader 27 preparing to get airborne. Note that this aircraft is missing its spinner.

7. Hauptmann Hans-Joachim Marseille of Fighter Geschwader 27, the most successful German fighter pilot in North Africa. At the time of his death in September 1942, his victory score stood at 158.

8. Fighter ace Leutnant Werner Schroer, adjutant of IInd Gruppe of Fighter Geschwader 27, with his personal aircraft. At the end of the war his victory score stood at 114. (Schroer)

dense pattern of fire that proved very effective against enemy fighters and light bombers. Against the four-engined bombers, with their tougher structures, it was another matter however.

■ FIRE POWER ■

From mid-1942 the Me 109F units operating over western Europe and North Africa encountered the American B-17 Flying Fortress and B-24 Liberator heavy bombers with increasing frequency. On average it needed about twenty hits with 20mm rounds to knock down one of these rugged aircraft. When in formation the heavy bombers put up a powerful defensive cross-fire which

forced the fighters to make high-speed firing passes. Under those conditions only an exceptionally good shot could achieve the required number of hits using a single cannon.

Greater fire power was needed, and in answer to this problem the Friedrich was modified to carry a blister under each wing containing an extra 20mm cannon and ammunition. The change trebled the fighter's fire power, but at no small cost in terms of its performance and general handling. It was the first ominous sign of a problem that would afflict the Me 109 and other German piston-engined fighter

Above: 'Friedrich' of Fighter Geschwader 77 operating on the Leningrad front in 1942. (Pichler via Obert)

types for the remainder of the war. In short, any fighter that had sufficient fire power to engage Allied heavy bombers successfully would be too heavy and too unwieldy to engage Allied fighters on equal terms.

That critical shortcoming would become all too evident when the next variant of the fighter entered production, the 'Gustav', which is described in the next chapter.

THE EASY TIMES IN RUSSIA

Initially the German fighter pilots had an easy time over Russia, and the more talented of them built up huge victories scores. There were plenty of opportunities for everyone, however, even the inexperienced pilots. In the summer of 1942 Unteroffizier Walther Hagenah was posted from training to Ist Gruppe of Fighter Geschwader 3 operating the Me 109F. He flew as wing man to Oberfeldwebel Otto Wessling, a skilful and experienced pilot. Hagenah told this author: 'Wessling was a superb leader who seemed to be able to score hits from ranges as great as 400m [1,312ft]. He would manoeuvre into a position of advantage above his enemy, dive on his prey and open fire from long range, hit his enemy and pull away without getting close to his foe. My first weeks as an operational fighter pilot were a disappointment. To be sure I fired at enemy aircraft, but all I seemed to hit was the air. I was beginning to get discouraged. One day Wessling took me to one side on the ground and said "Now it is time that you made your first victory!" On 12 August 1942 we were on patrol on the central Russian front and he spotted a pair of LAGG-3 fighters. He took us round into an attacking position on their tails and down we went. We came from out of the sun and achieved surprise. He hit one of them from about 400m [1,312ft] and down it went. Then he called me and said "Now you go ahead and hit the other one!" But the second Russian pilot had a lot of pluck and he really threw his aircraft about the sky in an effort to shake us off his tail. Then Wessling joined in the dogfight, but at the same time telling me what I had to do to get "my" kill. Eventually he succeeded in manoeuvring both me and the Russian fighter into a position where I could open fire at it – just as a gamekeeper will chase a deer into a position where a wealthy man can hit it with his gun. All I had to do was follow Wessling's instructions and fire when he said, and I hit the enemy fighter. So I achieved my victory. I was very proud. Wessling was big enough to keep quiet about how I got it.'

During the Second World War the principal fighter types in the major warring nations underwent courses of development to improve their fighting capability. They were fitted with more powerful (and heavier) engines, more effective (and heavier) armament, larger (and heavier) fuel tankage and additional (and heavier) protective armour and items of equipment.

As the fighter steadily gained weight, from time to time the airframe had to be stiffened to restore its original strength factors. That added a further twist to the spiral of increasing weight. Since the fighter's wing area usually remained constant, each increase in weight led to increase in wing loading. And that, inevitably, led to a deterioration in the fighter's handling characteristics. Stalling speeds became higher, control forces heavier, turning performance worsened and, in many cases, the aircraft developed vicious traits.

No fighter design suffered more from this remorseless process than the Me 109. Even at the start of the war, it will be remembered, the Me 109 had already passed through several variants. By the spring of 1942 it had reached the end of its effective development and ideally it should then have passed out of production. However Messerschmitt's planned replacement fighter, the Me 209, was still on the drawing board.

The Me 109G-2 was 660 pounds heavier than its predecessor, the Me109F

At that time the war was still going well for Germany. Her leaders confidently expected that the campaign on the Eastern Front would come to a victorious end in the autumn of 1942. Until a replacement fighter type was ready, the Luftwaffe opted to squeeze a little more speed from the Me 109 and keep the fighter in full production.

The new variant, the Me 109 'Gustav', was designed around the Daimler Benz 605 engine. In essence this was a DB 601 with the cylinder block rebored to increase the engine's capacity from 33.9 litres to 35.7 litres. The additional capacity gave an extra 175 horse power at full throttle, for no significant increase in the engine's external dimensions. That fact did not prevent the new variant of the Me 109 from putting on weight, however. The first major production version, the 'Gustav-2', was 660 pounds (300kg) or about 10 per cent heavier than the earlier 'Friedrich' and its handling characteristics were

Top: Me 109 'Gustav' of Fighter Geschwader 54 pictured at a forward airfield in Russia, showing the difficult conditions encountered during the spring thaw.
Above: Me 109 'Gustav' of Fighter Geschwader 53 pictured at a forward airfield in Sicily in 1943. (via Rigglesford)
Opposite: Pilots of Fighter Geschwader 53 at readiness snatching a quick meal beside one of their aircraft. (via Schliephake)

correspondingly worse; compared with the Me 109 'Berta' the figures were 2,200 pounds (1,000kg) and 46 per cent respectively! During May 1942 a total of 234 Me 109s came off the production lines in Germany and Austria, most of them 'Gustavs'.

MESSERSCHMITT 109 G-2

Type Single-seat general purpose fighter.
Armament One Mauser 20mm cannon firing through the spinner (150 rounds). Two Rhein-metall-Borsig 7.9mm MGs synchronized to fire through the airscrew (500 rounds per gun).
Power Plant One Daimler Benz DB 605A inverted V-12 liquid cooled engine developing 1,475hp for take off.
Dimensions Span 32ft 6in (9.92m); length 29ft 0in (8.85m).
Weight Normal operational take off 6,832lb (3,100kg).
Performance Maximum speed 406mph at 28,535ft (654km/hr at 8,700m). Service ceiling 39,360ft (12,000m).

Soon after the 'Gustav' entered service with Fighter Geschwader 27, Hans-Joachim Marseille lost his life while flying the type. In September 1942 his victory score passed the 150 mark, making him the first fighter ace in history to achieve this total. On the final day of the month he flew a newly-delivered 'Gustav-2' on a bomber escort mission over Egypt. There was no contact with the enemy and the flight was uneventful, until on the return flight the aircraft's engine started to smoke. Then it caught fire. The cockpit filled with fumes and, escorted by his comrades, Marseille stayed with the aircraft until he reached German-held territory. Then he jumped from the stricken fighter, but his luck had deserted him. As he left the Messerschmitt it appears that his head struck some part of its structure and he was knocked unconscious. His parachute did not open and he was killed on hitting the ground. Subsequent examination of his parachute revealed that it was still in the pack, held closed by the ripcord which had not been pulled.

Marseille jumped from his aircraft, but for once luck had deserted him

Small numbers of 'Gustav-2s' were modified for the tactical reconnaissance role, with the cannon removed and a vertical camera mounted in the rear fuselage. The use of the Me 109 (and also the FW 190) for this purpose

became necessary because the increasing enemy fighter opposition on each of the battle fronts meant that slower reconnaissance types incurred heavy losses. Modified versions of each of the new main variants of the Me 109 would be used for tactical reconnaissance for the remainder of the war.

The next major production version of the fighter, the 'Gustav-6', started to

leave the assembly lines in the autumn of 1942. This differed from the G-2 in that it carried two 13mm heavy machine guns on top of the engine cowling, in place of the earlier rifle-calibre weapons. To cover the larger breech mechanism of the 13 mmguns, the fighter had two large bulges on the cowling in front of the windscreen.

■ 210mm ROCKETS ■

The Luftwaffe issued a range of field modification kits to allow units to 'customize' the new fighter for specific operational roles. The R-1 kit, for example, provided an under-fuselage rack to carry a single bomb weighing up to 550lb (249kg). The R-2 kit provided for a tubular launcher under each wing to carry a 210mm rocket, for use against enemy bomber formations or ground targets. The R-4 kit provided a blister mounting for a 30mm heavy cannon and ammunition, one to fit under either wing.

'WILD BOAR' MESSERSCHMITT 109s

Me 109G-2s operating in the 'Wild Boar' single-engine night-fighter role to counter R.A.F. bomber attacks, summer 1943.

From mid-1943 the Luftwaffe began to employ small numbers of single-engined fighters, including Me 109s, to engage R.A.F. night bombers attacking cities in Germany. Over the target the concentrations of searchlights, the fires on the ground and the Pathfinders' marker flares often combined to illuminate the bombers. The single-seaters patrolling high above the target could then make visual attacks on the raiders. To prevent conflict with the flak defences it was agreed that the latter would engage bombers flying below a certain altitude, typically 18,000 feet (5,500 metres). Above that altitude, the fighters would engage bombers. The single-engined night fighter tactics bore the apt title 'Wild Boar'. For the remainder of the war these methods were an integral part of the German night air defence system.

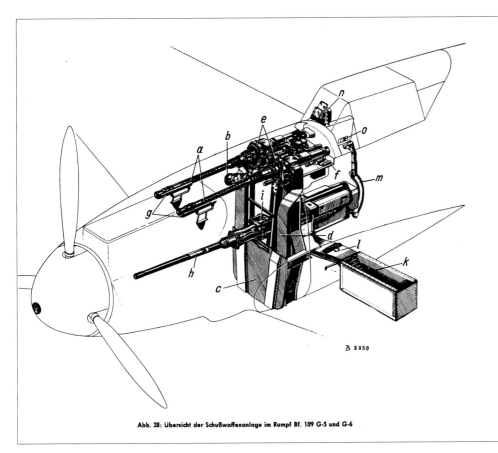

The Weapons Installation Fitted to the Me 109G-5 and G-6

Key:
a. MG 131 13mm heavy machine guns
b. Electrical synchronization unit for firing MG 131s through the airscrew disc
c. Magazine for MG 131 ammunition
d. Empty case chute for port MG 131
e. Mountings for MG 131s
f. Ignition coil, to provide high voltage for electrically fired MG 131 ammunition
g. Mounting brackets for nose fairing
h. MG 151 20mm cannon firing through propeller spinner
i. Front mounting of MG 151
k. Magazine for MG 151 ammunition
l. Feed chute for MG 151 ammunition
m. Control column, with firing button for weapons
n. Revi 16B reflector sight
o. Arming switch for weapons

B 5950

Abb. 28: Übersicht der Schußwaffenanlage im Rumpf Bf. 109 G-5 und G-6

Also the 'Gustav-6' had provision to carry one or two separate power-boosting systems, to inject a fluid into the supercharger of the DB 605 engine. To boost power at altitudes above 20,000 feet (6,096m), the GM-1 system injected nitrous oxide (laughing gas) into the engine. The nitrous oxide was held in liquid form in a heavily lagged pressurized container in the rear fuselage and the complete system weighed 670 pounds

Above: Diagram from an official Luftwaffe handbook, showing the fuselage armament fitted as standard to Me 109 Gustav-5 and Gustav-6. These fighters had a 20mm Mauser cannon firing through the airscrew hub, and two 13mm Rheinmetall-Borsig heavy machine guns above the engine cowling synchronized to fire through the airscrew. On some later aircraft the engine-mounted cannon was replaced by a Rheinmetall-Borsig 30mm weapon.

Below: The 'Gustav' did not suffer fools gladly. If the pilot opened the throttle too quickly during takeoff, the powerful engine torque was liable to lift the fighter off the ground before it attained flying speed. Often the fighter rolled upside down and smashed on the ground under full power, giving the pilot little chance of escape. (Schliephake)

Top: Me 109 'Gustav-2s' belonging to a tactical reconnaissance Gruppe. This version had the nose-mounted cannon removed, and a vertical camera fitted in the fuselage immediately behind the cockpit. *Above:* Me 109 'Gustav-2' of Fighter Geschwader 11 at Jever during 1943, fitted with underwing launchers for two 210 mm air-to-air rockets for use against US heavy bomber formations.

orated. On each battle front in turn the Luftwaffe was thrown on the defensive. More and more fighters were required and the 'Gustav', originally introduced as a stopgap type, was built in ever-greater numbers. During 1943 production of the Me 109 was twice that in the previous year, with more than 6,400 'Gustavs' delivered to the Luftwaffe.

One factor that led to demands for increasing numbers of air defence fighters was the daylight attacks by U.S. heavy bombers on targets in Germany. What had started as infrequent raids by a few dozen bombers against fringe targets had grown into deep penetration attacks by several hundred bombers able to inflict severe devastation. To meet the new threat, several fighter Gruppen were withdrawn from the battle fronts to bolster the defences of the homeland.

In the summer of 1943 Unteroffizier Hans Seyringer was posted to IInd Gruppe of Fighter Geschwader 27, a day

The young pilot had only about 200 flying hours in his log book

fighter unit based at Wiesbaden and equipped with the 'Gustav-6'. The young pilot had come straight from training and had only about 200 flying hours in his logbook. His recollections give a good impression of what it was like to serve with such a unit.

During bomber-interception missions the fighters usually carried a 66-gallon (300l) drop tank under the fuselage. The standard armament fitted to 'Gustavs' on Seyringer's unit was three 20mm cannon and two 13mm machine-guns. Some of the aircraft also carried two 210mm rocket launchers under the wings, though as an inexperienced pilot Seyringer never flew with these weapons.

When waiting on the ground at readiness the aircraft were usually drawn up by Staffeln in line abreast. The four Staffeln, each with about a dozen 'Gustav-6s', were dispersed separately at 90-degree intervals around the perimeter of the grass airfield. Once the pilots had

(304kg). To boost power at altitudes below 20,000 feet, the MW system injected a water/methanol mixture into the engine (the water cooled the charge and provided the extra power, the methanol prevented the water freezing at high altitude). The complete MW system weighed 300 pounds (136kg).

As the 'Gustav-6' entered service Germany's war fortunes suddenly deteri-

Above: A close-up of the rocket installation on a 'Gustav'.
Left: Me 109 'Gustav' of the Finnish Air Force. The type entered that service in March 1943 and remained in use until 1954.

the opposite direction accidentally loosed off a couple of rockets. The missiles came scorching past Seyringer's Staffel just as the fighters were getting airborne. Their proximity caused considerable consternation but, fortunately for the pilots involved, no damage!

■ TACTICS ■

Once the ground controller had brought a fighter Gruppe within visual range of an enemy formation, the Gruppe leader decided on the type of attack to employ. Usually Seyringer's Gruppe attacked bombers from the rear, the fighters flying in four-aircraft units in line abreast or line astern. After their initial attack, the fighters split into pairs to make further firing runs. Sometimes Seyringer's Gruppe made head-on attacks, though he did not like this method. He felt that the time spent manoeuvring into position for such an attack was out of proportion to the very short firing pass that resulted.

been brought to cockpit readiness, the order to scramble was given by firing a green flare from the control tower. From then on was important to get the Gruppe into the air and assembled into battle formation as rapidly as possible. To achieve this two of the Staffeln on opposite sides of the airfield began simultaneous take-off runs, moving on parallel headings separated by a few hundred yards. As the first two Staffeln passed each other at the centre of the airfield, the other two Staffeln began their takeoff runs also heading in opposite directions.

After takeoff the leader orbited once over the airfield so the individual Staffeln could start to move into position behind him. Then he turned on to his intercept heading and began a slow climb away. Once the formation was fully assembled he increased his rate of climb.

These tactics provided the most rapid means of getting a Gruppe into the air and assembled into formation. There was little small margin for safety if anything went wrong, however. Seyringer recalled a nerve-racking incident when, due to incorrect fitting, a fighter taking off in

Above: 'Gustav-6' carrying the white fuselage band and wing tips of a unit operating on the Mediterranean front.
Right: Unteroffizier Hans Seyringer of Fighter Geschwader 27, whose experiences are described in the text, pictured with his 'Gustav-6'. With a victory score of four enemy aircraft destroyed, he was shot down and wounded during an engagement with American escort fighters in February 1944. (Seyringer)

Until late in 1943 the American escort fighters lacked the range to penetrate deep into Germany. Seyringer's unit had few encounters with them and he thought that was as well, for a heavily laden 'Gustav-6' was no match for a Thunderbolt.

To Hans Seyringer the effect of the fighter's extensive development process on handling was all too evident. To put it simply, the 'Gustav' was too heavy and its engine too powerful for the fighter's small wing and tail surfaces. When carrying a full armament and drop tank the aircraft required careful handling during the takeoff. If there heavy-handedness of the controls the fighter was liable to react viciously. If, for example, the pilot opened the throttle too quickly the powerful engine torque was liable to lift the fighter off the ground before it attained flying speed. The 'Gustav' would drop its left wing, roll on its back and smash into the ground, giving the pilot little chance of escape. Certainly the 'Gustav' did not suffer fools gladly.

During 1943 the Luftwaffe tactics to counter the American heavy bomber raids were in a continual state of development. Home defence units used any type of weapon that came to hand. Fighter Geschwader 11 carried out experiments in air-to-air bombing, using

DISASTER FOR THE GERMAN DAY FIGHTER FORCE

In the spring of 1944 the American escort fighters were able to reach almost every part of Germany. The new Mustang was superior in performance to the Me 109 and it was usually present in greater numbers. As a result the German day fighter units took increasingly heavy losses. At the end of April 1944 Generalmajor Adolf Galland reported: 'Between January and April 1944 our day fighter arm lost more than 1,000 pilots. They included our best Staffel, Gruppe and Geschwader commanders. The time has come when our force is within sight of collapse.' Now the German pilots had to fight for their very survival, and one by one even the best of them were being picked off. Gone were the days when the aces could 'play' enemy planes to allow their less experienced colleagues to get easy kills, as over Russia a couple of years earlier. One of those who died in action with the American fighters in April 1944 was Leutnant Otto Wessling, then credited with 83 victories, who had set up Walther Hagenah's first 'kill' described earlier.

time-fused 550lb (249kg) released from above the bomber formation. Initially it seemed this tactic might have a good chance of success. Even if the bombs did not destroy the enemy planes, they might damage some of them sufficiently to force them to leave their formation. Other fighters could then finish off the wounded birds as easy prey. There were serious problems with this method, however. Carrying a bomb in place of a drop tank, the 'Gustav' had a short radius of action. Also it proved difficult to vector the heavily laden fighter into position above a high-flying bomber formation. Moreover, since there was no effective proximity fuse then available, the problem of getting the bomb to

MESSERSCHMITT 109 G-2 VERSUS HAWKER TEMPEST

At the beginning of 1944 a captured Me 109 'Gustav-2' was flown in a comparative trial against the latest R.A.F. fighter type, the Hawker Tempest Mark V. These extracts from the official report show that the German fighter was outclassed in almost every respect.
Maximum Speed: The Tempest possesses an advantage of 40–50mph [64–80km/hr] at heights below 20,000 feet [5,850m] but at heights in excess of 20,000 feet [6,096m] the advantage possessed by the Tempest rapidly diminishes. **Climb:** The climb of the Me 109 is superior to that of the Tempest at all heights but this advantage is not pronounced at heights below 5,000 feet [1,520m]. When both the aircraft commence a dive at the same speed and are put into climbing attitude, the Tempest is slightly superior, but providing the Tempest possesses the initial advantage in speed, it has no difficulty in holding it providing the speed is kept in excess of 250mph [400km/hr]. **Dive:** Comparative dives between these aircraft show that the Tempest will pull away from the Me 109. This is not so marked in the early stages of the dive, but in a prolonged descent the Tempest is greatly superior. **Turning Circle:** It was found that in this aspect of manoeuvrability the Tempest was slightly superior to the Me 109. **Rate of Roll:** At speeds below 350 IAS [mph indicated, 564km/hr] there is practically nothing to choose between the two aircraft, but when this speed is exceeded the Tempest can out-manoeuvre the Me 109 by making a quick change of bank and direction. **Conclusions:** In the attack the Tempest can always follow the Me 109, except in a slow steep climb. In the combat area the Tempest should maintain a high speed, and in defence may do anything except attempt a climb at low speed.

Comparative trials revealed that the Hawker Tempest Mark V, which entered service in the R.A.F. early in 1944, was superior to the Me 109 'Gustav-2' in almost every respect.

detonate as it passed the target aircraft defied solution. Most of the bombs detonated well clear of their intended victims, and after a month or so the unit abandoned this form of attack.

During the spring of 1944, following the introduction of new and larger drop tanks, the American escort fighters were able to reach almost every part of Germany. The new Mustang fighters were superior in performance to the defending Me 109s, Me 110s, Me 410s and FW 190s. Moreover the escort fighters operated in large numbers and as a result the German fighter units took heavy losses.

■ HOME DEFENCE ■

By now the greater part of the Luftwaffe fighter force was committed in the defence of the homeland. And it was losing pilots faster than the German flying training schools could provide replacements. The Luftwaffe was being bled white. The only possibility of reversing this trend was with the large-scale deployment of the Messerschmitt 262 jet fighter. Yet this type was still not ready to enter mass production (see next section of this book).

Although the 'Gustav' was now well beyond its effective development life, new sub-types continued to appear. By optimizing it for a narrow range of combat roles, the fighter might survive in action. Thus the 'Gustav-10', for example, was built specifically to engage in high altitude fighter-versus-fighter combat. These aircraft carried the new Daimler Benz 605D engine with an

enlarged supercharger and the GM-1 power boosting. Their armament was reduced to one 20mm cannon and two 13mm machine guns. They were assigned to units whose task was to provide top cover for more heavily armed fighters delivering attacks on bomber formations. In addition, small numbers of 'Gustav-10s' were modified for the tactical reconnaissance role with the two heavy machine guns removed and a fixed vertical camera mounted in the rear fuselage.

■ A DESPERATE TIME ■

In the spring of 1944 the German aircraft industry underwent a major reorganization. The

Above: Damaged Me 109 'Gustav' trailing glycol smoke, after being hit in the cooling system during an engagement with a US escort fighter. Soon after this picture was taken the 'Gustav' was shot down. (USAF)
Below: Me 109G-6s of IIIrd Gruppe Fighter Geschwader 27 waiting at readiness at Wiesbaden-Erbenheim in 1944. The broad red band around the rear fuselage indicated that the aircraft belonged to a Reich air defence unit. (Schroer)

IN ACTION DURING THE FINAL MONTHS OF THE WAR

Leutnant Hans-Ulrich Flade flew the Me 109 'Gustav' and the 'Kurfurst' with IInd Gruppe of Fighter Geschwader 27 early in 1945. In previous months the production of these fighters had reached an all-time high, and if an aircraft was damaged it was usually simpler to get a new fighter than repair the old one: 'We simply went to the depot nearby, where they had hundreds of brand-new 109s – G-10s, G-14s and even the very latest K models. There was no proper organization any more; the depot staff just said: "There are the aircraft, take what you want and go away." But getting fuel, that was more difficult. Flade's Gruppe had a strength of about twenty pilots, but it was losing these at a rate of two or three each day. Morale on the unit was low. 'Each morning we pilots had breakfast together, and the replacements would come in. The older pilots regarded the newcomers as though they had only days to live – and with reason, for the standard of fighter conversion training was now so low that most of the new pilots flew only two or three missions before they were shot down. I remember many conversations along these lines – not exactly a cheerful subject for a young man who had just joined his first operational unit!' The Gruppe operated in the top-cover role, to keep the American escort fighters off the backs of other German fighters making for the bombers. 'We followed the old rules: dive as a pair or a four out of the sun, make a quick attack to break up their formation and make them drop their tanks, then climb out of danger and assess the situation. If conditions were favourable, we would go down for a second attack. Always the escorts were so numerous that it would have been foolish to get into a dog-fight.'

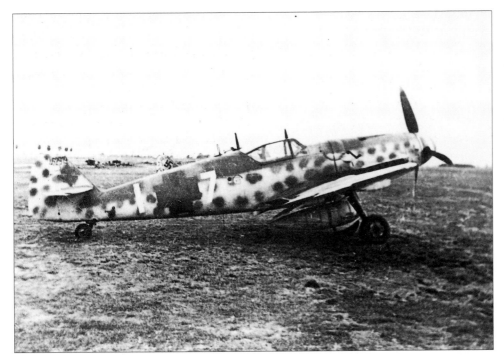

Left: The Me 109G-14 featured a larger rudder and a redesigned cockpit canopy to give better vision to the sides and the rear. This example belonged to IIIrd Gruppe of Fighter Geschwader 3, a unit that flew escort missions for more heavily armoured fighters delivering attacks on US heavy bomber formations. (Romm)

Below: Me 109 'Kurfurst', the final version of the fighter to go into production in Germany before the end of the war. As well as the revised tail surfaces and redesigned canopy fitted to the late production 'Gustavs', this variant featured a more powerful Daimler Benz 605 engine and carried two 15 mm cannons mounted on top of the engine.

Luftwaffe, by this time in a desperate situation, needed every modern fighter it could lay its hands on. Under the new Luftwaffe procurement plan, almost the entire capacity of the industry was turned over to the manufacture of fighter-type aircraft. At the same time, to render the industry less vulnerable to air attack, a large part of the aircraft construction and assembly work was dispersed into small factories and workshops dotted throughout the country.

Once the new system was in place, production of the Me 109 rose in leaps and bounds, despite the heavy and continual raids on German cities and industrial centres. For the Me 109 September 1944 was the peak month, with the Luftwaffe taking delivery of

Above and left: The unusual 'Mistel' weapon, a Me 109F mounted rigidly on top of a Junkers 88 bomber that had the cabin removed and a large warhead fitted in its place. The Me 109 pilot aligned the bomber on the target, then fired explosive bolts to separate his aircraft so he could make his escape.

Below: The Avia S.199, manufactured in Czechoslovakia after the war using components for the Me 109 'Gustav' built in that country. The fighter was fitted with a Jumo 211 engine which gave the unusual nose contours. (Hurt)

1,605 new aircraft. That year 14,212 examples of this type of aircraft were delivered, more than twice as many as in the previous year which had itself been a record. At this stage of the war the units equipped with Me 109s always had plenty of aircraft, although there were worsening shortages of trained pilots and fuel as the tide turned inexorably against the German forces.

Despite the known poor handling qualities of the Me 109 'Gustav', work continued in attempts to squeeze yet more speed and combat capability out of the basic design. The final variant of the Me 109 to enter large-scale production was the 'Kurfurst', deliveries of which began at the end of September 1944. The initial production sub-type, the 'Kurfurst-

2', had a pair of 15 mm cannon in place of the 13 mm weapons mounted above the engine. The 'Kurfurst-4' was a high-altitude fighter with a pressurized cabin. The 'Kurfurst-6' was a specialized bomber-destroyer version, with a 30 mm high-velocity cannon firing through the airscrew spinner. The final sub-type to enter production before the end of the war was the 'Kurfurst-14', which was powered by a DB 605L engine with a two-stage supercharger. This aircraft was the fastest Me 109 of them all, with a maximum speed of 452mph at 19,700 feet (728km/hr at 6,000m).

During the early months of 1945 the Allied ground forces were thrusting into Germany from both the east and the west. As the factories building components and assemblies for the Me 109 came under threat from these forces, they were blown up to prevent capture. Also at this time attacks on the German road,

No other fighter design was producd in greater numbers than the Messerschmitt Me 109

rail and canal systems made it difficult to deliver aircraft components to the assembly plants. However, despite these obstacles, the Me 109 continued to be turned out in large numbers until the very end of the war.

Incredibly, in the final four months of the conflict the Luftwaffe took delivery of nearly three thousand Me 109s. It is estimated that several hundred more of these aircraft were probably completed, but in the chaos and confusion of the final collapse they never reached the units for which they were intended and remained in the factories where they had been assembled.

The precise number of Me 109s built before the war finally ended will never be known with certainty, but without doubt it can be stated that the figure exceeded 33,000. So, to the type's other 'firsts' can be added the distinction that no other fighter design, anywhere else in the world, was produced in greater numbers.

Me 109 FRONT-LINE UNITS

9 APRIL 1945

Note: this date, four weeks before the end of the war, was the last for which an official strength return was made. First figure aircraft total, second figure serviceable.

Unit	Aircraft total	Serviceable
Air Fleet Reich		
Fighter Geschwader 4		
III Gruppe	61	56
Fighter Geschwader 27		
I Gruppe	29	13
II Gruppe	48	27
III Gruppe	19	15
Night Fighter Geschwader 11		
1 Staffel	16	15
4 Staffel	14	9
7 Staffel	21	19
Tactical Recon Gruppe 1	6	9
Fighter Geschwader 51 Air Fleet 4 (Eastern Front)		
II. Gruppe	7	5
Fighter Geschwader 52		
II. Gruppe	43	29
Fighter Geschwader 53		
I. Gruppe	27	27
Fighter Geschwader 77		
Staff Flight	1	1
Tactical Recon Gruppe 12	30	26
Tactical Recon Gruppe 14	42	19
Croatian Tactical Recon Staffel	17*	16*
Air Fleet 6 (Eastern Front)		
Fighter Geschwader 3		
III Gruppe	47	46
Fighter Geschwader 6		
III Gruppe	21	17
Fighter Geschwader 52		
Staff Flight	8	7
I Gruppe	40	37
III Gruppe	32	30
Fighter Geschwader 77		
Staff Flight	1	1
I Gruppe	30	26
II Gruppe	36	30
III Gruppe	34	25
Fighter Conversion Geschwader 1	109	97
Tactical Recon Gruppe 2	30	20
Tactical Recon Gruppe 3	37	22
Tactical Recon Gruppe 4	2	2
Tactical Recon Gruppe 8	35	21
Tactical Recon Gruppe 15	31	26
Luftwaffe Kommando West		
Fighter Geschwader 53		
Staff Flight	1	1
II Gruppe	39	24
III Gruppe	40	24
IV Gruppe	54	27
Tactical Recon Gruppe 13	39	26
Luftwaffe Kommando East Prussia		
Fighter Geschwader 51		
I Gruppe	10	8
III Gruppe	23	7
Tactical Recon Gruppe 4	26	17
Luftwaffe General Norway		
Fighter Geschwader 5		
Staff Flight	about 3	
III. Gruppe	about 20	
IV. Gruppe	about 20*	
Reconnaissance Gruppe 32	about 15*	
Tactical Recon Gruppe 5	25*	18
Luftwaffe General Italy		
Tactical Recon Gruppe 11	24	14

* Figure includes other aircraft types flown by the unit

MESSERSCHMITT 262

In the autumn of 1937 the Heinkel company began ground-running tests with the first German turbojet engine. Early the following year a new engine based on that unit underwent flight tests carried in a pod under the fuselage of a dive-bomber.

In the months that followed two other major German engine companies, Junkers and BMW, also began design work on jet engines of their own. Compared with the piston engine, the attraction of the jet was that it gave a far higher thrust for a given weight. Also it produced that thrust directly, with none of the conversion losses incurred by using a propeller. The disadvantage of the jet engine, in engineering terms, was that it ran at temperatures and rotational speeds far greater than those encountered in piston engines. Engineers working on the first-generation turbojets faced a range of new problems that they had to resolve from first principles.

■ JET FIGHTER STUDY ■

In October 1938 the Messerschmitt company began work on a design study for a jet-powered aircraft. This was an experimental fighter powered by two of the latest model BMW turbojets, each with a forecast thrust of 1,320 pounds (600kg). It was calculated that the maximum speed of the new aircraft would be around 560mph (900km/hr).

The German Air Ministry received details of the proposed Messerschmitt jet fighter in June 1939. As might be expected, the predicted performance figures aroused a lot of interest. If they were true the new fighter would be nearly one-third faster than the Me 109E that had recently entered service.

Right: **The third prototype Messerschmitt 262 pictured immediately after its first flight solely on jet power, 18 July 1942. After the first few prototypes, later Me 262s were fitted with tricycle undercarriages.**
Opposite: **Me 262 in flight, showing the aircraft's distinctive wing and engine arrangement.**

THE RATIONALE FOR THE GAS TURBINE

The concept of the gas turbine engine had first been suggested early in the 20th century. Only in the late 1930s, however, did serious work begin to produce such an engine to power a military aircraft. Two factors spurred this development work. First there were the war clouds gathering over Europe, which led to the need – and the money – to improve fighter performance. Secondly there was a dawning realization among aircraft designers that the laws of physics imposed a finite limit to the maximum speed that could be derived from a propeller-driven plane. That limit was somewhere around 500mph (805km/hr). This fundamental problem centred on the use of the propeller to convert the rotational power from the engine into thrust. In a nutshell, the efficiency of the propeller fell away drastically as the plane's speed neared that limit.

A few figures will serve to illustrate the point. In round terms, the Messerschmitt 109E attained a maximum speed of about 300mph (483km/hr) at sea level with an engine that developed about 1,000hp. At that speed the propeller was about 80 per cent efficient, and the 1,000lb (454kg) of thrust that it produced equalled the drag from the fighter's airframe. Now consider the engine power that would be needed to propel the Me 109 at twice that speed, 600mph (965km/hr). Drag rises with the square of speed, so if speed doubled the drag quadrupled. Thus 1,000lb (454kg) of drag at 300mph (483km/hr) became 4,000lb of drag at 600mph (965km/hr). To overcome that amount of drag the aircraft needed 4,000lb (1,814kg) of thrust. But at 600mph (965km/hr) the efficiency of the propeller was slightly over 50 per cent, so to drive the aircraft at that speed a piston engine would have needed to develop about 12,000hp. In 1945 the best piston engines produced a fraction over one horse power for each pound (.5kg) of weight. Thus a piston engine developing the power to propel our notional fighter at 600mph (965km/hr) would have weighed about 11,000lb (4,990kg) – about double the all-up weight of an early production Me 109. For flight at high speed the turbojet was a fundamentally more efficient form of power. It produced its output in the form of thrust, and since there was no propeller there were no conversion losses. Moreover the amount of thrust developed by a jet engine remained more or less constant throughout the aircraft's speed range. The two Jumo 004 turbojets fitted to the Me 262 each delivered 1,850lb (839kg) of thrust for a weight of 1,590lb (721kg), and gave the fighter a maximum level speed of 514mph (827km/hr) at sea level and 540mph (869km/hr) at 19,500 feet (5,944m). No piston-engine and propeller combination could offer a thrust-to-weight ratio to compare with that, and it was clear that for use in high performance aircraft their days were numbered.

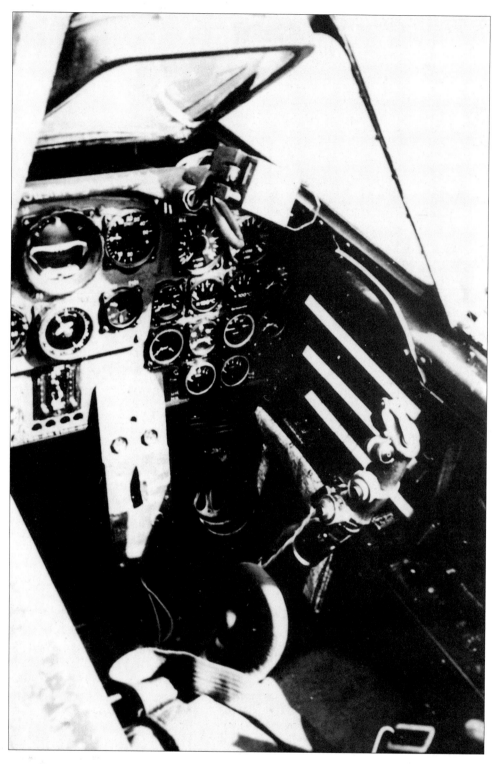

Above: **The cockpit of the Me 262. The jet fighter had noticeably fewer instruments than an equivalent fighter type with two piston engines.**

turbojet, however, and still no flight-cleared engines were available. As a temporary expedient, the Messerschmitt company decided to mount a 750 horse-power Jumo piston engine in the nose of the aircraft so that flight trials could begin. In April 1941 test pilot Fritz Wendel conducted the maiden flight in the new aircraft to determine its handling at low and medium speeds.

■ FLAME OUT ■

Towards the end of 1941 a pair of flight-cleared BMW 003 engines, each rated at 1,015lb (460kg) thrust, finally arrived at Augsburg. These were fitted to the Me 262 and, as a back-up, it was decided to retain the piston engine in the nose. On 25 March 1942 Wendel took off in the unusual three-engined aircraft. The flight nearly ended in disaster. Soon after take off the BMW units flamed out in succession. Using only the power from the piston engine, Wendel flew a wide circuit in the underpowered aircraft and returned to the airfield for a safe landing. Later, when the jet engines were stripped down, engineers found that several of the compressor blades had broken away. The intakes for both jet units were behind the propeller, and the turbulent airflow from the latter probably caused the problems. Beyond that, the BMW 003 compressor was not strong enough and required some redesign. Thereafter the unit played no part in the Me 262 story.

Messerschmitt test pilot Fritz Wendel made the Me 262's first flight on jet power alone

Within a few weeks Germany was at war against the forces of both Great Britain and France, yet there was no sense of urgency to get the jet fighter into production. For one thing, the Me 109 was thought superior to any enemy fighter type it was likely to meet in action. For another, despite their immense promise, during ground-running trials the early turbojets proved highly unreliable. In March 1940 the Messerschmitt company received a low-priority contract to build three prototypes of its twin-jet fighter now given the official designation 'Messerschmitt 262'.

By the spring of 1941 the first Me 262 airframe was ready for the engines. Still there were problems with the BMW

In the meantime the Junkers company's first-generation turbojet unit had reached the flight test stage. This, the Jumo 004A, had a rated thrust of 1,850lb (839kg). It was decided to redesign the Me 262 to take the new and more powerful Junkers engine.

In May 1942 a pair of pre-production Jumo 004 units arrived at the Messerschmitt plant. These fitted easily into the modified nacelles on the third prototype

Above: A ground crewman pulls the lanyard to start the two-stroke Reidel starter motor fitted in the nose bullet of the Jumo 004 turbojet. The two-stroke engine could be started manually, as in this case, or electrically from the cockpit.

Right: With a high pitched whine and a spurt of flame out the rear, a Jumo 004 turbojet bursts into life. This engine required very careful handling and if there was any heavy handedness with the throttle it was liable to flame out or catch fire.

Me 262. This time there was no piston engine in the nose to serve as a back-up; the aircraft would fly on jet power or it would not fly at all. On 18 July 1942 Fritz Wendel took off from Leipheim, to make the Me 262's first flight on jet power alone. During the brief initial 12-minute hop he encountered no serious problems, and later that day he took the fighter up for another short flight.

Soon the new aircraft was achieving speeds over 430mph (692km/hr) in level flight, rising to more than 500mph (805km/hr) as more powerful engines became available. When its Jumo 004s worked properly the aircraft had a sparkling performance. Often this was not the case, however (see Box on following page). As far as the Luftwaffe was concerned, in the summer of 1942 the jet fighter was a pointer to the future but no more than that. The main battle fronts were deep in the Soviet Union or in North Africa, and there was no threat of large-scale daylight attacks on targets in the German homeland. The latest versions of the Me 109 and the FW 190 had shown that they could deal effectively with any air opposition mounted by the enemy. Moreover these well-proven piston-engined fighters could operate from primitive front-line airfields in any climatic conditions. There simply was no operational requirement for an extremely fast but unreliable short-range jet fighter that required long runways and continual pampering from ground crews to keep it working.

At that time senior Luftwaffe officers regarded the Me 262, with good reason, as a white elephant. To keep abreast of the new technology, however, the Luftwaffe ordered fifteen pre-production examples of the jet fighter. In October 1942 that order was doubled to thirty aircraft. All too soon, the course of the war would force a dramatic change in that service's view of the Me 262.

■ THE WHITE HOPE ■

At the beginning of June 1943 there were three Me 262s flying and the aircraft regularly exceeded 500mph (804km/hr) in level flight. During the first six months of that year Germany's military situation

deteriorated rapidly on all fronts. Axis forces had been ejected from Africa and they had also suffered heavy defeats on the Eastern Front. In the west the Luftwaffe had been forced on the defensive, and American heavy bomber formations were mounting daylight attacks on targets in Germany itself. Now the operational requirement for the

Above and opposite below: Early production Me 262s belonging to Test Kommando 262, photographed at Lechfeld, Bavaria, probably in July 1944

Me 262 was clear enough; with its excellent turn of speed and powerful armament of four 30mm cannon, it would make a fine bomber-destroyer.

In the confident expectation that the reliability problems of the Jumo 004 turbojet could soon be solved, the Luftwaffe ordered the Me 262 into large-scale production. This plan called for production to begin in January 1944, and to achieve output of sixty aircraft per month by the end of May. The Me 262 had become the chosen replacement fighter for the Luftwaffe, and its white hope for the future.

PROBLEMS WITH THE GERMAN JET ENGINES

A problem that dogged the German jet engine programme throughout the war was that the nation was unable to import sufficient nickel, chromium and other steel-hardening ores to meet the needs of its war industries. Thus, in the case of the Jumo 004 turbojet, Junkers engineers had to do without the high-temperature-resistant alloys they would have liked to use in critical parts of the jet engine. The flame tubes, for example, were one of the hottest parts of the engine. The ideal material would have been a nickel-chrome-steel alloy with small amounts of silicon, manganese and titanium to serve as hardening elements. In the Jumo 004, however, these components were fashioned from mild steel sheet. To prevent oxidation (rust) the tubes had a spray coating of aluminium baked in an oven. This inelegant combination could not survive long at extreme temperatures, and while the 004 was running its flame tubes were slowly buckling out of shape. Another critical area was the turbine, where temperatures often exceeded 1,292º F (700º C). The high centrifugal forces on the blades imposed tensile stresses of up to 15 tons per square inch (14.7 tonnes per 6.5cm². The turbine blades fitted to the 004 were manufactured from a steel-based alloy containing 30 per cent nickel and 15 per cent chromium. Again, this material was insufficiently resilient for the task. As a result during running the blades developed 'creep', that is to say the metal began to deform and the blades gradually increased in length. When blade 'creep' reached a laid-down limit, the engine had to be changed. Limited by flame tube buckling and blade 'creep', the running life of pre-production Jumo 004 engines rarely exceeded ten hours. Then the Me 262 had to be grounded for an engine change.

The Junkers Jumo 004 engine had a very short running life – of around ten hours

In the spring of 1944 pre-production Me 262s started to come off the production lines. The short running life of the 004 engine, around ten hours, continued to dominate the project however. The jet fighters spent most of their time in hangars being fitted with new engines.

MESSERSCHMITT 262A

Role Single-seat jet interceptor fighter or fighter-bomber.
Armament (fighter role) Four Mk 108 30mm cannon, could also carry twenty-four unguided air-to-air rockets. (fighter-bomber role) Two 30mm cannon and two 550lb (249kg) bombs.
Power Plants Two Jumo 004A axial flow jet engines each developing 1,980lb (898kg) thrust.
Dimensions Span 40ft 11in (12.51m); length 34ft 9in (10.60 m).
Weights Normal operational take-off (fighter version): 14,105lb (6,400kg).
Performance Max. speed (fighter version) 540mph at 19,500ft (870km/hr at 5,950m).

Junkers engineers worked hard to improve the running life of the 004, but it was an uphill struggle. Until they succeeded, the design of the engine could not be 'frozen' to allow mass production to begin.

At Lechfeld a group of hand-picked Luftwaffe pilots was given an insight into jet power

Meanwhile, at Lechfeld in Bavaria, a service test unit formed to introduce the fighter into service. There, picked Luftwaffe pilots gained an insight into the mysteries of flying a jet-powered aircraft. Quite apart from its short running life, the Jumo 004 was a temperamental beast that needed very careful handling. Over-rapid movement of a throttle could cause an engine to flame-out or else catch fire. Another problem stemmed from the slow

build up of power, a factor common to all of the early jet engines. Once the pilot had throttled back on the landing approach he was committed to making a landing. If he tried to abort the approach and advanced the throttles, the Jumo 004s responded so slowly that the aircraft would probably strike the ground before it gained sufficient speed to start to climb away. Clearly the Me 262 was not a plane for inexperienced service pilots.

In May 1944, when the Me 262 was still in the service trials stage, Adolf Hitler issued his much-publicized order that initially the plane should be used only as a fighter-bomber. Several writers have poured scorn on the order, yet at the time there were sound tactical reasons behind it.

Since the previous autumn the German dictator had been worried by the prospect of an Anglo-American invasion of north-west Europe in 1944. If the landings succeeded, the German army would have to fight a two-front war against forces that were numerically far superior. Adolf Hitler believed, probably correctly, that if the invasion was to be defeated at all it had to be during its early stages. If his Panzer divisions could deliver their counter-attack before the Allied troops were established in defensive positions ashore, it might be possible to hurl the invaders into the sea with heavy losses. Hitler wanted a force of fighter-bombers to bomb and strafe the troops as they came ashore. He believed such attacks would cause great confusion, and might possibly delay the creation of the beachhead, allowing the Panzers to get their attack in first.

■ FRONT-LINE FORCE ■

Given the scale of likely Allied fighter cover over the landing area, only jet aircraft had any real prospect of delivering the required attacks. During discussions in the autumn of 1943 Hitler had asked Willi Messerschmitt if the Me 262 could carry bombs. Twice the designer had assured him that he could modify the aircraft

Above: **A series of shots from a cine film depicting an Me 262 of Test Kommando 262.**

to carry a 1,100-pound (499kg) bomb or two 550-pound (249kg). From then on the Me 262 featured prominently in Hitler's anti-invasion plans. On 20 December 1943 he confidently informed senior officers from all three services:

'Every month that passes makes it more and more probable that we will get at least one Gruppe of jet aircraft. The most important thing is that they [the enemy] get some bombs on top of them just as they try to invade. That will force them to take cover, and in this way they will waste hour after hour!

'But after half a day our reserves will already be on their way. So if we can pin them down on the beaches for just six or eight hours, you can see what that will mean to us . . .'

Certainly Me 262s could perform that task, provided enough of them could reach the area during the critical period. If a landing operation ran into serious trouble, as would happen at Omaha Beach on D-Day, such attacks might tip the balance and cause the landing to fail.

Those Luftwaffe officers familiar with Hitler's views did not attempt to sway them. Generalfeldmarschall Milch, controlling the Luftwaffe aircraft production programme, acknowledged the importance of the Me 262 as a fighter-bomber. However, he devoted his efforts to getting the type into service as quickly as possible, and that meant initially with the fighter force.

Matters came to a head on 23 May 1944, exactly two weeks before the D-Day landings. Senior Luftwaffe officers,

including Goering and Milch, assembled at Hitler's headquarters for a routine conference on aircraft production. The Fuehrer listened passively until someone mentioned the Me 262. Then he asked, 'I thought the 262 was coming as a high-speed bomber? How many of the 262s already manufactured can carry bombs?' Milch replied 'None, my Fuehrer. The Me 262 is being built exclusively as a fighter.'

Hitler wanted the Me 262 adapted to carry bombs for use as a fighter-bomber

Everyone was silent as the Fuehrer pondered the implications of that statement. After the assurances that the Me 262 could be modified to carry bombs, none of these aircraft could yet do so. The Allies might invade at any time, and the weapon on which had pinned his

hopes did not exist. Hitler exploded in anger and delivered a blistering attack on the Luftwaffe officers present. Before he stormed out of the room, he made Goering personally responsible for ensuring that every new Me 262 delivered from the factories was modified for the fighter-bomber role. One consequence of the revelation was that Erhard Milch was sacked from his post.

It should be stressed, however, that the short running life and poor reliability of the Junkers Jumo 004 engine still precluded the Me 262 from front-line service in any role. Nothing changed during the two weeks between Hitler's conference and the invasion. On D-Day itself the crucial period lasted from the initial landings at dawn on 6 June, until the troops established defensive positions ashore at noon. Not a single Me 262, nor any other German aircraft for that matter, delivered a damaging attack on the lodgement areas during those critical hours. By the afternoon of 6 June the opportunity had passed, and no power at

Above: **Three of the principal players in the controversy regarding the operational use of the Messerschmitt 262. Left, Adolf Hitler. Partially hidden by him is General-feldmarschall Erhard Milch, who was sacked from his post as head of aircraft production for not ensuring that the Me 262 was modified for use as a fighter-bomber. Shaking hands with the Fuehrer is General Adolf Galland, the Inspector of Fighters, who made unsuccessful attempts to persuade the Fuehrer to reverse his decision. Later Galland led Fighter Unit 44 with Me 262s in action during the final weeks of the war. (via Ethell)**

Adolf Hitler's command could dislodge the invaders.

The Me 262 was not yet in operational service but, given the high priority accorded to the aircraft, it would soon be. In the next chapter we shall observe the extent to which the jet plane would live up to the high hopes that had been placed in it.

The first Luftwaffe fighter-bomber unit to receive the Messerschmitt 262, the 3rd Staffel of Bomber Geschwader 51, began to re-equip with the new type at the end of June 1944. A month later the unit, with a strength of nine Me 262s, moved to Chateaudun near Paris and flew its first operational missions. Normally the fighter-bomber carried two 550-pound (249kg) bombs, which it released in shallow-dive attacks.

To lessen the chances of one of the advanced planes falling into enemy hands, pilots had strict orders not to descend below 13,000 feet (4000m) while over enemy territory. Releasing the bombs from so high an altitude reduced the accuracy of the attacks, however, and they achieved little against small battlefield targets such as bridges or armoured vehicles.

Also in July, the Me 262 fighter proving unit at Lechfeld received a new commander. Major Walter Nowotny, an Austrian who had amassed 255 victories while flying on the eastern front, moved into that post. The unit, now with about fifteen aircraft, was re-named Kommando Nowotny. All of the machines were early-production Me 262s that could not be modified to carry bombs, and their serviceability was poor. Rarely were more than four of these aircraft flyable at the same time. In addition to its programme of training flights, the unit flew practice interceptions against Allied reconnaissance aircraft passing over the area. During August the jet fighter achieved its first aerial victories: it shot down two Mosquitoes, a Spitfire and a P-38 Light-

Above: **A pair of Me 262 fighter-bombers of Bomber Geschwader 51 taking off for an operational mission, each carrying two 550-pound bombs under the nose. This unit was the first to take the Me 262 into action when** it began operations from Juvincourt in France at the end of July 1944.
Below and bottom: **Close ups of the bomb installation on the Me 262.**

Opposite: **The P-51 Mustang escort fighters, which penetrated deep into Germany to support bomber attacks, posed severe problems for the Me 262 fighter units. Although the American fighter was not as fast as the jet in level flight, when it had sufficient height advantage it could often exceed the latter's speed during a diving attack. (USAF)**

ning, all unarmed reconnaissance machines, and a damaged B-17 Flying Fortress limping home after an attack.

■ MASS PRODUCTION ■

At the beginning of September 1944 the running life of the Jumo 004 engine finally reached 25 hours. This was hardly an impressive figure, but it meant that the design could be frozen so that mass production of the turbojet could begin. That month the Luftwaffe took delivery of ninety-one Me 262s, more than four times as many as in August. Also in September, Hitler rescinded his edict that all new Messerschmitt 262s should be delivered equipped for the fighter-bomber role. Now the way was open for the aircraft to enter service with the fighter force. By that time more than a hundred Me 262 fighter airframes were sitting on the ground awaiting engines. As the necessary Jumo 004s arrived, these aircraft could be completed and flown. In fact the Fuehrer's order that the Me 262 be employed initially as a fighter-bomber delayed its entry into action as a fighter by less than a month.

At the end of September Kommando Nowotny possessed twenty-three Me 262s, all of them new aircraft fitted with new engines. The unit moved to the airfields at Achmer and Hesepe in north-west Germany, close to the battle area. The aircraft's career as a front-line fighter got off to a poor start, however. Still there were problems with the

Above: Major Walter Nowotny, the Austrian fighter ace, amassed 255 victories on the Eastern Front. In July 1944 he assumed command of the Me 262 Test Kommando and this unit was renamed after him. In September he led Kommando Nowotny in action, but was killed during air combat on 8 November 1944.
Below: The Me 262 was at its most vulnerable after the pilot had throttled back on the landing approach, as in the case of this aircraft framed in the gunsight of a marauding US escort fighter. (USAF)

engines and the serviceability of the aircraft remained poor.

As with any new aircraft, there were teething troubles. One of these centred on the undercarriage. The jet fighter's very high landing speed, around 125mph (200km/hr), placed a heavy strain on the tyres, which were made from poor quality rubber including recycled materials. Burst tyres were a common problem, causing the aircraft to swerve off the runway and make a bumpy ride across the grass until it came to a halt. After each such incident it was necessary to jack up the aircraft to inspect the undercarriage, and usually to carry out repairs. Another problem centred on the Rheinmetall-Borsig Mk 108 cannon. Pilots made the unhappy discovery that the links joining the hefty 30mm rounds were liable to break if they fired the guns during a high 'G' turn.

> *Lieutenant Drew rolled his fighter into a high-speed dive . . . and shot down both Me 262s*

Allied fighter pilots were quick to discover the Achilles' heel of the jet fighter: it was vulnerable while flying slowly immediately after take off or on the approach for landing. On 7 October Kommando Nowotny scrambled five Me 262s, the largest number to date, to intercept American bomber formations heading for oil targets in central Germany. As the bombers headed east, Mustang fighters patrolled high above the airfields of the Me 262s. From his vantage point 15,000 feet (4,592m) above Achmer, Lieutenant Urban Drew of the 361st Fighter Group watched a pair of the jets taking off. He rolled his fighter into a high-speed dive, levelled out behind them and shot down both before they could accelerate to fighting speed. A further Me 262 was lost in a separate action. In its first multi-aircraft action, Kommando Nowotny lost three Me 262s destroyed and one pilot killed. For its part, the German jet fighter unit shot down three American bombers.

ME 262 FRONT-LINE UNITS

10 JANUARY 1945

	Aircraft total	Serviceable
Bomber Geschwader 51		
Staff Unit	1	0
I. Gruppe	51	37
Kommando Braunegg (Recon)	5	2
Kommando Welter (Night Fighters)	4	2

During only its first month in action Kommando Nowotny claimed the destruction of four American heavy bombers, twelve fighters and three reconnaissance aircraft. In achieving these victories the unit lost six Me 262s in combat. In addition a further seven jet fighters were destroyed and nine were damaged in accidents.

Then, on 8 November, the unit suffered the most grievous blow of all. Following a high-speed skirmish with Mustangs of the 357th Fighter Group, Nowotny's aircraft crashed into the ground and the fighter ace was killed. By chance Generalmajor Adolf Galland was at Achmer that day, on an inspection visit to determine why the Me 262 unit had not performed more successfully in action. Galland saw enough to realize that Nowotny had been given an impossible task of trying to bring a completely new high-performance fighter into action with a pilot force that had for the most part received only a sketchy conversion training. Serviceability of the Me 262 remained poor and rarely could the unit fly more than half a dozen sorties per day. The big mistake, Galland realized, had been to commit the jet fighter into combat in such small numbers and before it was ready for action. In that area the Allied air forces had massive numerical superiority, and they dictated the terms on which the jets had to fight. Galland ordered the Me 262 unit to

return to Lechfeld for further training and so the aircraft could be modified to overcome some of their defects. He could see that if the new fighter was to achieve a decisive effect, it was necessary to assemble a far larger force before sending them into action. Fighter Geschwader 7, the first full Geschwader of Me 262 fighters, had already started to form. But it would take some time to get the unit fully ready for action.

Meanwhile, what had happened to the Me 262 fighter-bomber units? By the late autumn of 1944, Bomber Geschwader 51

had two full Gruppen equipped with the jet fighter-bomber, with a total of about forty aircraft. There, too, serviceability was poor and rarely was the Geschwader able to fly more than ten sorties per day. Single aircraft carried out attacks on Allied airfields and troop positions in France, Holland and Belgium. Due to the small number of aircraft involved, however, and the modest weight of bombs they could carry, the attacks achieved little.

By November 1944 there were sufficient Me 262s available for a few of these aircraft to be released to perform other important roles. A tactical reconnaissance unit, Kommando Braunegg, was formed at Herzogenaurach near Nuremberg. Initially its equipment comprised half a dozen aircraft each modified to carry two cameras in the nose. Flying from forward airfields, these machines operated over the Western Front and photographed Allied dispositions and troop movements at will. The intelligence thus gained proved extremely

Right, top and below: **Me 262 fighters belonging to Replacement Training Fighter Geschwader 2 operating at Lechfeld late in October 1944. Poor serviceability slowed the pace of training and greatly extended the time required to bring pilots to combat readiness.**

useful for the planning for Adolf Hitler's offensive in the Ardennes area launched in December.

Also in November an experimental night fighter unit, Kommando Welter, moved to Burg near Magdeburg and began flying interception missions with radar-equipped Me 262 single-seaters. At Burg the unit was well positioned to engage night raiders making their way to and from Berlin. Its main prey was the Royal Air Force Mosquito night bombers and long-range night-fighters which had previously operated over Germany almost with impunity.

■ THE FINAL BATTLES ■

By the beginning of January 1945 the Luftwaffe had taken delivery of about six hundred Messerschmitt 262s. Production of these aircraft was running at some 36 per week, yet on the 10th of that month only sixty Me 262s, one in ten of those built, were serving with front-line units (see Box on previous page). Most of these were fighter-bomber versions serving with Bomber Geschwader 51, the rest flew in the night fighter and tactical reconnaissance roles.

Right, top and below: These photographs show an experimental installation to increase the weight of bombs the Me 262 could carry. During a trial carrying a 2,200-pound (1,100kg) bomb the trailer began to porpoise and the movement was transmitted to the aircraft via the rigid towing bar. This became so serious that the pilot lost control and had to bale out of the aircraft. The method, described as 'hazardous and unsatisfactory', was abandoned.

Left: A few Me 262B two-seat trainers were modified for the night-fighter role with the installation of the 'Neptun' airborne interception radar. The large aerial array lopped about 38mph (about 60km/hr) off the fighter's maximum speed, but even so the aircraft retained a substantial performance advantage over the Mosquito high-speed bomber.

It was four months since Hitler had rescinded his order that the Me 262 should serve only in the fighter-bomber role. Certainly there was no shortage of jet fighters, yet none was serving with front-line day fighter units. What had gone wrong?

In fact, although several Me 262 fighter Gruppen were in the final stages of preparing to go into action, the training process was taking longer than expected. There were about 150 of these aircraft serving with day fighter units working up to go into action, or with operational training units. The IIIrd Gruppe of Fighter Geschwader 7 had its full complement of aircraft and was almost ready to go into action from airfields near Berlin. The Ist Gruppe was forming at Kaltenkirchen near Hamburg, as was the IInd Gruppe at Brandenburg/Briest.

■ A DIVERSION ■

Another unit that was working up with Me 262s was Bomber Geschwader 54, in the process of converting to the bad weather fighter role. For this new role the unit was redesignated as 'Bomber Geschwader (Fighter) 54'. This diversion of Me 262s from 'pure' fighter units has been linked to Hitler's earlier insistence that the type be used as a fighter-bomber. But now the issues were quite different.

Above: Me 262s of the Bomber Geschwader (Fighter) 54, a bad weather fighter interceptor unit. During its first two engagements the unit suffered heavy losses and it saw little action after that. (Baetcher)

Most Luftwaffe day-fighter pilots lacked training in instrument flying, a move calculated both to shorten training time and to save resources. Pilots assigned to bomber units received this training as a matter of course, and such skills were essential if the high-speed jets were to fly in marginal weather conditions.

At the beginning of the year there were about thirty Me 262s serving at the various Luftwaffe test centres. And by that time approximately 150 of these aircraft had been destroyed by enemy action in the air or on the ground, or lost in flying accidents. That accounted for about four hundred Me 262s. What had happened to the remaining two hundred Me 262s, about one-third of those built?

A large proportion of the missing planes were 'marooned' in the German rail system. To save precious aviation fuel, after their test flights most Me 262s were dismantled and crated, then transported to Luftwaffe holding depots by rail. The rail network was now under systematic attack from Allied strategic bombers, however. Many important marshalling yards had been devastated to such an extent that lines of undamaged trucks were isolated from the main tracks. Unless the lines could be repaired or new ones laid, the trucks and their loads would remain cut off for the rest of the war. This situation rendered many of the crated aircraft unusable.

The attacks on the rail network also impeded the movement of fuel, replacement engines and other spare parts to the front-line jet units. To add to these problems, the airfields operating jet aircraft suffered repeated bombing attacks. And on top of everything else, poor flying weather over Germany throughout much of the winter of 1944 restricted the flying time available to trainee pilots. Even without such obstacles it is difficult enough to introduce a

Below: A Rheinmetall-Borsig 30mm cannon pictured with one of its 11oz (330g) rounds. Four of this type of armament were fitted to the Me 262.

TRAINING TO FLY THE Me 262

In March 1945 Leutnant Walther Hagenah, an experienced fighter pilot, was posted to IIIrd Gruppe of Fighter Geschwader 7 based at Laerz near Berlin. He described the cursory training he received before flying the Me 262: 'Our "ground school" lasted one afternoon. We were told of the peculiarities of the jet engine, the dangers of flaming out at high altitude, and about their poor acceleration at low speeds. The vital importance of handling the throttles carefully was impressed upon us, lest the engines caught fire. But we were not permitted to look inside the cowling of the jet engine – we were told it was very secret and we did not need to know about it! By the time I reached III./JG 7 there were insufficient spare parts and insufficient spare engines; there were even occasional shortages of J-2 [jet] fuel. I am sure all of these things existed and that production was sufficient, but by that stage of the war the transport system was so chaotic that things often failed to arrive at the front-line units. In our unit, flying the Me 262, we had some pilots with only about a hundred hours total flying time. They were able to take off and land the aircraft, but I had the definite impression that they were of little use in combat. It was almost a crime to send them into action with so little training. Those young men did their best, but they had to pay a heavy price for their lack of experience.'

Left: Leutnant Walter Hagenah, who flew Me 262s during the final stages of the war

new combat aircraft into large-scale service. But given the formidable array of impediments encountered by the Luftwaffe, it is not surprising that the formation of a sizeable jet fighter force incurred lengthy delays.

On 9 February Ist Gruppe of Bomber Geschwader (Fighter) 54 sent its Me 262s into action for the first time. It put up about ten aircraft to counter a multi-pronged attack by American heavy bombers against targets in central Germany. The ex-bomber pilots had received only sketchy training in air-to-air combat, and it showed. Escorting Mustangs pounced on the jet fighters and shot down six in quick succession, while the Me 262s inflicted damage on only one B-17. One of the German pilots who lost his life in this action was bomber ace Oberstleutnant Volprecht von Riedesel, the Geschwader commander.

■ LARGE-SCALE ACTION ■

Just over a week later, the IIIrd Gruppe of Fighter Geschwader 7 went into action in force for the first time. On 21 February Mustangs of the 479th Fighter Group were on patrol near Berlin when they ran into fifteen Me 262s, by far the largest

number yet encountered. Moreover for the first time the jet fighters were flown aggressively, as the American formation leader reported:

'Bounce was directed at Red Flight, as squadron was making a shallow turn to the left from an easterly direction. Bounce came from 3 o'clock position at our level by four Me 262s flying the usual American combat formation, looking like P-51s with drop tanks. Our Red Flight broke into jets but they crossed in front of our flight up and away. A second flight of four Me 262s flying in American combat formation then made a bounce from the rear, 6 o'clock high. Our flight turned into this second Me 262 flight and the Me 262s broke climbing up and away. At this time the first flight of Me 262s came back on us again from above and to the rear. We broke into this flight and this kept up for three or four breaks, neither ourselves or Jerry being able to get set or close in for a shot. Each time we would break they would climb straight ahead out-distancing us. Within the Jerry flight the Number 4 man, while turning, would fall behind and slightly above, so that it was necessary to take on this Number 4 man or he would slice in on our tail if our Flight would take on the rest of the Jerry flight.' The report exemplified the sort of inconclusive actions that took

place when well-handled jets confronted well-handled Mustangs. Unless they held the advantage of surprise, the Me 262s were no real threat to the latter.

On 25 February the IInd Gruppe of Bomber Geschwader (Fighter) 54 made its first entry into action in the new role. In the process it suffered even heavier losses than its sister Gruppe earlier in the month. The unit lost six Me 262s in air-to-air combat, four when American

Leutnant Rudolf Rademacher was credited with eight victories in February 1945

fighters strafed its airfield and a further two in flying accidents. Following this series of disasters the bad weather fighter Geschwader was withdrawn to undergo further training.

During February 1945 one pilot, Leutnant Rudolf Rademacher of IIIrd Gruppe of Fighter Geschwader 7, showed what a well-handled Me 262 could achieve in combat. That month he was credited with the destruction of six heavy bombers, a Mustang and a recon-naissance Spitfire.

At this time the fighter-bombers of

Bomber Geschwader 51 were also active against Allied troops advancing into Germany. Their largest attack, against British troops near Cleve on 14 February, involved fifty-five jet fighter-bomber sorties spread throughout the day. The total bomb load carried in these raids amounted to a puny 27 tons, however. The attacks caused so little damage to military targets that they receive scarcely a mention in British army records.

The winter was in its final stages before the Me 262 day fighter units were ready to operate in force against the American bomber formations. On 3 March the Luftwaffe flew twenty-nine Me 262 fighter sorties, to engage 1,069 US heavy bombers and 684 escorts attacking a spread of targets in Germany. It was by far the strongest showing by the jet fighters so far, yet they could achieve little. This is hardly surprising, however, given that the American raiding force outnumbered the jet fighters by a ratio of more than sixty-to-one! The Me 262s claimed the destruction of six U.S. bombers and two fighters, in return for one Me 262 lost. American records list nine bombers and eight fighters lost that day, but do not claim an Me 262.

During the next two weeks most of the Me 262 fighter force stayed on the ground preparing for its next great exertion. That came on 18 March, when 37 jets took off to engage 1,184 US bombers and 426 fighters making for Berlin. The jet fighters claimed the destruction of 12 US bombers and a fighter; from US records it seems likely that only eight of the heavy bombers fell to the Me 262s however. Two jet fighters were lost during the action. During each of the following seven days there were similar pitched battles between Me 262s and American formations.

On the 30 March the Luftwaffe put up 31 jet fighters to engage 1,320 U.S. bombers and 852 fighters attacking Hamburg, Bremen and Wilhelmshaven. On patrol over Kaltenkirchen airfield, Mustang pilot Captain Robert Sargent of the 330th Fighter Group saw two jet fighters taking off. With his wingman he dived to attack the enemy planes:

'Unfortunately due to their camouflage we lost them for a second and when we got down to their level I was able to pick up just one of them. From here on it was easy. My air speed was 430mph and I estimated his as about 230mph. As we closed, I gave him a long burst and noticed strikes immediately. The left [jet engine] unit began to pour white smoke and large pieces of the canopy came off. The pilot baled out. We were at 300 feet at this time and the plane dove into the ground and exploded causing a large oil-like fire which went out almost at once. The pilot's chute did not open fully and

Below: **The 30 mm cannon was an extremely effective air-to-air weapon, as shown by the result of a single hit by a high explosive round on a Spitfire fuselage during a ground firing test.**

the last I saw of him was on the ground near the plane with the chute streaming out behind him. Lt Kunz did a splendid job of covering my tail and after the encounter we pulled up and looked for the second jet. But when we sighted him he was going balls out for central Germany and we couldn't overtake him.' That same day the jet fighters claimed three enemy bombers and three fighters destroyed, for the loss of three of their own aircraft.

During this stage of the war RAF Bomber Command also mounted frequent daylight attacks on targets in Germany. On 31 March a force of 460 Lancasters and Halifaxes headed for the U-boat assembly yards at Hamburg. Near the target several Me 262s delivered a sharp attack on the formation and knocked down seven bombers, before the escorting fighters drove them away.

■ THE ZENITH ■

Also that day 1,302 US bombers and 847 fighters attacked Zeitz, Brandenburg, Brunswick and Halle. These raiding formations also came under attack from Me 262s. The jet fighter units flew a total of about 38 sorties that day. On the available evidence it seems likely that they shot down 14 Allied heavy bombers and two fighters, for a loss of four of their own. That victory total marked the zenith of achievement for the Me 262 units. Yet even on this, the jet fighter's

Above and below: Me 262 of Fighter Geschwader 7, with a rack for twelve 55mm air-to-air rockets mounted under each wing. First used in action in March 1945, these unguided weapons were fired in rapid succession at a single target.

most successful day of all, the losses they inflicted amounted to only 1 per cent of the huge Allied raiding force. The Luftwaffe had done its utmost, yet the effect on its enemy had been no more than a pin-prick.

Early in April Fighter Unit 44 (Jagdverband 44) became operational with Me 262s, flying from Riem airfield

near Munich. Commanded by General Adolf Galland, this unusual unit included among its ranks several fighter aces including Johannes Steinhoff, Guenther Luetzow, Heinz Baer and Gerhard Barkhorn. With a strength equivalent to a Gruppe (30 aircraft), FU 44 flew its first mission on 5 April when it sent up five jet fighters. They claimed the destruction of two enemy bombers, without loss to themselves.

By now the Allied ground forces were advancing deep into Germany and the Luftwaffe fighter control organization was on its last legs. Even the uniquely talented pilots of Fighter Unit 44 could make no impression on the air situation. Rarely would the unit fly more than half a dozen sorties, or shoot down more than a couple of Allied aircraft, in a day. Compared with the huge Allied air activity this was indeed a puny effort, and the entry of Galland's unit into action passed unnoticed by its opponents.

On 7 April the Me 262 fighter force mounted its largest defensive effort of all, with a total of 59 sorties. However, because of poor ground control most of the Me 262s failed to engage enemy aircraft. The jets claimed five Allied aircraft destroyed for the loss of two of their own.

On 9 April, the last date for which figures are available, there were about two hundred Me 262s on the strength of the various front-line units. Of these, 163

Me 262 FRONT-LINE UNITS

9 APRIL 1945
Note: this date, four weeks before the end of the war, was the last for which an official strength return was made. First figure aircraft total, second figure serviceable.

Bomber Geschwader 51		
I Gruppe	15	11
II Gruppe	6	2
Fighter Geschwader 7		
Staff Flight	5	4
I Gruppe	41	26
II Gruppe	30	23
Bomber Geschwader (Fighter) 54		
I Gruppe	37	21
Fighter Unit 44	abt 30	abt 15
Night-Fighter Geschwader 11		
10 Staffel	9	7
Tactical Recon Gruppe 6	7	3

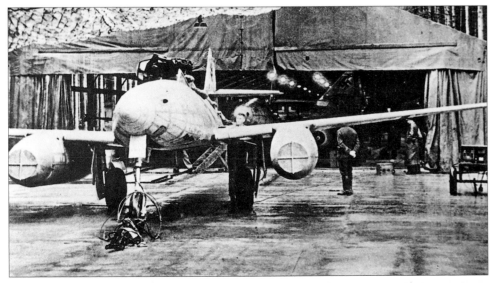

Left top: **An Me 262 of Fighter Geschwader 7 being refuelled after an air action near Berlin in April 1945.**
Middle: **Me 262 belonging to the tactical reconnaissance unit Kommando Braunegg. The aircraft carried a pair of cameras mounted vertically in the nose. The large bulge in front of the cockpit covered the film magazine for the port camera.**
Bottom: **A newly completed Me 262 leaving the heavily camouflaged factory at Leipheim near Ulm. Although more than 1,200 Me 262s were delivered to the Luftwaffe by the end of the war, only a small proportion were available for operations at any one time. (via Hans Selinger)**

served with day-fighter units, twenty-one with fighter-bomber units, about nine with night-fighter units and seven served with a tactical reconnaissance unit.

The final action of any note involving Me 262s occurred on 10 April. Fifty-five jet fighters took off to engage formations with more than two thousand US heavy bombers and escorts attacking targets in the Berlin area. The jets destroyed about

55042 A.C

Left: A dramatic combat photograph taken from a P-51 Mustang, showing an Me 262 under attack while it was engaging another Mustang. While the jet fighter maintained high speed it was a difficult target for the Allied piston-engined fighters. However, once a jet fighter slowed down to engage in a turning fight with Allied fighters, it was at a disadvantage. Several of the German jet fighters were shot down in combat. (USAF)

The high points of the Me 262's combat career were not especially impressive

In assessing the usefulness of the Me 262 as a combat aircraft, let's examine the statistics of what the aircraft achieved:

- Number of Me 262s delivered to the Luftwaffe by May 1945: more than 1,200.
- Largest number of Me 262s in front-line service (April 1945): about 200.
- Most Me 262 fighter sorties in a day (7 April 1945): 59.
- Most Me 262 victories in a day (31 Mar 1945): 16.
- Most Me 262 fighter-bomber sorties in a day (14 Feb 1945): 55.
- Highest tonnage dropped by Me 262s in a day (14 Feb 1945): 7 and a half.

These figures show the high points of the Me 262's combat career, yet in no case are they impressive.

■ CONCLUSION ■

With hindsight we can see that Adolf Hitler's edict, that initially the Me 262 should be used as a fighter-bomber, had remarkably little effect. The real problem lay with the aircraft's under-developed engines rather than its operational use, and the edict caused no great delay in the type's introduction in the fighter role. The Luftwaffe cannot reasonably be reproached for not pushing the Me 262 into production early enough. Indeed, if anything that service had initiated production of the Me 262 too early, before the Jumo 004 engine was ready to enter mass production. The Me 262 failed in action mainly because of the unreliability of its jet engines, coupled with the pressures – both direct and indirect – exerted by the powerful Allied air attacks.

In the chaos that existed in Germany during the final year of the war the Luftwaffe fighter units were unable to exploit the Messerschmitt Me 262's excellent performance and heavy fire power. In combat the jet fighters suffered heavy losses, and achieved little success. Given the huge numerical superiority of the forces arraigned against them, and the high quality of their equipment, it could hardly have been otherwise.

ten US bombers and seven fighters. However throughout this period the US escorts delivered vigorous counter-attacks in the course of which they shot down twenty-seven Me 262s, nearly half of those committed. Nineteen Lutfwaffe jet pilots were killed and five wounded. It was a major defeat for the Me 262 units, and one from which the force would never recover.

Now the German collapse was imminent, as Allied troops advanced rapidly into Germany from the east and the west. The Luftwaffe found itself squeezed into a progressively smaller area, and by the end of April the jet units had virtually ceased their operations.

Right: After the war the Czech Avia company assembled and flew eight Me 262s from components left in that country after the war. Five single-seater fighters (designated S-92s) and three two-seater trainers (designated CS-92s) served with the Czech Air Force until the early 1950s when they were replaced by Soviet-built jet fighters.

APPENDICES

COMPARATIVE RANKS

Luftwaffe	Royal Air Force	US Army Air Forces
Generalfeldmarschal	Marshal of the RAF	-
Generaloberst	Air Chief Marshal	General (4 star)
General der Flieger	Air Marshal	General (3 star)
Generalleutnant	Air Vice-Marshal	General (2 star)
Generalmajor	Air Commodore	General (1 star)
Oberst	Group Captain	Colonel
Oberstleutnant	Wing Commander	Lieutenant Colonel
Major	Squadron Leader	Major
Hauptmann	Flight Lieutenant	Captain
Oberleutnant	Flying Officer	1st Lieutenant
Leutnant	Pilot Officer	2nd Lieutenant
Stabsfeldwebel	Warrant Officer	Warrant Officer
Oberfeldwebel	Flight Sergeant	Master Sergeant
Feldwebel	Sergeant	Technical Sergeant
Unteroffizier	Corporal	Staff Sergeant
Obergefreiter	Leading Aircraftman	Corporal
Gefreiter	Aircraftman First Class	Private First Class
Flieger	Aircraftman Second Class	Private Second Class

ORGANIZATION OF LUFTWAFFE FLYING UNITS

The Staffel
During the early part of the war the Staffel (plural Staffeln) had a nominal strength of nine aircraft, and it was the smallest combat flying unit in general use in the Luftwaffe. By the late war period the strength of a Staffel could be much greater or much smaller, depending on the role of the unit. The Staffeln had Arabic numbers; 1st, 2nd and 3rd Staffeln belonged to the Ist Gruppe. The 4th, 5th and 6th belonged to the IInd Gruppe and 7th, 8th and 9th Staffeln belonged to the IIIrd Gruppe.

The Gruppe
The Gruppe (plural Gruppen) was the basic flying unit of the Luftwaffe for operational and administrative purposes. Initially it was established as three Staffeln each with nine aircraft, plus a Staff Flight with three, making 30 aircraft in all. After a period in action a Gruppe could be considerably smaller than that, as can be seen from the actual Luftwaffe orders of battle included in this book.

The Geschwader
The Geschwader (plural Geschwader) was the largest flying unit in the Luftwaffe to have a fixed nominal strength, initially three Gruppen with a total of 90 aircraft, and a Staff unit of four, making a total of 94 aircraft. Originally it had been intended that the Gruppen of each Geschwader would operate from adjacent airfields, but under the stress of war this idea had to be abandoned.

The Air Corps (Fliegerkorps) and the Air Fleet (Luftflotte)
The Air Corps and the larger Air Fleet varied in size, and the number of Gruppen assigned to them depended on the importance of their assigned operational area.

APPENDIX C

THE LUFTWAFFE FIGHTER ACES' VICTORY SCORES

The German fighter aces' victory claims were very much higher than those of their Allied counterparts. Over the years there has been controversy, much of it ill-informed, on the validity of these claims. For example Major Erich Hartmann, an Me 109 pilot and Luftwaffe top scorer, is credited with 352 victories. Thirty-five German pilots are credited with victory totals exceeding 150.

In comparison Group Captain 'Johnnie' Johnson, the top-scoring RAF pilot during the late-war period, is credited with 38 victories; Major Richard Bong, top-scoring US Army Air Force pilot, is credited with 40; and Guards Colonel Ivan Kozhedub, the top-scoring Soviet Air Force pilot, is credited with 62 victories.

At first sight it might seem, and several writers have said, that the German pilots scores were inflated by Dr Goebbels's propaganda service. This author has studied the German victory claims in some detail, however, and can say with confidence that this was not so. The Germans are nothing if not good bureaucrats, and before it received confirmation an individual pilot's victory claim had to undergo a lengthy period of checking; no claim was accepted unless there was an independent witness of the action in the air or on the ground, or if a wreck had been found which appeared to link with the claim. The confirmation process sometimes took several months, and was far more thorough than anything attempted by the RAF or the USAAF (or, almost certainly, by the Soviet Air Force). After the Luftwaffe was forced on to the defensive on the various fighting fronts, the majority of air combats took place over German-held territory. Under those conditions a German pilot would have difficulty getting a victory confirmed if the action took place over land and no wreck was

subsequently found. That is not to say that the victory score credited to every German fighter pilot is 100 per cent accurate in every case. The organization was as effective as could be expected in time of war, but it was not perfect and on occasions mistakes were made. The system was more thorough than its counterparts in the Allied air forces, however.

If the German pilots' victory claims are generally accurate, and this author believes they are, why was there so great a disparity between the claims of the different nations' best pilots? Were the top German fighter aces eight or nine times better than those of the Allied Air Forces? The answer is that they certainly were not.

The main difference between the two sides was that if he survived long enough, a German fighter pilot had a far greater opportunity to amass a large score than his Allied counterparts. During the early part of the war the Luftwaffe was often in action against air forces that were inferior in training, tactics and equipment. As a result the latter suffered accordingly. During the summer and autumn of 1941 it was relatively easy for an experienced German pilot on the eastern front to run up a large score. But the days of the easy victories soon passed as the Soviet fighter force improved, both quantitatively and qualitatively. From the mid-1943 the Luftwaffe had a hard fight on the Eastern Front and its losses were heavy. To survive for any length of time against numerically superior enemy forces, a German pilot had to be either very good or very lucky. But for those who knew their business, there were plenty of enemy aircraft to be picked off.

Another factor to consider is that German fighter pilots did not fly limited tours of combat duty like those in the R.A.F. or the USAAF For example Erich Hartmann joined Fighter Geschwader 52 on the Eastern Front in October 1942, and flew operations continually from then until the end of the war. His only breaks were during a few short spells of leave. By the end of October 1943 his victory score stood at 148, and in March 1944 it passed the two hundred mark. When the war ended Hartmann had flown more than 800 operational missions – an average of nearly one sortie per day over the 30-month period since he began operations. No British or American pilot flew combat missions at such an intensive rate and for so long, before being sent on a rest tour. Hartmann's victory total at the end of the conflict stood at 352 aircraft destroyed, or an average of one for every 2.25 sorties he flew. Several Allied fighter pilots at the peak of their careers achieved similar victory rates, but in the RAF or the USAAF they were not allowed to continue to do so for long.

To sum up, in this writer's view the German fighter pilots' victory scores were recorded as accurately as can be expected in time of war, and they were more carefully corroborated than those of their British or American counterparts. The German scores were higher than those achieved by other nations because their pilots had greater opportunities to achieve victories and their periods engaged in operational flying were longer.

Major Erich Hartmann (left), the top-scoring pilot in the Luftwaffe, credited with 352 aerial victories. In October 1942 he joined Fighter Geschwader 52 straight from training and remained with the unit, flying Me 109s on the Eastern Front, until the end of the war.

THE NORTH AMERICAN
P-51 MUSTANG

'The Forts were dropping their bombs, but the sky was so black with flak that we could only occasionally see them as they flew through the solid wall of sooty explosions. Don was the first to see the Me 109.

'"Johnny, at six o'clock high there's a single bandit."

'I looked back, and there he was, high above us. I gazed in disbelief as his nose dropped and he plummeted down on us.

'"Don, the crazy son of a bitch is bouncing us."

'"I know. When I yell 'Break', you break right and I'll break left."

'I watched as the 109 dropped closer and closer. "Break, Johnny."

'I pulled sharply to the right, and thought at first I had broken too late as the 109 pulled onto my tail. I tightened my turn and met Don halfway around as he tried to fire on the 109 in a head-on attack. I went around twice more with the Jerry on my tail before Don could reverse his turn and swing down for a rear attack. But this German pilot was a smart, capable flyer. As Don brought his guns to bear, he Split-S and dove to the ground. Don and I followed him, our motors roaring in pursuit. He pulled out of his dive and banked left, which brought him close to

me. I followed him and fired. He wasn't one to sit still, however, and changed his turn to swing into Don. I followed, firing intermittently. Don meanwhile had climbed for altitude, and I kept the Jerry busy in a tight turn. As I fired, I saw flashes on his wing, fuselage, and even his motor, but the pilot wouldn't bale out. Turning all the time and losing height, we were now just above the tree tops, and the 109's engine was spewing smoke. I had no forewarning that my ammunition was running out, but as I prepared for the final burst, only silence came as I pressed the tit.

'"Finish him, Don, I'm out of ammunition."

'Don, who had been maneuvring above us waiting for the Jerry to break out of the turn, zoomed down in front of me and made one pass on the courageous German flyer. His shots hit home . . .'

■ COMBAT DUO ■

The two Mustang pilots in this successful combat were two of America's finest; Don Gentile (21 victories) and John T. Godfrey (18 victories). Members of the 336th Fighter Squadron, 4th Fighter Group in the spring of 1944, the deadly duo became legendary for their teamwork, even though they only flew as a pair on five occasions.

This combat was notable on several counts. The Me 109G opposing them was in many ways the equal of the Mustang, and it started the combat with the dual advantages of height and position. The German pilot showed great confidence in engaging after it became clear that the element of surprise had been lost, when the safe move would have been to disengage and climb away, using the excess speed generated in his attacking dive. As it was, he was evidently banking on disposing of Godfrey before

Left: **Probably the greatest exponents of air combat teamwork in the USAAF were Captain Don Gentile, seen here in the cockpit of his P-51B** *Shangri-La,* **and Lieutenant John Godfrey, perched on the wing wearing flying helmet, goggles and Mae West (10 April 1944). On return to the USA, Gentile became an Air Force test pilot (KIFA 28 Jan 1951); Godfrey returned to action in August, was shot down by ground fire later that month, and became a prisoner of war (died 12 June 1958). (USAF)**

GENTILE AND GODFREY VERSUS ME 109

(1) the two Mustangs break in opposite directions, The Me 109 follows Godfrey's hard turn. (2) Gentile opens fire, misses, then turns away to reposition. Meanwhile Godfrey flies tight circles to deny the Messerschmit a shot. Gentile gets behind the German (3), who tries to disengage with a vertical dive (4) with Gentile in pursuit. Godfrey, now free, also dives to cut the 109 off (5). The German pilot pulls out of his dive (6) and turns towards Godfrey, but with Gentile still on his tail is forced to turn away. With Godfrey in an attacking position, Gentile pulls up and circles (7). Godfrey runs out of ammunition and calls Gentile, who dives and delivers a lethal burst (8).

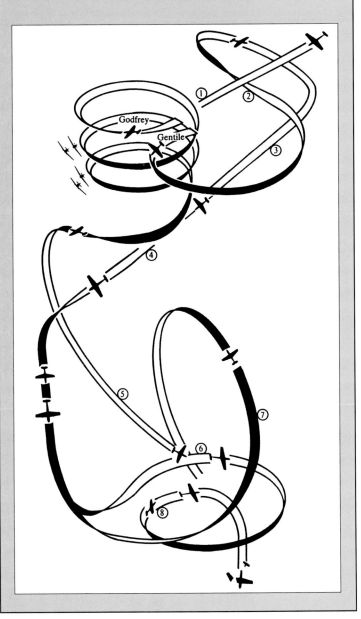

Gentile could intervene, then taking on the second Mustang in a one-versus-one combat.

That he failed was due to the excellence of the P-51B, which turned hard enough to deny him a valid shooting opportunity, and the skill of John Godfrey in holding him off until Gentile could take up an attacking position.

Having lost the initiative, and outnumbered two to one, he attempted to disengage with a near-vertical dive to ground level. The superb performance of the two Mustangs allowed them to follow him down with relative ease, with Gentile in hot pursuit. Even then he might still have escaped had it not been for the teamwork of the two Mustang pilots, one of whom held him in play while the other jockeyed for position, the leadership passing back and forth between them as opportunity offered. But against what was acknowledged to be the best fighting pair in the USAAF, flying aircraft fully the equal of his own, his bravery and flying skills availed him nothing.

■ PRECISION BOMBING RAIDS ■

When the United States of America entered the war, their policy in Europe was to carry out precision bombing raids on selected targets. The main bomber type was the Boeing B-17 Flying Fortress, which not only had adequate range for the task, but carried very heavy defensive armament. In theory this would allow the bombers, flying in close formation, to beat off massed attacks by German fighters. In practice this did not work at all well. With shallow penetrations of enemy airspace, casualties were sustainable, as the time spent in the combat area was limited. However, with deep penetrations the German fighter arm was able to react in force over a considerable period, and US losses rose to unacceptable levels.

The only possible answer was to match fighters with fighters, but there were problems. Single-seat, single-engined fighters of the time were traditionally short-legged, while the longer-ranged twin-engined fighters were outclassed by agile enemy single-engined fighters. Germany had learned this lesson during the Battle of Britain, when the Me 110 took a series of heavy beatings from the nimble British Spitfires and Hurricanes. Somehow a single-seater, single-engined agile fighter with the required range had to be found.

The solution came in the unlikely shape of an American airframe initially developed for the RAF, married to the outstanding Rolls-Royce Merlin engine. The Mustang had almost double the fuel capacity of the Spitfire and a correspondingly greater radius of action. On late models, the addition of a large fuel tank in the fuselage and two drop tanks under the wings increased the range to the point where the American fighter could rove the length and breadth of the Third Reich. Wherever the bombers went, Mustangs could accompany them, to the dismay and discomfiture of the defending German fighters.

■ MERLIN ENGINE ■

The Merlin engine had been adopted to provide the high-altitude performance lacking in the original Allison-engined aircraft. That the airframe was good there was no doubt; the early model Mustang had proved itself to be an outstanding fighter at low and medium altitudes. The RAF used it in roles where high-altitude performance was not required, such as ground attack, army co-operation and low-level reconnaissance.

The USAAF was not slow to follow suit, with the attack version redesignated the A-36 Invader and the tactical reconnaissance aircraft the F-6. The fighter variant was at first known as the Apache in USAAF service; only later were both names abandoned in favour of Mustang, which, already used by the British, in the long run saved a lot of confusion.

While the Merlin-engined Mustang variants were by far the most important of the breed, and the type

Above: **Wherever there was action, Mustangs were sure to be found. They ranged Europe from Norway in the north to Italy in the south, and from France in the west to Russia in the east. North African deserts, Burmese jungles, Chinese paddy fields, the vast wastes of the Pacific, even the skies over Japan – all heard the thunder of their engines. (Arvin Williams via JE)**

gained undying fame in the skies of Western Europe, it was used in virtually every theatre of operations during the Second World War. A handful of Mustangs was supplied to the Soviet Union, although these were far too few to have any real impact. B-17 Fortresses on the so-called 'Shuttle' missions, which flew on to Russian bases after bombing Germany, were accompanied by Mustangs, which sometimes operated briefly on the Eastern Front. Mustangs were also based in southern Italy, from where they could range as far afield as Romania, Bavaria, or the south of France.

In the Far East, the Japanese were made well aware of the presence of the P-51, units of which were at various times based in India, Burma and China. Even in the vast Pacific Ocean, traditionally the domain of the US Navy carrier fleets, the Mustang's immense radius of action was put to good use. Based on Iwo Jima towards the end of the war, Mustangs escorted the huge B-29 Superfortresses during raids on the Japanese home islands.

Like all fighters of the era, the Mustang underwent a process of continuous development, and its performance started to approach the limits of what was possible with the internal combustion engine and not very efficient propeller. The other limit which had been pushed very hard indeed was pilot endurance. After a seven-hour mission over Germany, a pilot was completely exhausted. The

Below: **The combination of the British Rolls-Royce Merlin engine and the American P-51 Mustang airframe resulted in a superb fighter. With the addition of extra fuel tanks, it was able to escort the heavy bombers over previously unheard-of distances.**

answer had to be a second pilot to share the load. But how was this to be done without compromising performance?

The answer was the P-82 Twin Mustang. In essence, two Mustang fuselages and tails were coupled together with a central wing and tail section, with the outboard wings remaining unchanged. This gave two cockpits, while range and performance remained largely unimpaired; only manoeuvrability suffered, and that not to any great degree. Still later an airborne interception radar was fitted, giving night and all-weather Twin Mustangs.

■ KOREA ■

The end of the Second World War coincided with the emergence of the new breed of jet fighters. Totally outperformed, the Mustang seemed as if its days as a front line combat aircraft were numbered. It had, however, one remaining advantage. Early jet engines were incredibly thirsty, and their acceleration was sluggish. Consequently endurance was almost non-existent by comparison with the Mustang, and they were unable to use short temporary airstrips from which the piston-engined fighter could operate with ease.

This endurance was to show to advantage in the war in Korea, which broke out in 1950. Japan-based jets could stay over the battle area for just a few minutes, whereas P-82s from the same base could loiter for much longer, and P-51s could be based 'in-country'. The final combat sortie of an American

P-51 took place from Korea in January 1953, but this was far from the final combat mission to be flown.

Above: **Even in 1944, the German Me 262 jet gave the Mustang a hard time in combat. A far greater mismatch nearly occurred in 1963. If the confrontation between Malaysia and Indonesia had resulted in open war, Indonesian Mustangs would have had to face missile-armed Mach 2 Lightnings of the RAF. (BAe via author)**

Israeli Mustangs flew in defence of the newly formed state from late 1948, and even in 1956 they took an important, if secondary, role in the Suez war before being phased out during the following year. In 1963, a confrontation took place between Malaysia and Indonesia. The main Indonesian fighter type was the Mustang. The air defence of Malaysia was largely in the hands of the Royal Air Force, equipped with the Mach 2-capable Lightning. In the event of overt hostilities, this would have been a tremendous mismatch; perhaps fortunately for the Indonesian fighter pilots it did not occur. Finally, in what was perhaps the most ridiculous war ever, Salvadorean Mustangs fought with Honduran Corsairs and Thunderbolts. This was the combat swansong of the Mustang, which was soon after relegated to airshows and unlimited-class racing.

In what was to prove a final renaissance for the fighter, the Cavalier Aircraft Corporation PA-48 Enforcer made its maiden flight on 9 April 1983. A heavily modified Mustang, it was offered to the South American market as a light tactical aircraft. There were no takers, and the programme was finally terminated in 1986. The Mustang is long gone from the military scene, but its proud legend lives on. This is its story.

Below: **1945 saw the Mustang the dominant fighter in the USAAF, but it was outclassed and superseded by the new jet fighters, typically the Lockheed P-80 Shooting Star shown here. (Author)**

NORTH AMERICAN P-51B MUSTANG

1 Rudder trim tab (plastics)
   construction
2 Rudder frame (fabric covered)
3 Rudder balance
4 Fin front spar
5 Fin structure
6 Access panel
7 Rudder trim tab actuating drum
8 Rudder trim tab control link
9 Rear navigation light
10 Rudder metal bottom section
11 Elevator plywood trim tab
12 Starboard elevator frame
13 Elevator balance weight
14 Starboard tailplane
   structure
15 Reinforced bracket
   (rear steering stresses)
16 Rudder operating horn forging
17 Elevator operating horns
18 Tab control turnbuckles
19 Fin front spar/
   fuselage attachment
20 Port elevator tab
21 Fabric covered elevator
22 Elevator balance weight
23 Port tailplane
24 Tab control drum
25 Fin root fairing
26 Elevator cables
27 Tab control access panels
28 Tailwheel steering mechanism
29 Tailwheel retraction mechanism
30 Tailwheel leg assembly
31 Forward-retracting steerable
   tailwheel
32 Tailwheel doors
33 Lifting tube
34 Fuselage aft bulkhead/
   breakpoint
35 Fuselage break point
36 Control cable pulley brackets
37 Fuselage frames
38 Oxygen bottles
39 Cooling air exit flap actuating
   mechanism
40 Rudder cables
41 Ruselage lower longeron
42 Rear tunnel
43 Cooling air exit flap
44 Coolant radiator assembly
45 Radio and equipment shelf
46 Power supply pack
47 Fuselage upper longeron
48 Radio bay aft bulkhead
   (plywood)
49 Fuselage stringers
50 SCR-695 radio transmitter-
   receiver (on upper sliding shelf)
51 Whip aerial

52 Junction box
53 Cockpit aft glazing
54 Canopy track
55 SCR-522 radio transmitter-
   receiver
56 Battery installation
57 Radiator/supercharger
   coolant pipes
58 Radiator forward air duct
59 Coolant header tank/radiator
   pipe
60 Coolant radiator –
   access cover
61 Oil cooler air inlet door
62 Oil radiator
63 Oil pipes
64 Flap control linkage
65 Wing rear spare fuselage attachment bracket
66 Crash pylon structure
67 Aileron control linkage
68 Hydraulic hand pump
69 Radio control boxes
70 Pilot's seat
71 Seat suspension frame
72 Pilot's head/back armour
73 Rearward-sliding
   clear-vision canopy
74 External rear-view mirror
75 Ring and bead gunsight
76 Bullet-proof windshield
77 Gyroscopic gunsight
78 Engine controls
79 Signal pistol discharge tube
80 Circuit-breaker panel
81 Oxygen regulator
82 Pilot's foot-rest and seat
   mounting bracket
83 Control linkage
84 Rudder pedal

85 Tailwheel lock control
86 Wing centre-section
87 Hydraulic reservoir
88 Port wing fuel tank filler point
89 Port 0.5in (12.7mm) machine
   guns
90 Ammunition feed chutes

91 Gun bay access door (raised)
92 Ammunition box troughs
93 Aileron control cables
94 Flap lower skin (Alclad)
95 Aileron profile (internal aerodynamic balance diaphragm)
96 Aileron control drum and

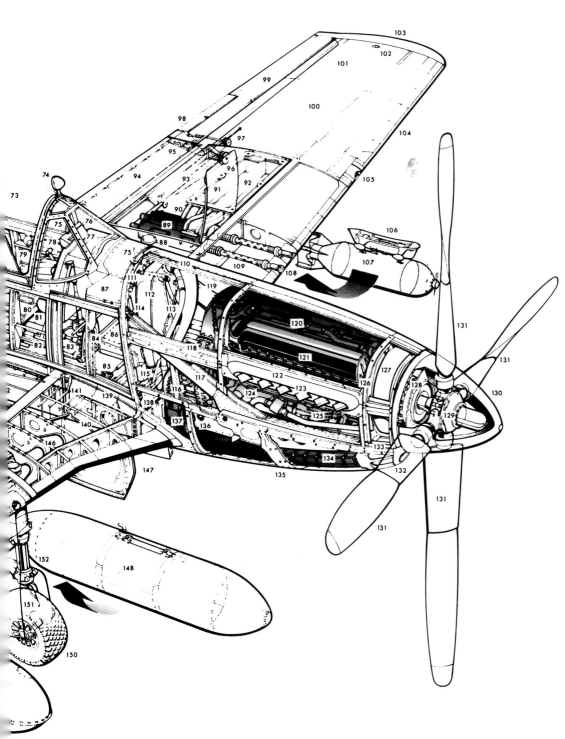

115 Oil tank metal retaining straps
116 Carburettor
117 Engine bearer assembly
118 Cowling panel frames
119 Engine altercooler
120 Engine leads
121 Packard (Rolls-Royce Merlin) V-1650 engine
122 Exhaust fairing panel
123 Stub exhausts
124 Magneto
125 Coolant pipes
126 Cowling forward frame
127 Coolant header tank
128 Armour plate
129 Propeller hub
130 Spinner
131 Four-blade Hamilton Standard Hydromatic propeller
132 Carburettor air intake, integral with 133
133 Engine mount front frame assembly
134 Intake trunking
135 Engine mount reinforcing tie
136 Hand crank starter
137 Carburettor/trunking vibration-absorbing connection
138 Wing centre-section front bulkhead
139 Wing centre-section end rib
140 Starboard mainwheel well
141 Wing front spar/fuselage attachment bracket
142 Ventral air intake (radiator and oil cooler assemblies)
143 Starboard wing fuel tank
144 Fuel filler point
145 Mainwheel leg mount/pivot
146 Mainwheel leg rib cut-outs
147 Main gear fairing doors
148 Auxiliary fuel tank (plastic/pressed paper composition); capacity 90 Imp gal (409l)
149 Auxiliary fuel tank (metal) capacity 62 gal (284 litres)
150 27in (68.6cm) smooth-contour mainwheel
151 Axle fork
152 Towing lugs
153 Landing gear fairing
154 Main gear shock strut
155 Blast tubes
156 Wing front spar
157 Gun bay
158 Ammunition feed chutes
159 Ammunition boxes
160 Wing rear spar
161 Flap structure
162 Starboard aileron tab
163 Starboard aileron
164 Starboard aileron tab adjustment mechanism (ground setting)
165 Wing rib strengthening
166 Outboard section structure
167 Outer section single spar
168 Wingtip sub-assembly
169 Starboard navigation light
170 Detachable wingtip

mounting bracket
97   Aileron trim tab control drum
98   Aileron trim tab plastics (phenol fibre) construction
99   Port aileron assembly
100 Wing skinning
101 Outer section sub-assembly
102 Port navigation light
103 Port wingtip
104 Leading-edge skin
105 Landing lamp
106 Weapons/stores pylon
107 500lb (227kg) bomb
108 Gun ports
109 Machine gun barrels
110 Detachable cowling panels
111 Firewall/integral armour
112 Oil tank
113 Oil pipes
114 Upper longeron/engine mount attachment

With war looming in the late Thirties, it became a matter of urgency for Britain and France to expand their air forces. With their home industries already heavily committed, it was only natural that they should turn to the United States.

The best of the American fighters of this period was the Curtiss P-40. The prototype of this had first flown in the autumn of 1938, more than two years after the Spitfire, but it was in fact little more than a re-engined Hawk 75 of rather earlier vintage. A large production order for the US Army Air Corps was placed in May 1939, and this meant that the manufacturers had little spare capacity to meet export orders for Britain and France in the immediate future. At this stage, the British Purchasing Commission, based

in New York, sought a second-source manufacturer. Their choice lighted on North American Aviation, based at Inglewood, California.

At that time, North American was mainly noted for its NA-16 Harvard trainer, and its sole experience of fighter design consisted of a handful of NA-50s and NA-68s for Thailand. These were in essence Harvards with more powerful engines and armament. This notwithstanding, the idea of licence-production of the Curtiss fighter did not really appeal to North American. Studies for a new fighter had been underway since the previous summer, and these appeared to indicate that the company could design a fighter around the same Allison engine used by the P-40, but which would have far better performance than the Curtiss.

A proposal was made to the British in January 1940, which resulted in a contract for a prototype, designated

FIRST ORDER

I am directed by His Majesty's Government to inform you that it is their intention to purchase from you 400 single-seat fighter aeroplanes, plus spare parts therefore in the amount of 20% of the value of the aeroplanes. (Author's note: this translates as 320 aircraft plus enough spares to make up another 80.)

Material ordered.
(a) 400 North American model NA-50B single-seater fighter aeroplanes fitted with Allison CV-1710 engines and three-bladed metal propellers all in accordance with North American specification No -1592 as finally altered and amended and agreed upon.

EXTRACT FROM LETTER OF INTENT FROM THE ANGLO-FRENCH PURCHASING COMMISSION

Left: Prior to the P-51, North American Aviation lacked experience in fighter design, its previous attempt in this field being a souped-up and armed version of the T-6 trainer, two of which are seen here with the Mustang prototype.
Below left: The NA-73X prototype. Sleek but angular, it was vaguely similar in appearance to the German Messerschmitt Me 109E, which gave rise to all sorts of unfounded rumours. From this angle, the wingtip shows the approximate configuration of the laminar flow section that was to play such a tremendous part in the Mustang's success. (AAHS via JE)
Far left: The instrument panel of the early Mustangs was tidily laid out, as can be seen in this photograph taken during assembly, although it followed American rather than British practice. Another departure from British practice was the wrap-around perspex windshield, with an armoured glass screen behind it. If the windshield misted up, as frequently happened, the pilot was unable to reach past the armoured glass to wipe it. The answer was a revised windshield with an armoured glass panel incorporated; this was implemented on the second production batch. Also visible here are the reflector sight and the rearview mirror. (Roger Freeman)

NA-73X. Part of the mythology of the Mustang's origins was that the British insisted that the new fighter should be produced from scratch in just four months. In fact, this arose from a statement by NAA President Dutch Kindelberger, but it was never an element in the contract. Of course, the dice were loaded; design studies had, as we have seen, been underway for almost a year, and when the contract was signed on 23 May 1940, much of the detail design was already complete. It was however a remarkable achievement that the NA-73X was rolled out just 102 days later, even though it lacked an engine and the wheels had been borrowed from a Harvard!

The NA-73X was sleek but angular. For ease of production, curves were never used where a straight line would do. This gave the aircraft a superficial resemblance to the Me 109E and thus started the canard that NAA designer Edgar Schmued was a German who had once worked on the Messerschmitt fighter. There was of course no truth in this, even though it was to appear in print many times.

One crucial decision was to use a laminar flow wing

Aerodynamic drag increases in direct proportion to the square of the speed; i.e. drag at 400mph is 16 times greater than the drag for the same aircraft at 100mph. The only way to obtain greatly improved performance over another fighter which uses the same engine is to substantially reduce drag, and NAA designers made every attempt to do this. At the same time they made every effort to keep weight down by making many items serve more than one purpose.

One of the really critical decisions was to use a laminar flow wing. This had been researched by the National Advisory Committee for Aeronautics (NACA, the forerunner of the modern NASA). The normal aerofoil sections for

DESIGN CONSIDERATIONS

Strictly for comparative purposes, we are including results of a study showing the difference in size and performance between the airplane offered and one which might be offered with a minimum of armament and without protective armor. This second design (P-509) incorporates only four machine guns and is not fitted with protective armor, but is otherwise the same. It will be noted that the high-speed in this condition is 400mph with a wing area of 190 sq. ft. With a full complement of armament and armor plate protection front and rear, the weight is increased from 6,450 lbs to 7,765 lbs and the wing area is increased from 190 sq. ft. to 230 sq. ft. in order to maintain the same landing speed. The resulting performance is materially reduced and the high-speed is 384mph under the same conditions.

EXTRACT FROM LETTER FROM NAA, 1 MAY 1940

the period had their maximum thickness at roughly 20 per cent of the chord, the chord being the distance from front to back. They also had a distinct camber, with a convex upper surface and a concave lower surface. After the airflow passed the thickest point, it had a tendency to 'burble', or become turbulent. The thickest point on a laminar flow wing was more than half-way across the chord, and for all practical purposes it had no camber; both surfaces were convex in shape. In practice this meant that the air tended to slip smoothly past both surfaces, giving a tremendous reduction in drag. There was of course a price to be paid for this; the lift generated was not as high as a more conventional aerofoil section, and for low speeds, large and powerful slotted flaps were needed.

■ ALLISON ENGINE ■

The NA-73X was of all-metal stressed skin construction. The wings, which had pronounced dihedral, contained a sheet-web main spar, and an almost equally strong rear spar, which carried the ailerons and flaps. The distance between spars was sufficient to fit the length of the 0.50in (12.7mm) Browning machine gun, leaving only the barrel to project ahead of the main spar. The main gear legs were widely spaced, giving excellent ground handling, and retracted inwards towards the centreline. The main gear wheels were large, and to house them within the wing, the leading edge was kinked forward inboard to increase wing depth at this point. To minimize drag, the tail wheel was also retractable.

The only engine considered was the Allison V-1710, which was a liquid-cooled 12 cylinder inline producing 1,150hp. Contrary to popular legend, it had a geared supercharger, but power, and with it performance, fell away rapidly above 15,000ft (4,570m). At that time the USAAC had no requirement for high-altitude combat fighters, and all American fighters of the era were equally limited. Even as the NA-73X was being built, combat experience in Europe was proving otherwise, but while a turbo-supercharger was briefly considered, it was discounted at this stage. Traditional engine mountings of the day consisted of a frame of welded steel tubes. NAA differed in designing cantilevered beams, with the engine itself resting on rubber blocks to damp out vibration.

Location of the radiator beneath the fuselage

Another attempt to minimize drag involved the cooling system. Heat from the engine was led to a radiator which dissipated it into the passing air. Heat is of course a form of energy which, unless some means could be found to harness it, was wasted. Theoreticians on both sides of the Atlantic suggested that if the heated air was discharged rearwards at high pressure it could actually provide a small increment of thrust, which in turn would partially offset the drag of the

Right: Fitting Browning 0.50in (12.7mm) guns and their ammunition feeds in the wings could initially only be done by canting them on their sides, as seen here. This frequently caused jams when they were fired during hard manoeuvres. (Roger Freeman)

Left: The Allison engine installation, showing the carburettor intake. The heavy machine guns mounted low on each side of the engine, together with their synchronization gear, ammunition tanks and feeds, made servicing difficult, and these were deleted on later models. (Roger Freeman)

installation. It demanded great care in designing the ducting for the intake and efflux, with moveable flaps to adjust the flow as necessary. While the principle was well known, early Mustang radiators did not produce thrust in this manner, and only later was this developed.

The optimum location for the radiator installation was found to be beneath the fuselage, just aft of the cockpit. A small penalty was paid in weight for the extra piping required, but in terms of performance it paid off. Not considered at that time was the danger of extra combat vulnerability, but even if this had been taken into account, it would probably have been deemed to be compensated for by increased performance.

■ 8MM SEAT ARMOUR ■

The controls were well harmonized, and instead of cables, which could slacken slightly, adversely affecting handling, the control runs were rods, again at a slight weight penalty. The control surfaces on the tail were fabric-covered, whereas the ailerons were aluminium.

The cockpit was roomy by British standards, with 8mm back armour to protect the pilot. To minimize drag, it was set low, and the roof line was faired into the fuselage. The view 'out of the window' was good, although, as with many contemporary fighters, rearward visibility could have been better. However, the canopy design drew adverse comments from some quarters. Whereas British fighters had sliding hoods, the canopy of the NA-73X was hinged. The panel on the left opened out and downwards, while the roof hinged open to the right. It could not be opened in flight, unlike the British-style canopies, although in an emergency it could be jettisoned. In this it was not unlike the Me 109.

The NA-73X carried no armament, although dummy gun ports were painted on the leading edges of the wings. The proposed armament was heavy by any standards. Two 0.50in (12.7mm) Browning machine guns were mounted

Above: Test pilot Paul Balfour came to grief on the fifth flight of NA-73X, when the engine cut. His forced landing in a cultivated field was a disaster, as can be seen here. Damage was extensive, and over seven weeks passed before the aircraft could be flown again.

low on the nose, synchronized to fire through the propeller. These were staggered to allow their magazines to fit one behind the other. Two more 0.50in (12.7mm) Brownings were set outboard in the wings, with four 0.30in (7.62mm) Brownings further out. The magazines for the wing guns, holding two hundred 0.50in (12.7mm) rounds each or five hundred 0.30in (7.62mm) rounds each, were set well outboard, and fed by conveyor chutes.

The United States being a far larger country than Britain, Americans are perhaps more distance-conscious than their trans-Atlantic cousins. This showed in

the design fuel capacity of the NA-73X, which consisted of two 75 imperial gallon (90 US gallon/341 litre) tanks in the inboard wing sections. This was three-quarters as much again as the normal capacity of the Spitfire, and gave the new fighter the remarkable endurance of about four hours.

Fuel capacity – two 75 imperial gallon tanks in the wings

Although the airframe had been rolled out early in September 1940, Allison engines, also used in the P-38, P-39 and P-40, were in short supply. Not until early October did one become available. It was fitted quickly, and taxiing trials commenced. Then, on 26 October,

freelance test pilot Vance Breese lifted the new aircraft off the Mines Field runway for its first flight.

Three more successful test flights were made, which revealed only minor snags apart from a tendency of the engine to overheat. Modifications to the radiator inlet were needed, but before these could be put in hand, near-disaster struck.

On 20 November, company test pilot Paul Balfour took the NA-73X aloft on its fifth test flight. As he approached the runway he throttled back, and as speed bled off the engine started to run roughly, then spluttered to a stop. With no power available, Balfour attempted a dead-stick landing in a cultivated field short of the runway. He selected gear down but, given the soft surface, this was an error. The wheels dug in and the aircraft nosed over onto its back. That there was no fire was fortunate on two counts. Balfour was trapped in the cockpit, the canopy of which was half-buried

Above: The first production aircraft, AG 345, in British markings. The short carburettor scoop has yet to be lengthened. The nose guns can be seen projecting, while some idea of the unorthodox layout of the wing guns is given by the vertically staggered ports, with the centre guns set lower than the others.

in the soft earth, and had to be dug free. Secondly, the precious prototype, although damaged, was repairable, and was returned to the flight test programme on 11 January 1941.

One of the more obvious modifications concerned the carburettor scoop. Due to the layout of the Allison engine, this was located on top of the engine cowling. Under certain flight conditions, low airspeed, low revs and increased angle of attack, air ram recovery was insufficient. This had been responsible for the crash of the first prototype. The cure for it was to extend the intake forward to the very front of the cowling.

Ultimately the incident did not jeopardize the project. The urgency of the British requirement meant that the North American fighter had been purchased 'off the drawing board', an order for 320 having been placed in August 1940, following the original letter of intent of 11 April. Then, during December of that year, it was officially named Mustang by the British.

The first production aircraft was scheduled for delivery in January 1941, but, due to various problems, it did not take to the air

until 23 April. This machine was not delivered to the RAF; instead it was retained as a development aircraft by NAA, who flew it intensively in conjunction with the prototype.

■ FIRST MUSTANG ■ IN THE UK

The first Mustang to reach Britain arrived at Liverpool docks in a crate in October 1941, having survived the attentions of the U-boats en route. It was taken to Speke airport, where it was assembled, and made its first flight in its adoptive country on 24 October. From Speke it went to the Aeroplane and Armament Experimental Establishment at Boscombe Down where all operational equipment, British gunsights, radios etc. were installed, and evaluation began. Further evaluation of this aircraft and one other was made by the Air Fighting

Left: The first production Mustang flew on 23 April 1941. From this angle, the short carburettor scoop above the engine and the radiator housing beneath the fuselage can clearly be seen. The control surfaces on the tail were fabric-covered, which accounts for the different colour. (Paul Coggan via JE).

FLYING REPORT

The aircraft is pleasant to fly, being extremely stable in all planes. The take-off is rather long, but with little tendency to swing, and as the engine is not fitted with an automatic boost control, care must be taken not to overboost. The landing is easy though the run is longer than taken by a Hurricane or Spitfire. The controls are well balanced and can be made light or heavy as required by adjustment of the servo-tabs fitted to ailerons and elevators. There is little tendency to heavy-up at high speeds. With the controls lightened by the tabs, the Mustang is as light as the Spitfire but far smoother in all manoeuvres. The aircraft handles extremely well in aerobatics and gives ample warning of the stall. In particular, it was found far more difficult to effect a high speed stall than in a Spitfire.

EXTRACT AFDU REPORT 5.5.42.

Development Unit at RAF Duxford from 28 January 1942. In fact, most of the first 20 Mustangs to arrive in Britain were initially used for evaluation and installation trials.

The AFDU at Duxford gave a very favourable report on the American fighter, praising in particular its handling. It noted that the cockpit, while generally spacious and comfortable, was a trifle cramped for a tall pilot. In addition it was excessively hot, even in freezing conditions. Compared to the Spitfire VB it was significantly faster at low and medium altitudes, but the speed advantage was lost at 25,000ft (7,600m). In rate of climb the Mustang was significantly inferior to the British fighter, by which it was outmanoeuvred at all heights. It did however perform far better in the dive as a result of its aerodynamic cleanness.

■ A MAJOR FLAW ■

The fall-off in performance with increasing altitude was the one flaw in an otherwise superb fighting aeroplane. From the first days of air fighting, altitude had always been regarded as the most important tactical advantage. By 1942, most air combat took place at altitudes where the Mustang was less agile. This being the case, RAF Fighter Command could not risk it, and the majority of the first batch of Mustang Is went to Army Co-operation Command squadrons, where their sparkling low-level performance and outstanding range could be fully utilized in the low-level armed reconnaissance role. For this they were fitted with an F24 oblique camera mounted behind the pilot's head armour.

Even as prophets are traditionally without honour in their own land, so the Mustang was for a long time ignored by the USAAF. Reasons were not hard to find; existing fighters such as the P-38 and P-40 were undergoing further development, while several new and promising designs were coming along fast, among them Republic's enormous P-47 Thunderbolt. Consequently there

Above: The seventh production Mustang I seen at the Air Fighting Development Unit, RAF Duxford, for which it had the yellow P in a circle painted on the fuselage. The carburettor scoop on this machine has been lengthened, and the adjustable outlet at the rear of the radiator farm can be seen open.
Right: The fourth and tenth production Mustangs were retained by the USAAC for evaluation under the designation XP-51. This was a departure from standard practice, as the X prefix was normally only given to true prototypes, which this was far from being. Seen here in RAF colours and apparently ready for delivery is AG 348, the fourth production machine, later renumbered as 41-038.

was little interest in what was primarily seen as a 'foreign' design. The USAAF did however acquire two examples of the type.

This had come about quite fortuitously. Before warplanes could be exported, the manufacturer needed a Foreign Release Agreement with the USAAC (as the USAAF then was). This agreement stated that the fourth and tenth production machines should be supplied for evaluation, with the designation XP-51. Although the first aircraft was flown on 20 May 1941, various delays ensured that it did not reach the test centre at Wright Field, Ohio (now Wright-Patterson AFB) until 24 August. The second XP-51 did not arrive until 16 December that year, by which time the official performance flight tests were all but complete.

The US government made credit available with lend lease

The first batch of Mustangs for the RAF was a straight sale, but with the costs of all-out war escalating, British funds ran short. At this stage the US government made credit available with Lend-Lease. Under this arrangement, the USAAF ordered aircraft as though for their own use, then passed them on. On 7 July 1941, the USAAF placed an order for 150 Mustangs on behalf of the RAF. These differed from the previous batch in that they were armed with four 20mm Hispano Suiza cannon in place of the previous eight machine guns, a change arising from extensive combat experience. In RAF service these became Mustang IAs; to the Americans they were plain P-51s, with no suffix letter.

With flight testing at Wright Field in full swing early in December 1941, the treacherous attack on Pearl Harbor by the Japanese catapulted the United States into the war. While this was to have a lasting effect on the future of the Mustang, at first it served only to obscure matters as American fighter development

Top: 41-038 seen at the Wright Field, Ohio, test centre (now Wright-Patterson AFB) some time after 24 August 1942. With the exception of an anti-dazzle panel on the cowling and bright national markings, the aircraft is in bare metal. Surprisingly, the carburettor scoop has not been lengthened, while the gun ports have either been blanked over, or airbrushed out by the censor. (USAF via JE)

Middle: 41-038 survived the war, albeit in a sad and careworn state. Seen here at Freeman Field in Indiana in 1945 and scheduled for the scrap yard, it was rescued for the National Air and Space Museum. (Haney Collection via JE)
Bottom: Completely refurbished by the Experimental Aircraft Association after 30 years in storage, 41-038 flew again in 1980 as part of the Warbirds of America fleet.

XP-51 OFFICIAL PERFORMANCE SUMMARY

Level Flight Speed at Design Altitude of 13,000ft (3,950m) with a Design Gross Weight of 7,934lb (3,600kg)

Maximum speed 382mph (615km/hr) 3,000 rpm/1,100bhp
High speed 370mph (595km/hr) 3,000rpm/1,100bhp
Cruising speed 325.5mph (524km/hr) 2,280rpm/750bhp

Optimum Range and Endurance with 170 imperial gallon fuel
Cruising speed 780 miles (1,255km) 2.4 hours

Climb Data with Gross Weight of 7,934lb(3,600kg)

Altitude	0/0	5,000/	10,000/	15,000/	20,000/	25,000/	30,800/
(ft/m)		1,524	3,0484	572	6,095	7,620	9,387
Climbing speed							
(mph/kh)	178/286	194/312	208/335	222/357	236/380	248/399	262/422
Engine (rpm)	3,000	3,000	3,000	2,600	2,600	2,600	2,600
Power (bhp)	1,050	1,095	1,140	820	680	550	–
Max climb							
ft/min	2,200	2,270	2,345	1,570	1,070	610	100
m/sec	11.18	11.53	11.91	7.98	5.44	3.10	0.51

and production was stepped up. The few Wright Field test pilots who had flown the Mustang were impressed, but they were lone voices crying in the wilderness. Only slowly were its sterling qualities recognized and accepted.

Of the 150 P-51s ordered for the RAF, only 93 were actually delivered to them. Of the remainder, 55 were retained by the USAAF, commencing in July 1942, by whom they were at first known as Apaches. Most of these were fitted with cameras to become F-6A tactical reconnaissance machines. The final two were

earmarked for the XP-78 project, which involved a change of engine.

Massive expansion had caused budgetary problems for the USAAF, and by the time that it decided that it wanted the Mustang, the budget for fighters was exhausted. There was however still money in the kitty for an attack aircraft. Consultations between NAA and the Pentagon resulted in the A-36A Invader. In essence this was a P-51 with the uprated -87 Allison engine, underwing racks to carry two 500lb (227kg) bombs, and dive brakes. Hydraulically actuated, these were of the perforated door type, set above and below the wings. The 0.30in (7.62mm) machine guns in the wings were deleted.

■ DIVE-BOMBER PLOY ■

At this stage the USAAF had no requirement for a dive bomber, but modifying the P-51 in this way was a useful ploy for getting it into USAAF service. Be this as it may, this did not prevent the USAAF from evaluating the A-36A as a dive bomber. On 16 April 1942, a massive order for 500 A-36As was placed, long before this variant flew.

This was followed on 23 June (when the next year's budget became available) by another order for 310 P-51As. These used the latest model Allison V-1780-81 engine, which developed maximum power at 18,000ft (5,490m) and thus significantly improved high-altitude performance, although it still did not give the Mustang parity in this sphere with its European contemporaries. The other major change was in weaponry; the nose-mounted guns with their heavy and cumbersome synchronization gears, the latter necessary to prevent damage to the propeller, were deleted, as were the wing-mounted 0.30in (7.62mm) machine guns. The number of wing-mounted 0.50in (12.7mm) Browning heavy machine guns was increased to four.

This change in the armament offered

Left: The angular lines of the Mustang made it easily mistaken for the rather smaller Me 109E. Seen here is the most heavily armed Mustang of all, the P-51 (no suffix letter), which carried four 20mm cannon in the wings. (Roger Freeman)

Left: **The A-36A Invader was the dive bomber variant, fitted with dive brakes above and below the wings. With an uprated Allison engine, it could carry one 500lb (227kg) bomb beneath each wing. The wing-mounted 0.30in (7.62mm) machine guns were deleted as seen here.**

several advantages. With the increasing use of armour plate and self-sealing tanks by the enemy, light machine guns had little to commend them, whereas the Browning .50s were adequate against all but heavy bombers, few of which were likely to be encountered. The projectile of the heavier gun had near-perfect ballistics (the world's first supersonic fighter, the Bell X-1, used the same shape for its fuselage) giving a long effective range. Weight saving was considerable. The complexity of the overlapping feeds for the wing guns was greatly reduced, while the logistical problems that arose from using two different sizes of ammunition were eliminated.

Right: **P-51A of the USAAF. The wide spread of the main gear legs made it particularly suitable for operations from semi-prepared airstrips. (Roger Freeman)**

USAAF reverted to the British name of Mustang

The A-36 made its maiden flight in the hands of test pilot Ben Chilton on 21 September 1942 – by which time the USAAF had reverted to using the British name of Mustang for all variants – and the same pilot also took the first P-51A into the air on 3 February 1943. With production by now in full swing,

Above: **Reconnaissance Mustang! The F-6B was a P-51A fitted with a twin K24 camera installation. This 9th Air Force example is from the 107th Squadron of the 67th Tactical Reconnaissance Group. It is fitted with the Malcolm hood, a field modification invented by the British to improve all-round view from the cockpit. (T. R. Bennett via JE)**

first deliveries of the latter took place during the following month. Of the 310 P-51As, 35 were fitted with the twin K24 camera installation to become F-6Bs, while 50 were allocated to the RAF as Mustang IIs.

The Mustang was by now well and truly launched in both RAF and USAAF service. But the best this fighter could produce was still to come.

FINAL REPORT

The A-36 has excellent diving characteristics from the standpoint of a fighter, but it dives too fast for a dive bomber, the dive breaks slowing the airplane down approximately eighty-three (83) miles per hour. This is insufficient from the dive bomber standpoint, as the airplane will still dive with the dive breaks open to speed in excess of four-hundred-fifty miles per hour, necessitating bomb release at approximately four thousand (4,000) feet in order to pull out of the dive. The best diving angle is approximately seventy (70) degrees.

EXTRACT FROM FINAL REPORT ON TEST OF THE OPERATIONAL SUITABILITY OF THE A-36 TYPE AIRPLANE, 15 APRIL 1943.

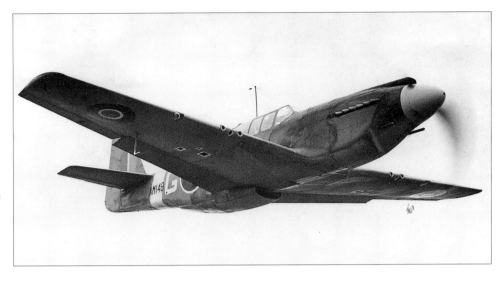

The first Mustang delivery to an operational unit was made in late January 1942. The lucky recipient was No. 26 Squadron of Army Co-operation Command (ACC) RAF, based at Gatwick where the international airport now stands, but then just a grass field.

■ BRITISH MUSTANGS ■ (WESTERN EUROPE)

Experience in the Battle of France (albeit at the receiving end) had convinced the British that the key to success in land operations lay in close co-operation with the air. Of course, the RAF had long possessed dedicated army co-operation

Left: It's all right, they're ours! Tactical reconnaissance Mustangs of No. 168 Squadron RAF overfly allied armour advancing across Normandy. They carry the invasion stripes adopted for instant recognition. (Roger Freeman)

squadrons, but on the outbreak of war these were equipped with antiquated Hawker Hector biplanes and lumbering Westland Lysanders. Both types of aircraft were far too slow and vulnerable for modern warfare.

Army Co-peration Command (ACC) was formed in December 1940 as a Command in its own right, with the object of building an effective tactical reconnaissance and close air support force against

Above: Mustang I of No. 26 Squadron poses for the camera with a few degrees of flap. The vertically staggered gunports indicate some of the problems of getting three machine guns in the wings. (Roger Freeman)

Below: Same engine, different aircraft. A P-40 Tomahawk I in RAF service. The slightly ungainly appearance is due to its development from the radial-engined P-36. (Crown Copyright via Bruce

Above: **The Mustang I supplanted the Westland Lysander in Army Co-operation Command. This is an aircraft of No. 225 Squadron. (via Bruce Robertson)**

the day when the war could be carried to the Third Reich. Its first task was to re-equip with faster and more modern aircraft, but these were in short supply. ACC had to take what was available, which in this case was the Curtiss P-40 Tomahawk, rejected by RAF Fighter Command because of poor high-altitude performance – although used effectively in North Africa with the Desert Air Force.

Re-equipment with the Tomahawk commenced in August 1941, but a high rate of unserviceability made this type unsatisfactory. The Mustang, also rejected by Fighter Command for short-comings at high altitude, but with an outstanding performance at low level, came at the ideal time to replace it.

The army co-operation mission was still in the throes of development at this stage. For this reason, conversion onto type was a fairly leisurely affair, with both types operated during the conversion phase. This had the advantage of keeping all the squadrons operational, rather than taking them out of the line

Below: **Mustangs of No. 400 Squadron RCAF, parked on a hardstanding at Dunsfold, Surrey, in 1943. These have flame dampers on the exhausts for Night Ranger missions. (Roger Freeman)**

MUSTANG I AND II SQUADRONS IN ACC SERVICE, OCTOBER 1942

Sqn	Service	Prev A/C
2	RAF	Tomahawk
4	RAF	Lysander
16	RAF	Lysander
26	RAF	Tomahawk
63	RAF	Hurricane
169	RAF	Beaufighter
239	RAF	Tomahawk
241	RAF	Tomahawk
268	RAF	Tomahawk
309	Polish	Hurricane
400	RCAF	Tomahawk
414	RCAF	Tomahawk
430	RCAF	Tomahawk
613	R (Aux)AF	Tomahawk

No. 241 Squadron never flew Mustangs operationally. In November 1942 it was sent to the Middle East to fly Hurricanes, and its aircraft were taken over by No. 168 Squadron.

to re-equip. By October of that year, no fewer than 14 squadrons had converted to the Mustang I or II. In all, 24 British squadrons flew Allison-engined Mustangs during the war, although there were never more than 16 at any one time.

■ MUSTANG ■ AND 109 LOOKALIKE

A major cause for concern was the superficial resemblance between the Mustang and the Messerschmitt Me 109, particularly the 109E, which had square-cut wingtips. To make for easier identification, most Mustang Is in front-line squadrons carried painted yellow bands around the wings throughout 1942.

The combat debut of the Mustang came on 10 May, when a single aircraft of No. 26 Squadron flown by Flying Officer G. N. Dawson left Gatwick at first light for an armed reconnaissance. Crossing the coast south of Le Touquet, he shot up hangars in the corner of the airfield north of Berck Plage, then attacked a goods train before returning safely. From such small beginnings, the Mustang legend grew!

The first major operation in which the

Mustang was committed was the amphibious landing at Dieppe on 19 August. Virtually a dress rehearsal for the later invasion, it was a test of effectiveness of the army co-operation concept. Four ACC squadrons were involved; the already operational No. 26 and 239, with elements from the Canadian No. 400 and 414 Squadrons, whose operational debut this was.

Nine Mustangs were shot down by flak and fighters

It was a hard baptism of fire. Nine Mustangs were shot down by flak and fighters in the course of 72 sorties, while two more were damaged beyond repair. On the credit side, information on the

Below: Practice run. Mustang Is of No. 63 Squadron hurtle low over Scotland in April 1943. The aircraft from which the picture was taken was obviously even lower than these two. (Roger Freeman)

tactical situation was available in England very quickly; the operation was valuable as a learning experience; and American pilot Hollis Hills, flying with No. 414 Squadron RCAF, claimed a Focke-Wulf FW 190 as the Mustang's first air combat victory. It was the first of many.

■ 'POPULAR' OPS ■

The low-altitude armed photo-reconnaissance sorties which were the ACC Mustang's basic mission were code-named 'Popular'. These sorties were normally flown by a section of two at 270mph (434km/hr) at very low altitude. The camera technique was to point the port wing at a likely target, then set the camera rolling. The task of the wingman was to protect his leader by keeping a sharp lookout for fighters. 'Populars' were only flown in conditions of seven-tenths cloud or more, with the cloud base at 1,500ft (460m) or less. This provided something in which to hide if the going got rough.

After the Dieppe raid, 'Rhubarbs' became fashionable. These were low-level incursions aimed at specific ground targets, flown by an element of two aircraft in weather conditions which would aid them in eluding the German defences. 'Rangers' were identical except

Below: **German flying boats moored on a lake in the south of France burn under the guns of attacking Mustangs in 1944. (Roger Freeman)**

LOW-LEVEL TACTICS

Attacks should be alternated between the two members of the flight, one covering while the other makes the attack. Each pilot of the pair should be constantly searching for enemy aircraft so as to avoid a surprise attack by enemy pursuit (aircraft). Attacks should be made from one side of the railway, canal or roadway, to the other – never along. An attack should never be repeated even though the objective has been missed, because the protecting element of surprise is no longer present. At a speed of 270mph and at zero altitude, the search area is comparatively limited and targets appear quickly. Experience and alertness are required to pick out those targets in time to make an attack . . . It has also been found that depressing the flaps 5° will have little effect on the speed, but it will change the attitude of the aircraft so that targets can more easily be seen over the nose.

BRITISH ARMY CO-OPERATION TACTICAL EMPLOYMENT OF THE MUSTANG, 26 AUGUST 1943.

that targets of opportunity were sought. Spitfires also flew these missions, but the fact that the Mustang could penetrate twice as far into enemy territory made the American fighter far more useful in this role. Some idea of the general effectiveness of these can be given by the fact that in the space of 18 months, a single Mustang squadron destroyed or severely damaged 200 railway engines, over 200 barges, and a considerable number of enemy aircraft on the ground. Losses during this period were eight Mustangs: five to flak, two to unknown causes, and one to enemy fighters. During the course of this saga of destruction Mustangs penetrated into Germany itself, their deepest incursion to just outside Wilhelmshaven, where on one occasion they shot up a railway engine. Air combat was avoided where possible, but nearly 30 German fighters fell to the guns of Allison-engined RAF Mustangs. No. 400 Squadron RCAF claimed a dozen in the first year of operations, three alone falling to the guns of Flight Lieutenant Duncan Grant. From June 1943, this unit also flew occasional night intruder patrols, attacking German aircraft over their own bases. For these night missions, flame-damping exhausts were fitted.

ACC was disbanded in June 1943, and the Mustang squadrons, after a spell with Fighter Command, transferred to 2nd Tactical Air Force, an organization set up specifically for the invasion of Europe. By this time production of Allison-engined Mustangs had ceased, and the attrition inherent in low-level operations

(more than twice as many were lost in accidents than to enemy action) caused a shortage of aircraft. Between June 1943 and January 1944, nine Mustang squadrons converted to other types.

In 18 months a single Mustang squadron destroyed or damaged 200 railway engines

---

By D-Day, 6 June 1944, only five British Allison-Mustang squadrons remained; Nos 2, 168, 268, 414 RCAF and 430 RCAF. The next eight months saw heavy losses, and by the end of the year only Nos 26 and 268 Squadrons still operated the type. In fact No. 26 ceased to fly Mustangs late in 1943, but reconverted in October 1944 for the photo-reconnaissance of V-2 rocket-launching sites in Holland. At the end of the war in Europe, only these two squadrons still flew Allison-Mustangs.

■ AMERICAN MUSTANGS ■ (WESTERN EUROPE)

With the invasion of Europe scheduled for mid-1944, the USAAF planned to have several squadrons of F-6As and F-6Bs in place in England for the event. However, the plan was foiled by the non-availability of Allison-engined Mustangs, and in fact only one unit was formed. This was the understrength 67th TRG, with a mere 24 F-6Bs, which took up residence at Membury in October 1943.

The first 'Popular' sortie was flown on 20 December. Although finally reduced to a single squadron, the type was operated up to the last days of the war as part of 2nd TAF.

■ AMERICAN MUSTANGS ■ (MEDITERRANEAN)

The first USAAF Mustangs in operation were the cannon-armed P-51s which

ALLISON-MUSTANG UNITS IN SERVICE IN ENGLAND, D-DAY, 6 JUNE 1944		
No. 2	Squadron	RAF
No. 168	Squadron	RAF
No. 268	Squadron	RAF
No. 414	Squadron	RCAF
No. 430	Squadron	RCAF
67th	TRG	USAAF

were appropriated from the British order from July 1942. Tactical reconnaissance training took place at Key Field in Missouri. They were followed into service in October by the A-36A Invader, four groups of which were formed over the next few months. Although the USAAF originally had no requirement for a dive bomber, training for this role began. It proved hazardous, as the air brakes sometimes extended unevenly due to varying hydraulic pressures. When this happened, it was nearly impossible to keep the aircraft aligned on its target. To make matters worse, structural failures sometimes occurred, causing the loss of both aircraft and pilot. As a direct result, the USAAF recommended that the type should be used for low attack only, but in practice many operational units later practised dive bombing with a great deal of success.

By March 1943, USAAF Mustangs were ready for action. Their combat debut came in North Africa, when the 68th Observation Group (later redesignated Tactical Reconnaissance Group), based in Morocco, received 35 P-51s.

Above: Some American aircraft types used by the RAF, seen at Speke in December 1941. In the foreground is a Mustang I, later allocated to No. 430 (Canadian) Squadron; behind is a P-40D Kittyhawk, while left to right in the background are a Lockheed Hudson and two Douglas Boston light bombers. (Roger Freeman)

They were really camera-equipped F-6As, but this designation was rarely if ever used. That same month, the A-36As of the 86th Bomb Group were also shipped to Africa, but for various reasons this unit was late getting into action. The combat debut of USAAF Mustangs took place on 10 April, a photo-reconnaissance mission to Kairouan airfield in Tunisia.

The build-up of A-36As in North Africa continued apace, and by the end of May over 300 had arrived. Many of these were used to re-equip the 27th Bomb Group. This Havoc light bomber outfit had arrived in theatre only to have its aircraft and crews used as replacements for casualties in other units. Like their British counterparts, the American

Above: December 1943, and an A-36A of the 27th FBG drops supplies to troops on Mount Maggiore in Italy. (Roger Freeman)
Opposite above: Desert conditions played havoc with aircraft, not least their paint schemes, as demonstrated by this camera-equipped P-51 in North Africa. The Stars and Stripes on the tail was adopted for the benefit of local inhabitants who might have been unfamiliar with standard USAAF insignia.
Opposite below: A-36A of 27th Fighter-Bomber Group in Sicily, 1943. The white bars on the nose carry the mission records. This aircraft, No 42-84067, is seen with a 500lb (227kg) bomb under each wing. (USAAF via Roger Freeman)

Mustang units in the Mediterranean theatre used yellow wing stripes for ease of identification.

It was the 27th BG that took the A-36A to war for the first time, when it dive-bombed the airfield on the Axis-held island of Pantelleria on 6 June. Attacks on Sicilian targets followed; then, shortly after the successful invasion of that island, the 27th moved to Sicily, where it was joined by the 86th. Both Groups then took part in attacks on the Italian mainland.

The sequence of events for a dive-bombing attack was as follows. Target approach was between 8,000 and 10,000ft (2,400–3,000m). Air brakes out, then half-roll directly above the target and pull through into a vertical dive. The bombs were released as the speed built up through 300mph (483km/hr), which was usually at an altitude of between 2,000 to 4,000ft (600–1,200m), with recovery on the deck. Against heavy flak defences, bomb release and recovery were made much higher. Attacks were made by sections of four, who went down one after the other. This had the fault of putting all aircraft in the same chute; if the ground gunners missed the leader, they might easily get one of those following. Tail-end Charlie in a dive bombing mission was not an enviable place to be!

■ DIVE-BOMBING ■

The difference between dive and glide bombing was purely the angle of dive on the attack run. Anything less than 72 degrees was regarded as glide bombing. A true vertical dive gave greatest accuracy, but it was not easy to tell when this was achieved. There was only one foolproof way; an aileron roll would cause the aim to wander off if the dive angle was less than 90 degrees! One final canard should be disposed of; it has often been stated that the air brakes were wired shut. There was an early recommendation that they should not be used, due to handling problems caused by differential deployment. The wiring

Above: An A-36A Mustang of the 27th FBG overflies the Vesuvius volcano south of Naples shortly before it erupted in 1944. (USAAF via Roger Freeman)

story, which is baseless, appears to have arisen from this. In fact, the problem was largely overcome by a simple modification.

While based on Sicily, the two A-36A groups several times provided escorts for B-17s and B-24s raiding targets in the Naples area. This was not a great success due to their lack of high-altitude capability but they were the only fighters in the theatre with the range to get there and back. German fighter and flak defences were fierce, and several aircraft were lost on these missions.

HIGH SPEED

It became an excellent fighter-bomber, capable of delivering its load with extreme accuracy. Its high speed and good manoeuverability make it an excellent aircraft for either dive or glide bombing, but it must be noted the accuracy obtained by glide bombing is much less than that obtained by using the dive brakes to secure vertical dives on the target.

NORTHWEST AFRICAN AIR FORCE TACTICAL BULLETIN NO. 23, 1 JULY 1943.

DIVE-BOMBER

'Our most dangerous flights were down the straits between the toe of Italy and the island of Sicily, when we were assigned the task of bombing enemy barges, which were being used to get troops out of Sicily. The anti-aircraft fire was intense during these missions, which were successful but costly in terms of pilots and planes. We were very successful in hitting the barges during dive bombing. I have no idea how many guns were mounted on the barges; we were too busy concentrating on our dive bombing and strafing runs to count guns.'

WAYNE RUTHERFORD, 86TH FBG.

The Salerno landing in September 1943 also saw the Mustang's long operational radius used to the full, although on this occasion they were not required to operate at high altitude. Then after a few days the 27th and 86th TRGs were moved to an airstrip on the beachhead itself. The missions were of short duration but very dangerous, as the Mustangs were under fire even during take-off and landing.

By March 1944 almost half the available A-36s had been lost or written off

The mountainous terrain in Italy made dive bombing necessary, even though losses in this form of attack were high. Where possible, low-level attacks were substituted. With no replacement aircraft forthcoming, the 27th and 86th, by now redesignated as Fighter-Bomber Groups, suffered a reduction in size from four squadrons to three. By March 1944, almost half the available A-36As had been lost or written off. Matters were made worse when a handful of A-36As were transferred to the 111th TRS of the 68th TRG, to supplement their F-6As. This situation could not last. The 27th FBG re-equipped with P-40s that month, while in July the 86th FBG converted to P-47s. At much the same time, the 111th TRS handed in their remaining P-51As and A-36As in exchange for Merlin-engined Mustangs. It was the end of an era.

■ AMERICAN MUSTANGS ■ (FAR EAST)

The 311th FBG arrived at Dinjan in north-east India in the late summer of 1943, having been shipped across the Pacific via Australia. Two squadrons were equipped with A-36As; the third flew P-51As. It was an all-can-do group, tasked not only with reconnaissance, attack and dive bombing, but interception and bomber escort. In these last two it was rather less than successful.

The main Japanese fighter in the

Below: **P-51A Mustangs of the 1st Air Commando Group at an airfield outside Karachi before moving to Burma. The first operation of the 1st ACG was in support of the Chindits, the long-range penetration force led by Orde Wingate which operated behind Japanese lines. (USAF via JE)**

Above: Conditions in the India/Burma theatre of operations were often primitive. This P-51A of the 1st ACG, seen here being laboriously refuelled by hand pump from 40-gallon drums, was flown by Captain Robert L. Pettit. (USAF via JE)

theatre was the Nakajima Ki-43 Haya-busa 'Oscar'. This very lightly wing-loaded Japanese fighter outclimbed and out-turned the P-51A at all altitudes and had a far higher ceiling. From low speeds it accelerated rapidly. It did have short-comings, however, the main ones being its relatively light armament of two 0.50in (12.7mm) machine guns, and general lack of protection for fuel tanks and pilot.

Tasked to provide protection for trans-ports flying the 'Hump' route over the Himalaya, the A-36As were forced to fight at higher than optimum altitudes, and three went missing very quickly. This notwithstanding, the P-51A-equipped 530th FBS was detached to Kurmitola in Bengal to provide fighter escort for bombing raids on the Rangoon area, some 450 miles(725km) away. Fitted with two 60 imperial gallon (75 US gallon/284 litre) drop tanks, these were the first long-range escort missions under-taken by Mustangs.

They were less than successful. While escorting Mitchells on a raid on Mingal-adon airfield, the 530th was bounced by four Hayabusas. Out-manoeuvred in a low-level turning fight, two Mustangs were lost. The next mission, to Insein, was even worse. Four Mustangs were lost for a single Hayabusa shot down and another badly damaged. After four escort missions, 530th FBS losses amounted to 50per cent of strength.

P-51As were also used by two Air Commando units set up to support the Chindits on their deep penetrations behind Japanese lines. Often they oper-ated from small strips carved from the jungle, carrying two 1,000lb (454kg) bombs, or triple Bazooka installations. A handful of P-51As also operated with USAAF units based in China.

THE ROLLS-ROYCE ENGINE

The margin between success and failure is always slim. As fighters sought ever greater altitudes, the British need for the Allison-engined Mustang diminished. As it was, the type was rejected for the pure fighter role due to its poor high-altitude performance. Had the RAF not had a requirement for low-level tactical reconnaissance it might easily have been shunted off to some less important theatre of operations, there to languish largely unseen and unsung, until attrition removed it from the inventory.

On the other hand, the great wonder is that the Mustang was not designed with a more suitable engine from the start. Such an engine was available from the outset; the Rolls-Royce Merlin which powered the Spitfire and Hurricane, and a dozen other aircraft as well. As the Mustang was designed for the British, it is extremely surprising that such a power plant was not suggested at a very early stage. That the superb American airframe was eventually mated with the equally superb British engine appears to have been due as much to chance as anything. Be that as it may, it produced one of the truly great fighters of the Second World War, albeit rather belatedly.

■ SOMETHING BETTER ■

Late April 1942. The Mustang prototype had made its first flight almost exactly 18 months earlier, and AFDU was finalizing the test report on the production articles at Duxford. Meanwhile a new German fighter, the Focke-Wulf FW 190A, had entered large-scale service on the Channel coast. It comfortably outclassed the standard British fighter of the day, the Spitfire V. Almost overnight the RAF had slipped from a slight technical advantage to a position of undoubted inferiority. Something better was needed, urgently. This was the state of play when Rolls-Royce test pilot Ronald Harker visited Duxford.

Part of Harker's brief was to evaluate the performance of aircraft powered by engines built by companies other than Rolls-Royce. This included not only British competitors, but American

Opposite page: P-51B Mustangs of the 354th FG shepherd B-24 Liberators of the 458th Bomb Group over the sea. In proximity to the enemy, the American fighters would maintain a healthy distance from the guns of the bombers. (Roger Freeman)

Below: The Mustang X, a Rolls-Royce company conversion with a Merlin 65 engine. The intercooler radiator beneath the nose rather spoiled the sleek lines of the original aircraft. (Roger Freeman)

Left: NAA converted two Mustangs to take Packard-Merlin V-1650 engines as XP-78s, later redesignated XP-51Bs. The first to fly, 41-37352 seen here, was originally built as a P-51 for the RAF but was taken over by the USAAF when America entered the war. The 20mm cannon armament was retained. (USAF via JE)
Below: Drop tanks beneath the wings, a P-51B of 354th FG based at Boxted in Essex taxies out ready for takeoff. This variant carried only four guns. (Associated Press via Roger Freeman)

and captured German machines.

On this particular day, 30 April, Wing Commander Ian Campbell-Orde, commanding AFDU, invited Harker to try out the Mustang. A 30-minute flight impressed him tremendously, although he noted the fall-off of power at altitude. At the same time he realized that the new Merlin 61, with a two-stage supercharger, would make all the difference.

On his return to Rolls-Royce, he asked the chief engineer to calculate performance figures for such a machine. The results were startling. Maximum speed was 441mph (710km/hr). Not only was this 70mph (113km/hr) faster than the Allison Mustang, but it was achievable at 25,600ft (7,800m) – almost double the best altitude of the American fighter! If the calculations were correct, the combination was a potential world-beater. In some parameters it was better than the new Spitfire VIII powered by the same engine.

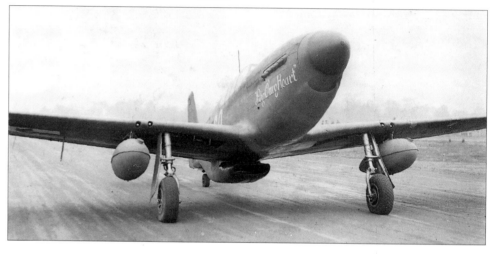

TEST FLYING

'Flying a new airplane I always put the power on easily at the start to get the feel of the airplane on the ground, then gradually gave it power. When I got airborne, a couple of hundred feet off the ground, I pulled up the gear and decided then I'd see how it would climb from scratch. I poured the coal to it and the aircraft snap-rolled! Rolls-Royce hadn't provided enough vertical fin area, and not enough offset.'

LT COL. CAS HOUGH, USAAF

■ TWO-STAGE MERLIN ■

The advent of the Merlin 61 was almost as fortuitous. By mid-1941, the engine had neared its development limits, and the future was thought to lie with the larger Griffon. There was however a requirement for a turbo-charged Merlin to power a high-altitude bomber. But turbo-superchargers, as American engine manufacturers knew well, were heavy, bulky, and complicated. As an alternative, Rolls-Royce hooked up two superchargers in series. The results were startling. Trial flights showed the full-throttle altitude as 29,750ft (9,070m); an amazing increase! Shortly after, the high-altitude bomber was cancelled and the new engine was developed for the Spitfire as the Merlin 61.

At first, interest in Harker's proposal was lukewarm, but as the new engine was expected to give the Spitfire little more than parity with the FW 190A, the prospect of a fighter which would clearly outperform the German machine was too tempting to resist. Five Mustang air-frames were acquired for trials.

The Americans had meanwhile been keeping a close watch on developments. Arrangements had been made for Packard to licence-build the Merlin as the V-1650 as long ago as October 1940. By 1942 American production of the British engine was in full flood, and arrangements for production of the Merlin 61 were well in hand. North American were fully in the picture, and also started planning a Mustang with the new engine.

■ HIGHER AND FASTER ■

Fortunately not too many modifications were needed. The Merlin was dimensionally similar to the Allison, although it was some 300lb (136kg) heavier. The extra weight was more than offset by about 600hp extra, plus the high-altitude capability that was so desperately needed. Rolls-Royce chose to design a new engine mount. The intercooler for the supercharger installation led to a small radiator under the nose, and this

Left: Fresh from the factory, this Block 1 P-51B shows off its beautifully clean lines, the low drag of which contributed materially to its superb performance.

Middle: Although seemingly a P-51B with USAAF insignia, this is actually a late-production Mustang III destined for the RAF (FX 883), and carries an RAF fin flash and RAF camouflage. The inboard kink of the wing leading edge is very apparent from this angle. (Paul Coggan via JE)

Bottom: A Texas-built P-51C. The only visible difference between this and a P-51B is in the radio mast at the rear of the cockpit. This is a late-production aircraft, completed at the time when bare aluminium was favoured over camouflage. While this was popularly supposed to increase maximum speed, differences between specific aircraft made it impossible to confirm. (Paul Coggan via JE)

location also housed the carburettor intake, giving a rather bulged effect to the front of the aeroplane and spoiling its clean lines.

The first flight of the Mustang X, as it was designated, took place at Hucknall on 13 October 1942. While all went well, it was quickly evident that the formerly pleasant handling qualities had been adversely affected by the changes. Torque from the more powerful engine and the four-bladed propeller reduced directional stability, particularly in the dive. To overcome this, a small dorsal spine was added to the rear fuselage just in front of the fin, to give extra keel area. Despite the draggy nose contours, the first Mustang X attained a level speed of 433mph (697km/hr), and reached 20,000ft (6,100m) in 6.3 minutes; barely two-thirds of the time taken by the Allison Mustang. But the P-51X was purely experimental, with Rolls-Royce feeding information back to NAA in California.

■ TWO-SEATER ■

Meanwhile NAA had also been moving fast. Authorization to convert two Mustangs to Merlins had been issued on 25 July. At first these were designated XP-78; only later did they become XP-51Bs. Whereas Rolls-Royce had spoiled the clean lines of the nose with

Above: A late-production P-51B, *Snoot's Sniper*, was given the Malcolm hood as a field modification. A sliding canopy, this could be opened in flight, unlike the previous 'lid and door' arrangement. This was an advantage on the landing approach in bad weather.

was easier said than done, and much redesign and intensive wind tunnel testing was needed to get it right.

Externally the P-51B differed little from the P-51A. The nose was slightly fatter, with the dorsal air scoop replaced by a less obvious ventral intake just behind the spinner. A Hamilton four-bladed propeller replaced the three-bladed one, and the radiator group under the mid-fuselage was slightly deeper. The structure had been beefed up internally, and hard points added beneath the wings to carry bombs. These were also plumbed for external drop tanks. Armament was standardized at four 0.50in (12.7mm) machine guns in the wings.

their conversions, with a consequent increase in drag and reduction in performance, NAA were extremely reluctant to do so. Urgent studies followed, which soon made it clear that the best location for the intercooler radiator was in with the group beneath the mid-fuselage. This

The first flight of the XP-51B took place on 30 November 1942, almost seven weeks later than the Rolls-Royce conversion, and immediately superior performance was evident. NAA test pilot Ben Chilton achieved a level speed of 441mph (710km/hr) at 29,800ft

Above: With a 75-gallon drop tank beneath each wing, the range of the P-51B was extended sufficiently to allow it to act as a long-range escort fighter. Its success in this role completely changed the bombing offensive against Germany.

Above right: This Mustang had a chequered career. Still crated, it was dropped in the sea while being unloaded, and badly damaged. Condemned to be reduced for spares, it was rebuilt as a two-seater, in which configuration it is seen here. It was finally lost in the Irish Sea in 1944 due to engine problems. (George Gosney via JE)

Right: P-51B of Don Blakeslee's 4th FG, seen late in 1944 after the switch from camouflage to natural metal finish. (Roger Freeman)

(9,080m), while the rate of climb against that of the P-51A was almost doubled. An order for 400 P-51Bs had been placed even before the prototype flew, and more large orders followed. Mass production was initiated, with a shadow factory at Fort Worth, Texas. Fort Worth Mustangs were virtually identical to those from Inglewood, but were designated P-51Cs.

The first production P-51B flew on 5 May 1943, and the first P-51C on 5 August of the same year. Photo-reconnaissance was still a requirement, and 71 P-51Bs and 20 P-51Cs were converted to carry two K24 oblique cameras, or a K17 and K22. In this guise they became F-6Cs, most of which retained their armament.

■ ESCORT FIGHTER ■

By mid-1943 the USAAF 8th Air Force was carrying the fight to Germany, but it was becoming increasingly evident that the heavy bombers were unable to protect themselves sufficiently. A long range escort fighter was needed. The P-47 Thunderbolt, although an excellent fighter in many ways, lacked range, while

Below: Winter 1943–44. An early shipment of P-51Bs lined up at Speke airport, awaiting allocation to front-line units. (Roger Freeman)

the twin-engined P-38 Lightning, though able to acquit itself well enough in theatres where the Allies held an overwhelming numerical advantage, was a turkey in the dogfight against the German single-engined single seaters.

The Fisher P-75A, an enormous, heavy, and complicated beast

Several large and expensive fighters were under development for the long-range escort role. Fairly typical of these was the Fisher P-75A, an enormous, heavy and complicated beast, which first flew in November 1943. Early trials were unpromising, and a requirement was issued for an extra fuel tank to be fitted in the fuselage of a P-51B. With two external drop tanks this increased the total fuel capacity of the Mustang to 348 imperial gallons (419 US gallons/1,586 litres). With this fuel load, the P-51B could do a round trip of over 1,200 miles (1,930km); rather more than the distance from England to Berlin and back.

Only the last few hundred P-51Bs and Cs were fitted with the fuselage tank as standard at the factory, although

P-51B/ MUSTANG III

Dimensions

Wingspan	37ft 0in (11.28m)
Length	32ft 3in (9.83m)
Height	13ft 8in (4.17m)
Wing area	233 sq. ft (21.65m²)

Weights

Empty	7,000lb (3,175kg)
Normal TO	9,200lb (4,173kg)

Power

Packard V-1650-7 inline rated at 1,720hp war emergency

Performance

Max. speed	422mph (711kph)
Climb	3,475fpm (18m/sec)
Range	950miles (1,529km)
Ceiling	42,500ft (12,953m)

Armament

4 x 0.50in (12.7mm) machine guns

some of the earlier production aircraft were retrofitted with it later. It did not feature on the Mustang III, as the P-51B was known in RAF and Commonwealth service.

There was of course a penalty to be paid. The extra weight so far back made directional stability rather marginal, and when half empty the petrol slopped about, affecting handling during what were quite mild manoeuvres. The drill was to take off, form up gently with the others, set course, then drone on steadily for the next hour or more, burning off fuel. Not until the fuselage tank was virtually empty could the pilot relax.

■ INTO SERVICE ■

Ordering a new aircraft type from the drawing board is unthinkable today, but during the war, things were different. A protracted development period, during which all the bugs were ironed out, simply meant that the in-service date might be delayed by a year, or even more. During this time, pilots would

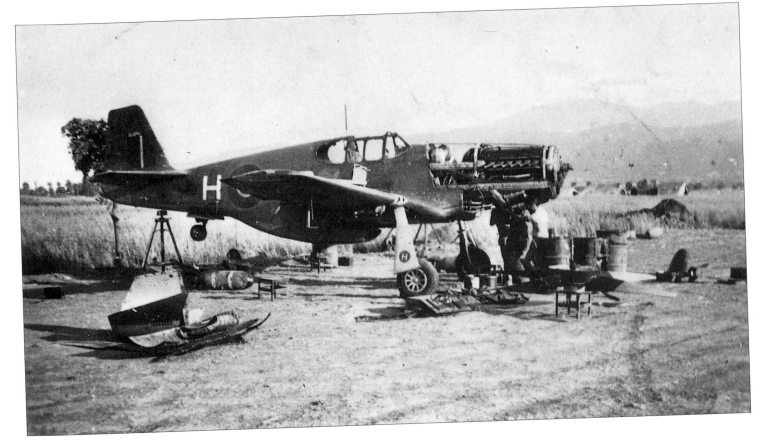

Above: RAF Mustang IIIs in the Mediterranean theatre of operations retained the original canopy. This example is a P-51C of No. 260 Squadron, seen having a thorough overhaul in Termili, Italy. (Roger Freeman)

ROLL

'Upon returning from a mission with the right drop tank still attached, I flared out for landing with a 45 knot crosswind from 90° to the right. The airplane was trimmed heavily to the left, to hold up the right wing, due to the extra drag from the drop tank. As the airspeed decreased, just prior to touchdown, the tank dropped off. The right wing came up, and the wind started to roll the airplane to the left. I immediately applied full power. The torque, the wind, and the extreme left trim caused an immediate roll of 180°. I found myself inverted 50 feet off the ground and looking up through the canopy at pierced steel planking going by at 100 or so mph. I throttled back and sort of washed out in a half roll to the right.'

LT WILLIAM G. COLONEY USAAF, 5TH FS, 52ND FG, 15TH AF

have to make do with inferior or outdated machines, and all too often pay with their lives for the privilege. An underdeveloped but superior-performing machine rushed into service could also be a cause of fatalities, but its performance gave its pilot a better chance in the hazard of battle. It was a question of which omelette required the fewest broken eggs, and in general this was the latter course of action.

The first Merlin-Mustang unit to see action reached England in October 1943. The 8th Air Force had been eagerly awaiting the arrival of the new long-range fighter, but an administrative error saw it assigned to 9th Air Force for ground attack. A compromise resulted in it being made available for bomber escort with the 8th until such time as further P-51B Groups arrived. Not until the following spring was the type operational in quantity.

Technical problems were rapidly encountered. Engines running rough, propeller seal leaks spilling oil onto the

Right: P-51Ds of three fighter groups in Italy. Left to right, 332nd FG; 52nd FG, to which William G. Coloney was assigned; and 31st FG. (Roger Freeman)

Below: Closeup of the Malcolm hood, which was fitted to all British-based Mustang IIIs, and not a few Mustang IIs. Not only did it give far better all-round visibility, but it could be opened in flight. (Roger Freeman)

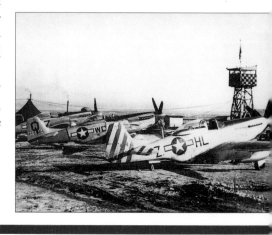

LOST WINGS

'In high speed dives, when the design or wing load velocity was exceeded, it could shed one or both of its wings. I witnessed this loss on two occasions. One wing was lost directly over the airfield at Madna, Italy, in the fall of 1944. The airplane and pilot went straight into the ground not far from the control tower.

'One other loss occurred there during an afternoon "rat race". Coincidentally we were discussing this wing loss with Johnny Typer, the civilian representative from NAA at the time. He was adamant that "no-one can pull the wings off a P-51". No sooner had he made that remark than I heard behind me the dull thumps of two wings separating. He asked "What's that?" and I answered that it had happened again. He asked how I knew that, to which I replied "Once you've heard that sound, you'll never forget it". We watched as the litter and tumbling wings fell slowly to the ground, long after the fuselage and pilot had crashed – an unforgettable sight and feeling.'

LT WILLIAM G. COLONEY USAAF,
5TH FS, 52ND FG, 15TH AF.

Above: Combat in Europe stressed the need for better rearward visibility from the cockpit. NAA took the ninth production P-51B, seen here, cut down the rear fuselage and fitted a teardrop canopy. Armament was increased from four 0.50in machine guns to six, with the mountings upright to avoid jamming. (NASM via JE)

Below: Distinguished aircraft, distinguished pilot. The P-51D was generally regarded as *the* Mustang. This example is being flown by Lieutenant-General Jimmy Doolittle, commander of 8th Air Force from January 1944, who on this occasion obviously neglected to wear a flying helmet. (Benjamin S. Kelsey via JE)

windshield, overheating for whatever reason, faulty engine mounting bolts. All were gradually cured. Sometimes the underwing drop tanks failed to feed; the solution was to pressurize them.

Far more serious was the problem of gun jamming. To fit the Brownings in the wings, they had to be canted at an angle, with the ammunition belts feeding over and down into the breeches. In a turn of more than 2g, the forces exerted exceeded the limits of the mechanism, and they jammed. In the middle of a dogfight this could be very embarrassing. Booster motors were fitted, but these were a long time arriving.

The 68 imperial gallon (85 US gallon/ 322 litre) fuselage tank not only led to directional instability in flight, it also caused such severe tail-heaviness that even take-off was an activity fraught with peril. Before long the load was restricted to 52 imperial gallons (65 US gallons/246 litres). A related problem was that a sudden pull on the stick caused a high-speed stall followed by a snap roll. This could however be put to good use by experienced pilots as an evasive manoeuvre that no enemy fighter was able to follow.

A procedure was initiated in which the fuel in the fuselage tank was used first, followed by that in the drop tanks. After a few instances in which Mustangs were

Below: **One Mustang IV ready for delivery to the RAF. This is actually a Texas-built P-51K. In all, 875 Mustang IVs entered service, two thirds of which were P-51Ks. (AAHS via JE)**

bounced by enemy fighters and forced to drop full wing tanks, this sequence was reversed.

Most serious of all was structural failure. Occasionally the wings came off a Mustang in a high-speed dive. There were two main causes for this. At very high speeds, the large doors of the ammunition bays began to bulge outwards. This distorted the wing to the stage where the stresses imposed were too great, and it parted company with the fuselage. The second cause was a tendency for the undercarriage to extend in flight, causing abnormal loads on the

Above: **F-6C Mustang of the 111th Tactical Reconnaissance Squadron, 12th Air Force, seen in southern France, late 1944. The oblique camera port can be seen in the lower rear fuselage. (Roger Freeman)**

wing. These faults were eventually cured, but too late for some pilots.

The P-51B entered RAF service as the Mustang III. However, at this late stage, it was decided that the cockpit canopy was 'totally unsuited to European conditions', something that could have been determined way back in

P-51/K, MUSTANG IV/IVA

Dimensions

Wingspan	37ft 0in (11.28m)
Length	32ft 3in (9.83m)
Height	13ft 8in (4.17m)
Wing area	235 sq.ft (21.83m²)

Weights

Empty	7,635lb (3,463kg)
Normal TO	10,100lb (4,581kg)

Power

Packard V-1650-7 incline rated
at 1,720hp war emergency

Performance

Max. speed	437mph (703kph)
Climb	3,475fpm (18m/sec)
Range	1,710miles (2,751km)
Ceiling	41,900ft (12,770m)

Armament

6 x 0.50in (12.7mm) machine guns

1940, before the first Mustang ever flew. In a series of field modifications, the Mustang III was fitted with a bulged sliding canopy similar to that of the Spitfire. This was the 'Malcolm Hood', which vastly improved the all-round view, especially rearwards. A few Mustang IIs were also modified in this way.

As previously noted, the P-51B/C had several operational shortcomings, and NAA commenced work to rectify these. With ever-greater importance being placed on the all-round view from the cockpit, NAA modified a P-51B to take a one-piece tear-drop sliding canopy, which involved cutting down the rear fuselage to accommodate it. First flown on 17 November 1943, the new canopy gave a first class view through 360 degrees. With other modifications, it formed the basis of the definitive Mustang, the P-51D, or P-51K when built at Fort Worth.

The next improvement made was to the armament. Four 0.50 guns were demonstrably inadequate, while the inability to fire in hard turns without them jamming was a serious handicap. Extensive redesign resulted in six 0.50s, all upright instead of canted, which virtually eliminated feed stoppages. The two inboard guns had 400 rounds each, while the other four each had 270 rounds.

The wing chord was increased at the root, making it slightly deeper and affecting the kink at the leading edge. The main gear was strengthened to take a much greater all-up weight, and the wheel bays were modified to suit.

The P-51D was supplied to the RAF as the Mustang IV

Directional stability with fuel in the fuselage tank was always marginal, and cutting down the fuselage made matters worse. To offset this, a small dorsal fin was added. The P-51D was supplied to the RAF as the Mustang IV, and the P-51K, which differed only in having a slightly different propeller, became the Mustang IVA in British service.

As was the case with all other Mustang variants, some were converted for photo-reconnaissance. Two cameras, a K17 and a K22, were fitted in the rear fuselage just ahead of the tailwheel. Camera ship designations were F-6D and F-6K, and so far as is known, all retained their armament.

■ AUSTRALIAN ■ MUSTANGS

Only a handful of Mustangs were built outside the USA. The Commonwealth Aircraft Corporation of Australia obtained a licence to build the P-51D in 1944, starting with the assembly of knocked-down kits supplied by NAA. These resulted in 80 CA-17 Mustang XXs, the first of which flew in April 1945, while indigenous production provided 40 CA-18 Mustang 21s; 14 Mustang 22s fitted with an F24 camera; and 66 Mustang 23s, which differed in having British-built Merlins. However, no Australian-built Mustangs became operational until after the war.

Below: **Many late P-51D/Ks had a small dorsal fin extension added to provide extra keel area and improve directional stability, which was always marginal with fuel in the fuselage tank. (Alvin Williams via JE)**

When in the early months of 1943 the heavy bombers of the US 8th Air Force commenced raids on targets inside Germany, it soon became clear that without fighter escort, losses were far higher than expected. The heavily armed bombers, flying in close formation, were unable to protect themselves adequately. Fighter escort was essential. Within certain constraints it was available from the outset; Spitfires could penetrate a short way, while Thunderbolts could almost reach the German border. Lightnings were longer-legged still, but in close combat they were no match for the latest German single-engined fighters.

From July of that year, drop tanks enabled Thunderbolts to reach the western extremities of Germany, but against targets beyond this, the bombers were forced to fly unescorted. Deep penetrations during the late summer and early autumn incurred swinging losses, and the 8th Air Force was forced to call a halt to the long-range raids.

The only American fighter that had sufficient range to escort the bombers on deep penetrations was the P-51B, and this was only just entering service. But there was many a slip . . . ! Back in the Pentagon, someone obviously regarded the new Mustang variant as an attack aircraft like the Allison-engined P-51A, and consequently the first P-51Bs to arrive in England were allocated to the 354th FG of the 9th Air Force, then in the course of being formed to assist in the forthcoming invasion of Europe. Fortunately 9th AF had only recently been established, and its fighter units came under the control of VIII Fighter Command. This circumstance allowed 8th AF to make use of them initially.

Above: The first unit in England to receive the P-51B was the 354th FG at Boxted, an aircraft of which is seen taking off. The white ring around the nose is an identification marking, supplementing those on the wings and tail. (USAF via JE)

Many 354th pilots were not long out of flying school, and the air combat mission which they now had to undertake was a world away from the close air support role which had previously been their lot. Air-to-air gunnery and tactics loomed large on their horizons. The basic formation within the squadron was the finger four, so called because the aircraft positions within it were like the fingertips of an outstretched hand. The advantages of height and sun were stressed, and also mutual support. The basic element was the pair; the leader or shooter, and his wingman, whose task it was to protect his leader's tail at all times. They were also carefully briefed on the strong and weak points of their fighter vis-à-vis those of the enemy. In order to increase experience levels, several 'old heads' from other units

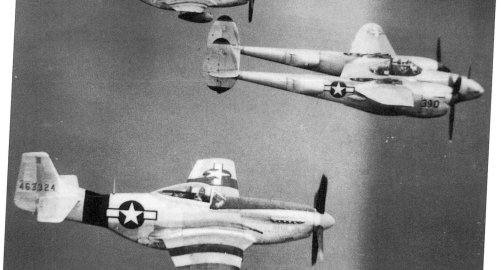

Left: P-51Ds formate on a Lockheed P-38 Lightning at high altitude. Despite its size, the P-38 was out-ranged by the Mustang; nor was it a match for the German single-engined fighters.

Far left: Mustang IIIs of No. 19 Squadron RAF, with identification stripes and Malcolm hoods. Despite the bulged effect, this type of canopy was actually less draggy than the original. (Roger Freeman)

COMPARISON MUSTANG vs FW 190A

Maximum speed: The Fw 190 is nearly 50mph (80km/hr) slower at all heights, increasing to 70mph (113km/hr) above 28,000 (8,500m).

Maximum climb: There appears to be little to choose in the maximum rate of climb. The Mustang is considerably faster at all heights in a zoom climb.

Dive: The Mustang can always out-dive the FW 190.

Turning circle: Again, there is not much to choose. The Mustang is slightly better. When evading an enemy aircraft with a steep turn, a pilot will always out-turn the attacking aircraft initially because of the difference in speeds. It is still therefore a worthwhile manoeuvre with the Mustang when attacked.

Rate of roll: Not even the Mustang approaches the FW 190.

Conclusions: In the attack, a high speed should be maintained or regained in order to regain height initiative. An FW 190 could not evade by diving alone. In defence a steep turn followed by a full-throttle dive should increase the range before regaining height and course. Dogfighting is not altogether recommended. Do not attempt to climb away without at least 250mph (400km/hr) showing initially.

COMPARISON MUSTANG vs Me 109G

Maximum speed: The Mustang is faster at all heights. Its best heights, by comparison, are below 16,000ft (5,875m) (30mph/48km/hr faster approx.) and above 25,00ft (7,600m) (30mph/48km/hr increasing to 50mph/80km/hr at 30,00ft (9,150m).

Maximum climb: This is rather similar. The Mustang is very slightly better above 25,00ft (7,600m) but inclined to be worse below 20,000ft (6,100m).

Zoom climb: Unfortunately the Me 109G appears to have a very good high-speed climb, making the two aircraft similar in a zoom climb.

Dive: On the other hand in defence the Mustang can still increase the range in a prolonged dive.

Turning circle: The Mustang is greatly superior.

Rate of roll: Not much to choose. In defence (in a tight spot) a rapid change of direction will throw the Me 109G's sight off. This is because the 109G's maximum rate of roll is embarrassing (the wing slots keep opening).

Conclusions: In attack the Mustang can always catch the Me109G, except in any sort of climb (unless there is a high overtaking speed). In defence, a steep turn should be the first manoeuvre, followed, if necessary, by a dive (below 20,000ft/6,100m). A high-speed climb will unfortunately not increase the range. If above 25,000ft (7,600m) keep above by climbing or all-out level.

were drafted in as a temporary measure. One of these was Major Don Blakeslee, a former Eagle Squadron pilot with the RAF, soon to gain a reputation as the greatest American fighter leader of the war.

On 1 December 1943, two 12-ship formations of P-51Bs took off from Boxted on the first operational mission for the type. Led by Don Blakeslee, they carried out an uneventful fighter sweep over Belgium and northern France. Other missions followed, and on 13 December they flew an escort mission to Kiel, where Lt Glenn Eagleston, later to become the top-scoring ace of 9th AF with 18.5 victories, damaged an Me 110. The first confirmed victory for the P-51B came just three days later, when Lt Charles Gumm downed an Me 110 over Bremen.

First victory: Lt Charles Gumm downed an Me 110 over Bremen

Two more 9th AF P-51B units made their operational debuts in February 1944. These were the 357th FG at Leiston and the 363rd FG at Rivenhall. The latter unit remained with 9th AF, but the 8th, failing to get the 354th transferred,

Below: **Lieutenant Glenn Eagleston of the 354th FG, on his return from the first American raid on Berlin, during which he shot down a Me 109. He went on to become the top scorer for 9th AF. (Roger Freeman)**

INTO ACTION

'The first days of March saw titanic battles fought as the bombers attacked Berlin and other distant targets. Now they had fighter cover. Our group was credited with 324 aircraft destroyed during this period (February 28–April 18; the day I got shot down.) Quite a bit has been written about mechanical problems with this new airplane, but I do not recall difficulties. Many of the pilots, especially the leaders, such as Beeson, Blakeslee, Goodson and others, had been privileged to fly the Spitfire while serving in the RAF. We changed over to the P-47 Thunderbolt in March of 1943 and most of us despised it. When we were given the Mustang in February 1944, we were for the most part delighted. At last we had a fighter similar to the Spitfire, but with substantially greater speed and three times the range.'

GEORGE CARPENTER, 336FS, 4TH FG:
14 VICTORIES.

horse-traded the established 358th FG equipped with P-47s for the untried 357th. Events were to show that it was a very good swap.

In the same month Merlin-Mustangs started reaching 8th AF units, starting with 4th FG at Debden. The oldest fighter group in 8th AF, the 4th had been formed from the three RAF Eagle

Below: Shuttle mission. P-51Bs of the 325th FG escorting B-17s on one of the long-range missions where, after raiding the target, they continued on to Russia to refuel and rearm. (Roger Freeman)

Bottom: Colonel Donald J. M. Blakeslee, widely considered to have been the finest fighter leader in the USAAF, is seen here on the right, having just been decorated by General (later President) Dwight D. Eisenhower. In the centre is fighter ace Don Gentile. Both flew with No. 133 Squadron RAF before the USA entered the war, which accounts for them wearing RAF pilot's wings above their right breast pockets. (Konsler via JE)

Squadrons, making its pilots by far the most experienced. This helped what was to become known as the '24 hour conversion'. Commanding Officer Don Blakeslee, by now returned from his stint with the 354th, was so taken with the P-51B that he promised VIII Fighter Command's General Kepner that he would have his group operational on type just 24 hours from receiving the Merlin Mustang. He kept his word; 4th FG became operational on 25 February, and over the next few weeks put on a bravura performance.

Meanwhile the old bogey of faulty

FINGER-FOUR FORMATION

The finger-four formation, varied occasionally by four abreast, was a standard fighter formation used by all combatants during the Second World War. The fighters operated as elements of two, with pairs giving mutual support. Spacing between aircraft was roughly 600ft (180m), and generally they were stepped down towards the sun. In this way, all blind spots were covered. the other great advantage of this formation was that it could be used to make rapid changes of course, by having all aircraft cross-over with each turning at its maximum rate.

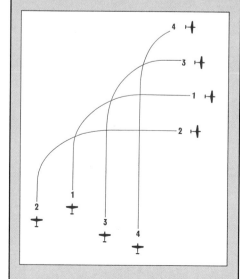

aircraft recognition had once again surfaced; all too often Mustangs were mistaken for Me 109s. White stripes were painted on the nose, wings and tail surfaces, but even this was not foolproof. An early victim was Glenn Eagleston, who was badly shot up by a P-47 near Brunswick on 10 February. Fortunately he just managed to nurse his torn and tattered Mustang back to England before baling out.

The first Mustang IIIs for the RAF arrived in December 1943 and were assigned to No. 65 Squadron, based at Gravesend. Nos 19 and 122 Squadrons followed shortly after. While assigned to 2nd TAF and earmarked for the invasion, they still assisted in escorting the American heavies until the P-51B strength of the USAAF reached acceptable levels. Lacking the extra fuel tank in the fuselage, the British Mustangs did not possess the endurance of their USAAF counterparts, but could still reach well into western Germany. The combat debut of the Mustang III took place on 15 February, when Nos 19 and 65 Squadrons carried out a fighter sweep over the French coast. That same afternoon they escorted American heavy bombers attacking V-1 launch sites in the Pas-de-Calais.

■ ESCORT TO BERLIN ■

By March 1944, with three Mustang groups available for long-range escort, it appeared that Berlin could now be

VICTORY

'I jumped three other Me 110s just as they let go their rockets, which burst behind the last of the bombers. I raked the three Me 110s which were flying wingtip to wingtip. As the No. 1 enemy aircraft broke into me, I saw strikes all over the cockpit and both engines as he disappeared beneath me. I cleared my tail, noticing a P-51 covering me behind and to the side. I closed in, firing on the No 2. Me 110, and saw pieces falling off and an explosion in the back cockpit. I pulled up over him, and last saw him in a vertical dive pouring black smoke.

LT NICK SEGURA, 4TH FG

attacked in force without incurring unacceptable casualties. The first raid on the German capital was scheduled for 3 March, but was foiled by heavy cloud at high altitude. An attempt on the following day failed for the same reason, although on this occasion the recall signal was not received by some units and a small force reached the target and bombed ineffectively. The defenders were hampered by cloud almost as much as the raiders, and losses were moderate. Two days later weather conditions were finally suitable.

On 6 March, 776 heavy bombers set course for Berlin. They were escorted by 644 fighters. Of these 109 were P-51Bs of the 8th and 9th Air Forces, and three squadrons of Mustang IIIs of the RAF. Many shorter-ranged fighters flew twice on this day.

Top: Home again! Two P-51Ds of the 357th FG escort a B-17G Flying Fortress back to its base in East Anglia. (Roger Freeman)
Above: Lieutenant Colonel James Howard scored six victories against the Japanese before arriving in England to command the 356th FS. On 11 January 1944, he became separated from his unit, and single-handedly took on the protection of the 401st BG. The guns of his P-51B jammed one by one, but he continued to make feint attacks on the German fighters. For this action he was awarded America's highest decoration, the Medal of Honor. (Roger Freeman)

The task of the escort fighters was far from easy. They could not simply fly in formation with the bombers, but were forced to maintain a far higher cruising speed to enable them to engage enemy fighters successfully. To stay in the vicinity of the bombers they weaved above them, occasionally ranging ahead or out on the flanks, ready to break up a massed German attack. This used up fuel, and consequently the fighters operated in relays, flying by a direct route to a predetermined rendezvous. They then took station on their charges, protecting them until fuel ran low. This was for about half an hour or so during which time roughly 100 miles (160km) was covered. At this point they would be relieved by a fresh unit. In practice this meant that a bomber stream about 90 miles (144km) long was protected by a mere 150 fighters at any one time.

On this first Berlin raid, relays of Thunderbolts made up the escort to a point east of Brunswick (now Braunschweig). The long-legged P-51Bs then took over for the target area, and were relieved by Lightnings north-west of Berlin after the attack. RAF Mustang IIIs then met the bombers to the north-east of Hanover and escorted them to a point south of Bremen, where fresh units of Thunderbolts awaited them.

The first fighter action of the raid took place before the Mustangs arrived, but they were in place in time to meet the second German massed attack, consisting of 72 single and 41 twin-engined fighters. The 4th Fighter Group, led by the indomitable Don Blakeslee using the call-sign 'Upper', was in place escorting the leading bombers. The 354th FG was protecting the next bombers in the stream. At this point the 357th arrived. Several Mustangs had by this time turned back with mechanical or electrical failures, reducing the strength of the escorts to 92 P-51Bs.

The first sign of the presence of German fighters was a line of condensation trails coming from head-on and high. Blakeslee positioned his group up-sun, just below contrail height, and waited for the attack to commence. As the first German formation came in against the bombers, he led his men down to intercept. The result was what a watching B-17 pilot later described as 'one of the damnedest dogfights of the war. It was off to the right of us as we headed east and several thousand feet higher – about one and a half miles away. It looked like a giant swarm of bees, P-51s, Me 109s, FW 190s'.

EMERGENCY

'I knew I was somewhere to the south of Berlin but having chased the 109 I had no idea exactly where I was. However the sight of the 109s nearby was enough to stimulate me to lift the little latch on my throttle arm for War Emergency Power. This gave me a little more power but only for about five minutes or the engine would suffer severe damage. It was strictly an emergency measure – but at that moment I deemed it something of an emergency.'

LT ROD STARKEY, 357TH FG

With so many aircraft involved, the level of confusion was tremendous. Lieutenant Rod Starkey of the 357th FG was split off from his unit and embroiled with several Me 109s. To make matters worse, three of his four guns jammed. In answer to his urgent radio call, his squadron commander replied that he would be glad to help if only he knew where Starkey was!

Massed guns of the bombers were blazing away at all and sundry

The confusion of the ferocious fighting that took place in this encounter makes it difficult to establish scores with any certainty, especially as the massed guns of the bombers were blazing away at all and sundry. Five Mustangs were lost on this mission, four of them from the 4th FG, the other from the 354th. Of the German losses, at least 13 can definitely be credited to the Mustangs, and possibly more. American bomber losses were high, but not enough to stop them returning to Berlin within a matter of days. Luftwaffe chief Hermann Goering reportedly said that he knew the war was lost when he saw Mustangs over Berlin.

With Merlin Mustangs pouring off the production lines, re-equipment of 8th AF fighter groups with the new aircraft was rapid. In March the 355th FG handed in

Right: Major George Preddy was the top Mustang ace of the war with 27 aerial victories. He was killed over Belgium at Christmas 1944 by 'friendly' ground fire. (Roger Freeman)
Below: The carriage of two 86 imperial gallon drop tanks, seen here on these P-51ds of the 20th FG, gave the Mustang the range to go anywhere in Germany. The tanks were of impregnated paper, a non-strategic material. (Roger Freeman)

Top: A 'buzz job' on their base by Mustangs of the 20th FG. They would be much lower than this if attacking an enemy airfield. (Roger Freeman)

Above: Bare metal finish solved the recognition problem in 1944, when camouflage schemes were abandoned. It did nothing to ward off 'friendly' ground fire however, and broad black and white Invasion Stripes were painted on the undersides of wings and fuselage, as seen on this 348th FG P-51D. (Rocker via JE)

its P-47s, followed by the 339th and 352nd in April and the 359th and 361st in May. June saw the arrival of the far superior P-51Ds; these naturally went to the crack 4th FG, which also became the first to operate the P-51K in December of that year. P-38 units also started to receive the new fighter, commencing with the 55th FG.

Thus equipped, the 8th AF fighter

groups became even more aggressive than before. Their stint of protecting the bombers complete, they frequently came home at low level, shooting up targets of opportunity on the way. Whereas at one time the German fighters routinely disengaged by diving, then found their way home on the deck, now they were even hunted down over their own airfields. Airfield attack became a routine Mustang diversion after a bomber escort mission, although these were carefully planned beforehand.

The long-established problem of recognition was finally solved in 1944, when camouflage paint schemes were finally abandoned. The shiny bare metal of the P-51Ds and Ks made them instantly identifiable from far away. A German joke of the period ran: 'Silver aircraft are American, camouflaged aircraft are British, and if they're not there at all, they're German!'

■ AIR SUPERIORITY ■

In many areas, the opposing German fighters were as good as, and in some respects better than, the Mustang. How then did the Mustang come to dominate the skies over Germany so completely?

In part the overwhelming range of the American fighter allowed it to seek out its adversaries anywhere; they had no safe haven. Also the war was in its fifth year. German casualties had been high, and fuel shortages had disrupted the training of new pilots. The result was that by mid-1944 the German fighter arm consisted of a few 'old heads', very experienced and very dangerous, but worn out by constant combat, gradually melting away in the crucible of battle. They were supplemented by undertrained youngsters. By contrast, American fighter pilots were the best-trained in the world at this time. The fighter must be good, but the real difference is the man in the cockpit. And so it proved.

Of the 10,720 air combat victories claimed by the USAAF in Europe, no fewer than 4,950 were credited to Merlin-engined Mustangs, which is quite remarkable when one considers it was in

STRAFING

'Once I hit the drome, I really get down on the deck. I don't mean five feet up; I mean so low the grass is brushing the bottom of the scoop.

'For a squadron attack on a Hun airfield I do not recommend sending sections in waves. This is a good way to get half the outfit shot down. In my own group, I want want as many as eight in at one time, if possible. These should be well abreast and, knowing our target beforehand, we go right in full bore in a straight line. Once you start an attack of this kind, don't turn or swerve. If you do there is a danger of collision or entering another man's pattern of fire . . . After the attack on the field stay on the deck for a good mile beyond the dome before pulling up. The break should consist of rudder yawning. Never cock a wing up. If you must turn on the drome, do flat skidding turns . . .'

LT COL DONALD J M BLAKESLEE

EARLY MERLIN MUSTANG PRODUCTION BATCHES

P-51B	P51-C	Mustang III
USAAF Serials	USAAF Serials	RAF Serials
43-12093 to 12492	42-102979 to 103328	FB100 - FB399
43-6313 to 6352	42-103329 to 103378	FR411 -
43-6353 to 6752	42-103379 to 103778	FX848 - FX999
43-6753 to 7112	42-103779 to 103987	FZ100 - FZ197
43-7113 to 7202	43-24902 to 25351	HB821 - HB961
42-106429 to 106538	44-10753 to 11152	HK944 - HK947
42-106541 to 106738		HK955 - HK956
42-106739 to 106908		KH421 - KH640
42-106909 to 106978		SR406 - SR438
43-24752 to 24901		SR440 -

action for a mere 18 months. At the same time, they accounted for just over half of the 8,160 aircraft claimed destroyed on the ground by strafing.

The only German fighter to outclass the Mustang in sheer performance was the superb Me 262 jet. Vastly superior in speed, rate of climb and firepower, it was defeated by the Mustang's three advantages. The ability to turn tightly prevented the German fighter from getting more than the most fleeting shooting opportunities. Long endurance meant that it could outlast the Me 262 in the air, forcing it to break off through shortage of fuel. Finally, greater numbers allowed the Mustang not only to protect the bombers, but to patrol the airfields of the German jets in order to catch them on takeoff or landing, when they were slow and at their most vulnerable.

Above: Pilot quality was the factor which enabled American fighter units to grind down the German defenders. Chuck Yeager of the 357th FG, seen here with P-51B *Glamorous Glen*, named after his fiancée, always claimed that his superb distance vision gave him the initiative in combat. (W. Bruce Overstreet via JE)

Right top: 'I got a good trade on the old model!' Dan Zoerb of the 52nd FG taxies out in a new and gleaming P-51B, having just turned in his Spitfire on Corsica in April 1944. (Dan Zoerb via JE)

Right middle: From bases in Italy, 15th AF Mustangs flew escort missions to as far afield as Romania. P-51B *Sweet Clara* of 325th FG took part in these missions some time in 1944. (Hans-Heiri Stapfer via JE)

Below: Late in 1944 the distinctive chequerboard markings of 325th FG were extended forward of the tail, across the top of the stabilizers, and onto the wingtips. This is a P-51D with the added dorsal fin.

Below left: Lieutenant Edward 'Buddy' Haydon of the 357th FG, who on 8 November 1944 engaged an Me 262 jet near the Dummersee. Surprised on his landing approach, the German pilot, who had engine problems, took violent evasive action and snap-rolled into the ground. Thus died Walter Nowotny, the fifth-ranking German ace, credited with 258 air combat victories. (Edward Haydon via JE)

P-51D PRODUCTION BATCHES

P-51D USAAF Serials	F-6D USAAF Serials	F-6K USAAF Serials
44-13253 to 14052	44-13020 to 13039	44-11554
44-14053 to 14852	44-13131 to 13140	44-11897 to 11952
44-14853 to 15252	44-13181	44-11993 to 12008
44-15253 to 15752	44-84059 to 84540	44-12216 to 12237
44-63160 to 64159	44-84566	44-12459 to 12471
44-72027 to 72126	44-84773 to 84788	44-12523 to 12534
44-72127 to 72626	44-84835 to 84855	44-12810 to 12852
44-72627 to 73626	44-11655 to 11689	
44-73627 to 74226		
44-74227 to 75026		
44-11152 to 11352		
44-84390 to 84989		
45-11343 to 11542		
45-11543 to 11742		

Right: **A P-51D of 7th Air Force is serviced in the Philippines. In the background is a Curtiss Commando transport. (Rocker via JE)**

Above: **Photo-reconnaissance F-6Ks of the 26th Squadron, 51st Fighter group, 14th Air Force, are prepared for their next sortie at Nanning, China, 27 July 1945. (USAAF via JE)**

■ OTHER ■
US AIR FORCES

Total Mustang production amounted to 15,675 of all types. Merlin-Mustangs equipped several Fighter Groups of the 15th AF based in Italy, including the 31st, 52nd, 325th, and the all-African-American 332nd. In the Far East, 14th AF had the 23rd, 51st and 311th Fighter Groups, mainly flying P-51Bs and Cs by the end of 1944. In the Pacific theatre, the first Mustang unit was the 3rd Air Commando Group with P-51Ds. This was followed by the 71st Reconnaissance Group, which turned in its elderly P-40s for F-6Ds. The 35th and 348th re-equipped with P-51Ds in March 1945.

In the same month, the 15th and 21st were sent to Iwo Jima; their task was to act as long-range escorts for B-29s bombing the Japanese home islands. However, other priorities intervened. The north of the island had not been cleared of Japanese, and these attacked the camp

Left: Mustangs of the 14th AF were commonly fitted with a teardrop housing over the radio direction-finding antenna. This is the aircraft of former Flying Tiger Ed Rector, commanding 23rd FG. (Don Lopez via JE)

Below: Mustang IIIs of No. 260 Squadron RAF. Previously having operated P-40 Kittyhawks, the squadron converted to the Mustang in Italy. (Frank F. Smith via JE)

Bottom: The Southern Cross on the rudder denotes the Royal Australian Air Force. This is a Mustang IV of No. 3 Squadron, seen at Foggia in February 1945. The large combat flaps are evident from this angle. (A. F. Lane via JE)

of the 21st, causing many casualties. The following few days saw the long-range fighters flying very short-range strafing missions as the defenders were finally eliminated.

The first escort mission to Japan was flown on 7 April. Unlike Europe, there was no need to provide fighter escort over the entire route; it was sufficient to rendezvous with the bombers as they approached the target area and stay with them until they cleared it.

The 15th and 21st, joined in mid-May by the 506th, now found themselves flying the longest and most exhausting single-seat fighter missions of the war. Distances were extreme – a round trip of 1,500 miles (2,400km) lasting for seven

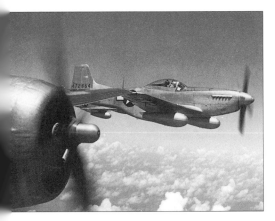

Above: Laden with external fuel 'jugs', a 7th AF P-51D based on Iwo Jima tucks in tight to a B-29 Superfortress 'shepherd' for the long flight to the Japanese home islands in July 1945. Beneath its rear fuselage can be seen the wing and jug of another Mustang. (USAAF via JE)

or eight hours was not uncommon. To make matters worse, most of the route lay over the featureless ocean, while such islands as there were all looked much the same. With no margin for navigational errors, a B-29 was assigned to each fighter group to shepherd it safely across the vast wastes of the Pacific.

As if the risks posed by Japanese fighters, plus a long overwater flight dependent on a single engine, were not bad enough, other hazards had to be faced. Dust from the crudely constructed airstrips on Iwo Jima rose in clouds on every takeoff. Not only did it obscure visibility, but it clogged air filters, causing many an engine to cut. Crashes shortly after takeoff were commonplace. But the worst enemy of all was often the weather. The violence of tropical storms was unimaginable to those who had never experienced them.

On 1 June 1945, 148 Mustangs set off to rendezvous with a B-29 raid on Honshu. Halfway they encountered a weather front, and in trying to penetrate it, 27 fighters went down, taking 22 pilots with them. It was the heaviest Mustang loss of the war.

■ OTHER AIR FORCES ■

The second largest Mustang user of the war was the Royal Air Force which, by the cessation of hostilities, had taken delivery of 910 Mustang IIIs – 59 going to the Royal Australian Air Force; 280 Mustang IVs, and 594 Mustang IVAs, although the latter did not see action before the end of the war in Europe.

■ RAF SQUADRONS ■

Fighter Command or 2nd TAF: Nos 19, 26, 64, 65, 118, 122, 126, 129, 154, 234, 237, 268, 303 Polish, 306 Polish, 309 Polish, 315 Polish, 316 Polish, 345 French, 441 Canadian, 442 Canadian, 611. Mediterranean: Nos 94, 112, 213, 241, 249, 250, 260. Also No. 5 South African Air Force; No. 3 Royal Australian Air Force.

Other air forces to operate Merlin Mustangs at the end of the Second World War apart from the British Empire countries of Canada, Australia and South Africa, were the Free French (about 100); Sweden (54 including four interned examples which force-landed there), and China (about 50).

Although it was designed to the same load factors and of similar size and configuration to the Spitfire, the airframe of the Mustang was considerably heavier. As there was obviously room for improvement, NAA embarked on a weight reduction programme early in 1943, the aim of which was to improve performance. As this involved considerable redesign, the opportunity was taken to simplify many systems, thereby improving maintainability. What emerged was virtually a new aircraft under the skin, even though in appearance it was virtually indistinguishable from the P-51D.

The main secret of the Mustang's success had been the low-drag laminar flow wing. A new and even lower drag profile was adopted, while the formerly kinked leading edge was straightened, slightly increasing the wing area. The entire cooling system was redesigned to give greater efficiency, less drag, and reduced vulnerability to battle damage. The engine remained the same, but its mounting was much simpler and lighter, and gave better access for servicing. One propulsion change was the use of a hollow steel three-bladed propeller.

The cockpit layout conformed closely to British practice while the pilot's back armour was moulded to form part of the seat, and a much longer but less draggy sliding canopy was fitted. The tail surfaces were made larger, the control surfaces improved, and the ailerons given 15 degrees of travel instead of the previous 12 degrees. The wheels, now with disc brakes, were reduced in size. The main gears were redesigned in line with the reduced maximum all-up weight, and the hydraulic system was simplified.

■ MUSTANG V ■

The fuselage fuel tank, which played such havoc with stability when it was full, was deleted, while the inboard wing tanks were increased in size to hold 81.6 imperial gallons (102 US gallons/ 386 litres) each; an increment of 13 per cent. Finally, and rather surprisingly, the two inboard machine guns were deleted, and the remaining four were given 440 rounds each.

The first lightweights were built as XP-51Fs, and the third, finished in British camouflage, became the Mustang V. NAA test pilot Bob Chilton made the first flight on 14 February 1944. Although it was very fast (466mph/ 750km/hr at 29,000ft/8,845m), it lacked directional stability. Two more lightweight Mustangs were built, designated XP-51G. These were powered by the experimental Rolls-Royce Merlin 145,

Opposite: Jean Landis, seen here about to climb into the cockpit of a P-51D, was a WASP. With Mustangs rolling off the production lines at the rate of one every 22 minutes, and most men able to handle high-performance fighters already with front-line units, ferry pilots were at a premium. The answer, as in Britain with the Air Transport Auxiliary, was to use women pilots. The Women's Airforce Service Pilots was formed in 1943 as a ferry organization, and by the end of the war, over 1,000 women had piloted virtually every type in service with the USAAF. (Jean Landis via JE)
Below: The absence of the kink in the wing leading edge, coupled with the small wheels, at once identifies this Mustang as a lightweight variant. It appears to have a three-bladed propeller, which makes it a P-51F. (NAA via JE)

P-51H

Dimensions

Wingspan	37ft 0in (11.2m)
Length	33ft 4in (10.13m)
Height	13ft 8in (4.17m)

Weights

Empty	7,040lb (3,193kg)
Max TO	11,500lb (5,216kg)

Performance

Max. speed	487mph (784kph)
Climb	3,600fpm (18m/sec)
Ceiling	42,00ft (12,800m)
Range*	1,160ml (1,866km)

*with two drop tanks

Above: **The only lightweight Mustang to enter production was the P-51H. While the definitive version of this model featured an extended fuselage and a taller fin and rudder for greater longitudinal stability, not all P-51Hs were so modified, as evidenced by this machine, seen at Fort Dix, New Jersey, in December 1945. (AAHS via JE)**

driving a five-bladed propeller. First flown on 10 August 1944, the second of the two is reported to have achieved 495mph (796km/hr) six months later, making it the fastest Mustang of all.

Neither the XP-51F or G ever entered production, but work done on the former was used for the next production variant, the P-51H. Power for this model was the -9 engine, tweaked to give a war emergency rating of 1,900hp at about 19,000ft (5,800m) using 150 grade fuel and water/alcohol injection, and with a four-bladed propeller. The airframe of the P-51H differed considerably from that of the XP-51F. A longer fuselage and a taller vertical tail with a dorsal spine finally provided a cure for the lateral instability that had so bedevilled the P-51D.

The most difficult part of air combat gunnery is deflection shooting, which involves aiming ahead of the target by an amount which varies according to target speed and crossing angle. Pulling the correct amount of lead often meant

that by the time that the correct amount of deflection had been achieved, the target had vanished beneath the long nose of the Merlin-engined fighter. In an attempt to prevent this, the cockpit of the P-51H was raised to give a downward angle of sight over the nose of eight degrees. At the same time, the armament reverted to six 0.50in (12.7mm) Browning machine guns. The fuselage fuel tank was reinstated, although capacity was reduced to 40 imperial gallons (50 US gal/191 litres).

With a maximum level speed of 487mph (784kph), the P-51H was the fastest propeller-driven production fighter of the war. Large orders were placed for this and the similar P-51M built at Fort Worth, but production was barely into its stride before the war ended in August 1945.

Other Mustang variants curtailed by the end of hostilities were the P-51L, basically a P-51H fitted with the -11 engine and a Stromberg injection-type carburettor, rated at 2,270hp with water injection; and the XP-51J. The J model reverted to the Allison V-1710-119 engine, with two-stage super-charging which was able to provide more than reasonable altitude performance. Only one prototype ever flew, for a brief period which started in April 1945, but the full test flight programme was not completed.

■ ENDURANCE ■ PROBLEMS

Until 1943, the pilot had traditionally outperformed the fighter. He could use war emergency power until the engine blew up, tug on the pole until the wings came off, or point upwards until the thin air failed to support his machine and it fell spinning into the abyss. But when deep penetrations of the Third Reich began, with sorties of six or seven hours, the machine outlasted him. The strain was such that some pilots became so exhausted that they had to be lifted from the cockpit at the end of a mission. And when that mission ended with a return to base through foul English weather, with the rain clouds scraping the tree tops, landing accidents were all too common. Another consideration was the Pacific. There the distances were even greater, and the problems of providing fighter escort more intractable.

The obvious answer was to have two pilots to share the workload, but this in turn posed problems. A few Mustangs had been built or converted as two-seaters. However, the rear seat displaced the fuselage fuel tank, thus reducing range. Not only this, but with the extra weight of second pilot and his seat aft, they were useless for combat. The purpose-built two-seat fighters of the era lacked the agility to take on single-seaters on level terms, and in any case, most of

Above: The raised cockpit and high fin and rudder, plus the twin radio masts, mark this as a late-built P-51H. This example was diverted to cold weather testing at Edmonton, Alberta, in 1945. (L. L.Coombs via JE)

Below: Contrast in styles. The 82nd FG operated both the P-51H (nearest) and P-51D (farthest from camera) in the early postwar era. While the tall tail of the H is easy to spot, close examination also shows the deepened fuselage and downsloped nose resulting from the raised cockpit of the P-51H.

Below right: Sheer pilot fatigue coupled with poor weather, or perhaps a damaged or malfunctioning aircraft, caused many a crash on return. This P-51B of the 339th FG, interestingly enough fitted with a Malcolm hood, came to grief at Manston. (Roger Freeman)

them were optimized for night missions.

The problem then became how best to produce a two-seater which could hold its own in a sky infested with agile German single-seaters. The answer was to perpetuate a trend which had been evident since 1915. The agile biplane had long been superseded by the higher performing but less agile monoplane. Agility was an advantage only when the enemy was willing to fight, whereas superior performance allowed a fighter to make slashing attacks before breaking off. This had particularly been the case in the Far East, where the agile Japanese fighters had been defeated by dive and zoom tactics, the American pilots keeping their speed high at all times.

The other factor in the equation was time. Designing a fighter from scratch, testing it, and getting it into production, was a lengthy business. Was there a quicker way?

■ TWIN MUSTANG ■

There was! In November 1943, NAA proposed a long-range fighter based on not one Mustang, but two. Two Mustang fuselages, with engines, cockpits, outer wings and vertical tails, could be joined together using common inner wing and horizontal tail surfaces. Four prototypes, designated XP-82, were ordered in January 1944, although only three, including one XP-82A, were built.

Although the airframe of the production aircraft was based on the P-51H, Packard-Merlin-powered XP-51Fs with standard fins and rudders were utilized for both XP-82s. The engine for the production aircraft was however the latest version of the Allison V-1710, the two-stage geared supercharger which gave more than adequate high-altitude performance. The Allison fitted with few changes, while when at the end of the war Packard ceased to licence-build Merlins, it posed no supply problems. The single XP-82A was used as a test-bed to integrate the V-1710-119.

In the production aircraft, the engines were handed (as the -143 and -145 respectively), with the propellers rotating inwards in opposite directions. This arrangement minimized torque, so that in the event of engine failure on one side, asymmetric handling problems in single-engined flight were reduced.

Adding the wing and tail centre sections posed few problems; the former housed six 0.50in (12.7mm) Browning machine guns with 440 rounds per gun. A slotted flap occupied the entire length of the trailing edge. Lateral stability appeared questionable; to improve matters the fuselages were lengthened by 4ft 9in (1.45m), and the dorsal strakes ahead of the fins considerably enlarged. Based on the P-51F, both prototypes

Six 0.50in Browning machine guns with 440 rounds per gun

had vertical tails similar to those of the P-51D, although production P-82s carried the taller vertical surfaces of the P-51H.

One area which underwent considerable redesign was the main landing gear, which had to carry roughly double the weight of a standard P-51. The legs were located beneath the fuselages, and the wheels retracted into the wing centre

Above: Details of a field-modified two-seater Mustang P-51B of 4th FG based at Debden. (Roger Freeman)

Above right: The second prototype XP-82 Twin Mustang, cobbled together from two XP-51Fs. As can be seen here, the fuselages were considerably extended in length and large dorsal strakes added ahead of the fins. Production aircraft had taller vertical tails. (NASM via JE)

section. Increased weight also called for structural redesign of the wings, the total area of which was considerably less than that of two P-51s, giving altogether higher loadings.

To improve manoeuvrability in the rolling plane, which suffered due to both the increased wing span and the inertia of the two widely spaced fuselages, much longer two-piece ailerons were fitted, and given hydraulic boost. Four self-sealing fuel tanks, two in the outer wings and two beneath the fuselage, gave a total capacity of 459.2 imperial gallons (574 US gallons/2,180 litres), promising greater range than any previous fighter.

Surprisingly, standard P-51 cockpits,

RAMJET MUSTANG

Ramjet engines were mounted on the wingtips of this P-51D a year or so after the end of the Second World War. The purpose was not to add to the performance of the Mustang, but to measure the capability of the ramjet engines. The throttles developed for the ramjets were basic, to say the least; fuel flow was controlled by a global valve (like a bath tap) on the floor on each side of the pilot's seat. Both engines had to be operated simultaneously, which meant that

to hold the stick while adjusting the ramjets really required a pilot with three arms! This notwithstanding, all went well until 19th August 1948, when test pilot Paul Chell tried to restart the starboard ramjet after a flameout, only to be greeted by a violent explosion and flames coming from the wing. He immediately jettisoned the canopy, rolled inverted, and baled out.

LONG MISSIONS

'In all we went to Berlin four times that week (March 1944) and I've never been so tired in my life – six-hour missions one right after the other just knocked the pee right out of you. I'd swear I could have given you the serial number off my oxygen bottle and dinghy pack by reading it off my left cheek.'

LT GLENN EAGLESTON, 354THE FG

adapted for the twin-engined configuration, were not used. The command pilot flew from a fully-equipped port cockpit, while his copilot, expected to take over only intermittently, occupied a far more austere starboard hole, with only enough instrumentation for relief and emergency operation. At one point an interceptor variant with the starboard cockpit faired over was considered, but not taken up.

■ 500 ORDERED ■

An order for 500 Twin Mustangs was placed in the early summer of 1944 as the P-82B. First flight of the XP-82 took place on 15 April 1945, and from the outset the aircraft was a winner, reaching a maximum speed of 482mph (776kph) at 25,100ft (7,650m), while range on internal fuel alone was 1,390 miles (2,237km). But the war ended before the P-82B reached the production line, and all except 20 aircraft were cancelled. These never entered squadron service, but instead were used for training and operational trials. Two were converted to prototype night fighters, as the XP-82C and D respectively.

The USAAF became the USAF in 1947, and in the following year fighter designations changed from P (pursuit) to F (fighter). The first Twin Mustang to enter service was the F-82E, which was operated by the 27th Fighter Escort Wing (FEW) of Strategic Air Command in 1948. But the new generation of swept-winged jets quickly made piston-engined fighters obsolete, and the F-82Es were finally phased out in July 1950.

■ NIGHT FIGHTER ■

At the end of the war, the USAAF lacked an effective night fighter. The Black Widow was unmanoeuvrable, too slow and lacked altitude capability, and jet night fighters were still a long way from entering service. The Twin Mustang had obvious night-fighter potential, with the starboard cockpit adapted to take a radar operator. All that was needed was to fit it with air interception radar.

This was easier said than done. The scanner had to be located ahead of the propellers to avoid interference from them, and this meant a long way forward of the wing leading edge. The obvious

Above: Sinister black finish proclaiming that it is a night fighter, the XP-82C demonstrates the long and unwieldy pod that had to be developed to locate the radar scanner ahead of the propellers. The landing lights were positioned on the main gear legs beneath the fuselages. This was not a good idea; when switched on at night, the lights reflected back from the propeller discs, half-blinding the pilot. (NASM via JE)

place to mount it was in a pod under the wing centre section. A tremendously long pod was thus needed, which could only be secured at its rear end. This caused problems. Under loads caused by manoeuvring flight the pod, with its long moment arm, could flex; the line of sight of the scanner then moved out of alignment with the axis of the aircraft, causing inaccurate indications on the radar scope. Greater rigidity was needed, not only of the pod, but of the wing centre section that carried it. A great deal of experimentation was needed to overcome this.

> ### Other night-flying kit added included marker and radar beacons

The first aircraft to carry the SCR-720 search radar was the XP-82C, converted from the tenth production P-82B. In a belt-and-braces move, the eleventh production P-82B was also converted as the XP-82D, its similar underslung pod fitted with the AN/APG-28 tracking radar – less capable but smaller and lighter than the SCR-720, and therefore less prone to flexing.

Twin Mustangs carrying both radar types were ordered in September and October 1946; 100 P-82Fs with AN/APG-28 radar, and 50 P-82Gs with SCR-720C. Other specifically night flying kit added included marker and radar beacons, and an AN/APS-13 tail warning radar. Prior to delivery, a further requirement was added. Service in Alaska called for the ability to operate in extreme conditions, and nine P-82F airframes with SCR-720C instead of AN/APG-28, and five P-82Gs were modified to suit, mainly with improved heating systems. These, the final Mustangs built, became P-82Hs. Deliveries took place during 1948 and early 1949, by which time the new USAF designations had come into effect. F-82Fs went to the 52nd and 325th Fighter (All Weather) Groups and the 51st Fighter (Interceptor) Group, while the 347th F(AW)G received F-82Gs. The handful of F-82Hs were assigned to the 449th F(AW) Squadron at Ladd AFB in Alaska, where they soldiered on until the end of 1953 – the last propeller-driven fighters operational with the USAF.

The jet engine spelt the beginning of the end for the Mustang. In the ongoing development of fighter aircraft, performance had always taken precedence over manoeuvrability, and jet fighters had overwhelming performance advantages over their piston-engined brethren. Mustang ace John C. Meyer (23 victories) and later to become Vice Chief of the USAF, concluded after an action against the German jet that eight P-51s were the equal of a single Me 262 if each knew of the other's presence. This was not an inspiring ratio. Had Germany been able to get the Me 262 into service in really large numbers, with adequately trained pilots, the American daylight raids on the Third Reich would have gone very differently.

Above: **Even more than the jet fighter, it was the concept of the fast jet bomber, pioneered by the Arado Ar 234 seen here, that sounded the knell of the piston-engined fighter. (Author)**
Opposite: **The USAF donated F-51Ds to the South Korean Air Force. Initially these were flown by American pilots, but after 80 hours training on type, ROKAF pilots became operational and took over. (USAF via JE)**

■ THE OLD ORDER ■

The performance advantages conferred by the jet engine were not confined to fighters, as the German Arado Ar 234 jet bomber clearly demonstrated during the final months of the Second World War. Although vulnerable at low level, and in the acceleration phase after take-off and the slowing down phase prior to landing, at operating speeds and altitudes the Ar 234 was virtually uninterceptable by piston-engined fighters. This was the shape of the future, and the only effective counter was the high-performance jet fighter, which would eventually supersede all piston-engined types.

The first American jet fighter, the Lockheed P-80A, entered service with the 412th FG at the end of 1945, and re-equipment of numerous other fighter groups followed rapidly. Other, more advanced jet fighters were in the pipeline, and Mustangs became obsolescent almost overnight.

The few USAAF Mustang units which remained in front-line service were re-equipped with the P-51H, and hundreds of their now outdated P-51D/Ks were handed to the Air National Guard,

which had been re-formed in May 1946. At its peak in 1952, no fewer than 68 ANG squadrons, just over two-thirds of the total, flew Mustangs. Other P-51s were scrapped, placed in storage, or sold at knock-down prices to neutral or aligned nations. Apart from those countries already mentioned, Bolivia, the People's Republic of China, Cuba, Dominican Republic, Guatemala, Haiti, Holland, Honduras, Indonesia, Israel, Italy, Nicaragua, New Zealand, Philippines, Salvador, Somalia, South Korea, Switzerland and Uruguay all operated Mustangs, usually P-51Ds or Ks, at one time or another.

The USAAF shrank to barely a quarter of its former size

In the 57 months following the end of the Second World War, the front-line fighter strength of the USAF shrank to barely a quarter of its former size. About 1,850 were jets, including 419 examples of the superb swept-winged fighter that had replaced the Mustang on the NAA production lines; the F-86 Sabre. The rest were obsolescent piston-engined types.

The most numerous was the Mustang, but with the proliferation of jets in the air forces of potential threat nations, it was

difficult to foresee a scenario that envisaged more than a peripheral role for the F-51. Even the comparatively new F-82 Twin Mustang was regarded as a mere stop-gap, awaiting the arrival of the first jet all-weather fighters, after which it would be discarded. This was the situation in mid-1950.

OUTCLASSED

'We were eight against one but the 262 didn't break off the attack. Instead he would turn away and we would break back and we would find that he could fly the circumference of the circle around the crippled Fortress in the time it took us to fly the diameter to cut him off. Thus if we followed him, he was so much faster he could fly around to the other side and cut back in without allowing us an opportunity to use our guns. I then positioned four Mustangs on each side of the B-17.'
LT COL JOHN C. MEYER, 352ND FG

Left: **Supplanted as an interceptor, first by the F-80 Shooting Star, then by the F-86 Sabre, the Mustang was used in the attack role, only to be replaced by the F-84 Thunderjet. (Author)**

■ RETURN TO BATTLE ■

The Korean War started on 25 June 1950. That afternoon, a USAF transport was destroyed by strafing North Korean fighters. The evacuation of foreign nationals was commenced immediately, and the USAF Far Eastern Air Force (FEAF) provided air cover. This was far from easy; the nearest FEAF bases were in Japan, roughly 400 miles (650km) from the South Korean capital, Seoul. Once more, the need was for aircraft which were designed for long range and endurance.

Two aircraft types were available; short-legged F-80 Shooting Star jets, and F-82G Twin Mustangs of the 347th F(AW) Group. The latter both had the necessary range, and could outperform the propeller-driven North Korean fighters. They quickly deployed to the airfield at Itazuke in southern Japan, and flew their first patrols of the Korean War the next day.

Under orders to keep a low profile, a pair of F-82Gs from 68th F(AW)S easily evaded a half-hearted attack by two North Korean Lavochkin La-7s that afternoon. The rules of engagement were promptly changed, and on 27 June the Twin Mustangs bit back. Attacked at low level near Seoul, they accounted for three North Korean fighters, plus a probable.

Having covered the evacuation of civilians, the next task was to stop the onward roll of the North Korean army. The Twin Mustangs were switched to day and night interdiction against enemy supply routes, using 500lb (227kg) general purpose bombs, 5in (127mm) high-velocity aircraft rockets (HVARs), and napalm.

The following weeks were critical. Although the small North Korean Air Force was quickly reduced to a state of impotence, the numerically strong army, backed by Russian-built T-34 tanks, came close to overrunning the entire south. With hardly any suitable airfields left, FEAF was forced to provide close air support and interdiction from Japan. For this the F-82 was invaluable. Whereas the endurance of the F-80 in the target area was a bare 15 minutes, the Twin

Below: **Bucket of Bolts**, an F-82G, scored the first air victory of the Korean War on 27 June 1950, downing a North Korean Yak-7U. It was flown by Lieutenant William 'Skeeter' Hudson, with Lieutenant Carl Fraser as his co-pilot. (James Gasser via JE)

Mustang could stay around for an hour or more, as well as ranging far deeper into enemy territory than the jet. These missions were often flown by singletons. Under these conditions, the tail warning radar, with a range of about 4,000ft (1,220m) astern, was an asset. It could however give very realistic false alarms if the beam touched the ground in mountainous terrain, or if the nose was pulled up at low level, thus projecting the beam downwards.

Right top: **No. 77 Squadron of the Royal Australian Air Force joined the United Nations contingent in Korea in July 1950. It flew Mustangs until March 1951, when it converted to the Gloster Meteor jet. One HVAR remains beneath the wings of this example as it taxies in after a mission in August 1950. (USAF via JE)**
Right: **With what looks like napalm tanks underwing, Mustangs of No. 2 Squadron South African Air Force, the Flying Cheetahs, run up their engines prior to their first mission in Korea on 16 November 1950. All appear to have different coloured spinners. (USAF via JE)**
Below: **Taegu airstrip, with USAF F-51Ds of the 18th FBG and ROKAF sharing the field. The hill to the left was perfectly lined up with the main runway and, while no problem in clear visibility, was a hazard in poor weather. It was known locally as Mount Bustyourass. (USAF via JE)**

Above: HVARs and napalm on an F-51D of the 8th FBG. *Bad Check*, with the subtitle 'Always Comes Back' in smaller letters, was the personal mount of James A. Gasser. (Jim Gasser via JE)

■ REVERSE RE-EQUIP ■

In mid-1950, FEAF had three fighter groups based in Japan which had only just finished converting from the F-51D to the F-80C Shooting Star. On the outbreak of hostilities, they flew their first war missions with the Lockheed jet. Most Korean airfields were relics of the Second World War, and were unsuitable for fast jets so, like the large and heavy Twin Mustangs, the F-80s were forced to operate from Japanese bases. At such extreme range, the lack of endurance proved critical.

The F-51s that were previously operated by these units had been placed in storage prior to being scrapped, not because they were worn out, but because the USAF had no further use for them. It so happened that their destruction was fortuitously delayed, and when South Korea was invaded they formed an immediately available reserve of perfectly serviceable aircraft.

The decision to make the three units (8th Fighter Bomber, 35th Fighter Interceptor, and the 49th Fighter Bomber Wings) trade in their shiny new jets for their old Mustangs seemed a retrograde step to some, but there were sound operational reasons for it. First, the F-51D could loiter over the target area for at least an hour and a quarter, five times as long as the F-80. Secondly, the small and ill-equipped North Korean Air Force posed little threat, and F-51Ds were perfectly adequate to counter it. Thirdly, the F-51 was in many ways better suited to the close air support mission than the F-80C by reason of its slower speed, greater agility, longer endurance and better weapons-carrying capability. Fourthly, when circumstances demanded, the F-51 could use basic

Right: Conditions in Korea were often appalling. Heat and dust for part of the year alternated with rain and mud. Runways and taxiways were normally of pierced steel planking (PSP), which wore out tyres at an amazing rate. Here a P-51D of 18th FBG throws up spray as it takes off from a waterlogged airstrip in August 1951. (USAF via JE)

Korean airstrips to refuel and rearm, reducing turn-round time. Finally, having only recently relinquished the type, the three fighter groups (pilots and equally important, ground crews) took minimal time in reconverting back onto it.

The Republic of (South) Korea had no combat aircraft; just a handful of liaison and training machines, most of which were knocked out on the ground in the first few days. It was hastily reconstituted by an initial gift of ten F-51Ds from the

Above: **Ground fire was the greatest threat to the attacking Mustangs. Lieutenant David Gray of 18th FBG, unable to lower his landing gear due to hydraulic system damage, makes a perfect belly-landing in September 1952. (USAF via JE)**

USAF, complete with American pilots and ground crewmen commanded by Major Dean Hess.

Based well forward at Taegu, this small unit did fearful execution among the advancing North Koreans, but was too small to influence events to any great extent. The unfamiliar South Korean markings also caused confusion among friendly forces, not least because the personal Mustang of Dean Hess carried the legend 'By faith I fly' on the nose. No great problem about that, except that it was written in Chinese!

With the Mustang established as the best machine for the job, another 145 were withdrawn from ANG units, flown to the west coast of the USA, loaded onto the aircraft carrier USS *Boxer* and rushed across the Pacific, arriving at Tokyo on 23 July. To operate them, a provisional unit, the 'Dallas Squadron', was formed from personnel drawn from

the 18th FBW, whose home base was in the Philippines.

The 40th Fighter Interceptor Squadron left their comfortable base and their fast and modern F-80s in Japan, converted to Mustangs, and took up residence in the dusty hell of Pohang, close behind the battle area. Operational within only three days, the squadron averaged 35 close air support sorties each day during the first week.

The 40th FIS took up residence in the dusty hall of Pohang

Nor was this all. The United Nations Security Council, in an unprecedented display of determination, backed the American moves and turned the Korean War into a UN operation. This brought two more Mustang squadrons into the fray: No. 77 Royal Australian Air Force, which for operational purposes was attached to the 39th FBW, and No. 2 Squadron South African Air Force, which

was attached to the 18th FBW. Both units flew F-51Ds; in fact the F-51D/K was the only Mustang type to participate

OPERATIONAL RECORD, 12TH FBS, 15 JULY 1950 TO 30 AUGUST 1950

Aircraft type	F-51D
A/C available	20
Sorties flown	1,438
Avge sorties per day	33
Hours flown	2,650
Munitions expended	
500lb (227kg) bombs	2,300
5in (127mm) HVARs	8,500
0.50in (12.7mm) bullets	860,000
Losses	6
Pilots killed	4

This record is typical for a Mustang Squadron at that time.

MUSTANG VS MIG-15

7th November 1950

'The MiG leader had selected the worst possible firing position and the flaming tennis balls (37mm shells) came nowhere near us. As each MiG passed in front of us, all four of us would squeeze off a burst from our six 0.50 calibre guns at it. The #4 MiG pilot must have seen us shooting the other three so he decided to alter his attack. As #4 left the perch, he began firing way out of range. In fact he was still out of range when he stopped firing and began a right turn. At the time, I called for Cousin Willie (the F-51 flight callsign) to break left and I turned inside the MiG.

'I had everything going for me except the speed. But I was able to pull lead on him and fire about a two second burst. We were using API ammo and I could see strikes along his fuselage. The MiG driver immediately zoom-climbed to about 20,000ft (6,100m) . . .'

CAPT HOWARD TANNER, 36 FBS

Below: **The Russian-built MiG-15 was a second-generation jet fighter. When it first appeared over Korea in November 1950, it not only totally outperformed the Mustang, but the American F-80 and F-84 jet fighters also. Only the superior quality of the United Nations pilots prevented a disaster. (Author)**

in the conflict. The lightweight F-51H was considered unsuitable for the hurly-burly of close air support, and none was sent to the theatre.

■ NAPALM ■

The momentum that was built up by the numerically strong North Korean army, spearheaded by armoured columns, was difficult to stop. At first, the best that could be done was to slow it, and here the Mustangs were in their element. Operating mainly from Japanese bases, they flew in pairs and fours. Once in the target area, they linked up with a forward air controller who directed them where and what to attack.

All weapons were effective against troops and soft targets, but the heavily armoured Russian-built T-34 tanks were another matter. Bombs or HVARs were effective only if a direct hit was scored, but the inaccuracy of these weapons made this a rare event. Napalm, a fire bomb made from jellified petroleum, proved the best answer, as on impact it covered a wide area.

Attacks had to be made at low level, where even small-arms fire could be deadly. It was hazardous work, and F-51 losses were high. As in the Second World War, the coolant system proved vulnerable to even small hits which otherwise would have caused little damage.

Eventually the situation on the ground stabilized, then reversed. The broken North Korean army was pursued up the peninsula, while Mustangs, some of them by now based in-country, ranged almost to the Chinese border. It was during this phase that Mustangs scored their only air combat victories of the war, five in all, with 'Moon' Mullins of the 67th FBS accounting for three Yakovlev fighters.

■ ACTION REPLAY ■

On 1 November, a new factor entered the equation. A flight of Mustangs was escorting a T-6 spotter aircraft near the border when they were intercepted by Chinese MiG-15s. Evading hard, they escaped unharmed, but it was clear that luck had been on their side. Five years earlier, even with vastly superior numbers, Mustangs had been hard pressed to cope with the Me 262. The swept-winged Russian jet was as far advanced over the 262 as the latter had been over the P-51D then, and now the huge numerical advantage was lacking. It was a bleak prospect for the Mustang pilots.

Above and below: The US Air National Guard became the major operator of the Mustang. Of these two examples, one belongs to the California ANG; the other, with mysterious wing markings, to an unidentified unit. (Roger Freeman)

Below: The small wheels and lightweight main gears of the F-51H, as seen on this aircraft of the Massachusetts Air National Guard, were only suitable for use from permanent airfields with hard runways. This was a major factor in preventing their use in Korea, where PSP surfaces were the norm.

'We would put the tank on the centre line of our nose, and at the last moment, when you felt you had to pull up not to hit the tank, you released the napalm bomb and then pulled up, and the bomb hit the tank. We always attacked from 90 degrees and dropped only one bomb at a time, so each Mustang, which carried two napalm bombs, six 5in rockets, and several hundred rounds for the six machine guns, could do a hell of a job. The rockets were huge but not very accurate. But when they hit a tank, they destroyed it.'

ELIEZER COHEN, ISRAELI PILOT.

Above: The F-51D became the J 26 in Swedish Air Force service. This aircraft, seen on 3 August 1950, belongs to F 21 based at Lulea, and is flown by Engineer Cadet Harald Werner. (Lars Olausson via JE)

Below: Long after the war of 1956, an Israeli Mustang undergoes a complete refurbishment. In 1948 Israeli Mustangs flew in natural metal finish; in 1956 they were camouflaged. (Author via Flypast)

Right: The final operational users of the Mustang were various small Latin American countries. This example is Guatemalan. (Roger Freeman)

A glimmer of hope shone through on 7 November, when four F-51Ds of the 36th FBS, callsign Cousin Willie, were flying a combat air patrol close to the Chinese border at 10,000ft (3,050m). Attacked from above by an equal number of MiG-15s, the Mustangs fought back hard, damaging three enemy aircraft while suffering no hurt to themselves. But this was a one-off action, and the Mustang pilots had been extremely lucky. Chinese leadership, tactics and pilot quality were very poor, but there could be no guarantee that this would always be the case, and against properly handled MiGs the Mustang would stand little chance; one or two hits from their heavy cannon armament would cause lethal damage.

Also in November, the 45th Tactical Reconnaissance Squadron received their first RF-51Ds, formerly F-6Ds. Operating at low level, they suffered high casualties at first, mainly to ground fire. Finally they were forced to fly two-ship missions, with one covering the photo aircraft from about 3,000ft (900m) above, searching for the guns.

■ KOREAN FINALE ■

Just when it seemed that North Korea would be overrun and the war ended, a massive military intervention by China reversed the process. The UN forces were rolled back, finally stabilizing the front near the original border between North and South Korea. Meanwhile the Mustang force was gradually wound down. No. 77 Squadron RAAF traded its F-51s for Gloster Meteor 8s in March 1951. By late summer, all except two USAF units had converted onto jets. The 18th FBW received F-86 Sabres in January 1953, as did the attached No. 2 Squadron SAAF, while the 45th TRS soldiered on until the armistice in July 1953. The only other Mustang units in theatre belonged to the South Korean Air Force.

In total, 194 Mustangs were lost in the course of the Korean War. Of these, 10 fell in air combat, mainly to MiG-15s, and a further 172 succumbed to ground fire. The fate of the remaining dozen is unrecorded.

■ POST-KOREA ■

Mustangs continued to serve their country of origin with the Air National Guard until early 1957, when the last of them was phased out. But even before this, the American fighter had been involved in another shooting war.

Four crated F-51s arrived in Israel in September 1948, and were quickly assembled and pressed into service. During the War of Independence that raged in the Middle East at that time, Israeli Mustangs accounted for two of the 35 air combat victories gained.

The Israelis found napalm the best weapon against tanks

More F-51s were purchased in 1953 from Sweden and Italy, and were used in the fighter-bomber role. In the 1956 Suez War, they cut Egyptian communications by pulling down telephone wires with a special hook. If this failed to work, they flew through the wires to cut them with their propellers. Strafing was also part of the job, and like the USAF in Korea, the Israelis found napalm the best weapon against tanks. But again like the USAF in Korea, losses to ground fire were high, and nearly one-third of the venerable Mustangs were lost to this cause. They were phased out shortly afterwards.

The combat swansong of the Mustang came in 1969, when El Salvadorean F-51s fought Honduran F4U Corsairs, in a war arising from an incident at a World Cup football match between the two countries. The final military user was the Dominican Republic, which phased out its Mustangs in 1983.

BIBLIOGRAPHY

ACE FACTOR, THE,
Mike Spick, Airlife, Shrewsbury, 1988.

AIRCRAFT OF THE ROYAL AIR FORCE SINCE 1918,
Owen Thetford, Putnam, London 1976.

DUEL FOR THE SKY,
Christopher Shores, Blandford Press, Poole 1985.

FAMOUS FIGHTERS OF THE SECOND WORLD WAR,
William Green, Purnell Book Services, London 1975.

FIGHTER PILOT TACTICS,
Mike Spick, Patrick Stephens Ltd, Cambridge, 1983.

FIGHTER PILOTS, THE,
Edward H. Sims, Cassell, London, 1967.

FIGHTER TACTICS AND STRATEGY 1914–1970,
Edward H. Sims, Cassell, London, 1972.

FIGHTERS OVER ISRAEL,
Lon Nordeen, Greenhill Books, London, 1990.

LOOK OF EAGLES, THE,
John T. Godfrey, Random House, New York, 1958.

MIG ALLEY,
Larry Davis, Squadron/Signal, Michigan 1978.

MIGHTY EIGHTH, THE,
Roger Freeman, MacDonald & Janes, London 1970.

MUSTANG, A DOCUMENTARY HISTORY,
Jeffrey Ethell, Janes, London 1981.

MUSTANG AT WAR,
Roger Freeman, Ian Allan, London, 1974.

NORTH AMERICAN P-51 MUSTANG,
Bill Gunston, Salamander Books, London, 1990.

TARGET BERLIN,
Jeffrey L. Ethel and Alfred Price, Arms & Armour Press, London, 1981.

TEST FLYING AT OLD WRIGHT FIELD,
Ken Chilstrom and Penn Leary (Ed), Westchester House, 1993.

WORLD WAR II FIGHTER CONFLICT,
Alfred Price, Purnell Book Services, London, 1975.

Magazines.
Various issues of *Air International*, *Air Enthusiast* and *Asia Pacific Defence Review*.

ACKNOWLEDGEMENTS

The author wishes to thank Colonel Donald J. M. Blakeslee, Colonel Reade Tilley, Colonel William G. Coloney, and Dr George Carpenter, all USAF (ret), for their kind assistance in the preparation of this volume.

THE BOEING B-17 FLYING FORTRESS

PROLOGUE

Bremen, north-west Germany, 11 June 1943. 'We did not know that the lead plane of the group ahead of us had two of its engines blasted by flak and had slowed to a crawl over that landscape from which came bomb bursts and legions of Focke-Wulfs and Messerschmitts.

'Mo (Colonel Preston) was trying to avoid overrunning the bombers ahead of him. We were trying to avoid overrunning Mo, and so the group disintegrated . . . we had been taught that strict formation flying was as vital to us as the British square had once been to the infantry. Not for us the anarchic whooping attack en masse. To be uncovered from a formation's friendly fire was to be naked and next to dead.

'Seeing our ragged line zig-zagging on a bomb run, the enemy came at us like wolves after straggling sheep. We had moved in so close to Colonel Mo that our wing tip was almost within reach of his waist gunner. Bohn (the co-pilot) had never flown formation at high altitudes. Johnny (the pilot) was an experienced formation flyer, but he was sitting on an unexploded 20mm shell somewhere in his seat, and the thought paralysed him.

'Bohn's tactic was to follow Mo as a chick follows its mother. We were tucked in so tight that our spent shells bounced off the wings of a B-17 beneath us. We could see that in the low squadron there was not a single plane that did not have at least one feathered prop.

■ FLAK ■

'When we came to a wide bay we saw the German smoke pots cloaking our target, Wilhelmshaven. Out of the smoke rose a storm of flak, rocking *Tondelayo*, sending fragments through her metal skin, biting into her delicate electric nerves.

'I called out the heading for the target, but Bob was already on top of his sight. We could not bomb as a Group, but only in train, following the plane ahead, hoping to hit the submarine pens we could not see. The explosions billowed up above the veil of smoke, but we could not be sure of whether we were plastering the shipping, the bay, the harbour or the bistros, whorehouses, shops, and homes of Wilhelmshaveners.'

This was the first combat mission of Lieutenant Elmer Bendiner of the 527th Squadron of the 379th Bomb Group, based at Kimbolton, and a more frightening introduction to war could hardly be imagined. The cold at 25,000ft (7,600m) caused frost to form on the plexiglass windows of the bomber, obscuring the view and making enemy fighters hard to spot. Constant scraping was needed in order to keep them clear.

The Fortress's course had taken them over the German Bight, then a turn onto a southerly course towards Bremen, their primary target. Making landfall near Cuxhaven they encountered accurate flak, its shrapnel rattling against their aircraft. Still heading south, German fighters had come thundering in from the east with guns blazing, and the B-17 gunners fired back, filling their machine with cordite fumes. A nearby bomber caught fire and spiralled down.

Above: The 379th BG, one of whose early exploits is described here, returns to base at Kimbolton after a raid on Germany.

Above: The 379th BG lost 141 aircraft missing in action, but despite extensive flak damage to the nose this Fortress was not one of them. (USAF via Alfred Price)

■ ALTERNATE TARGET ■

Almost simultaneously *Tondelayo* was hit by a 20mm cannon shell from an FW190. It made a jagged hole beneath Bendiner's window, grazed his helmet, penetrated a bulkhead and then passed through one of the rudder pedals and the pilot's seat before finally lodging in his seat-type parachute.

As if this were not enough, Bremen was obscured by cloud and haze and the bombers turned west for Wilhelmshaven, their secondary target, where, as related, the bombing proved fairly haphazard. On return, Bendiner's B-17 was found to have sustained multiple hits but, with the exception of damage to the hydraulic braking system, most were superficial.

From an Air Force point of view the raid was moderately satisfactory. Of the 168 bombers that set out that morning, only eight failed to return. But as so often happened, the brunt of the losses had been borne by a single unit. Bendiner's 379th Bomb Group lost six aircraft on this one mission, and of that six, four were from the 527th Squadron.

Narrow escapes were the order of the day, not only for Bendiner and his pilot. Another B-17F from Kimbolton was hit in the cockpit and both pilot and copilot were seriously wounded. The aircraft was flown back and successfully landed by one of the gunners under instruction from the pilot. The standard tour of duty was 25 operational missions, but to the survivors of the 527th Squadron it seemed that they would not have to go this far.

Above: The right tailplane of this 91st BG was knocked off by a 'friendly' bomb over Bremen in June 1943. (USAF via Alfred Price)

Above: Bombs go down on the Focke-Wulf aircraft factory near Bremen. Attacks on German aircraft production were given priority at an early stage of the American daylight bombing campaign. (USAF via Alfred Price)

■ TACTICS ■

American bombers flew in close formation for mutual protection against fighters, thereby unfortunately providing a massed target for flak as well as sometimes engendering problems on the bombing run. When the lead aircraft of the leading Group lost two engines on the same side, it threw the following 379th Group into total disarray. As luck would have it, the German fighters arrived on the scene, just when the formation was at its most vulnerable, and this, more than anything else, accounts for the heavy losses sustained by this unit. Throughout the war, formations and tactics were continually modified to find the best solutions to these problems.

As the war progressed, Fortresses ranged the length and breadth of Europe, the Mediterranean and North Africa, not to mention the Pacific theatre. Their first operational bombing sorties were made by the Royal Air Force even before the USA entered the war, and the type served with the British throughout, mainly with Coastal Command on anti-U-boat patrols over the Atlantic. Others flew over Germany at night in the electronic warfare role.

■ PACIFIC/FAR EAST ■

In American service they were present on Hawaii and the Philippines when Japan attacked Pearl Harbor, and were later seen in the skies of India, Java, New Guinea and Australia. Fortresses played a

Above: A German fighter pounces on a straggler from the 100th BG. (USAF via Alfred Price)

Above: While nose art was frequently of the 'girlie' type, it depended more on the predilections of the aircraft captain. The pilot of *Hard Seventeen* appears to have been a gamblin' man! (Ralph Trout)

peripheral role in the decisive naval Battle of Midway in June 1942, but were largely supplanted by B-24 Liberators in the Pacific Theatre of Operations from September 1943. But it is the strategic bombing of Germany for which they are best remembered, penetrating to the farthest corners of the Third Reich. Even when casualties were at their highest, the Fortress raids never turned back. The operational swan song of the Fortress came long after the war, when Israel used it against Egypt.

The practice of naming individual aircraft was almost universal in the United States Army Air Force, and was usually illustrated by graphic nose art. For example, *Tondelayo* was a character portrayed by Hedy Lamarr in a Hollywood film called *White Cargo,* depicted on the aircraft in a state of semi-undress. But not all the inspiration came from the cinema. Some aircraft bore warlike names, while others were references to crewmen or home towns. The most famous of all was of course *Memphis Belle,* the first B-17 to complete a full tour of 25 operational missions before returning to the USA in triumph to help sell war bonds.

Naming endowed a machine with a personality and carried with it the tacit belief that she – never it, always she – would bring her crew safely through. The aeroplane thus became a lucky charm, an amulet belonging to the entire crew, within which they were protected. When the aircraft's luck ran out, as it so often did, the crew went with it. But if, as happened from time to time, a Fortress brought its crew back but was so badly damaged that it had to be scrapped, it was sometimes the case that the replacement aircraft was given the same name with the suffix II added, thus transferring the luck from the old to the new.

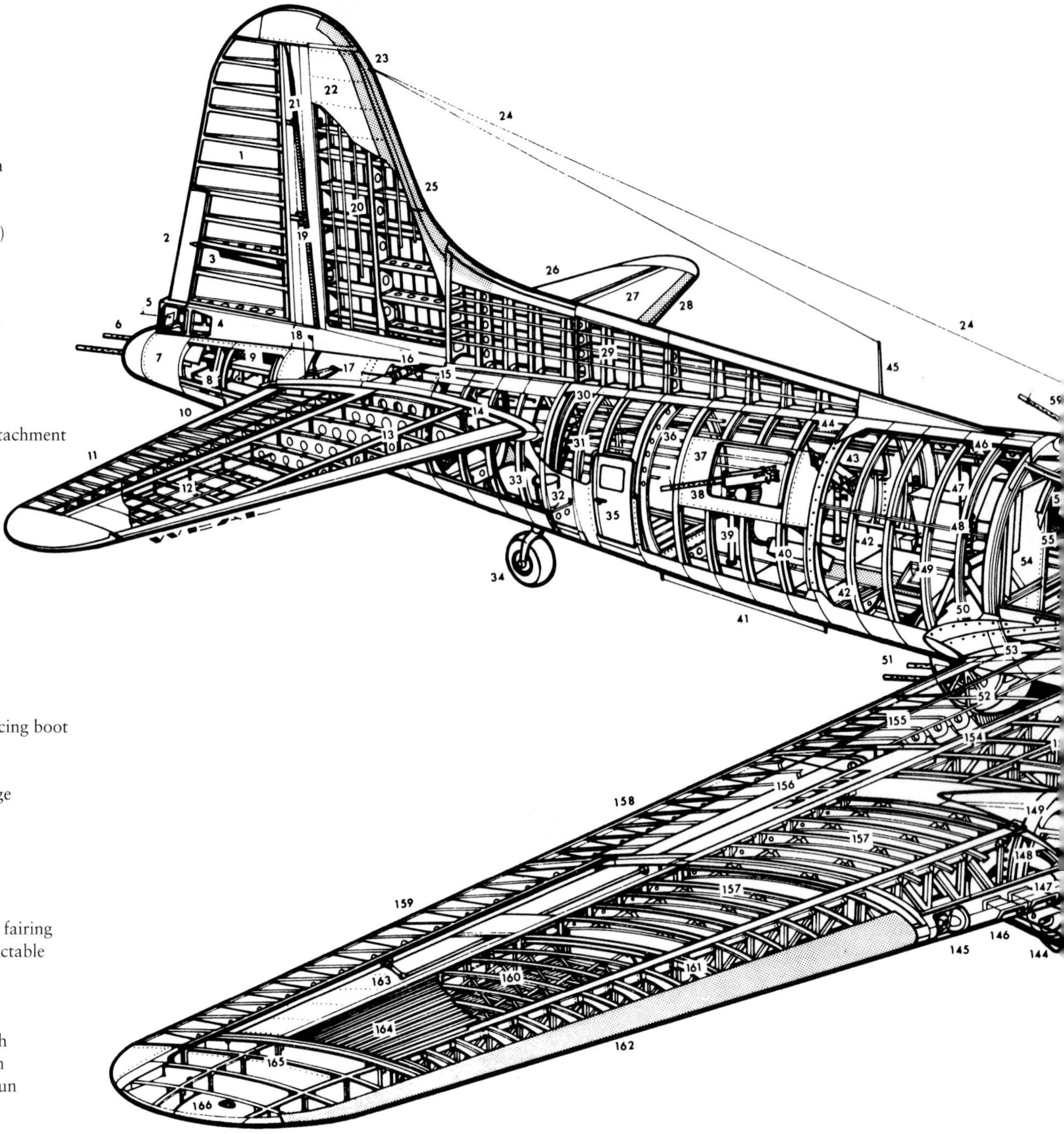

1 Rudder construction
2 rudder tab
3 Rudder tab actuation
4 Tail gunner's station
5 Gunsight
6 Twin .50in (12.7mm) machine-guns
7 Tail cone
8 Tail gunner's seat
9 Ammunition troughs
10 Elevator trim tab
11 Starboard elevator
12 Tailplane structure
13 Tailplane front spar
14 Tailplane/fuselage attachment
15 Control cables
16 Elevator control mechanism
17 Rudder control linkage
18 Rudder post
19 Rudder centre hinge
20 Fin structure
21 Rudder upper hinge
22 Fin skinning
23 Aerial attachment
24 Aerials
25 Fin leading-edge de-icing boot
26 Port elevator
27 Port tailplane
28 Tailplane leading-edge de-icing boot
29 Dorsal fin structure
30 Fuselage frame
31 Tailwheel actuation
32 Toilet
33 Tailwheel (retracted) fairing
34 Fully-swivelling retractable tailwheel
35 Crew entry door
36 Control cables
37 Starboard waist hatch
38 Starboard waist .50in (12.7mm) machine gun
39 Gun support frame
40 Ammunition box
41 Ventral aerial
42 Waist gunners' positions
43 Port waist .50in (12.7mm) machine gun
44 Ceiling control cable runs
45 Dorsal aerial mast
46 Ball turret stanchion support
47 Ball turret stanchion
48 Ball turret actuation mechanism
49 Support frame
50 Ball turret roof
51 Twin .50in (12.7mm) machine guns
52 Ventral ball turret
53 Wingroot fillet
54 Bulkhead
55 Radio operator's compartment
56 Camera access hatch

57 Radio compartment windows (port and starboard)
58 Ammunition boxes
59 Single .30in (7.62mm) dorsal machine gun
60 Radio compartment roof glazing
61 Radio compartment/ bomb bay bulkhead
62 Fire extinguisher
63 Radio operator's station (port side)
64 Handrail links
65 Bulkhead step

66 Wing rear spar/ fuselage attachment
67 Wingroot profile
68 Bomb-bay central catwalk
69 Vertical bomb stowage racks (starboard installation shown)
70 Horizontal bomb stowage (port side shown)
71 Dinghy stowage
72 Twin .50in (12.7mm) machine guns
73 Dorsal turret

74 Port wing flaps
75 Cooling air slots
76 Aileron tab (port only)
77 Port aileron
78 Port navigation light
79 Wing skinning
80 Wing leading edge de-icing boot
81 Port landing light
82 Wing corrugated inner skin
83 Port out wing fuel tank (nine inter-rib cells)
84 No. 1 engine nacelle

BOEING B-17 FLYING FORTRESS

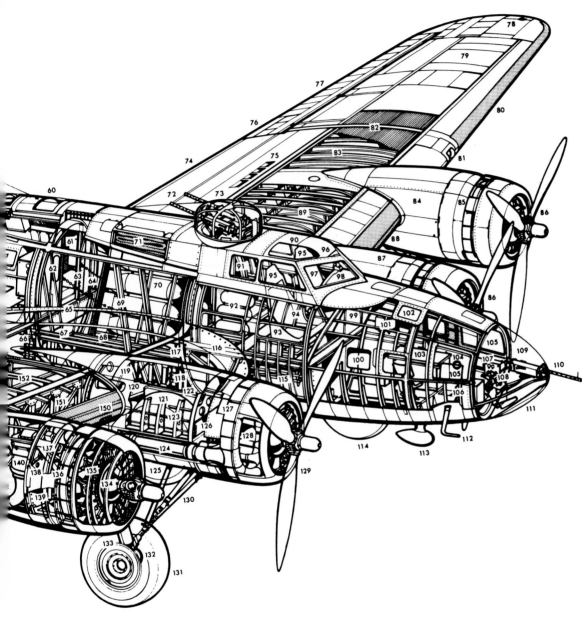

115 Flight deck underfloor control linkage
116 Wingroot/fuselage fairing
117 Wing front spar/ fuselage attachment
118 Battery access panels (wingroot leading-edge)
119 No. 3 engine nacelle spar bulkhead
120 Intercooler pressure duct
121 Mainwheel well
122 Oil tank (nacelle inboard wall)
123 Nacelle structure
124 Exhaust
125 Retracted mainwheel (semi-recessed)
126 Firewall
127 Cooling gills
128 Exhaust collector ring assembly
129 Three-blade propellers
130 Undercarriage retraction struts
131 Starboard mainwheel
132 Axle
133 Mainwheel oleo leg
134 Propeller reduction gear casing
135 1,000hp Wright R-1829-65 radial engine
136 Exhaust collector ring
137 Engine upper bearers
138 Firewall
139 Engine lower bearers
140 Intercooler assembly
141 Oil tank (nacelle outboard wall)
142 Supercharger
143 Intake
144 Supercharger waste-gate
145 Starboard landing light
146 Supercharger intake
147 Intercooler intake
148 Ducting
149 No. 4 engine nacelle spar bulkhead
150 Oil radiator intake
151 Main spar web structure
152 Mid-wing fuel tank rib cut-outs
153 Auxiliary mid spar
154 Rear spar
155 Landing flap profile
156 Cooling air slots
157 Starboard outer wing fuel tank (nine inter-rib cells)
158 Flap structure
159 Starboard aileron
160 Outboard wing ribs
161 Spar assembly
162 Wing leading-edge de-icing boot
163 Aileron control linkage
164 Wing corrugated inner skin
165 Wingtip structure
166 Starboard navigation light

85 Cooling gills
86 Three-blade propellers
87 No. 2 engine nacelle
88 Wing leading-edge de-icing boot
89 Port mid-wing (self-sealing) fuel tanks
90 Flight deck upper glazing
91 Flight deck/bomb-bay bulkhead
92 Oxygen cylinders
93 Co-pilot's seat
94 Co-pilot's control column
95 Headrest/armour

96 Compass installation
97 Pilot's seat
98 Windscreen
99 Central control console pedestal
100 Side windows
101 Navigation equipment
102 Navigator's compartment upper window (subsequently replaced by ceiling astrodome)
103 Navigator's table
104 Side gun mounting
105 Enlarged cheek windows (flush)

106 Ammunition box
107 Bombardier's panel
108 Norden bombsight installation
109 Plexiglass frameless nose-cone
110 Single .50in (12.7mm) machine gun
111 Optically-flat bomb-aiming panel
112 Pitot head fairing (port and starboard)
113 D/F loop bullet fairing
114 Port mainwheel

The Boeing Airplane Company was nothing if not versatile. It survived the lean years following the First World War, and the world recession that succeeded them, by building a wide variety of aircraft: fighters, seaplanes, mail planes, transports and even, in small numbers, a twin-engined bomber, the B-9A. The vast experience gained on these projects stood it in good stead when, in May 1934, the United States Army Air Corps mooted the idea of a really big bomber.

The standard USAAC bomber at that time was the Martin B-10, developed two years earlier and only just entering service. The B-10 was state of the art, an all-metal cantilever construction monoplane with retractable main gears, enclosed crew positions, including a gun turret in the nose, and an internal bomb bay. Its two 775hp Wright Cyclone radial engines were fitted with variable pitch propellers, itself a considerable innovation, and gave it a maximum speed of 213mph (343km/hr); fast enough to make interception by the fighters of that era extremely problematical. At cruising speed it could haul a bomb load of just over one ton out to a target 300 miles (480km) away.

The proposed new big bomber was worlds away from the B-10 in concept. At that time, the United States had retreated into near-isolationism, and was concerned solely with its own defensive needs. Neither of the adjoining countries, Canada and Mexico, was regarded as potentially hostile, and the widths of the Atlantic and Pacific Oceans appeared to rule out the possibility of air attack across them. Therefore the perceived threat was of enemy fleets approaching the coast; not only of the continental USA, but of Alaska and Hawaii also. The proposed counter to this was a very long-range bomber.

Left: **Nose gun position, showing the ring and bead sight. The semi-kneeling position allows the gunner to move more freely.**

■ THE BIG BOMBER ■

It was a bold decision, as the operational requirements specified were far beyond anything yet attempted. They called for a wingspan in the region of 150ft (46m); a maximum weight of around 60,000lb (27,200kg); a still air range of 5,000 miles (8,050km) and a bomb load of 2,000lb (900kg). The project was called XBLR-1 (Experimental Bomber, Long Range, No. 1), later abbreviated to Project A. Basically it was a technology demonstrator rather than a prototype for an operational bomber, to determine precisely what was possible. Both Boeing and the Glenn Martin company were invited to submit proposals by 15 June of that year, just one month later.

A decision was quickly made, and on 28 June, Boeing received a contract for the design and construction of a single aircraft. This brought problems in its train, caused by the sheer size of the machine. Special jigs had to be made, and it was built in sections in two different plants. By the time it was complete,

XB-15, BOEING MODEL 294

DIMENSIONS
Wingspan: 149ft 0in (45.41m)
Length: 87ft 7in (26.69m)
Height: 18ft 1in (5.51m)
Wing area: 2,780sq. ft (258.27m²)

WEIGHTS
Empty: 43,000lb (19,505kg)
Max. loaded: 70,706lb (32,072kg)
Bomb load: 8,000lb (3,629kg)

ENGINES
4 x P & W R-1830-11 Twin Wasp radials rated at 850hp each.

PERFORMANCE
Max. speed: 200mph (322km/hr)
Cruise speed: 152mph (245km/hr)
Service ceiling: 18,900ft (5,760m)
Max. range: 5,130 miles (8,254km)
Endurance: 24 hours

XB-15

With nothing to give it scale, the sleek lines of the Boeing Model 294, military designation XB-15, belie its enormous size. Compared to the standard bomber in service with the USAAC at that time, it was double the size and nearly four times heavier, and was expected to carry a similar bomb load seven times further. The huge wings were so deep that crawlways in them enabled mechanics to make adjustments to the engines in flight. With round-the-clock endurance, it needed extra crew and sleeping and cooking accommodation. Its influence on the design of the smaller B-17 is obvious. (Bruce Robertson)

Above: 'Grandpappy', as the XB-15 became known, had a wingspan even larger than the gigantic B-29 Superfortress. Over an 18-month period it carried more than 100,000lb (45,000kg) of cargo and 5,350 passengers without incident.

more than two-thirds of a million man-hours had been expended on what had become the Boeing Model 294, while the USAAC had redesignated it the XB-15.

Like almost every military aircraft in history, the XB-15 suffered from galloping weight growth during its gestation period, and maximum all-up weight increased by nearly one-fifth, with the inevitable result that it was underpowered. This was not helped by the fact that while it was originally to have been powered by four Allison in-line engines each rated at 1,150hp, it finally emerged with four Pratt & Whitney Twin Wasp radials of a mere 850hp each. It did, however, have some very interesting features.

The wings contained crawlways for crewmen to reach the engines in flight to make minor adjustments. Endurance was long enough to make two sets of crews necessary, and bunk space and a small galley with cooking facilities was provided. Two petrol-driven generators were installed in the fuselage to provide power for the plethora of electrical systems. Other provisions were an automatic pilot, de-icing and fire protection systems, plus large flaps to reduce take-off and landing speeds. Defence against air attack consisted of four .30 and two .50 calibre machine guns, in nose, dorsal, ventral and two side blister positions.

First flight took place at Boeing Field, Seattle, on 15 October 1937, 40 months after the contract was issued. Test pilot Eddie Allen was at the controls. One thing was quickly evident; the power of the four Pratt & Whitney Twin Wasp radials were insufficient to provide the required level of performance. But, like many other underpowered aeroplanes, the XB-15, quickly dubbed 'Grandpappy', handled well enough by the standards of the era. Accepted by the USAAC in March 1938, it served through most of the Second World War as the XC-105 troop and cargo-carrier, and was extensively used as a flying test bed.

One thing was certain. Mass-producing an aircraft as large as the XB-15 would be a tremendous drain on resources, both technical and financial. If on the completion of flight trials it could be shown to be a resounding success, then it might be worth the effort. But flight trials were still three years in the future, and in those days it was neither usual nor practicable to wait so long. The USAAC hedged its bets and thought smaller.

■ RETHINKING ■

Less than eight weeks after the contract for the XB-15 was placed, a new requirement was issued in the form of Circular 35-26. What was wanted was a 'multi-engined', which in those days usually meant twin-engined, bomber.

As was usual procedure then, the specification came out in the form of firm requirements that must be met, combined with a 'wish list' of 'nice to have' parameters. The proposed new aircraft would carry a bomb load of 2,000lb (900kg) and have a maximum range of at least 1,020 miles (1,640km) and hopefully 2,200 miles (3,540km), which was quite a jump. Maximum speed was to be at least 200mph (322km/hr) but preferably 250mph (402km/hr), and cruising speed 170mph (274km/hr) or 220mph (354km/hr). Finally, the service ceiling fluctuated from a low of 20,000ft (6,100m) to a high of 25,000ft (7,600m). A flying prototype had to be ready in just 12 months, August 1935, and worse still, no development funding was available. There was however one feature which made it very attractive. The maker of the aircraft selected would receive a contract to build no fewer than 220 bombers,

Below: Minus engine cowlings and with nose shrouded, Model 299 is prepared for its press debut on 16 July 1935. The *Seattle Daily Times*' report of the event called it a '15-ton flying fortress', which was later adopted by Boeing. (G.S.Williams)

later cut back to 185. This was quite a substantial order for the time, which made Boeing very keen to compete.

While it was expecting the contenders to be twin-engined, the USAAC had no objection to four. This would normally have been surprising when one considers not only the added initial cost, but the extra servicing, spares and maintenance that would be needed throughout the operational life of the aircraft. But the service knew what it was about. The order placed would be for either 185 twin-engined bombers, or 65 four-engined types.

While the lesser number may have appeared less attractive Boeing's decision to use four engines was made to enhance flight performance, thereby greatly increasing their chance of success. Prior to this time, four engines were traditionally used to improve take-off rather than the flight envelope.

Work on the Boeing Model 299, as it became, was conducted under conditions of semi-secrecy. Technology was taken from the XB-15, which was proceeding more or less in parallel, and the rather earlier Model 247, a small twin-engined transport. The former provided much of the wing design, scaled down and given tubular truss spars, while the latter influenced the shape of the fuselage. The tail surfaces of all three showed a strong family resemblance.

The urgency of getting the Model 299 ready in time caused it to race ahead of the XB-15, and it was rolled out and shown to the public on 16 July, only 11 months after the go-ahead had been given. And it was on that day that it quite fortuitously acquired its emotive name; a name that was to echo around the world in the coming years.

■ 15-TON ■ FLYING FORTRESS

The *Seattle Daily Times* naturally was represented at the roll-out, and on the following day it carried a feature together with a photograph bearing the caption '15-ton Flying Fortress'. This caught the imagination of Boeing's management, and they duly registered the

BOEING MODEL 299

DIMENSIONS
Wingspan: 103ft 9in (31.62m)
Length: 68ft 9in (20.95m)
Height: 18ft 4in (5.59m)
Wing area: 1,420sq. ft (131.96m²)

WEIGHTS
Maximum: 32,432lb (14,711kg)
Bomb load: 4,800lb (2,175kg)

ENGINES
4 x Pratt & Whitney R-1690-E Hornet radials, each rated at 750hp.

PERFORMANCE
Max. speed: 236mph (380km/hr)
Cruise speed: 140mph (225mph)
Service ceiling: 24,620ft (7,500m)
Max. range: 3,010 miles (4,840km)

name. Apart from any other considerations, it was very suitable for an aircraft which, like the XB-15, was intended for the maritime reconnaissance and anti-shipping roles, and was thus a purely defensive weapon.

Seen on the ground, the Model 299 was impressive. Resplendent in polished aluminium and with colourful USAAC wing and tail markings, the sleek, cigar-shaped fuselage, merging gracefully with the mid-set wings and tall shapely tail, looked exactly right. The four radial engines spoke of power and to spare, while four streamlined blisters, one dorsal, one ventral and one on either side of the fuselage, concealed menacing machine guns. Yet another gun could be mounted in the cupola surmounting the semi-ovoid transparent nose. The abiding impression was of speed and grace.

The maiden flight of the Model 299 took place on the morning of 28 July, with Boeing test pilot Leslie Tower at the controls. All went smoothly, and several more flights followed before the prototype was delivered to the USAAC at Wright Field, Ohio, for official evaluation. The non-stop journey of 2,100 miles (3,380km) took just over nine hours, giving an average speed of 233mph (375km/hr), which in 1935 was quite exceptional.

Y1B-17

One of the major differences between the prototype and the Y1B-17 was a redesigned single strut main gear leg. This had several effects. It saved weight and complexity, and made changing a wheel or a tyre a far simpler operation. Many other changes had been made, but many were still to come. Also clearly visible from this angle is the turbo-supercharger exhaust above the engine nacelle, the efflux from which interfered with the slipstream and caused buffeting. This aircraft is the sole Y1B-17A. (Roger Besecker)

The two other contenders for the contract were Glenn Martin's B-12, a highly modified B-10, and Douglas' DB-1, which was based on the DC-2 airliner, forerunner of the immortal DC-3 Dakota. Against these the Model 299 demonstrated a clear performance advantage, which made it appear certain that it would be the winner. But an unkind fate intervened. On the morning of 30 October, the Model 299 stalled and crashed just off the end of the Wright Field runway. It was totally destroyed, and with it died Leslie Tower, and USAAC test pilot Major Ployer Hill. The cause was, as is so often the case, human error. Control locks, fitted to prevent the moving surfaces from being flapped around by wind while on the ground, had not been released prior to take-off. Once in the air, Model 299 had become uncontrollable.

At the time that the disaster occurred, the final stage of testing, consisting of

Despite a major set-back the Fortress won through

evaluation flights by service crewmen, had still to take place. With the Model 299 out of the competition, the DB-1 was declared the winner. It entered service as the B-18 Bolo, and after just a few years was to vanish quietly into obscurity.

The short while that Boeing Model 299 had been evaluated at Wright Field had, however, been long enough to convince many people of its worth. On 12 January 1936 a contract was issued for 14 aircraft, one of which was a static test bed. A new designation was issued, YB-17, the Y prefix denoting pre-production machines, which incorporated modifications that had been found to be desirable during the trials of the prototype.

The main modification was the use of the Wright R-1820-39 Cyclone engine, rated at 850hp. Fabric-covered flaps replaced the original metal items, and the

main gears were given single legs in lieu of the original doubles. This made wheel changing a much simpler process. Other modifications affected the fuel system, instrument layout, de-icing and oxygen systems. In November of that year, the designation changed once more to become Y1B-17, but this reflected funding arrangements rather than hardware changes.

The first Y1B-17 flew on 2 December 1936. Problems were encountered on only its third flight. Engine overheating caused the flight to be cut short; then on touch-down the aircraft tipped onto its nose, fortunately without any injury being suffered by the crew. Inspection revealed that the brakes had overheated on take-off, then on being retracted while still too hot had seized up solid. But these were relatively minor faults, which could be quickly rectified. A

particularly interesting feature of this model was that the panelled transparent nose was able to rotate through a complete circle, allowing the machine gun installed a wide field of fire.

■ INTO SERVICE ■

On completion of the trials, the first delivery to an active service unit was made on 1 March 1937, at Langley Field, Virginia. A further 11 followed, making the 2nd Bombardment Group the first four-engined bomber outfit in the USAAC. It was the first of many. The thirteenth Y1B-17 remained at Wright Field for development work.

It had originally been planned to have two B-17 Groups, one on the east coast, the other on the west. To this end, a further 50 B-17s were ordered for 1938, plus 11 more for development work. Meanwhile the 2nd Bombardment

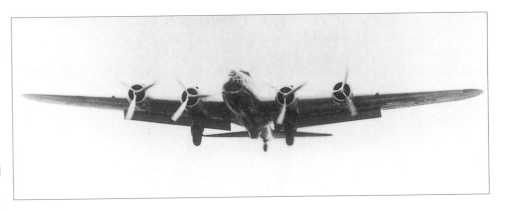

Above: Y1B-17 of the 2nd BG, which was charged with the operational evaluation of the type. (Author)

Below: Part of the 2nd BG over New York City on its way to Buenos Aires in February 1938.

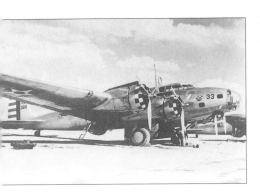

Above: The 38th Reconnaissance Squadron was unusual in that it operated Y1B-17s in other than the strategic bombing role.

Above: The Fortress was tough; *All American* of the 97th BG returned to base despite being nearly cut in half in a collision with a German fighter. (Boeing via Alfred Price)

Group was to develop and prove tactics and operational techniques for the new bomber. During this work, several records were broken, while the high spot was a goodwill visit to Buenos Aires in February 1938 by a formation of six aircraft. The 5,000 mile (8,050km) flight from Miami was made in just two stages, the big bombers calling at Lima, the capital of Peru, en route.

It was during this period that inter-service rivalry reared its ugly head. The US Navy had always justifiably regarded itself as the defender of the American coastline, and now watched the activities of the 2nd Bombardment Group with some suspicion. Their chance came in May 1938, when three Fortresses of the 2nd Bombardment Group carried out a practice interception of the Italian liner *Rex*.

What really upset the Navy was that the liner was more than 700 miles (1,100km) out in the Atlantic at the time, and the exploit received a lot of publicity. They reacted by accusing the USAAC of poaching on their patch; successfully, it would seem, because from then on, the 2nd Bombardment Group was restricted to within a limit of 100 miles (160km) of the coast! This was followed by a directive from the Secretary of State for War that in 1940 the USAAC was to procure only tactical bombers.

This was reversed by the Munich crisis in September, as a consequence of which it was planned to make a significant increase in air striking power. Meanwhile, the 2nd Bombardment Group had flown a total of 9,293 hours without a single serious accident, and had developed suitable navigation methods and tactics.

The development machines also provided valuable data, none more so than one that flew into a thunderstorm, where it was exposed to structural stresses far greater than those planned for the ground test article. The Y1B-17 ended in a spin, from which it recovered, remarkably for such a large aircraft. This unexpected evidence of structural integrity made the static test machine redundant, and it was assigned to flight trials with turbo-superchargers fitted to its Wright Cyclones as the Y1B-17A.

First flight was made on 20 November. The exhaust from the turbo-superchargers was initially expelled above the engine nacelles, but this interfered with the airflow above the wing, causing buffeting. A redesign brought the exhaust below the wing, which cured the problem.

■ TRIALS COMPLETED ■

The increase in performance was dramatic. Maximum speed increased from 256mph (412km/hr) to 311mph (500km/hr), while service ceiling went from 31,000ft (9,450m) to 38,000ft (11,600m). These figures were of course for a lightly loaded aircraft; a full load of fuel and bombs reduced these figures significantly, but they serve to illustrate the improvement obtained. To give some idea of operational capabilities, a little later, the Y1B-17A set a record by carrying 11,000lb (5,000kg) over a distance of 620 miles (1,000km) at an average speed of 238mph (383km/hr). Of course, bomb loads and fuel could be traded one against the other; a typical operational capability was 2,400lb (1,100kg) of bombs for 1,500 miles (2,400km).

With operational trials completed, Y1B-17s became B-17s, while the single Y1B-17A became the B-17A. The initial production batch of Fortresses was ordered. These started life as Boeing Model 299Es, but the performance advantages demonstrated by the B-17A resulted in the adoption of turbo-supercharged engines, among other things. They then became 299Ms or, in USAAC service, B-17Bs.

The maiden flight of a B-17B came on 27 June 1939. Externally it looked very similar to its predecessor. Engines apart, the main differences were a larger and reshaped rudder and a new nose transparency with an optically flat panel for bomb aiming replacing the previous ventral window.

Internally, crew positions were revised as a result of 2nd Bombardment Group experience; the pneumatic brakes were

Left: Nose cupola 'more appropriately located in an amusement park than in a war aeroplane' was the comment of Air Commodore Arthur Harris RAF on inspecting the Y1B-17.

B-17B

Only 39 B-17Bs were built. They were very similar in external appearance to the Y1B-17, the main changes being turbo-supercharged Wright Cyclone engines as standard, giving a significant performance increment, a larger, redesigned rudder for greater lateral stability at high altitudes, and a revised transparent nose with an optically flat panel in front of the bombsight. Many other changes took place under the skin. It was a step in the right direction.

supplanted by a hydraulic system, and the top-secret Norden bombsight was fitted. This last was to become notorious, less for its alleged accuracy than for the tight security measures that surrounded it. It was installed, still under wraps, in the aircraft shortly before takeoff, and removed again right after landing, always with an armed guard in attendance.

All 39 B-17Bs were delivered between 29 July 1939 and 30 March 1940, and this variant became the first to equip an operational Air Corps outfit. But even before the first arrived, work was in hand on an improved variant, of which 38 were ordered in 1939. This was the Model 299H, or B-17C.

This new aircraft featured several modifications, many of them influenced by the twin demands of greater survivability and improved performance. Externally, the greatest changes made were to the defensive gun positions. The lateral blisters had been found to provide an inadequate field of fire, and in any case caused unnecessary drag. They were consequently replaced by

Above: The Norden bombsight (just visible here) became as famous for its secrecy as it did for its accuracy. In the early days of Fortress operations, it was found that course corrections by each individual aircraft on the bomb run when flying close formation posed a collision hazard, and from then on, only the bombardier in the lead aircraft sighted; the rest of the aircraft dropped in unison with him. Most bombardiers became known as toggliers, as all they had to do was press the button when the leader's bombs went down. (USAF)

Y1B-17

The waist gun blisters of the Y1B-17 were innovative but not very practical. They were an attempt to provide the greater field of fire of a turret while minimizing aerodynamic drag. In service it was found that while they gave a reasonable arc of fire, elevation and depression were very limited, while drag was considerable, and disturbance of the slipstream adversely affected the tailplane and elevators. As protection against attacks from astern they were ineffective, as even at maximum traverse they left a considerable arc uncovered, while the tailplane shielded a significant area.

B-17C

The B-17C was the first Flying Fortress to see action. Among other changes it did away with the stylish but aerodynamically and defensively unsound gun blisters. The waist positions were made flush, although the original teardrop-shaped opening was retained so as to minimize structural changes. The ventral position was replaced by a much more solid 'bathtub', while the dorsal blister was omitted altogether and replaced by a sliding transparent fairing. The revised and enlarged rudder first introduced on the B-17B is seen to advantage here on this B-17C, in RAF service as the Fortress I.

B-17C DATA

DIMENSIONS
Wingspan: 103ft 9in (31.62m)
Length: 67ft 11in (20.70m)
Height: 15ft 5in (4.70m)
Wing area: 1,420sq.ft (131.96m²)

WEIGHTS
Empty: 31,150lb (14,130kg)
Max. loaded: 49,650lb (22,520kg)
Bomb load: 4,800lb (2,180kg)

ENGINES
4 x Wright Cyclone R-1820-65 turbo-super-charged radials each rated at 1,200hp.

PERFORMANCE
Max. speed: 320mph (515km/hr)
Cruise speed: 232mph (373km/hr)
Service ceiling: 36,000ft (11,000m)
Normal range: 2,100 miles (3,380km)
Climb rate: 1,300ft/min (6.60m/sec)

Right: The B-17E featured a complete redesign of the entire rear fuselage and tail unit to make room for a tail turret. (Frank F. Smith)

teardrop-shaped transparencies flush with the cylindrical fuselage, with pintle-mounted machine guns which gave a wider field of fire. The ventral blister gun was supplanted by a longer and more solid 'bathtub'. The dorsal blister was removed, and replaced by a sliding transparency faired to the contours of the fuselage. Finally, the central nose gun was replaced by two gun mountings in side windows.

Other changes included armour protection for the crew and self-sealing fuel tanks. All-up weight increased to 49,650lb (22,500kg), and the engines were Wright Cyclone R-1820-65 radials each rated at 1,200hp, driving constant-speed, fully-feathering three-bladed propellers.

■ THE B-17C ■

The first flight of a B-17C took place on 21 July 1940, by which time the Second World War had been running for ten months. While the ground war in Western Europe remained static until May 1940, British, French and German bombers had all been active. Much early combat experience, particularly that of the Royal Air Force, which set great store by heavily armed strategic bombers, had filtered back across the Atlantic, influencing American thinking.

This resulted in the B-17D, of which 42 were ordered. The USAAC recognized the need for greater defensive fire power and for increased survivability. The dorsal and ventral gun positions were modified to accept twin .50 calibre machine guns, while more armour was added. Cowl flaps were introduced on the engine nacelles, the bomb racks were redesigned, with a new release mechanism, and 24 volt electrics replaced the original 12 volt system. Deliveries of the B-17D began in February 1941, and the order was completed by the end of April. B-17Cs in USAAC service were also modified to D standard. But at the end of the day, the Dog was still an interim type.

By an irony of fate, the Flying Fortress did not make its combat debut in either its designed role of coastal defence, or even in the service of its country of origin. Instead it went to war as a high-altitude bomber with the Royal Air Force.

Even with the British, the Fortress got off to an unpromising start. With war looming, a British Purchasing Commission visited the United States in 1938 to investigate the possibility of acquiring American aircraft. With it was a certain Air Commodore Arthur Harris, later to become famous as Commander-in-Chief of RAF Bomber Command between 1942 and 1945. Among other types, he inspected a Y1B-17 of the 2nd Bombardment Group at Langley Field. Never a man for mincing words, Harris was scathing on the subject of its gun armament, and concluded that it was far

Left: As the Japanese swept across the Pacific, the Panama Canal took on a new importance. B-17s spent many weary hours patrolling the area. This is a B-17E with the early ventral turret. (USAF)
Below: A Messerschmitt Me 109 can just be seen in front of B-17F *Virgin's Delight* of the 91st BG, performing the Split-S breakaway manoeuvre. (USAF)

too vulnerable against any modern fighter. His comment on the nose cupola was that it was 'more appropriately located in an amusement park than in a war aeroplane'.

At the time, this was of course fair comment. But as we saw in the preceding chapter, Boeing and the USAAC were aware of these and other shortcomings, and were making every effort to correct them. By the end of 1940, the single most glaring deficiency was the lack of a power-operated gun turret.

By this time, the RAF had discovered

Above: Boeing got the serial letters wrong on the batch of Fortress Is for the RAF; they should be AN, not AM. On the left is Air Chief Marshal Sir Hugh Dowding, the former head of RAF Fighter Command during the Battle of Britain. (Bruce Robertson)

through hard and bloody experience that daylight raids on targets in the Third Reich, where strong fighter opposition might be encountered, were likely to incur unacceptable losses. There did, however, seem to be one possible solution to this.

ME 109E

The Messerschmitt Me 109E was the standard German interceptor during 1940 and most of 1941, and thus was the fighter that the Fortress I had to defeat. Powered by a Daimler-Benz 601 liquid-cooled engine, it could achieve a maximum speed of 354mph (570km/hr) at 12,500ft (3,800m). While its service ceiling was marginally better than that of the Fortress I, speed, rate of climb and manoeuvrability were all greatly reduced at extreme altitudes.

Above: Belly landing! A B-17 of the 379th BG touches down tail-first at Kimbolton. The ball turret has been jettisoned and all looks good. This group flew more sorties and dropped a greater weight of bombs than any other. (Bill Smith)

The standard German day fighter of the period was the Messerschmitt Me 109E. Leaving aside the brochure figures quoted for rate of climb and time to altitude of this aircraft, and instead allowing for a standing start scramble, time to join up, and a formation battle climb, which was always slower than could be accomplished by a single machine, it would take something over 30 minutes for the fighters to reach 30,000ft (9,150m). And once they did get there, both their maximum speed and their manoeuvrability would be greatly reduced.

■ WAS HEIGHT ■ THE KEY?

In the space of 30 minutes, a bomber cruising at 180mph (290km/hr) would cover a distance of 90 miles (145km). At that time there was little information about the German early warning system, but unless this could provide significantly more than half an hour's notice of impending attack, the chances were that the bombers would be able to do their work and be long gone before the fighters arrived. And even if adequate early warning was available, ground control would need to be very precise in order to position the fighters correctly for an interception.

Flying at such extreme altitudes appeared to offer bombers relative immunity from fighter interception, and almost total immunity from flak. A trio of British four-engined heavy bombers was entering service at about this time, but they were unable to reach such a high perch. Only the Flying Fortress had sufficient altitude capability, and of course this was coupled with the much-vaunted accuracy of the the top-secret Norden bombsight.

■ TRIALS AND ■ TRIBULATIONS

Initial British approaches for the Fortress were made in the summer of 1940, but not until the end of the year was the request approved, when 20 B-17Cs were released. Unfortunately these were not fitted with self-sealing fuel tanks, and had to be returned to Boeing for these to be installed. The delay thus caused was considerable, and not until April 1941 were the first four aircraft ready for delivery.

The first B-17C, known in RAF service as the Fortress I, arrived at Watton in Norfolk on 14 April. Others followed, and by the end of the third week in May, 14 had been delivered. Certain modifications were needed; standard British radio and signals equipment, identification lights etc., and all guns except the one in the nose were replaced by .50 Brownings. Most important of all

FORTRESS 1

Fortress I of No. 90 Squadron, RAF Bomber Command, the specially formed unit which pioneered very high altitude bombing, and with which the Flying Fortress made its combat debut. This aircraft, AN 530, *F for Freddie*, had an eventful career. It arrived in England on 10 July 1941; just too late to take part in the initial raid on Wilhelmshaven but, as one of the more reliable aircraft, it was selected for the abortive Berlin raid on 23 July. On 2 August it fought off attacks by three Me 109Fs of 3/JG 52, shooting down Feldwebel Wilhelm Summerer and damaging the other two. It was later transferred to No. 220 Squadron of Coastal Command and struck off charge in September 1943. (Bruce Robertson)

was the bombsight. The Norden was still top secret and had not been released; however RAF Fortresses were to have the Sperry Mk 0-1, similarly precise but rather more complex. This was duly installed, together with a Sperry auto-pilot system which, coupled to the sight, allowed the bomb aimer to make flat turns while lining up on target.

The recipient of the Fortress I was No. 90 Squadron, which was faced with the initial task of selecting men physically capable of standing up to the extremely demanding high-altitude operational environment. This was far from easy; nearly two-thirds of applicants failed for medical reasons. This made progress in forming the squadron slow.

As soon as sufficient personnel had been accepted and crewmen had been converted onto type (with the aid of a few selected American flyers and ground crew), high-altitude training was initiated. This revealed a number of problems.

The USAAC considered the optimum bombing altitude to be 20,000ft (6,100m), whereas the RAF proposed operating the Fortress I at least 50 per cent higher, and probably even more, in temperatures of – 40° Celsius or even lower.

■ PROBLEMS ■

Two related factors caused unexpected problems; the first was the extremely low temperature and atmospheric pressure encountered at 30,000ft (9,150m) and above; the second was the delta temperature and atmospheric pressure; the difference between ground level and high altitude. These played havoc with the engines and other systems.

The former caused many Cyclones (but not all) to throw oil from the crankcase breather pipes. The turbo-superchargers became unduly sensitive to hamfisted control movements, surging at the least provocation, with the turbine blower breaking up in consequence. Heated window panels were needed to keep them clear of frost, while the auto-pilot/bombsight coupling caused violent yaws if the gyros had not been synchronized beforehand. The extreme changes in temperature and pressure during the course of a standard mission caused engine exhaust flanges to fracture, and

was responsible for hydraulic leaks which allowed air to infiltrate the system; a circumstance that was hardly conducive to effective braking.

Watton was a grass field not really suitable for such heavy machines, and pending the completion of a new airfield at Polebrook, with hard runways and taxiways, No. 90 Squadron moved to Great Massingham. It was during a flight from here, shortly before the projected move to Polebrook, that the first serious accident occurred.

The first USAAF casualty on active service occurs

It was June, the month in which the US Army Air Corps became the US Army Air Force. A Fortress I on a training flight over Yorkshire failed to climb above a thunderhead, and instead entered it. Once inside, the giant bomber was pounded by huge hailstones, while a thick layer of ice built up on the wings. This destroyed the lift, forcing the huge bomber into a death-dive. As it tumbled from the sky, the forces exerted on the unlucky machine wrenched off a wing then tore the fuselage in half. The only

Above: The 305th BG which, under the command of Curtis LeMay, did so much to get the tactics right. Station-keeping in the formation ahead appears to leave much to be desired. (USAF via Alfred Price)

survivor was Flight Lieutenant Steward, a medical officer from the Royal Aircraft Establishment at Farnborough, who managed to parachute to safety. Among the dead was Lieutenant Bradley, an experienced American B-17 pilot. He was the first airman of the newly constituted USAAF to die on active service.

■ FIRST ACTION ■

The essentials for a very high altitude bombing mission were two-fold; clear weather and near-perfect visibility. However good the aircraft and its crew, and however accurate the bombsight may be, if the target area cannot be identified from many miles away, and what is more the actual target cannot be clearly seen from nearly 6 miles (9km) up, there is little point in even starting out. These conditions were met on 8 July, and three Fortresses were duly despatched from Polebrook. The crews, led by the squadron commander, Wing Commander MacDougall, were perhaps not as well trained as they might have been, but political pressure was exerted

Above: Damaged over Bremen, this 100th BG Fortress made a spectacular crash-landing when a propeller came off after touch-down. Over 800 holes were counted from the radio room aft. (John Kidd)

by those eager to see how the big bird would acquit itself in action.

The target was Wilhelmshaven. The three Fortress Is were to fly there in loose formation, closing up only if fighters were encountered. They would bomb the naval base individually from 30,000ft (9,150m) with four American-type 1,100lb (500kg) bombs, then, divested of their loads and homeward bound, climb away from the target area to make the task of interception even more difficult.

As Robbie Burns once observed, 'The best laid plans of mice and men gang oft agley!' He might have added aviators. On the climb-out from base, all four engines of one Fortress started throwing oil, which streamed back and froze on the tail surfaces. This set up intense vibration, forcing its pilot to abandon the main mission and seek a target of opportunity.

The other two pressed on. They reached Wilhelmshaven and attacked with no intervention from the defences, but two bombs on the leading aircraft failed to release due to a frozen solenoid. This was the first of many failures caused by a combination of extreme cold and high humidity. On trials the Americans had not gone so high, nor was there much humidity over the bombing ranges in Nevada or Utah. Humidity in particular bedevilled Fortress operations for the next two years. But even the bombs that did drop missed their targets. It was later concluded that the physical problems encountered at high altitude in unpressurized aircraft were greater than had been thought, and made bombing accuracy very hard to achieve. All in all, it was hardly to be regarded an auspicious combat debut.

After the Fortresses left the target area, two black specks were sighted climbing towards them by Tom Danby, a beam gunner in the squadron commander's aircraft. Fighters! The Fortresses lifted their noses and climbed labori-ously, but to no avail. The Messerschmitt Me 109s easily drew level with Danby's aircraft, passed across the nose as if taking the measure of this enormous stranger, then one started to turn in astern. Danby lined up his sight and took first pressure on the trigger. As he did so, his pilot commenced a gentle turn towards the direction of attack. This forced the German pilot to tighten his turn, but as he did so, his wings lost their grip on the rarified air and he literally fell out of the sky! No shooting was done by either side, which was probably just as well because there was more than a fair chance that the guns of the Fortress were frozen up.

The next raid was a complete fiasco. On 23 July, three Fortresses set out to attack Berlin in daylight. Over Denmark they started leaving long white contrails, pointers in the sky that led the fighters straight to them. Far below, the crewmen could see menacing black specks, frantically grabbing for height but as yet nowhere near them. Over Denmark, the three Fortresses turned southwards towards Berlin, only to be faced with a solid wall of cloud. With no chance of locating their targets through it, they turned back, frozen and frustrated.

Below: Pillars of dark smoke denote hits on an oil refinery by the preceding wave, as more bombers bore in to attack. (USAF via Alfred Price)

Above: Fortress I, formerly of No. 90 Squadron, seen here in the colours of No. 220 Squadron Coastal Command, escorting a convoy across the Atlantic. (Alfred Price)

Other raids followed. On 24 July Brest was attacked, and hits were claimed on the battle cruisers *Scharnhorst* and *Gneisenau*. Emden was raided two days later. So far the German fighters had failed to intercept, but this situation did not last. On 2 August a Fortress was attacked north of Texel at only 22,000ft (6,700m) by three Me 109Fs, which made seven passes at the bomber, hitting it, but fortunately not seriously. Remarkably, one German fighter was shot down into the sea, a second was damaged and force-landed, while the third suffered some minor damage from the Fortress's return fire.

The first high-altitude fighter engagement that took place was a much more

Below: Nineteen B-17Fs served with RAF Coastal Command as the Fortress II. This aircraft was written off in the Azores in 1944 after a taxiing accident. (Bruce Robertson).

deadly affair. The same crew was caught at 32,000ft (9,750m) over Brest by seven Messerschmitts on 16 August and subjected to 26 attacks in quick succession.

Even at high altitude the B-17 proved vulnerable to fighters

The pilot put the big bomber into a shallow dive for maximum speed, taking evasive action against each attack. Eventually he escaped into cloud, but not before two crewmen had been killed and another two wounded. The Fortress crashed on landing and burned. Then a four-aircraft attack against the German pocket battleship *Admiral Scheer* at Oslo on 8 September also encountered fighters. One bomber was shot down, another went missing without trace. The third returned too badly damaged to be repairable. The writing was on the wall.

Even at high altitude the Fortress I was proving too vulnerable in daylight, the bomb load was too small and the bombing too inaccurate.

The final Fortress operational mission from Polebrook was flown on 25 September, bringing the total to 48 sorties, 26 of which were aborted for various reasons, the most frequent of which was cloud obscuring the target. At this point, four aircraft were detached to Egypt, from where they carried out maritime reconnaisance missions over the Mediterranean, and night attacks on Tobruk and other North African targets. It was however found that the heat and dust of the desert reduced performance and serviceability quite spectacularly, and the two survivors of this period were sent to India, where they were eventually handed over to the USAAF.

Back at Polebrook, experimental high-altitude flights continued for a while. By this time the oil throwing and freezing-up of the guns had largely been cured, and the main purpose was to investigate the physiological problems more fully. This finally came to an end, and the remaining Fortress Is were transferred to No. 220 Squadron of Coastal Command, with whom they ranged far out over the Atlantic on anti-submarine patrols.

■ PACIFIC CRUCIBLE ■

By December 1941, the USAAF was in possession of about 150 Flying Fortresses. Mainly these were based in the continental USA, but some flew anti-submarine patrols from Newfoundland. These were reconnaissance missions only, because America was still officially neutral. Yet other Flying Fortresses were deployed in the Pacific.

Above: Action replay of the Pearl Harbor attack, as a 'Japanese Zero' swoops down on a landing Fortress at the annual air show at Oshkosh. The B-17 is specially modified to put one main gear and the tail wheel down to simulate battle damage. (Eric Lundahl)

Below: Conditions in the Pacific could be primitive. This aircraft made a wheels-down forced landing on a Papua New Guinea beach. After repair, the locals were enlisted to help lay a steel matting runway to allow it to take off. (Both Frank F. Smith)

The 19th Bombardment Group was based at Hickam Field, right next door to Pearl Harbour on Oahu in the Hawaiian Islands. In the Philippines, at that time an American Protectorate, were 35 B-17Cs and Ds of the 7th Bombardment Group, based at Clark Field. Both Groups were about to be reinforced, and a dozen aircraft were in transit to them. This was the situation when Japanese carrier aircraft made a surprise strike against the American fleet at Pearl Harbour on the 7th of the month, an attack which finally brought America into the war.

At Hickam Field, the 19th Bombardment Group was caught on the ground by the Japanese attack, and all 12 aircraft were destroyed. Worse was to follow. The reinforcements for the 7th and 19th Bombardment Groups arrived at the height of the raid; low on fuel and unarmed, they were unable to defend themselves. Four were destroyed and all the others damaged, some by Japanese fighters, others by 'friendly' ground fire.

Just hours later, the Japanese turned their attention to the Philippines, destroying 14 B-17s of the 19th Bombardment Group on the ground at Clark Field. It was fortunate that a single squadron from this group had been deployed to Del Monte on Mindanao, 200 miles (320km) further south, so some of the group escaped this attack unscathed.

The surviving Fortresses of the 19th were employed against the Japanese invasion force, with little success, for ships at sea proved elusive targets. Hits were often claimed, but in fact little damage was done.

Fighter opposition at this time was provided by the redoubtable Mitsubishi A6M2 Zero, and two notable encounters with Fortresses took place in the first few days of fighting. On 10 December, a Japanese landing force consisting of one light cruiser, six destroyers and four transports, was off-loading at Vigan on Luzon. At an altitude of 18,000ft (5,500m) above them flew 27 covering Zeros, one of them piloted by Saburo Sakai, later to become the top surviving Japanese fighter ace (62 kills).

ZERO ATTACK

'This was our first experience with the B-17, and the airplane's unusual size caused us to misjudge our firing distance. In addition, the bomber's extraordinary speed, for which we had made no allowance, threw our rangefinders off. All through the attack the Fortress kept up a steady stream of fire at us from its gun positions. Fortunately the accuracy of the enemy gunners was no better than our own.'

SABURO SAKAI, ZERO PILOT.

Six B-17Ds of the 14th Bombardment Squadron were sent against the invaders. They bombed from 25,000ft (7,600m), and succeeded in doing little damage. One of their number, piloted by Lieutenant Colin Kelly Jr, was spotted after the attack, and seven avenging Zeros set off in hot pursuit.

The Zeros were slower than their European counterparts, and in any case had additional height to gain. Not until 100 miles (160km) further on did they catch the speeding bomber. Even before they could gain a firing position, three other Zeros appeared ahead and attacked from above, but with absolutely no effect.

At last the pursuers caught up, and joined with the other three in line astern, making pass after pass, again with no apparent effect. The chase lasted a further 50 miles (80km), taking them over the US base at Clark Field. Sakai then took a hand. With two other fighters in attendance he closed right in, braving

ZERO FIGHTER

The Mitsubishi Zero was optimized for dogfighting rather than bomber interception. Japanese engines of the time lacked power, and to maximize manoeuvrability and performance by reducing weight, the Zero had no armour plating, no self-sealing fuel tanks, and often no radio. It was therefore very vulnerable to return fire.

Above: Some had it easier than others. General MacArthur's personal transport, *Bataan*, had reclining seats and hot and cold running water installed. (USAF)

Below: Declared 'war-weary' on the arrival of the B-17F, this E-model became a personal transport for General George Kenney. (USAF)

the defensive fire. Fuel streamed back from the ruptured tanks of the bomber, its gunners ceased firing, and fire broke out in the fuselage. It was the end. His crew baled out, but Kelly himself did not manage to escape. It was the first Flying Fortress to fall to Japanese fighters in the Pacific.

Four days later, a battle against even heavier odds ended differently. On 14 December, a B-17D of the 19th Bombardment Group piloted by Lieutenant Hewitt Wheless became separated from its formation. When he was just about to bomb a Japanese freighter from low altitude, he found himself bounced by 18 Zeros.

The Japanese fighters made attack after attack on the lone bomber, knocking out the left outboard motor, the radio and the oxygen system, shooting off the tail wheel, riddling the fuselage, holing the fuel tanks, damaging the control runs and killing one crewman. The Fortress gunners fought back desperately, claiming three fighters shot down, but their guns either jammed or ran out of ammunition. It looked like the end of the road, but fortunately the remaining Japanese fighters had also run out of ammunition.

This was perhaps less surprising than it may seem. Zeros carried a mere five seconds-worth of ammunition for their 20mm cannon, while their rifle-calibre machine guns were virtually useless

against a Fortress, which was an extremely tough aircraft indeed. Wheless' B-17D sustained over 1,000 hits and still kept flying, although it was eventually wrecked in the ensuing forced landing on Mindanao.

■ THE B-17 ■ ENTERS SERVICE

The Japanese overran the Philippines by the end of December, and the handful of Fortresses were pulled back to Darwin in Northern Australia. From here it was about 1,500 miles (2,400km) to targets in the southern Philippines, which meant that even with auxiliary fuel tanks in the bomb bay, the bomb load that could be carried was exceedingly small; less than two tons in many cases. Shortly after, the B-17s were sent to Java. There were so few of them, but they were the only aircraft available with the necessary range to reach Japanese bridgeheads in Borneo and elsewhere, and even then they needed to stage through those Allied airfields which had not yet fallen.

By now the improved B-17E was entering service, and more than 50 of these were sent to reinforce the theatre, although due to Japanese successes they were forced to come the long way round, via Africa and India. Attrition was heavy; nearly two-thirds of the available Fortresses were lost in the first three months of the Pacific War, to accidents as well as enemy action. During this period, Fortresses claimed to have sunk three warships, including the battleship *Haruna*, and eight transports, in the course of some 350 sorties. One bombardier actually claimed hits on ships when bombing from 35,000ft (10,700m) which says as much for his optimism as his eyesight. In fact, Japanese records showed that only two transports probably succumbed to air attack by Fortresses.

After two months operating out of airfields on Java the Allies had to evacuate in the face of Japanese advances, and once more the surviving Fortresses found themselves back in Australia. But by this time, very few of the original B-17Cs and Ds were left, and their replacement, the B-17E, was a very different bird indeed.

BIGGER AND BETTER

Even before the Royal Air Force took the Fortress I to war, many deficiencies of the early models had been recognized and the Boeing designers were working flat out to correct them. The two greatest failings were poor defensive armament and lateral instability at high altitudes, the latter not being conducive to accurate bombing. There was also the competition to consider; Consolidated's B-24 Liberator prototype had flown in December 1939, and, having incorporated more recent technology, looked likely to become a formidable rival.

The most widely favoured form of fighter attack against a bomber was the one that gave the easiest shot; an approach from astern to give a simple no-deflection firing opportunity. Against the early Fortresses, a slightly low approach was preferable to keep out of the wake of the big bomber, which was considerable, and could throw a fighter about, making accurate aiming difficult. The only defence for the bomber against this form

of attack was for the B-17 pilot to fishtail his giant aircraft from side to side in order to give his beam gunners the chance of a shot.

All British heavy bombers of the period were designed with a multi-gun powered turret in the tail in order to avoid this very situation. Something of the sort was obviously needed for the B-17, but equally obviously it would have to undergo a major redesign. Major changes were also needed to the tail unit in order to cure lateral instability at high altitudes.

■ B-17E FORTRESS ■

Boeing's designers were equal to the task, and, perhaps fortunately, the basic layout was capable of being adapted to take a completely new tail unit. The fin and rudder were

Left: **The navigator's station, a small cramped desk in the nose compartment. This is of course a posed picture on the ground. (USAF)**
Above: **The prototype Sperry ball turret. It covered the blind spot below and, although cramped, was by far the best ventral gun position of the war. (Wright Field)**
Below: **The early Bendix dorsal turret was sunk deep into the fuselage to minimize drag. Later it was positioned higher. (Boeing)**

B-17E

DIMENSIONS
Wingspan: 103ft 9in (31.62m)
Length: 75ft 10in (23.11m)
Height: 19ft 2in (5.84m)
Wing area: 1,420sq. ft (131.96m²)

WEIGHTS
Max. loaded: 54,000lb (24,500kg)
Bomb load: 4,800lb (2,180kg)
Engines: all as B-17D

PERFORMANCE
Max. speed: 318mph (512km/hr)
Cruise speed: 226mph (364km/hr)
Service ceiling: 36,000ft (11,000m)
Normal range: 2,000 miles (3,220km)

BROWNING M.2 MACHINE GUN

Calibre: .50in (12.7mm)
Length: 4ft 9in (1.45m)
Weight: 64lb (29kg)
Rate of fire: 750 rounds/min
Muzzle velocity: 2,850ft/min (869m/sec)
Effective range: 3,500ft (1,070m)

NB: Effective range in this case is the distance at which the projectile could do significant damage. The range at which the average gunner could expect to hit his target was less than half this.

Above: Two B-17Fs of the 43rd BG at Port Moresby in Papua New Guinea in 1942 as a DC-5 transport takes off. (Frank F. Smith)

B-17F

DIMENSIONS
all as B-17E

WEIGHTS
Empty: 34,000lb (15,435kg)
Normal max. takeoff: 56,000lb (25,400kg)
Overload takeoff: 65,000lb (29,500kg)
Max. bomb load: 9,600lb (4,350kg)
Normal bomb load: 4,000lb (1,814kg)

POWER
4 x Wright Cyclone GR-1820-97 turbo-supercharged radials each rated at 1,380hp war emergency.

PERFORMANCE
Max. speed: 325mph (523km/hr)
Cruise speed: 182mph (293km/hr)
Initial climb rate: 900ft/min (4.6m/sec)
Service ceiling: 38,500ft (11,700m)
Maximum range: 4,220miles (6,800km)

enlarged, with a dorsal strake extended forward along the fuselage, while the span of the tailplane was increased. These were mounted on a deepened rear fuselage section, at the end of which was a cramped rear gunner's station armed with two manually traversing .50in (12.7mm) Browning heavy machine guns.

The 'teardrop' transparencies in the waist were deleted and replaced by rectangular openings with sliding window covers, each with a single pintle-mounted

Below: Aircraft of the 91st BG being prepared for a mission at Bassingbourn, near Cambridge.

Above: Closeup of the tail gun position of a B-17F. The remote sight can just be made out in the transparent panel. (USAF)

heavy machine gun stowed internally. Cleared for action, both gunners stood in an icy blast, and in action frequently got in each other's way. Provision for a single .50 was made in the roof window of the radio room firing upwards and backwards only, while a Bendix electrically powered top turret with twin .50s was located just aft of the flight deck.

This left the blind spot below, and a powered ventral turret was installed just aft of the wing. This utilized a periscope sight, which in action was difficult to use. Aiming torpedoes at slow-moving ships from a submarine using a periscope was bad enough; aiming at fast-moving enemy fighters with the same device was extremely difficult! Yet another problem was that using the periscopic sight often caused disorientation and nausea.

Right: The main limitation on the size of bomb carried internally by the B-17 was the length of the bay, seen here open. (USAF via Alfred Price)

These factors made the initial ventral gun position well-nigh useless, and it was later supplanted by the Sperry ball turret, also armed with two .50 machine guns. Both dorsal and ventral turrets could travel through a complete circle, which meant that they could give cover ahead as well as astern and to the sides.

Nose armament remained as one or two rifle-calibre machine guns on pintle mounts. While something heavier was preferable, the front cabin was cramped at the best of times. The .30 Browning was shorter and lighter than the .50, and for this reason more suitable, although its relatively short effective range and lack of hitting power made it more of a 'scare' gun rather than a positive defensive asset. It might just deter an enemy pilot, even if it had little chance of shooting him down.

This heavily modified Fortress was the Boeing Model 2990, and in USAAF service, the B-17E. First flown in September 1941, it was the first true mass-production Fortress. Many early models were rushed to the Pacific in the first months of 1942, where their much heavier defensive armament came as a nasty surprise to the Japanese. However, the latter soon discovered that weak spots still existed. The ineffective ventral turret initially fitted allowed them to come in underneath, hang on their propellers and fire upwards. This mode of attack became far more hazardous when the Sperry ball turret was introduced.

Other B-17Es were used to form Bombardment Groups in the USA prior to their deployment to the European theatre of operations, while the RAF took delivery of 45 B-17Es in mid-1942, most of which went to Coastal Command as Fortress IIAs.

The B-17E was larger and considerably heavier than its predecessors, and as

Problems with engines – Wright Cyclones or Allisons?

it retained the same Wright Cyclones, performance suffered. More power was a possible answer, and the choice fell upon the Allison V-1710-89 12 cylinder inline engine rated at 1,425hp. The Allison was heavier but had a smaller frontal area than the Cyclone, giving less drag. Liquid-cooled, it was also more vulnerable to battle damage than the Wright radial, but the advantages of a significant increase in performance were felt to outweigh the risks.

The ninth production B-17E was duly modified by the Lockheed Vega Company to become the XB-38. First flight took place on 19 May 1943, and early trials showed promise, with a maximum speed of 327mph (526km/hr) attained. But then disaster struck. On 16 June the

XB-38 suffered an uncontrollable engine fire, and was destroyed. With a massive fighter production programme making heavy demands on the output of Allisons, the scheme was allowed to lapse.

■ B-17F FORTRESS ■

The B-17F was sufficiently similar to the E model for no prototype to be required, and superseded it on the production lines from April 1942. Outwardly it differed little from its predecessor: a single-piece nose transparency in Plexiglass with an optically flat bomb-aiming panel; paddle-bladed propellers; and engine cowlings modified slightly to allow the wider propeller blades to feather, and to accommodate filters. Like late models of the B-17E, it carried the new Sperry ball turret ventrally.

B-17F DEFENSIVE ARMAMENT

Location	Guns	Ammunition per gun (firing time)
Nose	1 x .30	500 (26 secs)
Waist (x 2)	1 x .50	300 (24 secs)
Dorsal	2 x .50	400 (32 secs)
Ventral	2 x .50	500 (40 secs)
Tail	2 x .50	565 (45 secs)

Internally, though, it had undergone considerable revision, with more than 400 modifications; some large, others small. Among the most important were self-sealing oil tanks, while in late production aircraft the so-called 'Tokyo Tanks' in the outer wings provided a massive 42 per cent increase in fuel capacity. While these increased maximum range to 4,220 miles (6,800km), they also increased vulnerability. Gasoline fumes leaking from these tanks accumulated in the wing tips, which enemy fire sometimes caused to explode. This was eventually cured by a venting system which carried away the deadly fumes. Finally the landing gear was strengthened to handle greatly increased take-off weights.

The internal bomb load of all Fortresses was limited by the dimensions of the bay, in which the bombs were stacked horizontally. Also limited was the size of the weapons which could be carried internally; the largest was a 2,000lb (900kg) bomb. Little could be done about this without redesigning the whole fuselage, but on the B-17F, provision was made for external bomb racks under the wings, bringing the maximum load up to 9,600lb (4,350kg). In practice these were rarely used, as the extra weight could only be accommodated by a reduction in fuel load, while the added drag combined to reduce the operational radius of action even further.

Later modifications allowed the maximum bomb load to be increased to a staggering 20,800lb (9,400kg), most of it carried externally, but this made

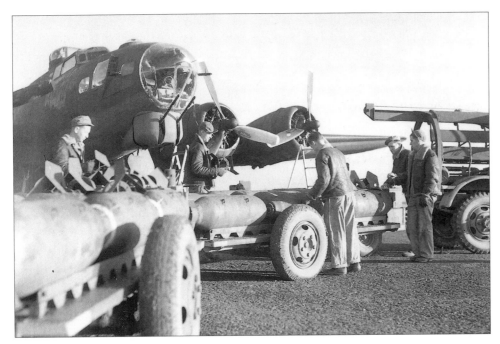

Left above: A typical load against Germany was ten 500lb (227kg) bombs, seen here being fitted with their fins prior to loading. (USAF)

Left: Bombs could be carried externally on racks as seen here on these B-17Fs of 94th BG, but this was rarely done. (USAF)

Left: A combination of firepower and tight formation, as seen here with the 96th BG early in 1943, proved insufficient protection against attacking fighters. The censor has obliterated the tail letter on the nearest aircraft only. (Garry Fry)

Left below: Still in close formation after a penetration to Mainz, B-17Fs of 381st BG begin their bombing runs. (USAF)

hoc arrangements were often made in individual units.

The B-17F served mainly in the European theatre of operations, primarily with the 8th Air Force, but 19 examples served with RAF Coastal Command as Fortress IIs until 1944. After this they were used for meteorological reconnaissance, for which their high-altitude capability was invaluable, and also for training purposes.

■ THE ESCORT ■ FORTRESS

Even before Fortresses of the USAAF commenced their daylight bombing campaign in Europe, consideration was given to the possibility of extra defence against German fighters. This could be provided by Allied fighters for short-range targets, but the need to range freely over Germany, far beyond the reach of any fighter then existing, was part of American bombing strategy. While it was widely felt that the massed fire power of B-17s in tight formation should be sufficient protection, doubts began to surface.

A possible answer was to kit out some B-17s as gunships, substituting bomb loads for extra guns, gunners, ammunition and armour, then flying these in the most exposed positions in the formations where they were best placed to add their massive fire power to that of the others. The idea was far from new; it had first been suggested by General Guilio Douhet in 1921, in his book *The Command of the Air*, and the French used the concept in the First World War with their Caudron R-4s.

Whether General Douhet, who was Italian, had influenced American thinking remains an open question. What is certain is that in August 1942, Lockheed Vega started to modify a B-17F as a

FIRE POWER

'There should on the whole be very little difference between one type of aeroplane and the other, which implies that combat planes (i.e. escorts), like bombers, ought to be capable of carrying a substantial load . . This increase in the carrying capacity of the combat unit should be made use of for increasing fire power and if possible, armour protection . . . A plane designed and constructed along these lines would, on the face of it, be so superior in intensity of fire power as to outmatch any pursuit ship now existing.'

GENERAL GUILIO DOUHET,
THE COMMAND OF THE AIR

manoeuvrability marginal and radius of action minimal. Typically, the B-17F carried a load of around 4,000lb (1,800kg) over a combat radius of about 800 miles (1,290km).

Late production models of the B-17F were powered by the more powerful Cyclone GR-1820-97 engines, rated at 1,380hp at 25,000ft (7,600m) for war emergency only. With a maximum speed of 325mph (523km/hr), the B-17F was the fastest Fortress of them all.

Defensive armament on the B-17F was never entirely standardized. A few later models featured two single .50 machine guns in cheek mountings on either side of the nose in lieu of the single .30, while ad

Left: Great hopes. A line of YB-40s seen at Bassingbourn during their combat trials phase. From this angle the second dorsal turret can be seen on the two nearest aircraft. (Marion Havelaar)

The revised tail section had made all B-17s from the E onwards tail-heavy. Although this could be trimmed out, it still adversely affected performance. On the YB-40, the added guns, turrets and armour plating, coupled with the lack of a bomb load, accentuated the tail-heaviness to the point where the aircraft became tricky to handle. Matters were not helped by the extra drag caused by the additional guns and turrets, which made further inroads into performance.

To state the obvious, all the fire power in the world is of little avail if the target is not hit. As a means of defence, the YB-40 possessed a tremendous weight of fire, but with little or no additional firing accuracy to back it up, this counted for nought. As an interesting footnote, the German fighter pilots were so impressed by the awesome firepower

gunship, with the designation XB-40. The initial trials appeared promising, and a further 22 B-17Fs were converted to YB-40s. In the following year they were sent to England to be proved in action.

Up-gunning of the YB-40 was basically as follows. A second dorsal turret with twin .50s was fitted above the radio room; the waist positions were modified to take twin .50s, with hydraulic boost power to ease the gunners' battle with the slipstream. The tail position was similarly modified and given a reflector sight to replace the original ring and bead; and a powered Bendix chin turret with two .50s was fitted beneath the nose to make defence against frontal attacks more effective. The ammunition supply was nearly tripled, and a considerable amount of armour plate added.

So much for the official modifications. The existence of many conflicting accounts make it seem possible that even more weapons were fitted at group or even squadron level, as up to 30 automatic weapons including 20mm and even 40mm cannon have been mentioned, although the latter seems unlikely.

The YB-40 was too heavy to keep in formation with B-17s

The YB-40 was a failure, primarily because its flying qualities and performance were inferior to those of its bomber stablemates, making it hard pressed to stay in formation with them. This was even more marked when the bombers had unloaded and were homeward bound at light weights. It was hardly to be expected otherwise. A laden YB-40 weighed in at 63,500lb (28,800kg), and its ammunition supply, even if all shot away, never lightened the aircraft to the same degree that unloading the bombs on a B-17 did.

Below: The YB-40 'flying battleship'. While the second dorsal turret above the radio room is hidden by the wingtip from this angle, other gun positions in the front cabin can clearly be seen, with both cheek positions and enlarged side windows to take extra guns. Also visible is the chin turret which supplanted the 'scare gun' in the nose. Many guns were mounted only just before takeoff, which is why the waist apertures, which should contain twin .50s, are empty. Had accuracy been upgraded to the same degree as weight of fire, the YB-40 would have been a formidable opponent. (Bruce Robertson)

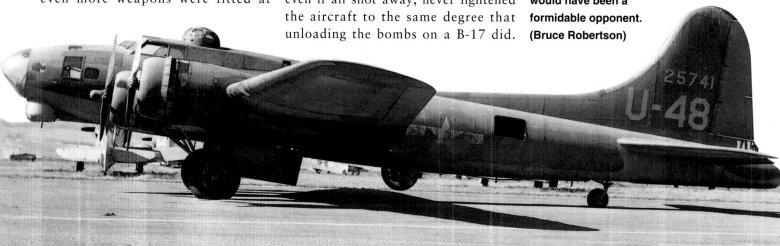

of the Boeing gunship that they were still reporting it several months after it had been withdrawn from service, the inference being that they were unable to tell the difference!

Above: The B-17G was the definitive Flying Fortress, differing from the B-17F in having the Bendix chin turret as pioneered by the YB-40, cheek gun positions in the nose cabin, and enclosed waist gun positions. (Barney Lucas)

Below: Comparison of nose armament between the B-17F and G. The F (seen here with combat damage) retains the nose gun, while the cheek guns cannot be brought to bear straight ahead. (USAF via Alfred Price)

■ B-17G FORTRESS ■

The B-17G replaced the F on the production lines from July 1943. Of the total 12,723 Fortresses built, no less than 8,680 (nearly 70 per cent) were B-17Gs,

B-17G		
DIMENSIONS		
all as B-17F except		
Length: 74ft 4in (22.65m)		
WEIGHTS		
Empty: 35,800lb (16,240kg)		
Max. takeoff: 65,500lb (29,700kg)		
Max. overload: 72,000lb (32,660kg)		
Bomb load: as B-17F		
POWER		
as B-17F		
PERFORMANCE		
Max. speed: 300mph (483km/hr)		
Cruise speed: 182mph (293km/hr)		
Service ceiling: 35,000ft (10,700m)		
Maximum range: 3,750 miles (6,030km)		
Endurance: 8.7hrs		

making this the definitive Flying Fortress. Externally the B-17G differed from the F in having a Bendix chin turret with twin .50 calibre machine guns as pioneered on the YB-40, added to the two cheek guns to give increased protection against

Above: The 'Cheyenne' tail position, seen here on this 457th BG aircraft, gave an improved arc of fire and field of view for the gunner. (USAF via Alfred Price)

frontal attack. The waist guns were enclosed for the first time, and staggered longitudinally, with the right-hand panel slightly farther forward to prevent the gunners getting in each other's way. The ammunition supply for these was doubled to 600 rounds per gun.

Late production models omitted the radio room gun, but incorporated the 'Cheyenne' tail mounting, which marginally increased what was a rather restricted field of fire and also the field of view. The 'stone-age' ring and bead was replaced by the N-8 reflector sight, about 5 inches (127mm) square with an illuminated red circle and central dot. This was much easier to use, and made for more accurate shooting. One modification not carried through from the YB-40 was armour protection for the tail gunner, even though he was a prime target for enemy fighters. The extra weight so far aft increased the inherent tail-heaviness to the point where aircraft handling was adversely affected.

■ RAF B-17Gs ■

The B-17G served with RAF Coastal Command as the Fortress III, and also with 100 Group of Bomber Command, specializing in radio countermeasures,

and with No. 233 Squadron on clandestine operations, dropping agents and equipment into France. In the former role they normally carried twelve 400lb (180kg) bombs, or sixteen 250lb (110kg) depth charges for use against U-boats.

In 100 Group service they were fitted with a battery of eight Mandrel and one Air-Borne Cigar jammers in the sealed bomb bay with two extra crew positions for the operators. Late in the war, these were replaced by Piperack and the extremely powerful Jostle IV jamming transmitter. Other modifications were flame dampers over the engine exhausts to reduce their visual signature at night, and an H_2S ground mapping radar in a radome beneath the nose.

■ CREW STATIONS ■

Young and agile crew members who flew in the front of the aircraft often entered the Fortress via a hatch on the underside, just in front of the wing leading edge,

although the easiest means of access was through a door on the right rear fuselage, just in front of the tailplane.

For take-off, all the gunners gathered in the radio room. Not only was this the safest place to be in the event of an accident, it also helped to keep the centre of gravity forward, minimizing the inherent tail-heaviness and improving controllability.

Once they were in the air, the gunners pulled on their electrically heated suits, sheepskin-lined jackets and trousers. Flak helmets and vests, flying boots, parachute harness and Mae West followed, and thus encumbered they took up their stations.

To reach the tail-gun cabin (not a turret in the accepted sense), the gunner

Below: Fortress III of 100 Group RAF Bomber Command. The bulge under the nose houses the H_2S ground mapping radar scanner. (Bruce Robertson)

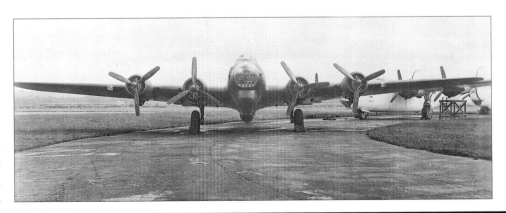

crawled past the tailwheel, which was retracted into the rear fuselage, making access difficult. On the homeward leg he left his station well before the pilot lowered the undercarriage; crawling past when the wheel went down could be a little too exciting!

The tail position was cramped and claustrophobic. The gunner sat on a sort of seat with knee supports in a semi-squatting position. Turning the head in either direction almost brought the oxygen mask into contact with the perspex. The guns were manually controlled by either hand via a spade grip. While the field of fire was very limited by comparison with that of a powered turret, it was adequate for the purpose.

The almost circular fuselage section allowed only a narrow catwalk, which made life difficult for the waist gunners, as they were forced to stand at their guns while rapidly changing position to keep their sights on enemy fighters. With the old ring and bead sight, this was not easy, especially as virtually all their

shooting was done at high deflection angles. Target precession and bullet trail were factors that few gunners ever mastered; having to aim behind an attacking fighter because the forward speed of the Fortress imparted a sideways component to the bullet trajectory seemed an unnatural activity to many of them.

Above: **Flying gear was heavy and cumbersome, and while often much of it was not donned until after takeoff, a frosty English pre-dawn sees this crew well wrapped up before climbing aboard. (USAF)**
Below: **Just how small the tail cabin really was can be gauged from the size of the figures alongside this crashed B-17G.**

time-consuming process in a situation demanding haste.

While the Sperry ball turret was the most effective means of ventral defence devised during the whole of the war, there were still complications in its use. Not the least of these involved the infamous 'pee' tubes. On the many long flights undertaken by Fortresses some arrangement was obviously necessary, but at high altitudes the spray from the outlets froze, covering the ball turret with unsightly yellow ice!

If the ball turret caught the runway the aircraft would usually break its back

Above: Unusual view of the interior of a Fortress fuselage, courtesy of the German anti-aircraft artillery, showing the circular cross-section which made the B-17 such a strong aircraft. Just visible to the left is the starboard waist gun position with its enclosing transparency, while the man standing on the ground occupies the space once taken by the ball turret, which has either been blown away or jettisoned. Above him can be seen the ball turret suspension gear. Hit on 27 September 1944, this B-17G returned safely to base. (USAF via Alfred Price)

gunner later commented: 'Presenting the family jewels to oncoming enemy fighters was not an entirely satisfactory way of waging war.'

Above the gunsight were two handles which worked electro-hydraulic valves to move the turret. A firing button was located on each handle, so that in action, the gunner's hands were higher than his head. But despite all this, it was not a particularly uncomfortable position to be in. The main worry was the lack of a parachute; the gunner had to vacate the turret in order to clip his on, and this could be a

Another problem was that in the event of hydraulic failure the turret might not retract. In a heavy landing, if the ball turret caught the runway, the aircraft would usually break its back, while in a belly landing this was always the case. In this event, the ball turret had to be jettisoned by undoing a series of large nuts and allowing it to fall away, having first

Below: Ball turret entry and exit was through this tiny armoured door, although normally it would be cranked up inside the aircraft.

A little further forward from the waist guns was the ball turret, which was enclosed in a low well. This could be partially retracted into the fuselage for take-off and landing, as in the extended position ground clearance was minimal. Ball turret gunners were small men; they had to be. The spherical turret was a mere 44in (112cm) in diameter, which had to accommodate the gunner, two .50 machine guns, and the Sperry lead-computing sight, which itself was quite sizeable.

Entry to the ball turret was gained through an armoured door in the rear. The gunner lay on his back and sighted his guns through an armoured glass plate between his raised legs. A pedal under his left foot controlled the rangefinder on the sight system. As one anonymous ball

Above: Flak damage to *Little Miss Mischief* of the 91st BG. Gunner Sergeant Ed Abdo survived. Statistically the ball turret was one of the safest places in action. (USAF via Alfred Price)

rescued the expensive computing sight system. A special tool was carried to undo the nuts, and the bottom of the Channel and North Sea became littered with discarded ball turrets.

In at least one well-attested case, the special tool was missing just when it was most wanted. An urgent radio message was sent, with the result that another B-17 flew above the offending machine, dangling the tool on the end of a long piece of string for the radioman in the lower aircraft to catch!

Just ahead of the ball turret was a bulkhead with a door leading to the

Right: Moths! A radio operator ruefully surveys the wreckage of his station after a near miss by flak.

radio room, in which the operator's station was a swivel seat on the port side. Above him was a roof hatch with a single .50 calibre machine gun, although the view aft and field of fire were so limited as to make its value questionable. The

gun was deleted from late models of the B-17G. Beneath the floor of the radio room was a well, containing a strike camera which automatically took photographs of the bombing run at 10-second intervals, for damage assess-

Left: **The sliding dorsal hatch of the radio room shows up well in this vertical shot of a 457th BG aircraft. (USAF via Alfred Price)**

more or less the pilot's assistant, his USAAF counterpart was an airborne crew chief and jack-of-all-trades, whose main function in combat was to man the Sperry dorsal turret.

Small and cramped, this turret was located at the rear of the flight deck. A sling seat was fitted, but in action the flight engineer usually stood on a stand mounted on the pivot post. Because the turret was sunk deep into the fuselage to minimize drag, the twin .50s could not be depressed below the horizontal, although on late model B-17Gs they did at least have a reflector sight and rangefinder.

Unlike British heavy bombers of the

ment purposes. The view from the small window was an uninspiring one; two engines and a large area of wing with its aluminium skinning quivering in the slipstream occupied much of it.

The radio operator was the odd-job man of the crew. In addition to his normal tasks, he was in charge of first aid, stood in as a waist gunner at need, and also checked whether any bombs had hung up after the bombing run. This last task could be a hair-raising one. The bomb bay was located just ahead of the radio room, and was spanned by a narrow catwalk bounded by rope handrails. To deal with hang-ups, he had to walk out over the void with the bay doors open and lean across to prise them loose by hand!

Whereas an RAF flight engineer was

Right: **A typical load for a moderate or deep penetration of the Third Reich consisting of ten 500lb (227kg) bombs, fins already fitted, is taken to a B-17F on dollies. Once there the bombs will be hoisted aboard using the shackles visible on top of them. Whereas larger and more destructive bombs had their advantages, as there would inevitably be fewer of them greater accuracy would be needed to achieve the same effect. Even with the Norden bombsight's vaunted accuracy, pattern bombing was the order of the day. (USAF via Alfred Price)**

Above: The Norden bombsight is carefully shrouded in the nose of *Marisika*, a B-17G of the 97th BG seen here at Amendola, Italy, in 1944. (USAF)

period, the Fortress carried two pilots – the aircraft commander on the left and the co-pilot on the right. Each of them had a yoke-type control column and rudder pedals, while the throttle controls were centrally mounted where both men were able to reach them. The main flight instruments were positioned on the left, while the co-pilot sat facing the engine and fuel gauges. The Fortress was remarkably easy to fly for such a large machine. It offered good directional stability, the ailerons and elevators were responsive and formation flying at high altitude posed few problems, unlike the B-24, which could be very hard work for the pilot.

Ahead of and lower than the flight deck was the forward compartment, the domain of the navigator and the bom-

bardier, reached by a narrow accessway between the two pilots. The former sat at a table on the left side, above which were the gyro and radio compasses. While on most missions all that was required was to stay in formation, if anything went wrong the aircraft might have to return alone. For this reason the navigator had to know where his aircraft was at all times.

■ ON THE BOMB RUN ■

The bombardier's seat was right in the nose, and the tool of his trade was the Norden M-7 bombsight, replaced from late 1943 by the M-9. This consisted of a gyro-stabilized platform on which was mounted a 2.5 magnification telescope. On the run-up to the target, the bombardier inserted the aircraft's speed and altitude, together with the ballistics of the bombs to be dropped, into the Norden computer. As the run continued, he would identify the target, then superimpose the crosshairs of the sight on it.

Corrections to the vertical crosshair by the bombardier were shown via a directional indicator on the flight deck to the pilot, who then adjusted his course to suit. The sight could be linked to the autopilot allowing the bombardier to control the aircraft laterally, but this was unreliable.

As the bomber neared the target, the changing angle of the telescope provided exact data on movement over the ground, thus giving range, while movement of the vertical crosshair provided the deflection needed to compensate (for example) crosswinds that would blow the bombs off course.

The bombing run was usually one of the more exciting events. The pilot had to hold a set heading, altitude and airspeed for a considerable time if the aiming requirements were to be met, which eased the task of the German flak gunners. But as bombs on target was the whole point of the mission, this just had to be accepted.

WAR IN EUROPE

When in December 1941 the USA entered the war, both the RAF and the USAAF were agreed on one thing: for the immediate future, the Third Reich could only be effectively attacked from the air. The primary disagreement was as to how. As a result of hard and bloody experience, the RAF had, with a few notable exceptions, abandoned daylight raids in favour of the cover of darkness, and argued strongly that the Americans should join them in this.

The USAAF, however, was not convinced. The British night effort at this time was fairly agricultural, with many crews unable to land their bombs within 5 miles (8km) of their targets. It consisted of little more than exporting bombs to 'somewhere in Germany'. Area bombing, which was to devastate German cities in the next three years, had not yet matured. The truth was that while night attacks tied down valuable

Left: Fortresses of the 381st BG leave contrails emblazoned across the sky, while two fighters hurtle across them high above. (USAF)
Below: Typical European weather made navigation, target finding and accurate bombing far more difficult than the USAAF expected. B-17F *Meat Hound* of the 306th BG in cloudy skies. (USAF)

Above: 8th AF commander General Jimmy Doolittle talks to a weather reconnaissance crew on their return. Second from left is Flying Officer Eldridge, an RAF weather observer. (USAF)

German resources in the shape of flak and night fighters, they were at that time doing little real damage.

The USAAF view was that precision attacks on industrial targets would be far more effective, and these could only be carried out in daylight. Daylight made accurate navigation much easier, and also the precise identification of industrial complexes. The American Norden

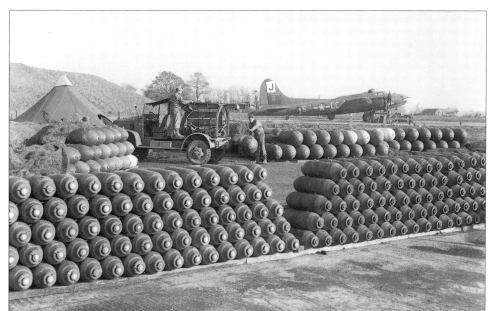

massed firepower of their defensive armament to beat off the German fighters. The new and better protected B-17E and F were coming on stream, and the vulnerability against attack from astern had been reduced. The British prophesied disaster, but the Americans were confident in adopting the 'wagon train' approach of their forebears.

But before operations could start, there was much to be done. RAF Bomber Command was expanding fast, and new airfields sprang up like mushrooms across England. Even more airfields were needed for their American allies, and providing these took time.

■ THE FIRST ■ BOMB GROUP

Nor was the USAAF ready initially. The basic unit was the Bombardment Group (BG), which consisted of a headquarters and three squadrons, quickly increased to four, each of which had an establishment of 8–10 aircraft. The demand for personnel, training and aircraft initially outstripped supply. Matters were not helped when many production Fortresses were sent to units in the Pacific. It was months before the first USAAF Bombardment Group (Heavy) was able to take off and point its Fortresses eastwards, across the cold grey Atlantic.

Above: **Airfields for the USAAF bombers were hastily prepared. An open-air bomb dump at Framlingham, with tented accommodation. (USAF).**
Left: **'Fill 'er up and check the oil, please!' For a raid on Germany, 2,000 gallons of fuel per aircraft was not exceptional. (USAF).**

tachometric bomb sight was inherently far more accurate than the British Mk XIV vector sight. On the bombing range in peacetime in clear visibility, releasing from an altitude of 10,000ft (3,050m), circular error probability (the radius within which the best 50 per cent of bombs fall) was about 300ft (90m) for the Norden and 775ft (235m) for the Mk XIV.

In combat, things were less simple. Heavy and accurate flak forced the bombers to much greater altitudes. Not only did circular error probability increase significantly with height, but shrapnel rattling against the wings and fuselage was a considerable distraction to the bombardier. European weather conditions bore no similarity to those of California, and frequently the target was obscured or semi-obscured by cloud. All these factors conspired against the highly accurate Norden bombsight. But all else being equal, there was no substitute for practical experience, and the USAAF

decided to press ahead and see for itself.

The ultra-high altitude bombing pioneered by the RAF in late 1941 was not repeated. Instead the American heavy bombers attacked in close formation from rather lower levels, relying on the

B-17 UNITS THAT BECAME OPERATIONAL IN ENGLAND 1942

Group No.	Squadrons	Base	First Mission	Notes
97	340, 341, 342, 414	Polebrook	17 Aug 42	to North Africa Nov 42
32	301, 352, 353, 419	Chelveston	5 Sept 42	to North Africa Nov 42
92	325, 326, 327, 407	Alconbury	Sept 42	training unit after four missions, returned to ops May 43 with YB-40.
306	367, 368, 369, 423	Thurleigh	9 Oct 42	Last mission 19 Apr 45
91	322, 323, 324, 401	Bassingbourn	7 Nov 42	Last mission 25 Apr 45
303	358, 359, 369, 427	Molesworth	17 Nov 42	Last mission 25 Apr 45
305	364, 365, 366, 422	Grafton Underwood	17 Nov 42	Last mission 25 Apr 45

ATTACKED!

First-hand account by Jim Fletcher.

'I'd never seen a fighter before from the perspective of the cockpit and the specks out ahead looked like the distant flak I'd seen the previous day. It wasn't until those specks started to grow rapidly in size and suddenly started blinking at us that I realized what was happening. Almost simultaneously the sky around us was lit up like the Fourth of July as 20-millimetres exploded all around our "17."'

LT JIM FLETCHER, CO-PILOT.

Above: **The Yanks are coming! Fortresses on Iceland, 21 July 1942.**

The first unit to arrive in England was the 97th BG, equipped with B-17Es; it was followed by other units with the newer B-17F. The recently formed US 8th Air Force had received its first weapons. Intensive training followed, and a period of acclimatization to European weather conditions.

The first mission was flown by the 97th BG, which was based at Polebrook, on 17 August 1942. Twelve B-17Es raided the Sotteville marshalling yards at Rouen, strongly escorted by four RAF Spitfire squadrons. Visibility was good, and about half the bombs landed in the target area. Two bombers were slightly damaged by flak. It was a promising

Below: **Early loss. A Fortress breaks up and goes down over northern France after being hit on the way to the target. (USAF)**

Above: They're here! Two B-17F Fortresses of the 91st BG arrive in England late in 1942. In the foreground are a Hurricane (left) and a Fairchild Argus (right) of the RAF. (Merle Olmsted)

debut, and all seemed set fair for the 8th AF, with the 301st BG in pre-combat training and the 92nd BG arriving. Due shortly were the 306th, 91st, 303rd and 305th BGs.

The 97th was given no time to rest on its laurels. Two dozen B-17Es bombed Abbeville airfield on 19 August during the Dieppe Raid, and the next day 12 aircraft attacked the Amiens marshalling yards, again with a Spitfire escort. All the bombers returned unscathed on both occasions, having seen little of German fighters.

Shallow penetrations over enemy territory continued for the rest of the month; sometimes the bombing was accurate, at others it was less so. In September the 301st and 92nd BGs became operational, and joined the fray. Then on 6 September, the Luftwaffe reacted strongly, penetrated the escorting fighters and shot down two of the 20 B-17s. The loss of 10 per cent of the raiding force came as a nasty shock.

In November, just as the B-17 force was getting into its stride, the 97th and 301st BGs were transferred to the 12th Air Force in North Africa, while the 92nd BG became a B-17 'finishing school', and did not return to action until September of the following year. This left only the 306th BG in the front line, although it was joined during the month by the 91st, 303rd and 305th BGs. The latter two units flew their first mission on 17 November.

It was not an auspicious start. The target was the U-boat base at St Nazaire, but it was obscured by heavy cloud. Those that managed to bomb were met with fierce flak, though they all returned. The 303rd had no such luck. They completely failed to find the target, and brought their bombs home. On the following day, the 303rd managed to bomb St Nazaire. The problem was that the briefed target was La Pallice, over 100 miles (160km) away! This was the very thing that daylight raiding was supposed to avoid. Then, four days later, only 11 out of 76 bombers despatched were able to find Lorient.

The final months of 1942 were very much a proving period for the B-17 units. Methods and tactics were in a continual state of flux. Formations were changed in an attempt to use the heavy defensive armament to its best advantage, while allowing concentrated bombing. The leader in this field was Colonel Curtis LeMay, commanding the 305th BG at Chelveston. One of the problems to be overcome was that of bomb aiming. It was impossible to keep a tight formation yet still have every aircraft aim individually, without risking multiple mid-air collisions. Having sorted out his optimum formation, LeMay solved the aiming problem by having everyone drop when they saw the leader's bombs go down. Sophisticated it was not, but against all but pinpoint targets it was good enough, and at least it ensured concentration. As 1942 drew to a close, the 8th had neither raided Germany nor attempted a deep penetration so far. But this was not far off.

■ **1943** ■
THE TEMPO INCREASES

The Casablanca Directive, signed on 21 January 1943, listed target types in

Below: The 91st BG returns to base at Bassingbourn after a sortie. (USAF)

REVISED 18-AIRCRAFT GROUP DEC 1942

The revised 18-aircraft Bomb Group formation, introduced in December 1942. The requirements were threefold; a concentrated bomb pattern which called for a narrow frontage; concentration of defensive firepower, which called for close formation, and freedom from masking the defensive guns, which demanded vertical staggering of aircraft. Formations changed throughout the course of the war, culminating in 1945 with a 36-aircraft BG occupying a frontage of 1,170ft (356m), with four nine-aircraft squadrons staggered through 1,150ft (350m) vertically.

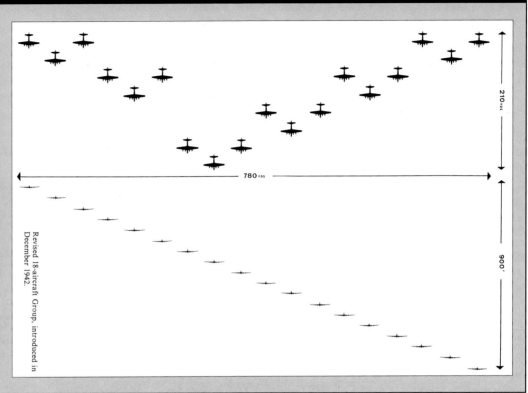

Revised 18-aircraft Group, introduced in December 1942.

210 YDS

900'

780 YDS

order of priority. They were: U-boat construction; aircraft construction; transport; fuel; other industries. Six days later, the 8th AF put this into practice as 67 B-17s set off to raid the U-boat construction yards at Vegesack, the first German target scheduled.

As was so often the case, the primary target was socked in by cloud, and the

The 8th AF begins its assault on Germany

secondary, which was Wilhelmshaven, was attacked instead, although with unimpressive results. Fortunately the flak was ineffective, and the FW 190 pilots of JG. 1, lacking experience in estimating range against anything as large as a B-17, failed to press home their attacks. Three

Right: A tight 'ladder' of bombs goes down from a B-17F of the 96th BG. In the background are other groups in rather ragged formations, while flak bursts stain the sky. (Boeing via Alfred Price)

bombers were shot down for 22 German fighters claimed, which seemed a good rate of exchange.

Appalling weather foiled planned raids on Germany over the next few months, while the Luftwaffe fighters polished their tactics and became ever more effective. Although much of the early bombing effort was directed against the U-boats, it quickly became apparent that measures against the fighters were badly needed. In the largest raid so far, 115 B-17s took off on 17 April, their

target the Focke-Wulf factory at Bremen.

Fighters arrived in force as the bombing run commenced, and wave after wave of them attacked from head-on. The leading wing, consisting of the 91st and 306th BGs, suffered the worst of the onslaught. In the former the entire low squadron went down, while the latter lost 10 out of 16 aircraft. Total losses for the mission were 16; one to flak, the rest to fighters. This amounted to 14 per cent of the entire force, while another 48 bombers returned with varying

54-AIRCRAFT COMBAT WING FORMATION INTRODUCED MARCH 1943

The 54-aircraft Combat Wing, consisting of three Bomb Groups each of 18 aircraft, was introduced in March 1943. Its aims were basically those of the Bomb Group formation; bombing concentration and defensive security. At first it occupied a box of sky some 1¹/₃ miles (2km) wide, 1,800ft (550m) from front to rear, and 2,900ft (880m) vertically. This proved unwieldy, and it was condensed into just over ¹/₂ mile (900m) wide, 1,275ft (390m) front to rear, and 2,700ft (820m) vertically.

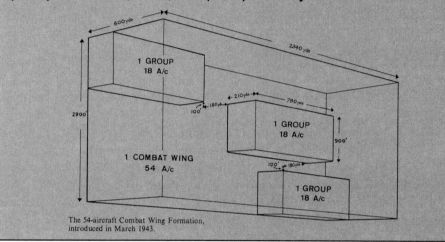

The 54-aircraft Combat Wing Formation, introduced in March 1943.

degrees of damage. This rate of attrition could not be sustained. The one apparent bright spot was the claim for 63 German fighters destroyed, but this turned out to be misleading.

■ GUNNER CLAIMS ■

Overclaiming has always been a feature of air warfare, and arises from confusion caused by the rapidity of events. This was inevitable. Several dozen gunners blazed away at one fighter; if it went down they all claimed it in good faith. Even the most expert debriefer could not sort out the tangle with any degree of accuracy. Figures for the period allowed 450 claims for fighters destroyed to be upheld, but the true figure was in all probability fewer than 50. Total bomber losses for the same period amounted to 103. The false picture thus presented gave rise to unfounded optimism in the USAAF.

Escort fighters were desperately needed. The British Spitfire was too short-legged for the task; the Republic P-47 Thunderbolt was better, but not by much, while the twin-engined Lockheed P-38 Lightning was no match for the agile Focke-Wulfs and Messerschmitts in a dogfight. It was at this point that the 92nd BG returned to operations, bringing with them the YB-40 gunship, of which so much was hoped. As related previously, these were a failure and were withdrawn from service in September of that year.

On 22 June came the deepest penetration yet when 235 Fortresses raided the synthetic rubber plant at Huls, in the Ruhr. To minimize fighter opposition, a feint course was flown to deceive the German fighter controllers, while both the RAF and USAAF mounted diversionary operations. This worked in part, but one of the diversionary forces suffered heavily. The main force landed just under 25 per cent of their bombs on target, which was a good result for the time. The plant was out of action for a month and production reduced for five months thereafter. Sixteen Fortresses of the main force failed to return, a more acceptable 6.8 per cent, one of them a YB-40 hit by flak, but no fewer than 170 were damaged.

The weather improved in late July, and a series of heavy raids was made by forces of 250–300 bombers. The deeper penetrations were often combined with raids on targets in occupied Europe by medium bombers, splitting the defender's strength. Then on 28 July, bombers returning from Oschersleben beset by German fighters were met at the Dutch border by more than 100 P-47s equipped

Right: **Not all losses were attributable to enemy action. A B-17F of the 91st BG sheds its load without realizing that another aircraft has strayed almost directly beneath it. The first bomb strikes the tailplane without detonating, bending it down. In the final picture the unfortunate Fortress goes down out of control; the victim of poor lookout and less than perfect station-keeping. (Boeing via Alfred Price)**

celebrated with the most ambitious deep penetration yet. Early that morning, 147 Fortresses took off to attack the Messerschmitt works at Regensburg, escorted by Thunderbolts as far as the German border. Shortly after, another 230 B-17s would take off, bound for the ball-bearing factories at Schweinfurt. These had no escort, as the German fighters would be on the ground refuelling and rearming. At least, that was how it was planned. In the event the second wave was delayed by fog, and got away hours later.

The German fighters waited for the Thunderbolts to turn back before launching their attack on the first wave. Then dozens of single and twin-engined fighters pounced. For the next 90 minutes they tore into the bombers, concentrating on the rearmost bombardment wing, which lost 13 Fortresses. Four more went down from the two leading wings. Only as the target hove in sight did the attacks cease. Visibility was excellent, and the bombing, led by Curtis LeMay, was accurate. The force then veered to the southwest, crossed Italy, and landed in North Africa, the first of the so-called 'shuttle' missions. On arrival, 24 B-17s were missing; one had crash-landed in Italy; two more, badly damaged, had sought sanctuary in Switzerland, while four had ditched in the Mediterranean out of fuel. Refuelled and rearmed, the German fighters waited in vain for the return flight.

They were however rewarded by the arrival of the second wave, now three

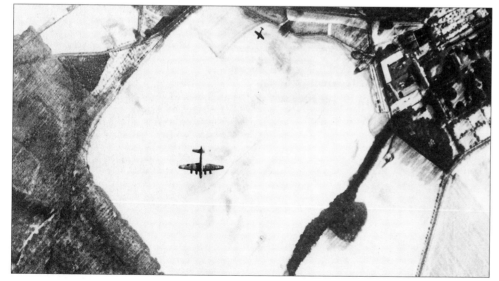

Top: Lockheed P-38 Lightnings escorting Fortresses of the 381st BG late in 1943. (USAF)

Above: Flames streaming from the starboard wing and separated from its formation, a Fortress is remorselessly hunted down by a FW 190 after raiding the aircraft plant at Oschersleben. (USAF)

with new drop tanks to extend their radius of action. These shot down nine of their assailants in short order. It was the shape of things to come.

■ SCHWEINFURT ■

It was 17 August 1943, the anniversary of the raid on Rouen, and the event was

The 8th AF lose 60 bombers against Regensburg and Schweinfurt

hours behind schedule. This time they concentrated on the leading bombardment wing. Twenty-one bombers were shot down by fighters on the way to Schweinfurt and one more was lost to flak over the target. The second wave did not head for North Africa; instead it returned to England, losing 14 more en

Above: Aircraft of the 381st BG lined up on the runway at Ridgewell prior to a mission. (USAF)

route. Schweinfurt was heavily hit, although accuracy was less than had been achieved at Regensburg.

Losses on this two-pronged raid were 60 Fortresses lost on the day, or 16 per cent. But worse was to come. When the remnants of the first wave returned from Tunisia, it was without 55 bombers too badly damaged to make the return flight. In all, the raid cost 118 aircraft, an unacceptable attrition rate of 31 per cent. American gunners claimed an incredible 288 fighters destroyed, later reduced to 148. Actual German fighter losses were just 25. Nor was the damage on the ground particularly rewarding. Production resumed a few days later, and was normal after a few weeks.

■ BOMBING THROUGH ■ THE WEATHER

The weeks following the Schweinfurt raid were quiet, with shallow penetrations only, as losses were made good. The B-17G started arriving in England at about this time, ready for its combat debut. The 8th did not sally forth in force again until 6 September, when 338 Fortresses set out for Stuttgart. This time the main enemy was the weather. Heavy cloud covered much of Western Europe,

Right: A Messerschmitt 110 curves away after attacking Fortresses of the 91st BG. (USAF)

Stuttgart was socked in and few so much as saw it; formation cohesion was lost. German fighters attacked in force over the target area, and again near Paris on the return flight. The result was a disaster. Eleven B-17s were lost to fighters; a round dozen came down in the Channel out of fuel; at least two more crashed on landing, while five lost or damaged machines set down in Switzerland. All this with hardly a bomb anywhere near the target.

The weather was kind to Germany over the following weeks, and the remainder of the month passed with raids on French and Belgian objectives. On 15 September two 1,000lb (450kg) bombs were carried on racks externally for the first time, one of the rare occasions on which this was done. Meanwhile, measures to overcome the worst effects of cloud were in hand.

In August 1943, the 482nd Bomb Group was formed at Alconbury, as the 8th Air Force's sole Pathfinder unit. It was made up of two B-17 and one B-24 squadrons equipped with British gadgets. The first was Gee, a comparatively short-ranged navigational device. The second was Oboe which, using signals from English ground stations, allowed fairly accurate blind bombing. The third was H2S, a primitive (by modern standards) ground mapping radar, later slightly improved to become H2X. The former was carried in a bathtub under the chin, the latter initially in a retractable dome in the same position, although production aircraft had this fitted in place of the ball turret. All Pathfinder aircraft carried smoke markers. Dropped above a solid undercast on radar indications alone, these left a distinctive trail above the clouds obscuring the target, providing a point at which successive waves of bombers could aim.

Pathfinding with H2S was pioneered on 27 September with an attack on

SCHWEINFURT

'I watched two fighters explode not far beneath, disappearing in sheets of orange flame, B-17s dropping out in every state of distress, from engines on fire to control surfaces shot away, friendly and enemy parachutes floating down and, on the green carpet far beneath us, numerous funeral pyres of smoke from fallen aircraft, marking our trail.'

COL. BEIRNE LAY

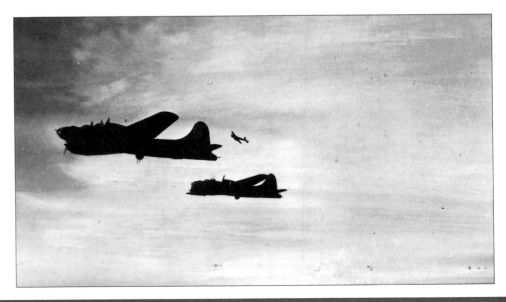

Above: A direct hit by heavy flak has torn the front fuselage and port inner engine clean away from this B-17, which goes down blazing furiously. (USAF)

Emden. The leading Wing dropped with the Pathfinder aircraft; the second Wing dropped on the smoke markers, while the third was able to find a gap in the cloud and bombed visually. Post-strike reconnaissance showed that only the Pathfinder-led units had hit Emden; the visual bombers were miles adrift. It was a promising start. A blind bombing leader was to become a standard part of most 8th AAF raids. But first the technique had to be refined, and sufficient crews trained.

In 1943, the life expectancy of a Fortress was a mere 11 missions; a tour of duty was 25 missions. When a crewman completed his tour – and a surprising number did – he was statistically dead twice over! However, progress was being made. Carpet, a gunlaying radar jammer, gradually entered service, and this equipment decreased the effectiveness of the flak. While flak destroyed only a small proportion of the bombers, it was responsible for most of those which returned damaged, while forcing them to bomb from ever higher altitudes, with a corresponding decrease in accuracy. Carpet was a British invention that saved many American lives.

The following month saw a return to Schweinfurt on the 14th by 291 Fortresses. As was by now standard procedure, the defending fighters held back until the bombers passed Aachen, when their escorts turned back. They then struck, in a way described by American official historians as 'unprecedented in its magnitude, in the cleverness with which it was planned, and in the severity with which it was executed'.

■ SCHWEINFURT ■ AGAIN!

By the time that Schweinfurt was reached, 28 bombers had gone down and many others were badly damaged. Despite this, the bombing was heavy and accurate, and only one aircraft was lost to flak in the target area. But now they had to run the fighter gauntlet once more on the homeward leg. Again they were assailed from all sides, and by the time that they reached the relative safety of the escorts, formations were breaking up, all cohesion lost.

Three ball-bearing factories had been hard hit, but once again the price was high. Sixty Fortresses were lost; five more crashed on reaching England, and 12 were written off with battle damage; over 26 per cent of the total. A further 121 were damaged but repairable. Barely one in every three returned unscathed, and these figures might have been still worse had it not been that the RAF sent fighters with long-range tanks to the aid of the hard-pressed American Thunderbolt and Lightning escorts.

The defenders had taken the measure of the Fortresses. They used 21cm rockets to break up the closely packed bomber formations, then attacked en masse from head-on. The B-17 was a tough bird, able to sustain severe damage and keep flying, and it normally took several attacks on one machine to bring it down. The essential thing, from the German point of view, was to isolate it so that it could be picked off at leisure.

The second Schweinfurt raid underlined what many had said all along; that unescorted bombers, no matter how well armed, could not fly daylight missions against determined fighter opposition without incurring unacceptable losses. The price was too high; long-range escort fighters were needed more desperately than ever.

Using drop tanks, P-47s were able to penetrate a little way into Germany; P-38s a bit further. Then in December came the answer to the problem. The P-51 Mustang was a happy marriage of an American airframe and a British engine. Using drop tanks it could range deep into Germany and go all the way to most targets.

■ BIG WEEK ■ AND BERLIN

Operations continued following the Schweinfurt raid, but increasingly poor weather meant that many of them were radar bombing missions led by Pathfinders. Few visual attacks could be made, and in January 1944 the 8th concentrated mainly on V-1 launch sites in the Pas-de-Calais. Not until late February did the bombers really get into their stride again, as the clouds parted, giving clear skies over Germany.

Big Week, the period from 20 to 25 February, saw a concerted attempt by the Allies to cripple the German aircraft industry. At last with escort fighters able to accompany them, the bombers raided Focke-Wulf plants at Tuetow and Oschersleben; Messerschmitt factories at Augsburg, Regensburg, Gotha, Brunswick, Furth and Erla/Leipzig; the Junkers works at Bernberg, Aschersleben and Halberstadt; and Heinkel's facility at Rostock. Immediate German production losses were estimated at 1,000 aircraft, and many more over the next few months. Total bomber losses, B-17s and B-24s, amounted to 226; just under 6 per cent of the 3,800 sorties flown. Fighter escort losses during Big Week amounted to 28, but the low figure of bomber loss underlined their worth.

On 4 March, the bombers set off to

B-17 UNITS THAT BECAME OPERATIONAL ENGLAND 1943

Group No.	Squadrons	Base	First Mission	Notes
94	331, 332, 333, 410	Bassingbourn	13 May 43	Last mission 21 Apr 45
95	334, 335, 336, 412	Alconbury	13 May 43	Last mission 20 Apr 45
96	337, 338, 339, 413	Grafton Underwood	14 May 43	Last mission 21 Apr 45
351	508, 509, 510, 511	Polebrook	14 May 43	Last mission 25 Apr 45. Film star Clark Gable flew with this group
379	524, 525, 526, 527	Kimbolton	29 May 43	Last mission 25 Apr 45; flew most sorties, dropped greatest bomb tonnage.
381	532, 533, 534, 535	Ridgewell	22 Jun 43	Last mission 25 Apr 45
384	544, 545, 546, 547	Grafton Underwood	22 Jun 43	Last mission 25 Apr 45, dropped last 8th AF bombs of war
100	349, 350, 351, 418	Podington	25 Jun 43	Last mission 20 Apr 45
385	548, 549, 550, 551	Gt Ashfield	17 Jul 43	Last mission 20 Apr 45
388	560, 561, 562, 563	Knettishall	17 Jul 43	Last mission April 45, flew 19 Aphrodite missions
389	568, 569, 570, 571	Framlingham	27 Sep 43	Last mission 20 Apr 45
482	812, 813, third sqn flew B-24s	Alconbury	27 Sep 43	Last mission 22 Mar 44, pioneer Pathfinder unit, also operational research
410	612, 613, 614, 615	Deenethorpe	26 Nov 43	Last mission Apr 45
447	708, 709, 710, 711	Rattlesden	24 Dec 43	Last mission 21 Apr 45

NB: The 422 BS commenced operations as part of 305 BG in Nov 42; then pioneered night bombing for 8th AF in Sep/Oct 43. Night leaflet sqn from 7/8 Oct 43. Based at Chelveston, redesignated 858 BS in June 44, re-equipped with B-24s the following month.

marker. They were intercepted on the homeward leg, but the Mustang escorts fought heroically to protect them, losing 23 of their number. Five Fortresses failed to return, a surprisingly small loss under the circumstances.

Two days later the 8th tried again. The force consisted of 561 Fortresses, tasked against a ball-bearing factory in the Erkner suburb and against the Bosch factory at Klein Machnow, plus 249 Liberators which were to attack the Daimler-Benz engine works. Fighter cover was provided by 691 Thunderbolts, Lightnings and Mustangs, some of the latter RAF, working in relays. The distance to Berlin ensured that no deceptive course changes could be used; the German fighters would have plenty of time to deploy.

Such a force could not be hidden. The time-consuming process of assembling such a massive armada in its correct order meant that it was under radar observation long before it left the English coast. In the occupied countries and in Germany, fighter units were brought to readiness; on this day they were to meet numbers with numbers.

The bomber stream was 94 miles (150km) long, thundering eastwards at 180mph (290km/hr), but some four hours after the first bomber had taken

Top: H₂X ground mapping radar, fitted in a retractable dome in the nose compartment, allowed blind bombing through cloud. This was an experimental installation.
Above: Radar-equipped pathfinder of the 401st BG, showing the retractable radome fitted in place of the ball turret. (Ralph Trout)
Right: A heavily armed Messerschmitt Me 410 commences its firing pass on a B-17F of the 390th BG.

Berlin, the only major German target not yet attacked in daylight. Once again the weather turned sour, and the recall signal was issued, but one combat wing of 29 Fortresses failed to receive it and carried on. Realizing this, headquarters allowed part of the escort to continue also. Fighters were encountered as the bombers neared the target, but they pressed on, releasing their loads on a Pathfinder's

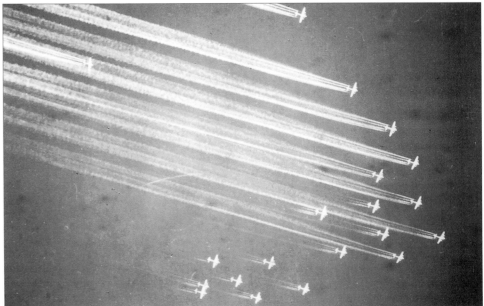

Above: Long-range escort fighters wheel protectively above B-17F Fortresses of the 390th BG. They tipped the balance against the defenders decisively. (USAF via Alfred Price)

Right: Flying Fortresses over the German capital. The low squadron is barely in the contrail belt. (USAF)

off, it had become disorganized. The head of the stream, well protected by Thunderbolts, had inadvertently veered southwards. The 13th Combat Wing was running behind schedule, and had lost visual contact with the aircraft in front. Not realizing this, it continued on the correct course, thus forming an offset in the formation.

The first German fighters attacked over Haselunne, just east of the Dutch border, to meet the 13th CW head-on. Only eight Thunderbolts were on hand to greet 107 Me 109s and FW 190s, and this was not enough to hold them off. The German fighters flashed between the bombers, guns blazing, and narrowly avoided collisions with them. Damaged Fortresses dropped out of formation in all directions; easy meat for the waiting fighters as they swung round to re-engage. Black smoke from burning air-craft stained the clear sky; white parachutes blossomed below.

Calls for help brought more P-47s from all directions; these took some of the pressure off, but there were simply not enough of them. The unengaged German fighters regrouped for another head-on attack. In all the battle lasted 45 minutes.

Above: **Target Berlin! Tempelhof airfield can be seen near the right wingtip of this 452nd BG Fortress as it lines up on its primary target. (USAF)**

one fell to unknown causes. This was the largest bomber loss ever suffered in one raid by the 8th Air Force. However, it was not enough to stop the 8th. Over the next three days, two raids of similar strength were visited upon the German capital, and a third on 22 March.

With the invasion of Europe looming, priorities switched. Attacks against communications centres intensified, while tremendous efforts were made to reduce

The 8th prepare for invasion; oil and transport the targets

Meanwhile the front of the bomber stream was faring almost as badly. Attempting to get back on course, it crossed several flak zones before meeting up with another huge German fighter formation. The escorting Mustangs were in the right place, but failed to avert the blow completely. More bombers went down, although the German interceptors paid a heavy price for their success.

At last the bombers reached Berlin, only to run into the most vicious flak

that most of them had ever seen. Partial cloud foiled the bomb runs on two of the primary three targets but widespread damage was caused in the city. The return flight was marked by skirmishes with small numbers of German fighters, which were generally held at bay by the escorts. There was however one exception. Forty-four German fighters managed to assemble near the Dutch border; they cost the 388th BG six Fortresses.

Losses on the Berlin raid amounted to 73, of which 56 were Fortresses. Of these, three reached Sweden in a damaged state, while four were struck off charge in England. Fighters accounted for 45, fighters and flak for four; flak alone for six, while

the German oil industry. On 12 May, 935 heavy bombers raided oil plants at Bruex, Bohlen, Leuna, Lutzendorf and Zwickau. Meanwhile 15th Air Force was raiding the Romanian oil fields at Ploesti. Raid followed raid, and aviation fuel production slumped from 175,000 tons in April to 52,000 tons in June; 35,000 tons in July, and a mere 7,000 tons in September. This caused a tremendous reduction of German fighter effectiveness.

Below: **A large hole through her fin making control difficult, *Boche Buster* of the 401st BG breaks formation to seek safety in neutral Sweden, 7 October 1944. (Bert Hocking)**

FORTRESSES THROUGH THE BERLIN FLAK

'A dark puffy veil that hung like a pall of death covered the capital city. It was the heaviest flak I had ever seen. It almost seemed to swallow up the bomber formations as they entered it. One ship blew up and three others dropped away from their formations . . . It didn't seem that anything could fly through that. But there they were, Flying Fortresses sailing proudly away from the scene of devastation.'

LT LOWELL WATTS, 388TH BG.

By October 1944 the bombing campaign against the Third Reich had sapped the strength of the German day fighter arm. Lack of aircraft was not the cause; widely dispersed plants scattered throughout Germany maintained production at record levels, and the depots were full of replacements.

The critical shortage was of trained pilots. Under the constant battering of the massive American raids, which were increasingly covered by long-range escorts, the German fighter units had suffered swingeing losses. Experienced men were irreplaceable; novices rarely lasted long. Then, as the fuel shortage bit ever harder, training was curtailed, and the quality of replacement pilots dropped still more. To make matters worse, even the ever-shrinking band of old stagers sometimes found themselves grounded for lack of fuel. From this time on, only on rare occasions were they able to put up serious opposition to the American armadas. Fortress operations over Germany gradually became safer, so much so that in the closing months of the war it was possible to fly a full tour and never encounter a German fighter in the air! On the other hand, the flak defences were strengthened, and losses to this cause began to exceed those of the fighters, although without reaching anywhere near the same proportions. This reduction in risk was acknowledged by the USAAF, who increased the number of sorties in a tour of operations from 25 to 30, and eventually to 35.

While in the early months the loss rate of Fortresses was horrendous, a few, and they were very few indeed, survived to complete more than 100 missions. Yet others had taken such a beating that they were no longer sufficiently reliable for operations, although still flyable. One

Left: The 91st BG unloads over Berlin on smoke markers dropped by lead aircraft in February 1945. The nearest aircraft is a late model B-17G, with the taller dorsal turret. (USAF)

use for some of these was as assembly ships. Shuffling a formation of many hundreds of bombers into the correct order before sallying forth was far from easy. One solution was to paint war-weary aircraft in brilliant colours and strange patterns. These unmistakeable psychedelic monsters were then launched and took up their assigned place in the assembly area, where their assigned formations took station on them. When all was in order, they returned to base.

■ APHRODITE ■

Another use for war-weary B-17s was as radio-controlled flying bombs. Stripped of all unnecessary equipment, these were packed with 20,000lb (9,000kg) of Torpex high explosive. For Project Aphrodite, as it was known, these were flown off by a two-man crew, who parachuted to safety near the English coast. Control was then handed over to a specially equipped 'mother' aircraft, which remotely guided the flying bomb to its target. The hazardous Aphrodite

Above: Mustangs escort B-17G *Patches* on a 15th AF shuttle mission to Russia. The long reach of the American fighter transformed American deep penetration missions. (USAF)

missions were flown by the 388th BG from Fersfield, an isolated airfield in the wilds of Norfolk, but the difficulties of accurately guiding them onto their targets, plus a couple of unfortunate accidents, ensured that only a handful of missions were flown.

Other experiments carried out from

B-17 UNITS THAT BECAME OPERATIONAL IN ENGLAND, 1944

Group	Squadrons	Base	1st Mission	Notes
	803	Oulton	5 Jun 44	Countermeasures Squadron, 8 B-17Fs and 2 B-17Gs. Largely replaced by B-24s from August 44.
486	832, 833, 834, 835	Sudbury	1 Aug 44	Last mission 21 Apr 45. (prev B-24s)
487	836, 837, 938, 839	Lavenham	1 Aug 44	Last mission 21 Apr 45. (prev B-24s)
490	848, 849, 850, 851	Eye	27 Aug 44	Last mission 20 Apr 45. (prev B-24s)
493	860, 861, 862, 863	Debach	8 Sep 44	(prev B-24s) Last mission 20 Apr 45. Last BG to become operational in 8th AF.
25 (R)	652 Sqn only with B-17, others with B-24	Watton	Nov 44	Composite unit, weather reconnaissance.
34	4, 7, 18, 391	Mendlesham	17 Sep 44	(prev B-24s) No losses to fighters over enemy territory.

Left: The 30mm cannon of the Messerschmitt Me 262 jet fighter packed a tremendous punch. This Fortress was lucky to survive. (USAF via Alfred Price)
Below left: In the final months of the war flak was the main hazard. On 10 April 1945, *Wee Willie* of the 91st BG went down on its 124th sortie. (USAF via Alfred Price)

remarkably low; less than one-third of a per cent. One B-17 was lost to a Me 262 jet fighter, while four more went down to flak, which damaged a further 85 aircraft. Just to show it was no fluke, 1,193 heavies went out on the following day, losing only two of their number. The pattern continued.

Whereas the British Lancaster routinely carried bombs of up to 12,000lb (5,400kg), Fortress (and Liberator) bays could not accommodate a bomb larger than 2,000lb (900kg). This was of little use against hardened targets, and the Disney bomb was introduced to correct this shortcoming. Weighing 4,500lb (2,000kg), it used rocket propulsion to pierce 20ft (6m) of reinforced concrete.

Nine B-17s of the 92 BG each carried four Disney bombs on underwing racks to the U-boat pens at Ijmuiden on 14 March 1945. Only one hit was scored, and a further raid was mounted, but

soon the Allied advance overran the area, making further attacks unnecessary.

Just four days later, the 8th mounted its final major attack on Berlin with 1,327 heavy bombers. They were met by an estimated 40–50 Me 262 jet fighters, which accounted for a mere eight Fortresses. The remaining 16 bombers which failed to return, plus a further 16 which force-landed in Russian-held territory, all fell to flak. The loss rate of three percent, while heavy for 1945, was a far cry from the first Berlin raid just over a year earlier.

Final rounds In Europe; operations continue in the Pacific

By now worthwhile targets were becoming few and far between, and on 16 April, General Spaatz stated that the strategic air war was over; from then on only tactical targets remained. The final 8th AF bombs of the war were dropped on the Skoda Armament Works at Pilsen on 25 April 1945, by a B-17 of the 384th BG.

Fersfield involved Batty, a system using a television-guided bomb. Rather ahead of its time, Batty was beset with technical difficulties, and achieved little.

To return to the bombing of Germany, some idea of the reduction of defensive effectiveness was given on 22 February 1945, when 1,411 heavy bombers attacked communication centres all over the Third Reich from the unprecedentedly low altitude of 10,000ft (3,050m), chosen to achieve bombing accuracy against small targets. Losses were

Above right: Not all losses were fatal. Damaged by fighters, this B-17G of the 96th BG force-landed in Denmark. Aided by the Resistance, the entire crew escaped to Sweden. (J. Helme via Alfred Price)
Right: B-17F *Talisman*, seen here at Port Moresby in 1943, was one of the last B-17s to operate in the Pacific theatre. (USAF)

B-17 OPERATIONAL STATISTICS 8TH AF

BG No.	Missions	Sorties	Bombs	A/c Missing	Sort/Miss (tons)
303	364	10,721	24,918	165	64.98
306	342	9,614	22,575	171	56.22
91	340	9,591	22,142	197	48.68
305	337	9,231	22,363	154	59.94
379	330	10,492	26,460	141	74.41
94	324	8,884	18,925	153	58.06
95	320	8,903	19,769	157	56.70
96	320	8,924	19,277	189	47.21
384	314	9,348	22,415	159	58.79
351	311	8,600	20,357	124	69.35
92	308	8,663	20,829	154	56.25
100	306	8,630	19,257	177	48.78
388	306	8,051	18,162	142	56.70
390	300	8,725	19,059	144	60.59
381	296	9,035	22,160	131	68.97
385	296	8,264	18,494	129	64.06
447	257	7,605	17,103	97	78.40
410	255	7,430	17,778	95	78.21
452	250	7,279	16,467	110	66.17
457	237	7,068	16,916	83	85.16
398	195	6,419	15.781	58	110.67*
97	14	247	395	4	61.75
301	8	104	186	1	104.00
TOTALS	**6,034**	**181,828**	**422,788**	**2,935**	**av61.95**

1) At least four BGs converted from the B-24 to the B-17 in the summer of 1944, but their records include data for both aircraft, and have not been included here.

2) Missing aircraft are just that; no allowance has been made for those that reached base but crashed on landing, or were struck off charge. A rough approximation based on available sources gives about one-third as many again.

3) At one point early in the war, the life expectancy of a B-17 was just 11 sorties. The sorties/missing aircraft ratio shows how much safer things had become in the later stages. This is particularly noticeable with BGs formed late in 1944. Three factors were decisive; sufficient numbers of long-range escort fighters; from Spring 1944 many missions were flown over occupied France; in the final months of the war, the Luftwaffe was a spent force.

As by far the majority of Fortress operations in the Second World War were flown by the US 8th Army Air Force based in England, it was only to be expected that the narrative would mainly concern itself with these. But the B-17 served well and faithfully with other air forces and in other theatres.

We have already touched on the early years of the Pacific War. While those Fortresses there at the start gave sterling service, ably backed by such reinforcements as could be got through, this period was essentially tactical. There was little scope for strategic bombing until the Japanese advance had been halted, which did not happen until mid-1942. While the Fortresses helped to hold the ring, there was little more they could do. Vulnerable to fighters at medium and low altitudes, they yet lacked the precision to hit either small fixed targets or moving ships from high altitude.

This was all too clearly demonstrated at the decisive Battle of Midway in June 1942, when 19 B-17s were based on the island. During the four days of battle, they flew over 80 sorties in the course of seven missions. They first attacked the invasion force; the main Japanese carrier force twice; two cruisers; a solitary destroyer; and finally an American submarine under the impression that it was a Japanese cruiser. They claimed hits on two battleships or heavy cruisers; two transports; three aircraft carriers, and finally 'sank' the 'cruiser'. During this flurry of activity, two B-17s were lost. In actual fact there was not even a near-miss. The sunk 'cruiser' had of course crash-dived to safety.

Below: The Boeing B-29 Superfortress commenced operations in the Far East in June 1944, as B-17 production was being run down. (Author)

293845

S034

Above: Tail gunners seem rarely to have carried cameras, which makes this view of B-17Gs of 15th AF setting out from their Italian base the more interesting.
Below: This 2nd BG aircraft of 15th AF was hit by flak over Hungary. Pilot Lt Miller brought it 520 miles (835km) back to Foggia in Italy by steering with the outboard engines and gaining and losing height by adjusting power settings. (Boeing via Alfred Price)

This is not to denigrate the efforts of the Army fliers, but it does provide an illustration of the difficulties; first of hitting moving targets from a level bomber, secondly of distinguishing bomb hits from other signs of battle, and thirdly of ship recognition by aviators, all from 3 miles (5km) up!

When at last the situation stabilized and the Japanese were forced onto the defensive, high-altitude bombing came once more into its own. However, the distances in the Pacific were so vast that the longer-ranged Liberator was preferred to the Fortress, which from mid-1943 had vanished from the scene. A few aircraft went to India, but the same factors applied.

■ SUPERFORTRESS ■

In any case, the days of the Flying Fortress were numbered; a specification for an ultra long-range bomber was issued in 1942. The B-29 Superfortress was far larger than its predecessor, better armed, longer ranged, and could carry a much bigger bombload as well as bigger bombs. B-29 bases in the Marianas Islands became operational from October 1944, and from then on, Japanese targets were under constant attack, culminating in the nuclear raids on Hiroshima and Nagasaki which brought the war in the Pacific to an abrupt close. B-17 production peaked in March 1944, but was thereafter run down in favour of the B-29 Superfortress.

■ MEDITERRANEAN ■ THEATRE

Two B-17 groups were detached from the 8th AF in November 1942 and transferred to the newly formed 12th AF, commencing operations from Maison Blanche in Algeria on the 16th of that month. They were joined in the spring of 1943 by the 2nd and 99th BGs, and carried out raids on targets in the western Mediterranean area.

Once German resistance in North Africa had ceased, they moved forward to raid Sicily, softening it up for invasion. It was a far cry from operations in Northern Europe. Distances were generally shorter; fighter escort, often from bases on Malta, was usually available; and the combined German and Italian flak and fighter defences far weaker. Generally the weather was better, and usually the primary target was bombed from high altitude. Just occasionally thick haze would rule this out. Making a virtue of a necessity, the Fortresses then flew in very low over the sea, under the enemy radar coverage, before pulling up to a moderate altitude to bomb.

When bases on the Italian mainland became available, a new command, 15th AF, was formed. While a considerable portion of heavy bomber strength in Italy consisted of Liberators, the Fortress strength was increased with the arrival of more B-17 BGs, although Fortress numbers never exceeded one fifth of the B-17 strength of the 8th AF. As the Axis forces were driven back in 1944, so 15th AF joined in the campaign against oil targets with raids on Ploesti in Romania.

Shuttle missions were not an 8th AF prerogative. On 2 June 1944, 130 B-17s of 15th AF bombed communications targets in Hungary before continuing to Russian airfields near Kiev. Two days later they attacked targets in Romania from the Kiev area, before once more raiding Romania while returning to Italy.

■ ROYAL AIR FORCE ■

Reference has already been made to Fortresses in RAF Coastal and Bomber Command service. In the former they were mainly used on anti-submarine patrols, operating from stations as diverse as Chivenor in Devon, Benbecula in the Hebrides, and the Azores, from where they helped to close the infamous mid-Atlantic Gap. The Azores, some 900 miles (1,450km) east of Lisbon, are part of Portugal, and Portugal was neutral during the Second World War. Permission to use Lajes airfield on the island of Terceira was granted when Britain invoked a Treaty of Alliance dating back to 1386!

European weather comes mainly from the southwest, and other Coastal units were Meteorological Reconnaissance squadrons, whose aircraft also ranged far out into the Atlantic, recording weather changes and conditions which would allow the accurate forecasting so necessary for planning bombing raids.

Finally two squadrons equipped with Fortress IIIs (B-17Gs) flew with No. 100

Below: Coastal Command Fortress IIs and IIa's of No. 220 Squadron at Lajes in the Azores, December 1943, from where they played a sterling role in containing the U-boat menace. (Bruce Robertson)

Group of Bomber Command from Tempsford and Oulton, packed to the gills with black boxes on electronic countermeasures sorties.

■ BLACK-CROSSED ■ BOEINGS

There was however a third major combatant which operated the B-17. The Luftwaffe was naturally very interested in this new opponent, which was frequently encountered in the autumn skies of 1942. What were its strengths and weaknesses? Shot-down Fortresses were eagerly examined and deductions made. Then, with Christmas approaching, the Germans received a present when a fairly intact B-17F made a

wheels-down landing in northern France.

It was taken to the flight test centre at Rechlin where all its secrets were laid bare, after which it was used for fighter affiliation trials. Nine months after its capture, it was sent to I/KG.200, a unit engaged in clandestine operations. Over the next 15 months it was joined by two more B-17s, and they were given the fictitious designation Dornier Do 200.

The usual task of the black-crossed Fortresses was the dropping of agents behind Allied lines. The area covered by these operations was vast, from Ireland in the west to Trans-Jordan in the east and Algeria in the south. Just one of these aircraft survived the war, and was recaptured at Altenburg in April 1945.

■ ODDBALLS ■

During and shortly after the war, many Fortresses were converted for purposes other than bombing. Transport was an obvious choice, although the circular fuselage cross-section did not particularly lend itself to this.

At an early stage, four Fortresses were evaluated as transports. One, fitted with side windows and 38 seats, became the XC-108; it was later used in the Pacific by General MacArthur as a personal transport. The second was fitted with a large side-loading cargo door to become the XC-108A. The third was fitted out as an executive transport as the YC-108, while the fourth was converted to a fuel tanker as the XC-108B. None entered production. More numerous was the CB-17, a conversion of war-weary bombers to the transport role.

Yet another wartime conversion was the F-9. This was a long-range reconnaissance machine based on the B-17F, which carried both vertical and oblique cameras. Depending on the equipment carried, these became F-9As, Bs and Cs.

At the end of the war, the USAAF converted B-17Gs to the search and rescue role as the B-17H. This was fitted with a sea search radar under the chin, and a para-droppable lifeboat under the belly. The US Navy also had its own uses for the type; fitted with an APS-20 search radar it became a pioneer airborne early warning aircraft, with the designation PB-1W. A few machines carried the

Above: **Dornier Do 200. A captured B-17 rather incongruously wearing Luftwaffe markings at Orly Airport, Paris, in December 1942. (Roger F. Besecker)**

radome dorsally, but in most cases this was fitted in a ventral position. The PB-1W also carried out maritime reconnaissance and anti-submarine missions. Yet another user was the US Coast Guard with the PB-1G, a long-range air-sea rescue machine, which was on occasion used for iceberg reconnaissance sorties. But despite these conversions, there were far too many Fortresses to be put to use. While many became drone targets or drone director aircraft, and a lucky few served with foreign air forces, the vast majority were scrapped.

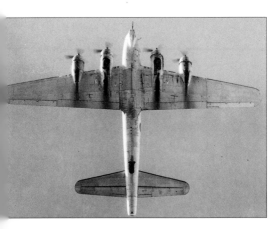

Above: **This RAF Fortress IIa has had the ball turret removed, and a 40mm Vickers S gun mounted in the nose with a sighting position in a gondola beneath it. (Bruce Robertson)**

RAF SQUADRONS OPERATING FORTRESSES

BOMBER COMMAND
No. 90, high-altitude bombers, Fortress I
Nos 214 & 223, electronic counter-measures, No. 100 Group, Fortress III

COASTAL COMMAND
Nos 206 & 220, anti-submarine, Fortress I, II, IIa and III
Nos 59 & 86, anti-submarine, Fortress III
Nos 251, 517, 519 & 521, meteorological, Fortress III

POST-WAR B-17 DESIGNATIONS

Transports	CB-17G
	VB-17G
Reconnaissance	FB-17F
	FB-17G
	RB-17F
	RB-17G
AEW/Maritime Reconnaissance	1PB-1W
Air/Sea Rescue	PB-1G
	SB-17G
Target Drone	MB-17G
	QB-17G
	QB-17L
	QB-17N
	QB-17P
Drone Remote Controller	CQ-4
	DB-17G
	DB-17P
Engine Test Bed	EB-17G
	XPB-1W
Pilot Trainer	TB-17G

As four-engined bombers went, the Fortress was a decidedly elderly design by the time that the Second World War ended in 1945, having first flown 10 years earlier. In many ways, such as the limitations of the internal bomb bay and the relatively low operational cruising speed, its age was showing, and by this time it was already being supplanted in USAAF service as a bomber in favour of the far superior B-29 Superfortress. Although a few other roles had been found for it, these involved only a small proportion of what was then a massive fleet. Inevitably, hundreds, if not thousands, were up for sale at bargain basement prices.

In a world impoverished by and tired of war, there were few takers. France, Portugal, Denmark, the Dominican Republic and Bolivia each took small quantities,

while Brazil acquired a handful of search and rescue B-17Hs in the early Fifties. Sweden operated a few in the transport role, but these were all aircraft that had been interned after force-landing there during the war. There was just one country that wanted Fortresses badly, but ironically it was a nation to which few were willing to sell.

The state of Israel came into being on 14 May 1948, when the British Mandate to run what was then known as Palestine, given at the Treaty of Versailles in 1919, expired. The country was regarded by the Jews as a national homeland, but its Arab neighbours, Egypt, Jordan, Iraq, Lebanon and Syria, didn't see it quite that way and were prepared to settle matters by force of arms.

What the fledgling Israeli state needed desperately was warplanes, of virtually any description as long as they were able fly. In a world full of surplus equipment they should have had little difficulty in acquiring it, but on paper, what became known as the War of Independence looked a David and Goliath affair, with the Arab Goliath an almost certain

winner. The state of Israel was an unknown quantity internationally; its future prospects were far from bright, while many countries that could have assisted had trade and other ties to the Arab world, and were therefore reluctant to give support.

Acquiring the hardware was not the problem. For example, a Jewish group in Hawaii gave the new-formed Israeli Air Force (the Chel Ha'Avir) 10 Mitchells, 10 Hellcats, five Venturas and two Avengers, but these could not be delivered. Export licences for arms to Israel were impossible to come by, and smuggling was the only alternative.

The acquisition of three B-17Gs by Israel was a minor epic in itself. Cover companies set up in the USA bought four aircraft cheaply. They had of course been

Opposite: **Waist gun positions in a B-17F, June 1943, showing the gun mounting and ammunition feeds.**
Below: **Post-war conversion. A B-17H fitted with sea search radar and a paradroppable lifeboat for the search and rescue role. (Roger F. Besecker)**

B-17G

Flight deck of a B-17G, showing the pilot and aircraft commander's seat (left), and co-pilot's seat (right). The control column moves forwards or back to command the elevators to give a dive or climb, while the wheel portion commands the ailerons, which, moving differentially, give a bank to left or right. Solid rudder pedals are visible on both sides, while the handy gate-type throttle levers are central where both pilots can reach them. On a mission, turns would be taken at formation flying, as this could be tiring, even though the B-17 was noted for its docile handling. (Merle Olmsted)

demilitarized; gun positions had been taken out and faired over, bomb racks and sights removed; even the oxygen system had been taken out.

Refurbishing them in the United States was not really a practical proposition; this would best be done at Zatec in what was then Czechoslovakia. The problem than became how it would be possible to get them to Zatec without the authorities finding out.

■ SECRET FLIGHTS ■

The flight could not be done overtly, neither could it be done in a single hop. Three aircraft left Miami for Puerto Rico on 12 June 1948, where they filed flight plans to Brazil, a country for which an export licence was not needed. This gave them sufficient fuel to reach Santa Maria in the Azores without arousing suspicion, where arrangements had been made for a quick turn-around. Taking off again in dense fog, they flew on to Zatec, reaching there on 14 June. Only one thing

Right: **With all gun positions except the waist and rear faired over, an Israeli B-17G formates over the Mediterranean. If any guns were in evidence these have been erased by the censor, as has the number on the fuselage. (via Barry Wheeler)**

went awry. The flight plan filed in the Azores was for Corsica, and the authorities there were to notify the Azores that they had arrived. When this was not done it at first appeared that all three aircraft were missing, but the truth soon emerged.

The fourth B-17G was at Tulsa, Oklahoma, and on 14 July it was flown to Westchester on the east coast. Once there the pilot filed a flight plan to the west coast but headed instead for St John's

in Newfoundland. Unfortunately bad weather forced him to land at Dartmouth in Nova Scotia, where Canadian customs found small arms and B-17 spares on board. The USA demanded their return, and the Fortress was given enough fuel to fly back to Boston. Taking off, it headed instead for the Azores, but was interned there.

In command at Zatec was former B-17 squadron commander and American volunteer pilot Ray Kurtz. He and his team

worked around the clock to get the three Fortresses more or less battleworthy. Most of what was available was ex-Luftwaffe and Czech Air Force equipment, and improvisation was the order of the day.

With Czech guns and ex-Luftwaffe equipment the B-17s flew to Israel

For example, no powered turrets were available, while the only guns to be had were rifle-calibre Czech BZ 37s, with a low rate of fire. A single hand-held gun was fitted in each of the tail and waist positions; a far cry from the heavily armed B-17Gs in USAAF service. Bomb racks of German design enabled each aircraft to carry four 550lb (250kg) and eight 150lb (70kg) bombs. A single bombsight (not a Norden) and an oxygen system were obtained; these were both fitted in same aircraft. The others were forced to use makeshift arrangements.

The three Fortresses were ready to leave on 15 July, by which time the War of Independence was in full swing. The original plan was to bomb Cairo on the delivery flight, but at that time British

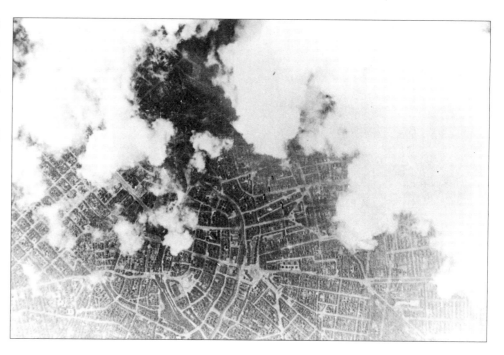

Above: Broken cloud could obscure the target even while the bomb run was in progress. (USAF via Alfred Price)
Below: With a Wright R-3550 Constellation engine mounted in the nose, this B-17G was used as an engine testbed and redesignated EB-17G and later still JB-17G. (Tom Cuddy)

Above: **Seen here in September 1957, this all-black RB-17G was used for dropping agents into South East Asia. (Merle Olmsted)**

fighters were based in the Canal Zone, and the risk of interception by these was judged too high for the aircraft without proper oxygen equipment. It was therefore decided that the machine with a bombsight and proper oxygen should bomb Cairo, while the others attacked Gaza and El Arish.

■ CAIRO BOMBED ■

On leaving Zatec the three bombers flew in formation down the east coast of the Adriatic, fired on by Albanian flak for good measure. Having crossed the Mediterranean, they split up. The B-17 that was scheduled to bomb Cairo flew in over the desert while the others stayed over the sea.

There was no blackout in Cairo, and the bombs were aimed at the King's Palace and the barracks of the Army Officer's School. There was no opposition to be faced from flak or fighters. Egyptian sources stated that casualties amounted to 30 dead and 55 injured. The other bombers failed to find their assigned targets in the darkness; they

probably hit Rafah in northern Sinai. All three of them landed safely afterwards at Tel Nof.

There was no time for congratulations, for the bombers were needed urgently. The very next morning they bombed the airfield at El Arish; at noon they were over Egyptian positions at Ashdod and Majdal, then at dusk, two of the three raided Syrian positions at Mishna Ha'Yarden. On this last mission, a shortage of bombs saw them using mortar shells dropped by hand. That evening, they were constituted as No. 69 Squadron, the Hammers, based at Ramat David.

The pace of the Hammers' bombing

was unrelenting. They returned to Mishmar Ha'Yarden on the morning of 17 July, then were off to attack Iraqi forces at Nablus and Tul Karrem. Three more raids were carried out on 18 July, including a single sortie to Damascus, before a truce on the following day allowed them to catch their breath.

No. 69 Squadron flew day and night missions without loss

The truce ended on 15 October, by which time the Israelis were planning to take the offensive. No. 69 Squadron was quickly in action, targeting an Egyptian headquarters at Majdal at dusk, with solo attacks on Gaza, El Arish, and Majdal again later that night. The first attack went awry. The Fortresses took off late and instead of Majdal, bombed a small village in error. The later singleton raids were little better; Gaza was not even found. This was not the last time that targets were misidentified, or even not located at all at night.

Most raids after this were carried out in daylight. Often a Spitfire escort was scheduled, but equally often it failed to appear. Fortunately enemy fighters were never encountered on these missions.

Day after day the pace continued with

Right: **North Africa was no picnic. A B-17 of the 97th BG returns to its base at Bliskra on three engines, December 1942. (VMI)**